# GOOD GIRLS DON'T MAKE HISTORY


CREATED BY: ELIZABETH KIEHNER, KEITH OLWELL

WRITTEN BY: ELIZABETH KIEHNER, KARA COYLE

ILLUSTRATION / DESIGN: MICAELA DAWN, MARY SANCHE


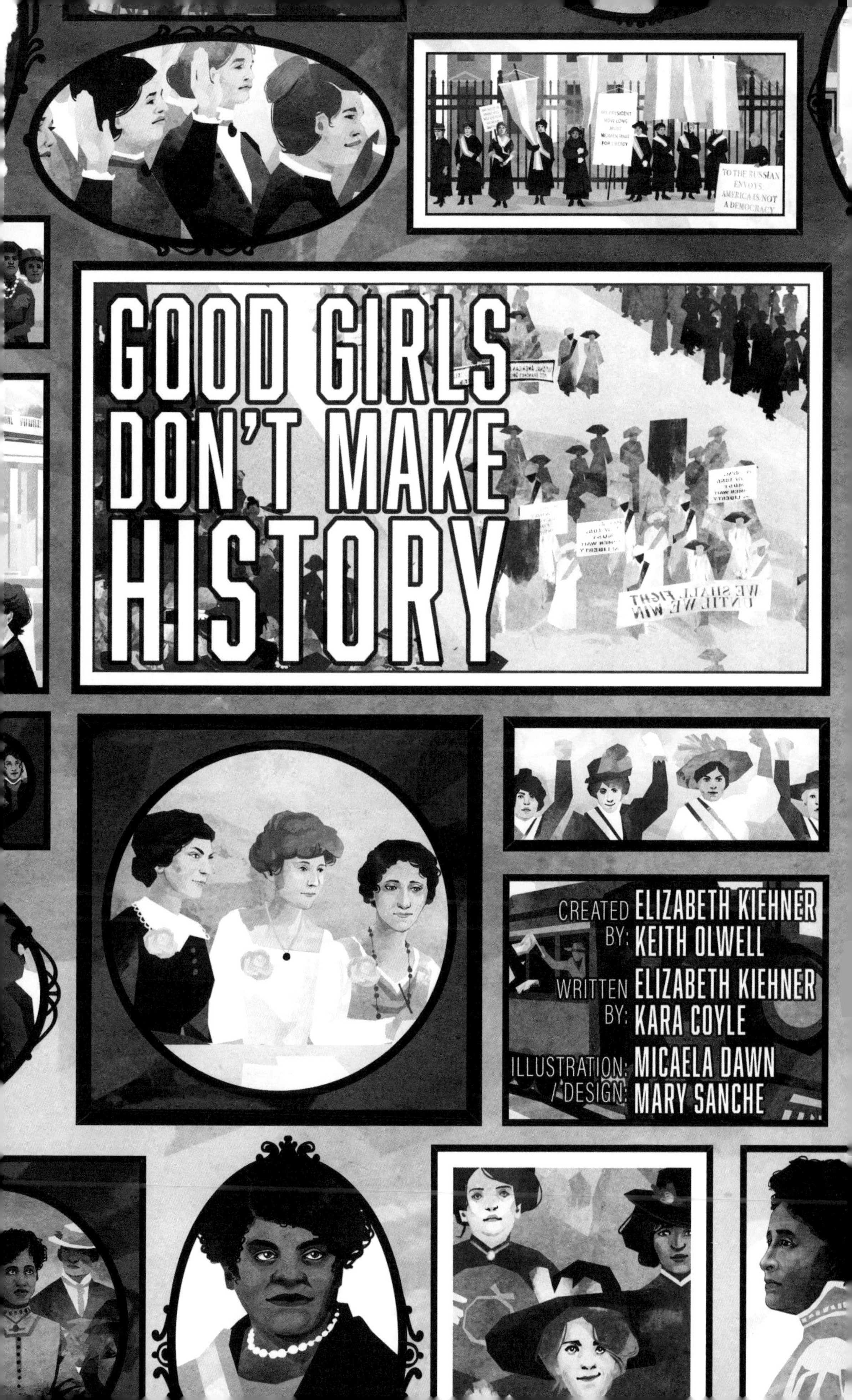

TO THE RUSSIAN ENVOYS AMERICA IS NOT A DEMOCRACY
WE SHALL FIGHT UNTIL WE WIN

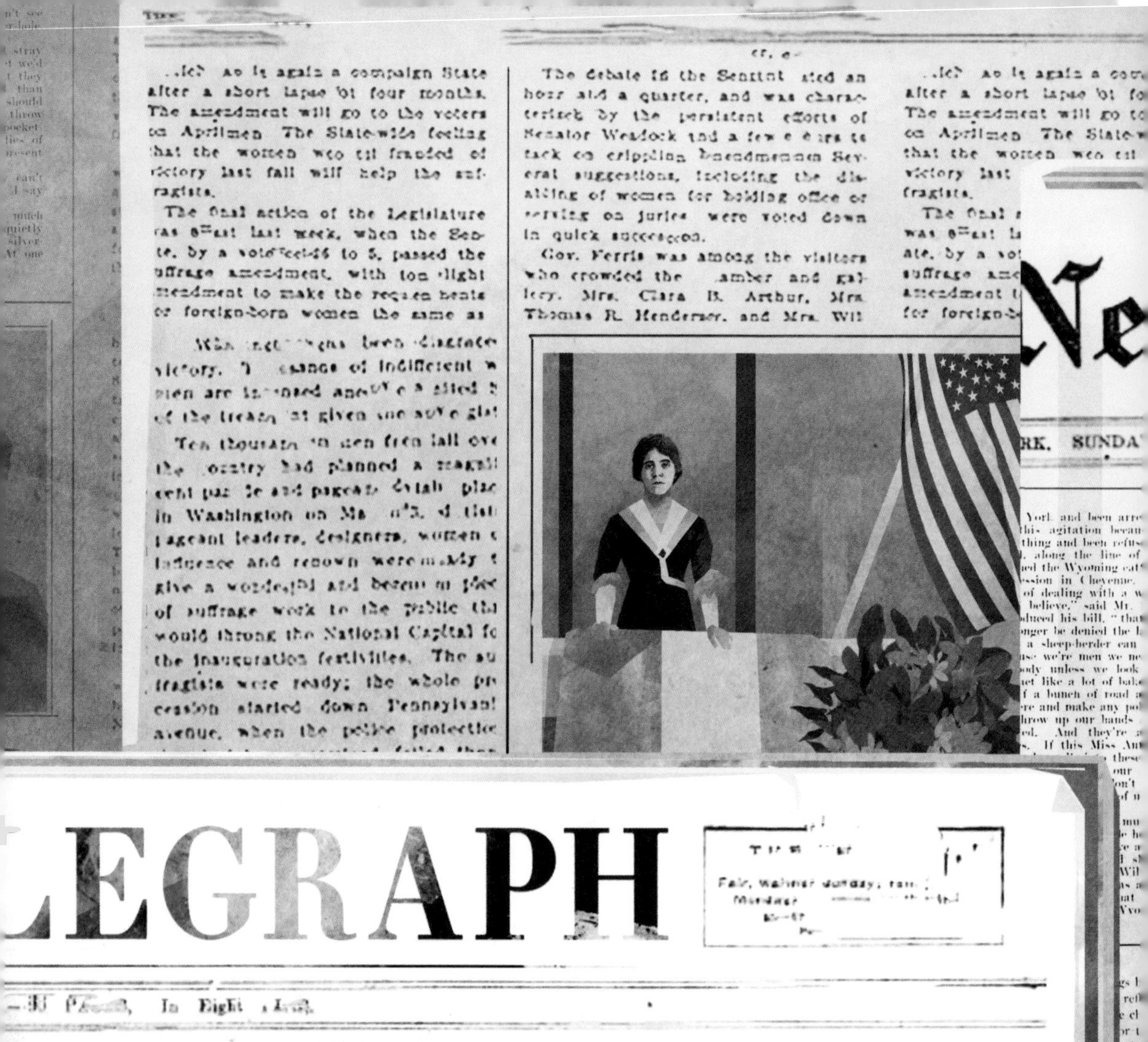

Brimming with creative inspiration, how-to projects, and useful information to enrich your everyday life, Quarto Knows is a favourite destination for those pursuing their interests and passions. Visit our site and dig deeper with our books into your area of interest: Quarto Creates, Quarto Cooks, Quarto Homes, Quarto Lives, Quarto Drives, Quarto Explores, Quarto Gifts, or Quarto Kids.

Inspiring | Educating | Creating | Entertaining



First published in 2021 by Wide Eyed Editions, an imprint of The Quarto Group. 100 Cummings Center, Suite 265D, Beverly, MA 01915, USA. T +1 978-282-9590 F +1 078-283-2742 www.QuartoKnows.com



A CIP record for this book is available from the Library of Congress.
Hardback ISBN 978-0-7112-6542-4 • Paperback ISBN 978-0-7112-7164-7

The illustrations were created with digital media.

Published by Georgia Amson-Bradshaw • Created by Elizabeth Kiehner and Keith Olwell
Written by Elizabeth Kiehner and Kara Coyle • Illustrated by Micaela Dawn and Mary Sanche
Edited by Hattie Grylls • Designed by Myrto Dimitrakoulia • Production by Dawn Cameron
Manufactured in Guangdong, China TT052021

1 3 5 7 9 8 6 4 2

FSC www.fsc.org
MIX
Paper from responsible sources
FSC® C016973

The title of this book, **Good Girls Don't Make History**, was inspired by Pulitzer Prize-winning historian Laurel Thatcher Ulrich who wrote that "well-behaved women seldom make history." This statement has been attributed to people as varied as Eleanor Roosevelt, Marilyn Monroe, and Kim Kardashian, yet it comes from Ulrich's 1976 article about Puritan funeral services. This often-quoted phrase speaks to the prevailing, and chronic, way that women frequently fail to receive proper attribution or credit for their work. Too often female lives, points of view, and accomplishments have been excluded from history altogether.

Many people might have heard of Susan B. Anthony and know that she fought for women's right to vote, but the rest of the narrative is perhaps the best-kept secret of political history. We created this graphic novel because this story is not taught in the American public school system. We aspire to give people a better view of the diverse women and men who fought for women's liberty, and use the graphic novel format to make the story vibrant, dynamic, and accessible. Unfortunately, we do not teach more of this inspiring story in America—it simply gets a paragraph in a thick textbook.

The systematic disrespect, abuse, and imprisonment of women during their campaign to win the right to vote is both an embarrassment to our history and a badge of honor to those who bravely fought for what is right. Just as we should be doing more to educate ourselves on this country's tragic racial history, we should also be aware that women's history is too often hidden or overlooked.

We are proud to share the story of 70 years of socially and economically diverse women with one clear goal: to win the right to vote. As we celebrate the first female vice-president of the United States, Kamala Harris, it is important to acknowledge the decades of persistent female leaders who paved the way to this historic moment. We hope you enjoy the following pages about an American movement, and draw inspiration and motivation for the battles that still lie ahead. Together, with voices united, we are unstoppable.

**Elizabeth Kiehner and the whole GGDMH team**

*This novel is based on actual events that occurred during the political struggle and debate over the right for women to vote in America. Some characters in the book are fictional and some scenes and pieces of dialogue are invented for creative and storyline purposes.*

"It was we, the people; not we, the white male citizens;
nor yet we, the male citizens; but we, the whole people,
who formed the Union... Men, their rights, and
nothing more; women, their rights, and nothing less."

Susan B. Anthony
1820–1906

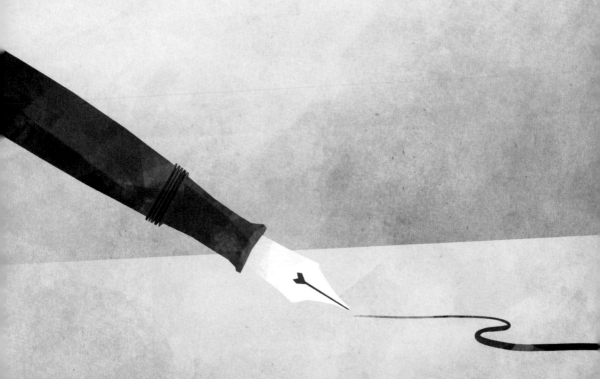

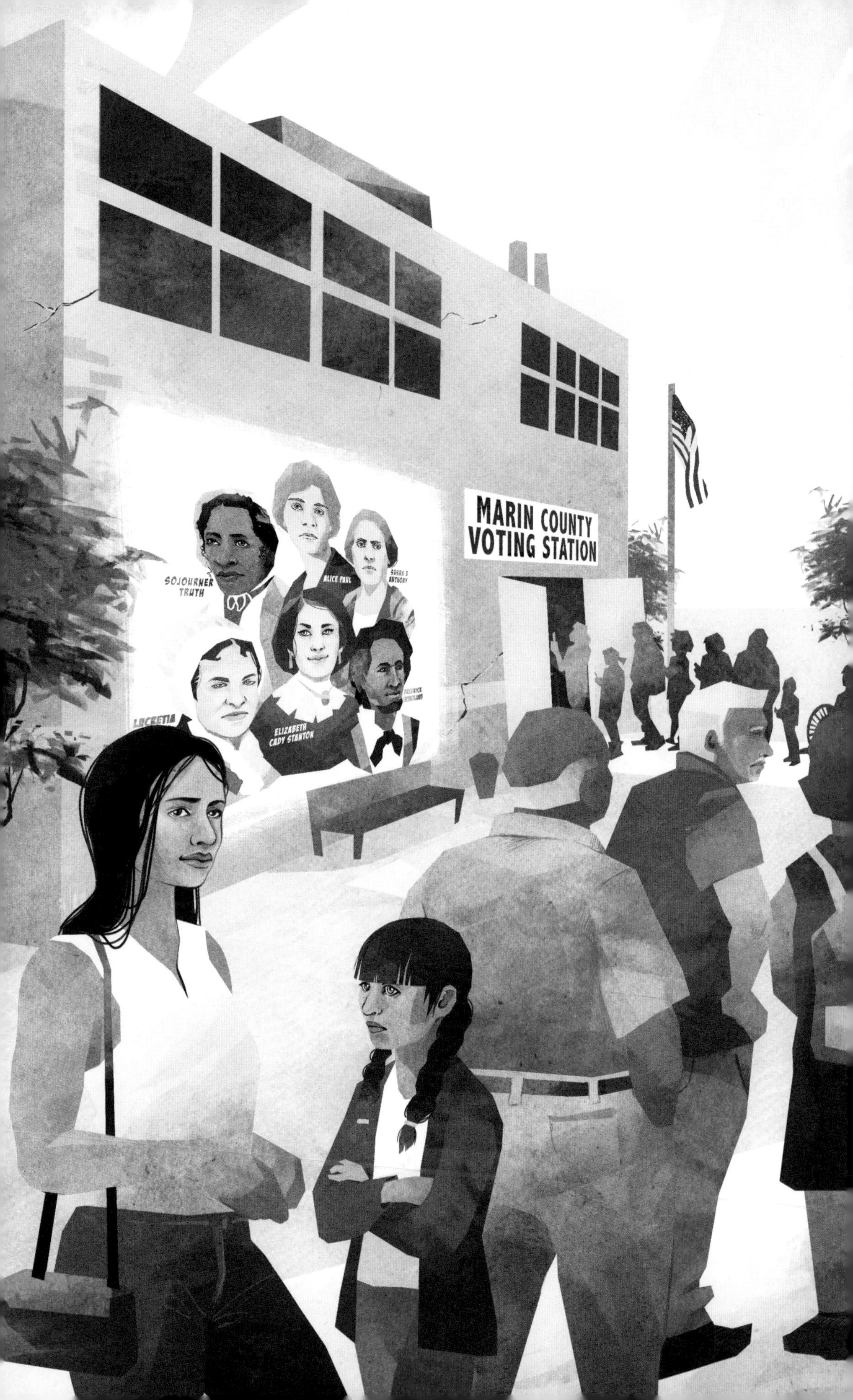

MARIN COUNTY
VOTING STATION
SOJOURNER
TRUTH
ALICE PAUL
SUSAN B
ANTHONY
LUCRETIA
ELIZABETH
CADY STANTON

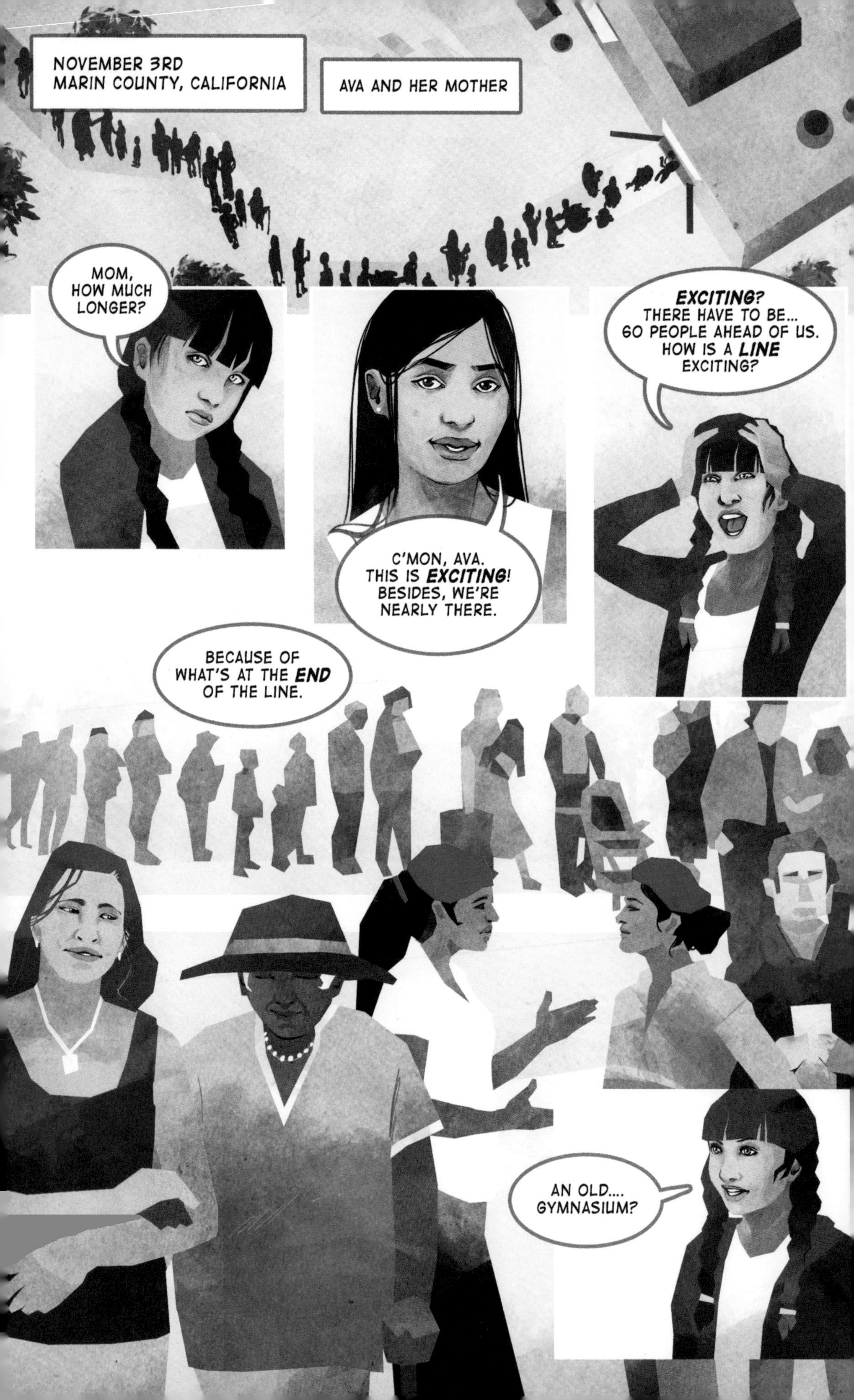
NOVEMBER 3RD
MARIN COUNTY, CALIFORNIA
AVA AND HER MOTHER
MOM, HOW MUCH LONGER?
C'MON, AVA. THIS IS EXCITING! BESIDES, WE'RE NEARLY THERE.
EXCITING? THERE HAVE TO BE... 60 PEOPLE AHEAD OF US. HOW IS A LINE EXCITING?
BECAUSE OF WHAT'S AT THE END OF THE LINE.
AN OLD.... GYMNASIUM?

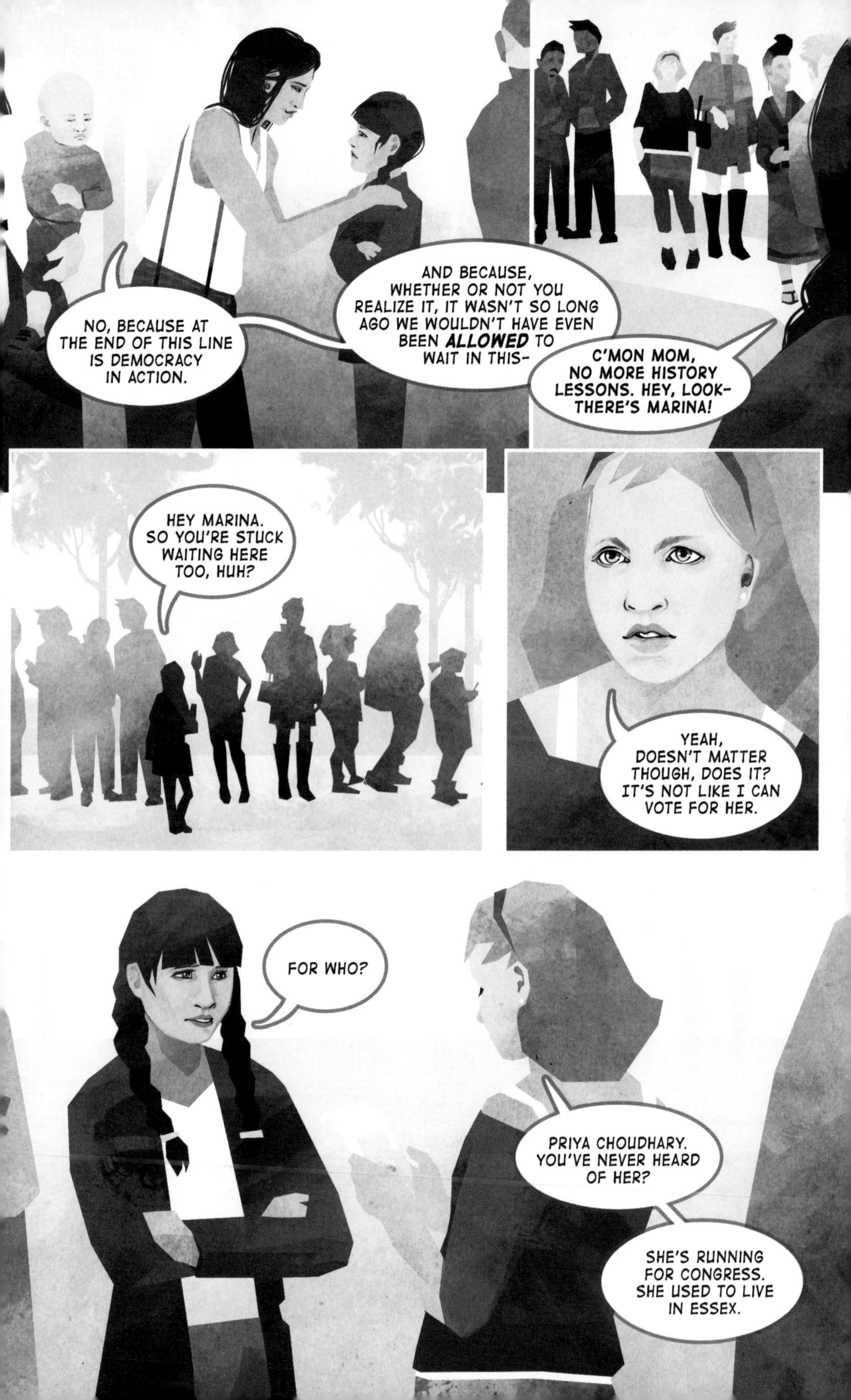
NO, BECAUSE AT THE END OF THIS LINE IS DEMOCRACY IN ACTION.
AND BECAUSE, WHETHER OR NOT YOU REALIZE IT, IT WASN'T SO LONG AGO WE WOULDN'T HAVE EVEN BEEN ALLOWED TO WAIT IN THIS-
C'MON MOM, NO MORE HISTORY LESSONS. HEY, LOOK- THERE'S MARINA!
HEY MARINA. SO YOU'RE STUCK WAITING HERE TOO, HUH?
YEAH, DOESN'T MATTER THOUGH, DOES IT? IT'S NOT LIKE I CAN VOTE FOR HER.
FOR WHO?
PRIYA CHOUDHARY. YOU'VE NEVER HEARD OF HER?
SHE'S RUNNING FOR CONGRESS. SHE USED TO LIVE IN ESSEX.

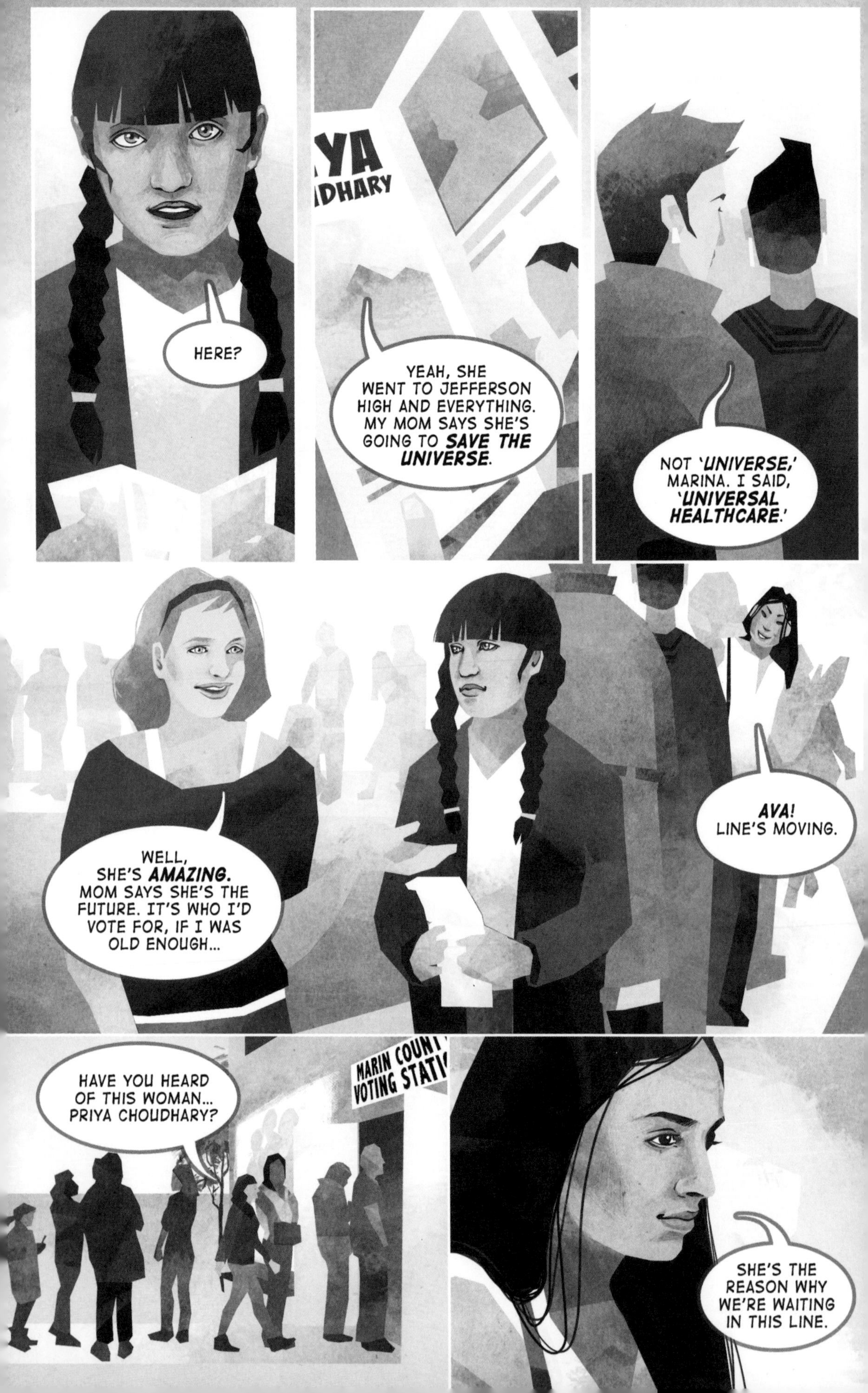
HERE?
YA
DHARY
YEAH, SHE WENT TO JEFFERSON HIGH AND EVERYTHING. MY MOM SAYS SHE'S GOING TO SAVE THE UNIVERSE.
NOT 'UNIVERSE,' MARINA. I SAID, 'UNIVERSAL HEALTHCARE.'
WELL, SHE'S AMAZING. MOM SAYS SHE'S THE FUTURE. IT'S WHO I'D VOTE FOR, IF I WAS OLD ENOUGH...
AVA! LINE'S MOVING.
HAVE YOU HEARD OF THIS WOMAN... PRIYA CHOUDHARY?
MARIN COUNT
VOTING STATI
SHE'S THE REASON WHY WE'RE WAITING IN THIS LINE.

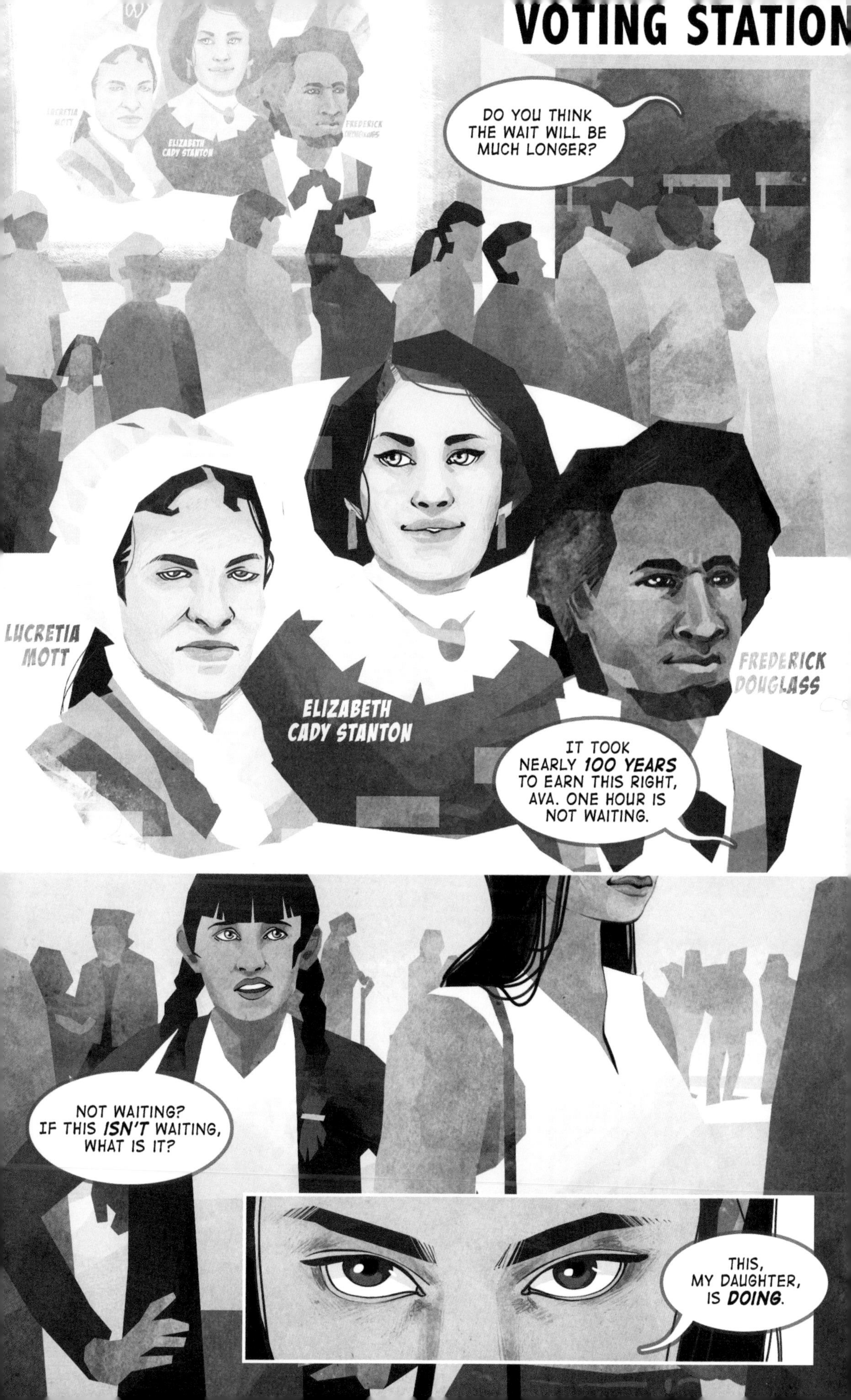
VOTING STATION
DO YOU THINK THE WAIT WILL BE MUCH LONGER?
LUCRETIA MOTT
ELIZABETH CADY STANTON
FREDERICK DOUGLASS
IT TOOK NEARLY **100 YEARS** TO EARN THIS RIGHT, AVA. ONE HOUR IS NOT WAITING.
NOT WAITING? IF THIS ***ISN'T*** WAITING, WHAT IS IT?
THIS, MY DAUGHTER, IS **DOING**.

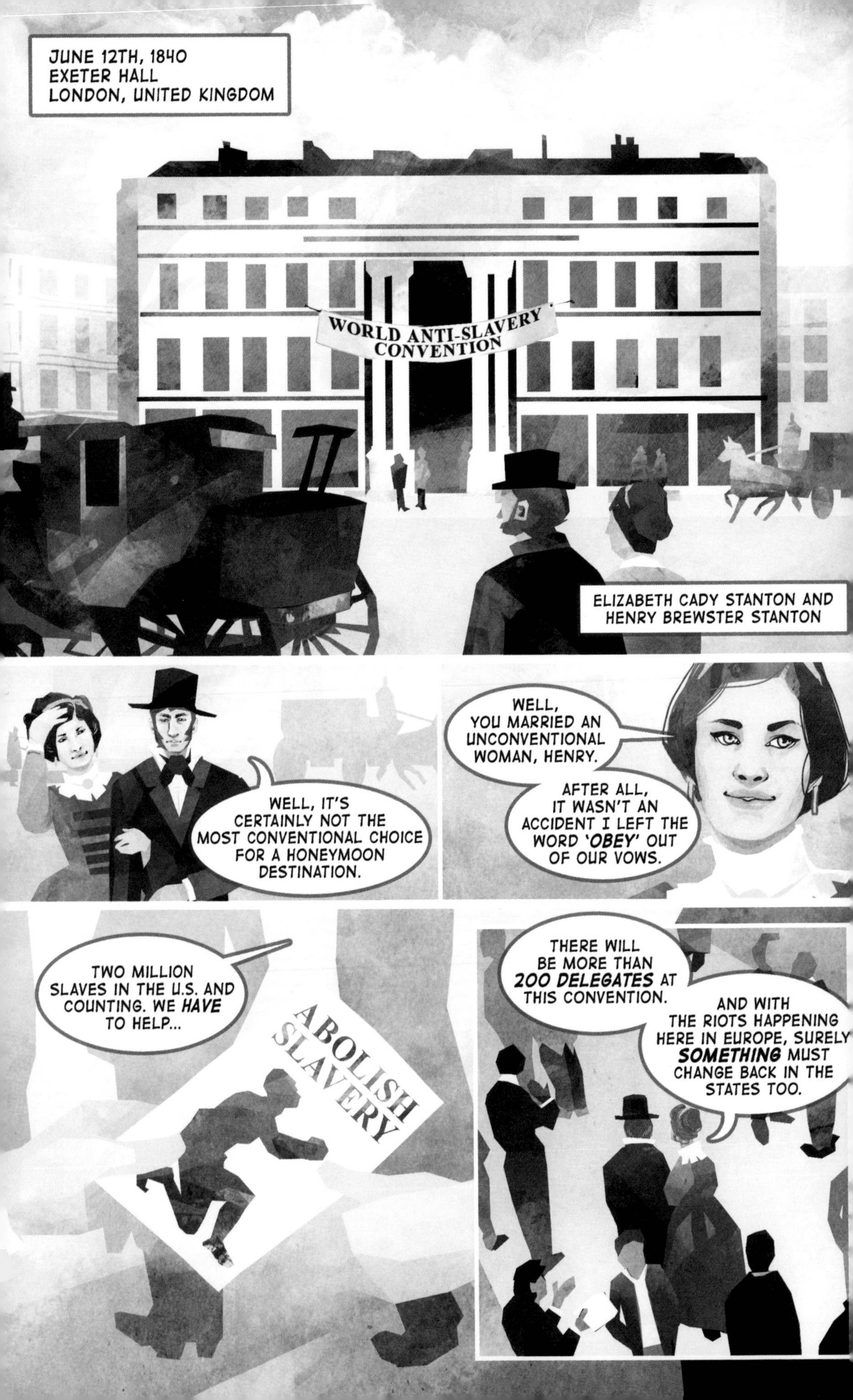
JUNE 12TH, 1840
EXETER HALL
LONDON, UNITED KINGDOM
WORLD ANTI-SLAVERY CONVENTION
ELIZABETH CADY STANTON AND HENRY BREWSTER STANTON
WELL, IT'S CERTAINLY NOT THE MOST CONVENTIONAL CHOICE FOR A HONEYMOON DESTINATION.
WELL, YOU MARRIED AN UNCONVENTIONAL WOMAN, HENRY.
AFTER ALL, IT WASN'T AN ACCIDENT I LEFT THE WORD '*OBEY*' OUT OF OUR VOWS.
TWO MILLION SLAVES IN THE U.S. AND COUNTING. WE *HAVE* TO HELP...
ABOLISH SLAVERY
THERE WILL BE MORE THAN **200 DELEGATES** AT THIS CONVENTION.
AND WITH THE RIOTS HAPPENING HERE IN EUROPE, SURELY **SOMETHING** MUST CHANGE BACK IN THE STATES TOO.

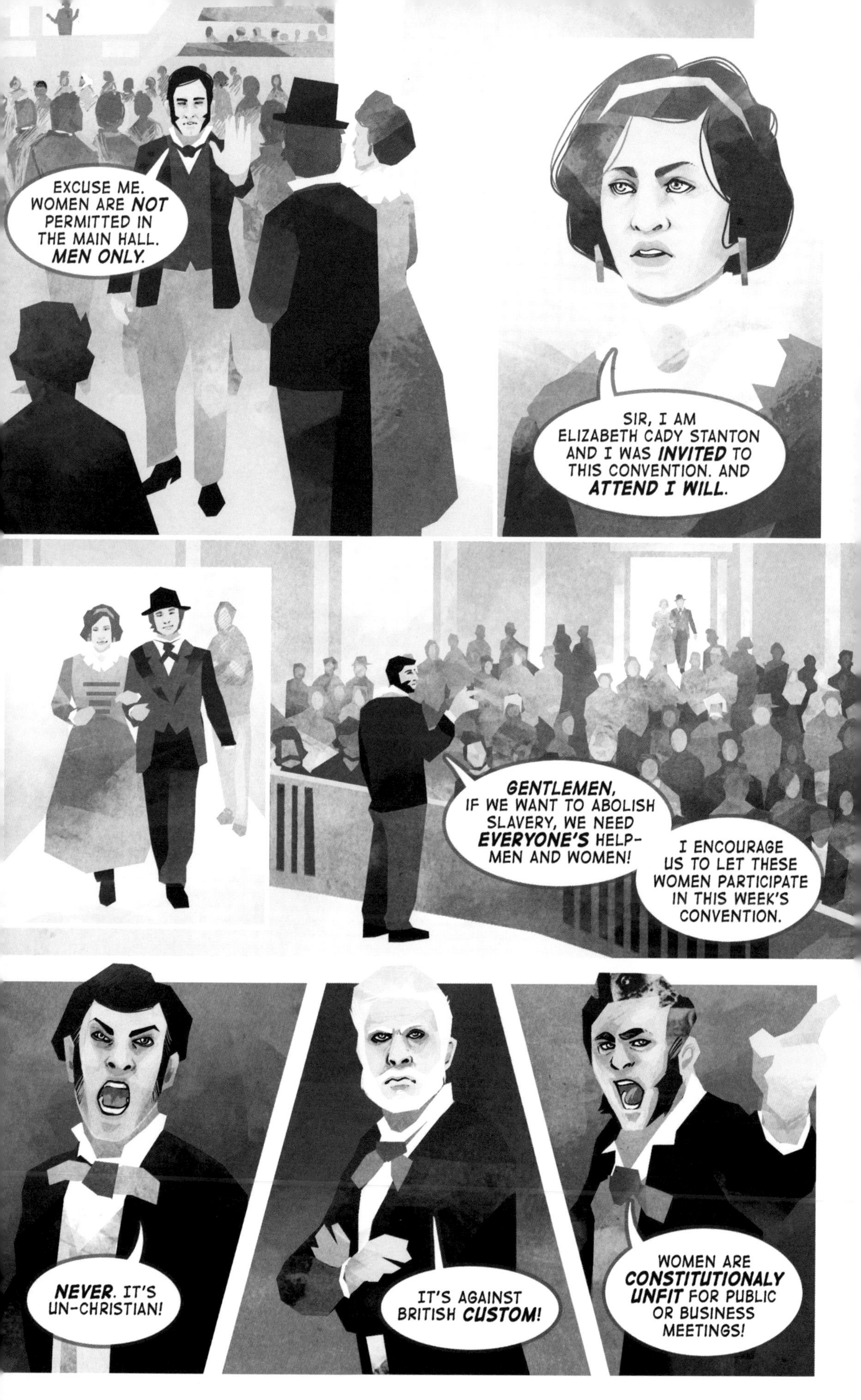
EXCUSE ME. WOMEN ARE NOT PERMITTED IN THE MAIN HALL. MEN ONLY.
SIR, I AM ELIZABETH CADY STANTON AND I WAS INVITED TO THIS CONVENTION. AND ATTEND I WILL.
GENTLEMEN, IF WE WANT TO ABOLISH SLAVERY, WE NEED EVERYONE'S HELP-MEN AND WOMEN!
I ENCOURAGE US TO LET THESE WOMEN PARTICIPATE IN THIS WEEK'S CONVENTION.
NEVER. IT'S UN-CHRISTIAN!
IT'S AGAINST BRITISH CUSTOM!
WOMEN ARE CONSTITUTIONALY UNFIT FOR PUBLIC OR BUSINESS MEETINGS!

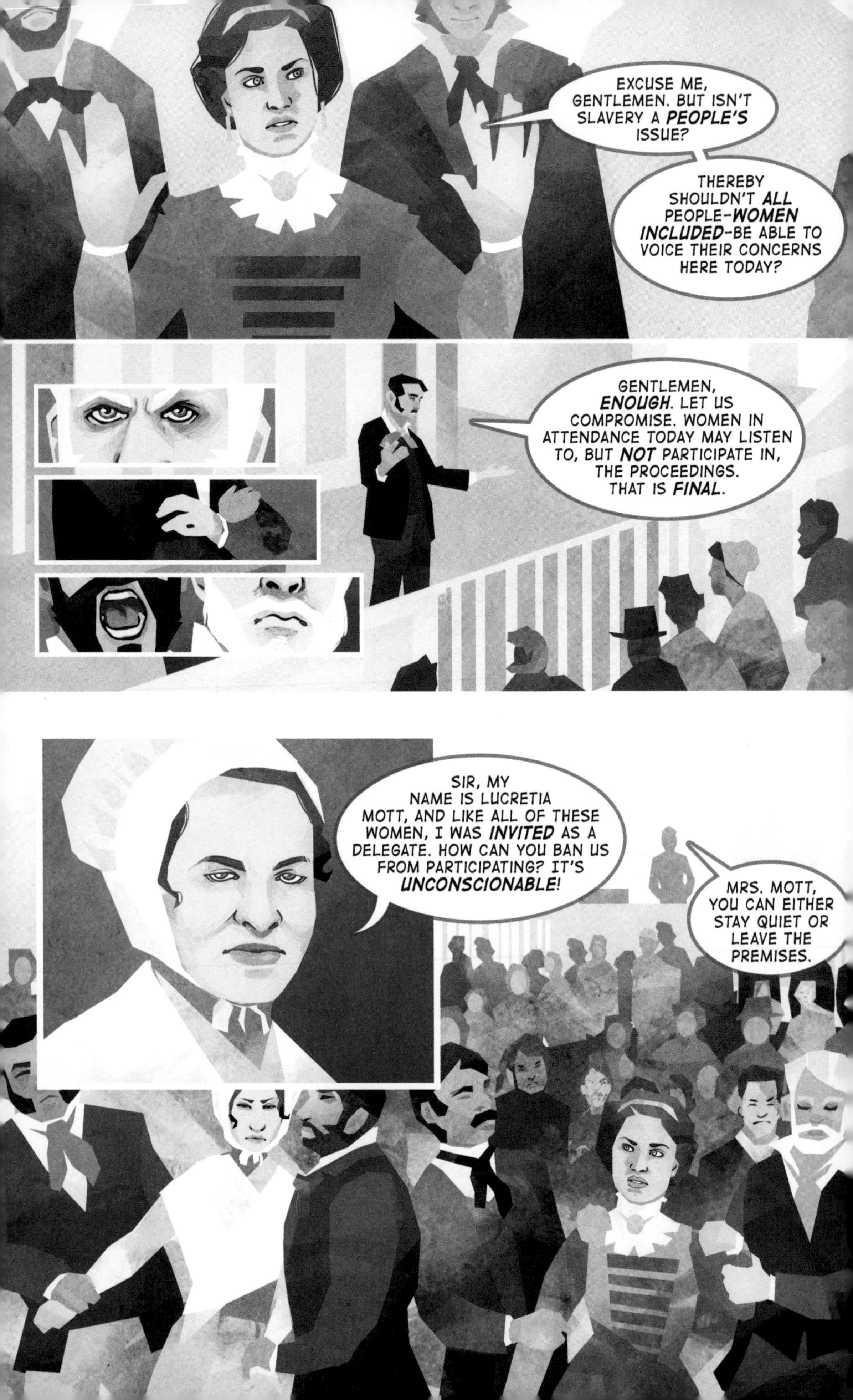
EXCUSE ME, GENTLEMEN. BUT ISN'T SLAVERY A **PEOPLE'S** ISSUE?
THEREBY SHOULDN'T **ALL** PEOPLE-**WOMEN INCLUDED**-BE ABLE TO VOICE THEIR CONCERNS HERE TODAY?
GENTLEMEN, **ENOUGH**. LET US COMPROMISE. WOMEN IN ATTENDANCE TODAY MAY LISTEN TO, BUT **NOT** PARTICIPATE IN, THE PROCEEDINGS. THAT IS **FINAL**.
SIR, MY NAME IS LUCRETIA MOTT, AND LIKE ALL OF THESE WOMEN, I WAS **INVITED** AS A DELEGATE. HOW CAN YOU BAN US FROM PARTICIPATING? IT'S **UNCONSCIONABLE**!
MRS. MOTT, YOU CAN EITHER STAY QUIET OR LEAVE THE PREMISES.

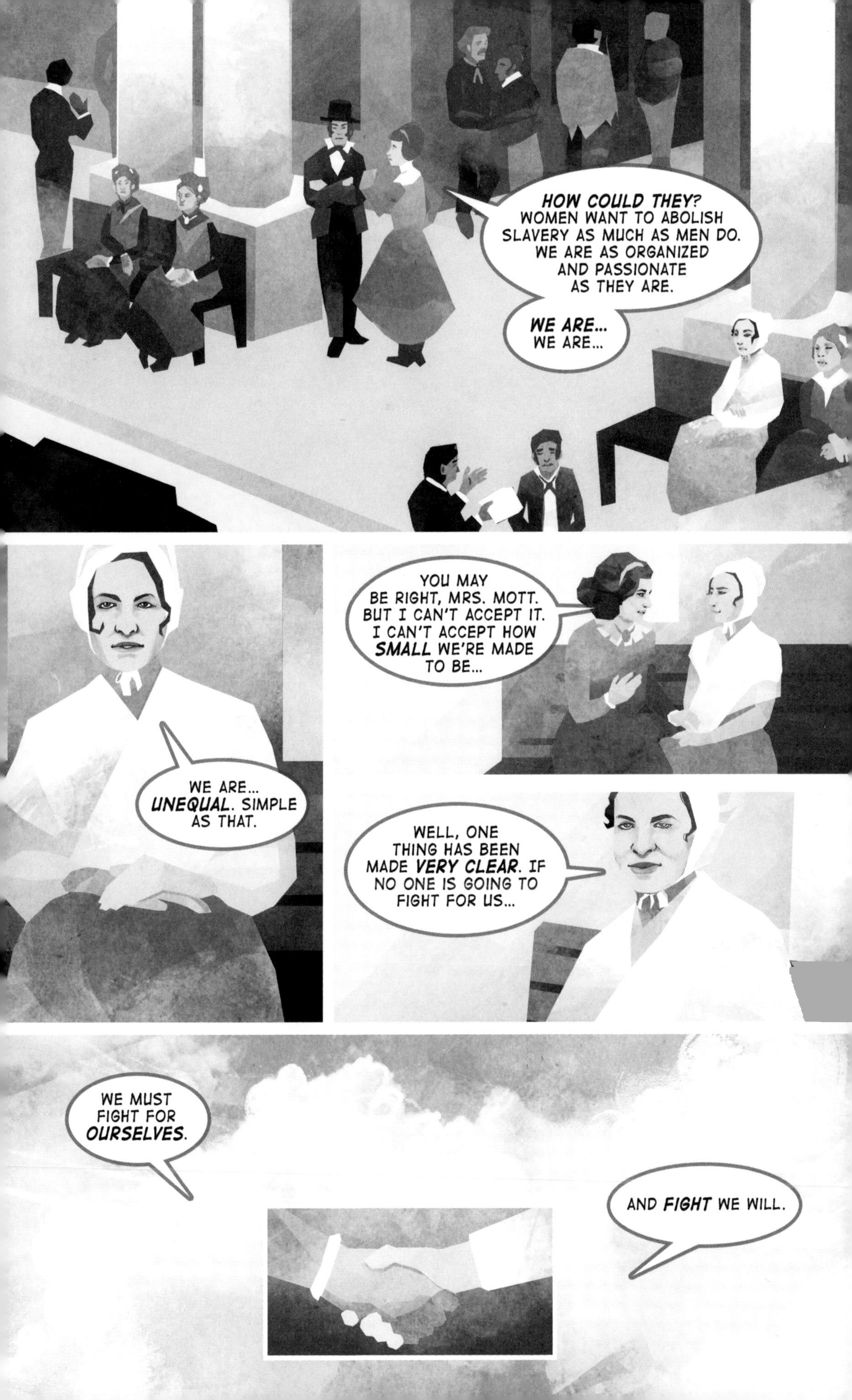
HOW COULD THEY? WOMEN WANT TO ABOLISH SLAVERY AS MUCH AS MEN DO. WE ARE AS ORGANIZED AND PASSIONATE AS THEY ARE.
WE ARE... WE ARE...
WE ARE... UNEQUAL. SIMPLE AS THAT.
YOU MAY BE RIGHT, MRS. MOTT. BUT I CAN'T ACCEPT IT. I CAN'T ACCEPT HOW SMALL WE'RE MADE TO BE...
WELL, ONE THING HAS BEEN MADE VERY CLEAR. IF NO ONE IS GOING TO FIGHT FOR US...
WE MUST FIGHT FOR OURSELVES.
AND FIGHT WE WILL.

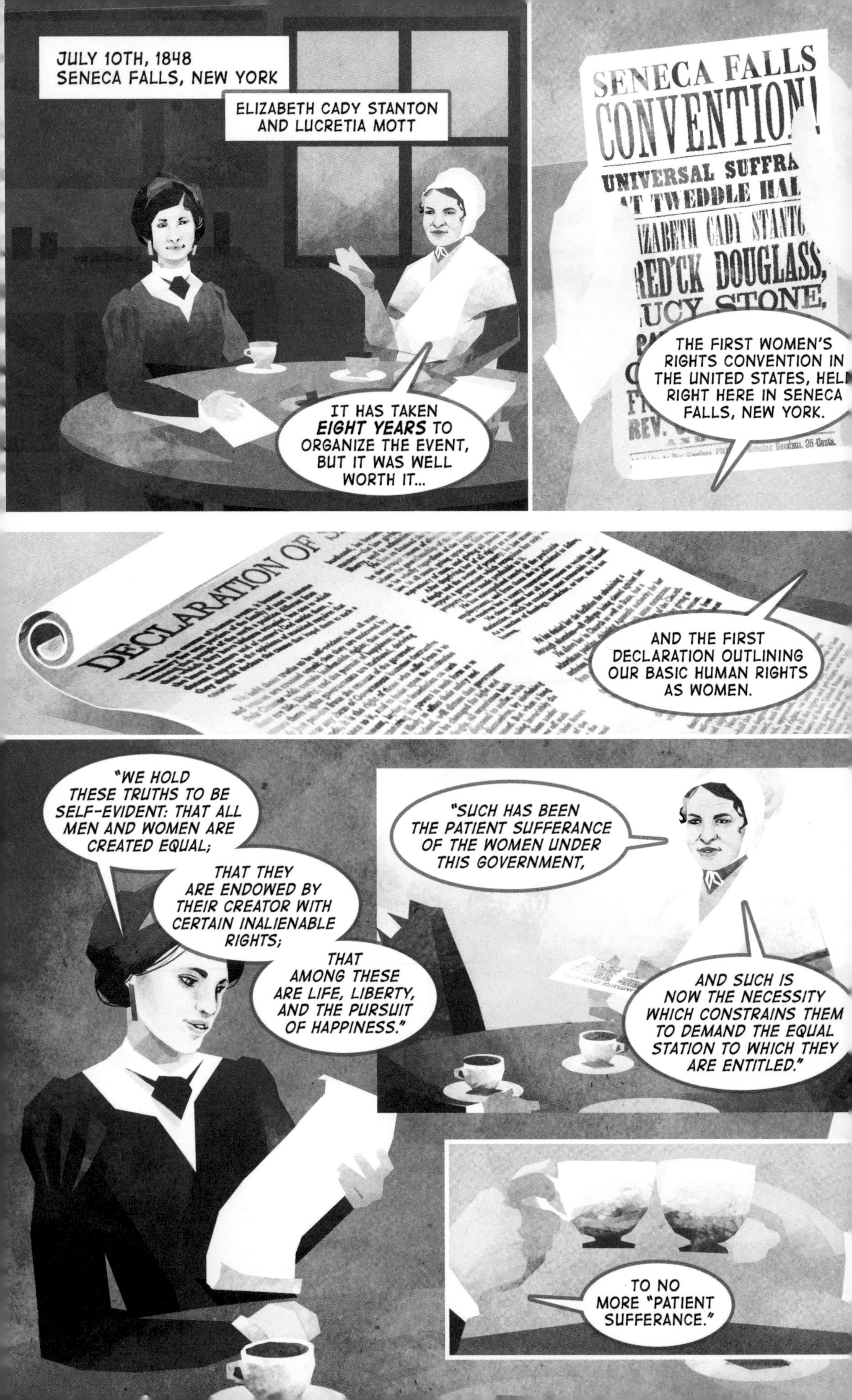

JULY 10TH, 1848
SENECA FALLS, NEW YORK
ELIZABETH CADY STANTON AND LUCRETIA MOTT
IT HAS TAKEN **EIGHT YEARS** TO ORGANIZE THE EVENT, BUT IT WAS WELL WORTH IT...
SENECA FALLS CONVENTION!
THE FIRST WOMEN'S RIGHTS CONVENTION IN THE UNITED STATES, HELD RIGHT HERE IN SENECA FALLS, NEW YORK.
DECLARATION OF
AND THE FIRST DECLARATION OUTLINING OUR BASIC HUMAN RIGHTS AS WOMEN.
"WE HOLD THESE TRUTHS TO BE SELF-EVIDENT: THAT ALL MEN AND WOMEN ARE CREATED EQUAL;
THAT THEY ARE ENDOWED BY THEIR CREATOR WITH CERTAIN INALIENABLE RIGHTS;
THAT AMONG THESE ARE LIFE, LIBERTY, AND THE PURSUIT OF HAPPINESS."
"SUCH HAS BEEN THE PATIENT SUFFERANCE OF THE WOMEN UNDER THIS GOVERNMENT,
AND SUCH IS NOW THE NECESSITY WHICH CONSTRAINS THEM TO DEMAND THE EQUAL STATION TO WHICH THEY ARE ENTITLED."
TO NO MORE "PATIENT SUFFERANCE."

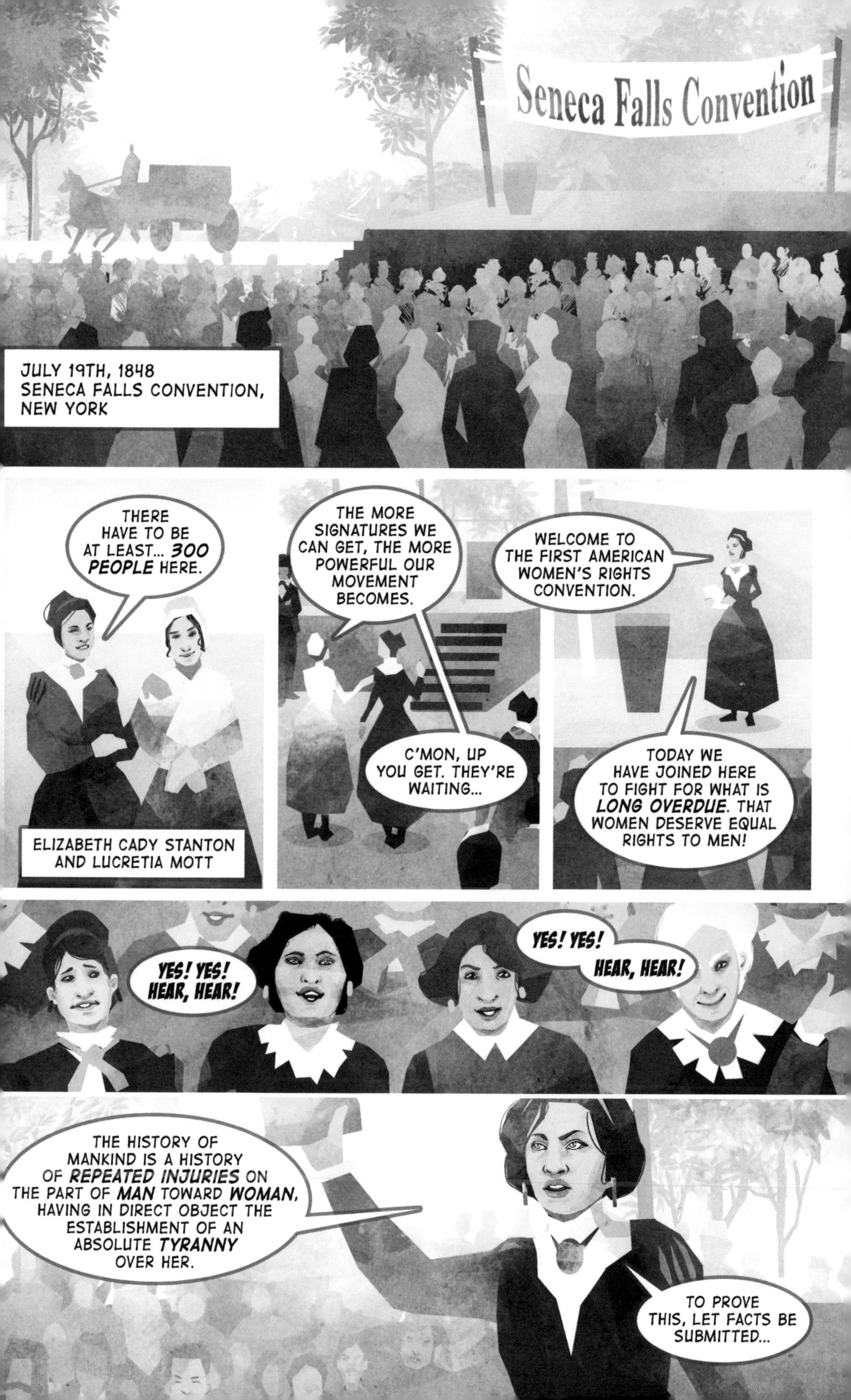
Seneca Falls Convention
JULY 19TH, 1848 SENECA FALLS CONVENTION, NEW YORK
THERE HAVE TO BE AT LEAST... 300 PEOPLE HERE.
ELIZABETH CADY STANTON AND LUCRETIA MOTT
THE MORE SIGNATURES WE CAN GET, THE MORE POWERFUL OUR MOVEMENT BECOMES.
C'MON, UP YOU GET. THEY'RE WAITING...
WELCOME TO THE FIRST AMERICAN WOMEN'S RIGHTS CONVENTION.
TODAY WE HAVE JOINED HERE TO FIGHT FOR WHAT IS LONG OVERDUE. THAT WOMEN DESERVE EQUAL RIGHTS TO MEN!
YES! YES! HEAR, HEAR!
YES! YES!
HEAR, HEAR!
THE HISTORY OF MANKIND IS A HISTORY OF REPEATED INJURIES ON THE PART OF MAN TOWARD WOMAN, HAVING IN DIRECT OBJECT THE ESTABLISHMENT OF AN ABSOLUTE TYRANNY OVER HER.
TO PROVE THIS, LET FACTS BE SUBMITTED...

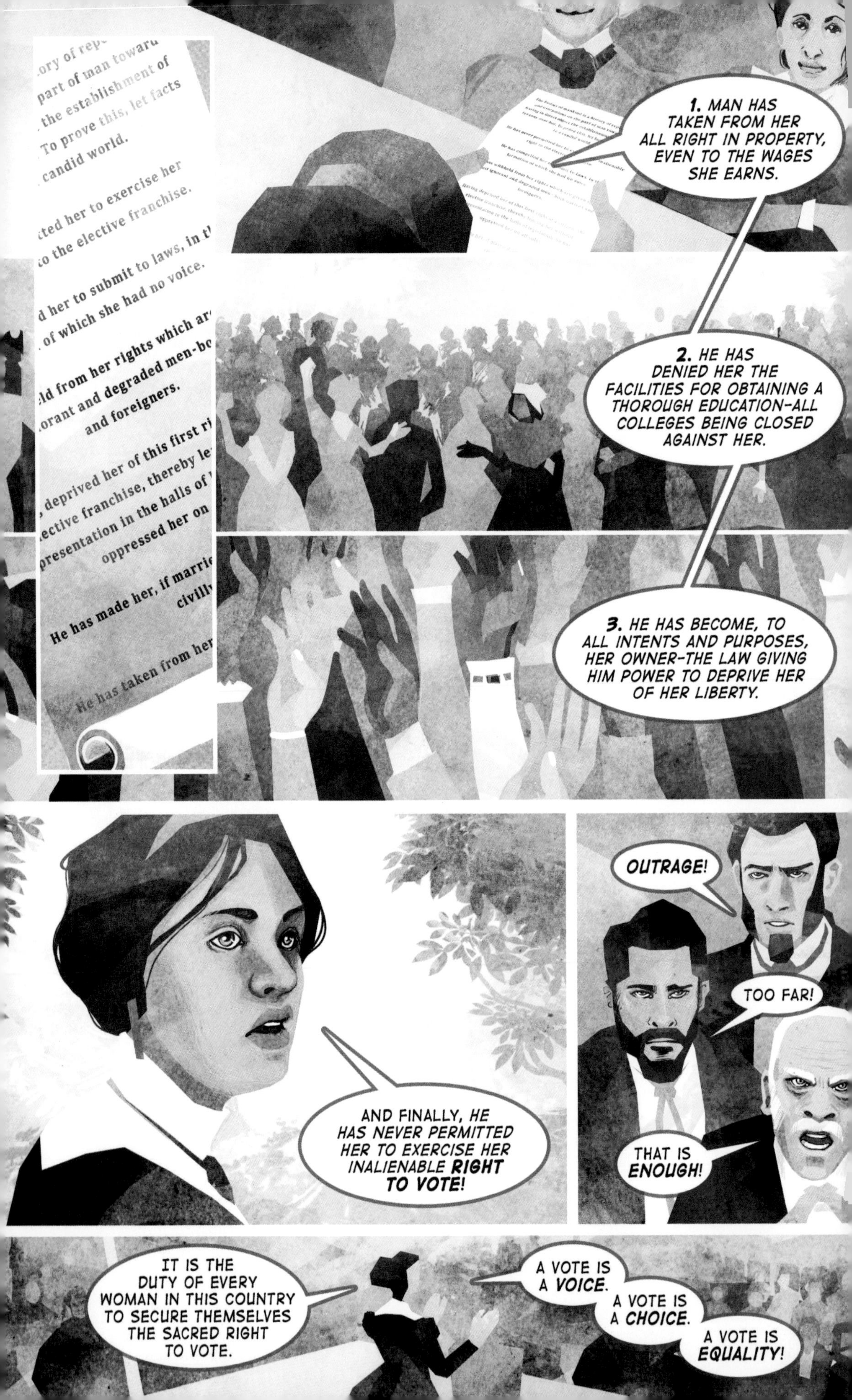
1. MAN HAS TAKEN FROM HER ALL RIGHT IN PROPERTY, EVEN TO THE WAGES SHE EARNS.
2. HE HAS DENIED HER THE FACILITIES FOR OBTAINING A THOROUGH EDUCATION–ALL COLLEGES BEING CLOSED AGAINST HER.
3. HE HAS BECOME, TO ALL INTENTS AND PURPOSES, HER OWNER–THE LAW GIVING HIM POWER TO DEPRIVE HER OF HER LIBERTY.
AND FINALLY, HE HAS NEVER PERMITTED HER TO EXERCISE HER INALIENABLE RIGHT TO VOTE!
OUTRAGE!
TOO FAR!
THAT IS ENOUGH!
IT IS THE DUTY OF EVERY WOMAN IN THIS COUNTRY TO SECURE THEMSELVES THE SACRED RIGHT TO VOTE.
A VOTE IS A VOICE.
A VOTE IS A CHOICE.
A VOTE IS EQUALITY!

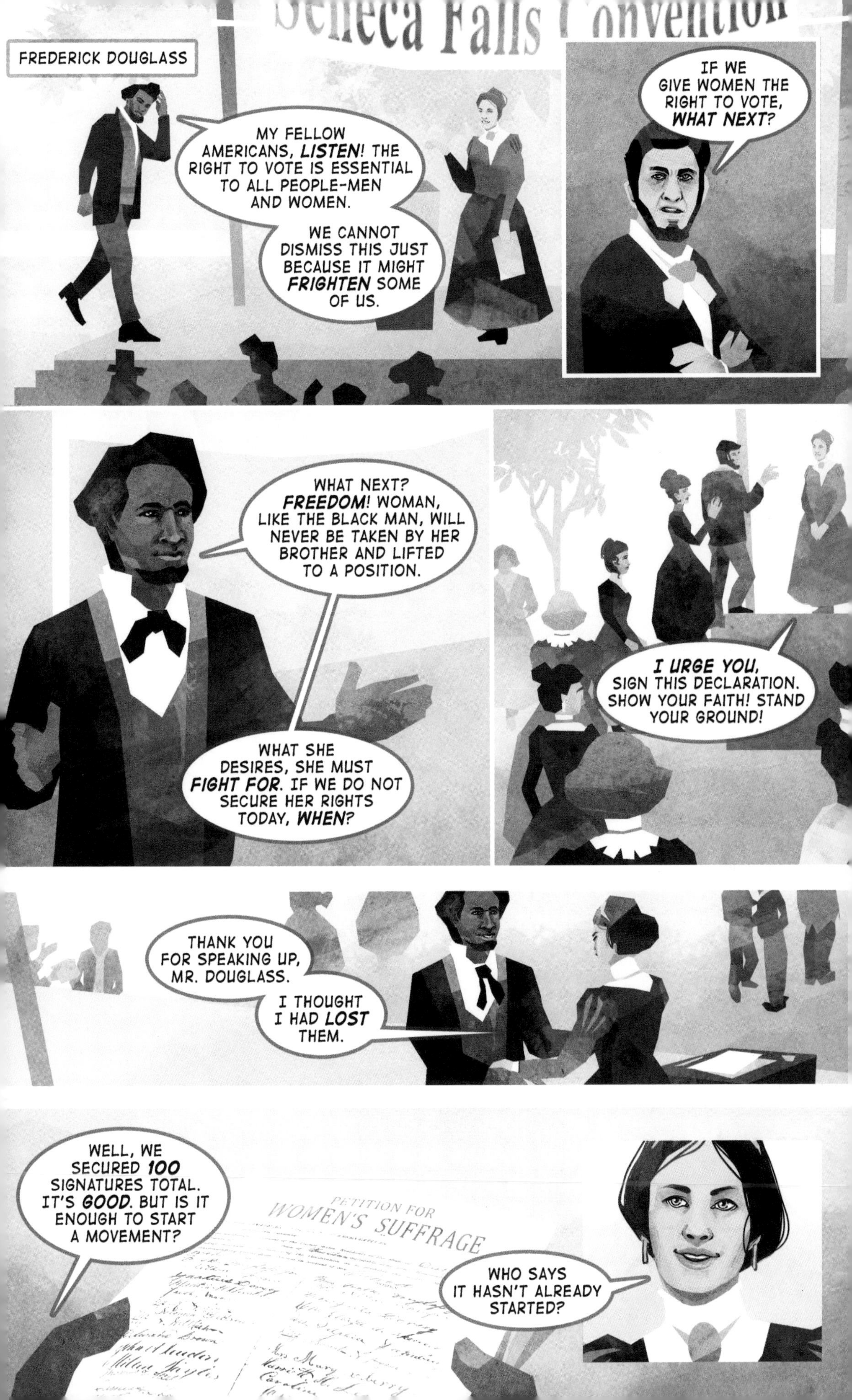

Seneca Falls Convention
FREDERICK DOUGLASS
MY FELLOW AMERICANS, LISTEN! THE RIGHT TO VOTE IS ESSENTIAL TO ALL PEOPLE-MEN AND WOMEN.
WE CANNOT DISMISS THIS JUST BECAUSE IT MIGHT FRIGHTEN SOME OF US.
IF WE GIVE WOMEN THE RIGHT TO VOTE, WHAT NEXT?
WHAT NEXT? FREEDOM! WOMAN, LIKE THE BLACK MAN, WILL NEVER BE TAKEN BY HER BROTHER AND LIFTED TO A POSITION.
WHAT SHE DESIRES, SHE MUST FIGHT FOR. IF WE DO NOT SECURE HER RIGHTS TODAY, WHEN?
I URGE YOU, SIGN THIS DECLARATION. SHOW YOUR FAITH! STAND YOUR GROUND!
THANK YOU FOR SPEAKING UP, MR. DOUGLASS.
I THOUGHT I HAD LOST THEM.
WELL, WE SECURED 100 SIGNATURES TOTAL. IT'S GOOD. BUT IS IT ENOUGH TO START A MOVEMENT?
PETITION FOR WOMEN'S SUFFRAGE
WHO SAYS IT HASN'T ALREADY STARTED?

"IF THE FIRST WOMAN GOD EVER MADE WAS
STRONG ENOUGH TO TURN THE WORLD UPSIDE
DOWN ALL ALONE, THESE WOMEN TOGETHER
OUGHT TO BE ABLE TO TURN IT BACK AND GET
IT RIGHT SIDE UP AGAIN! AND NOW THEY IS
ASKING TO DO IT, THE MEN BETTER LET THEM."

SOJOURNER TRUTH
1797–1883

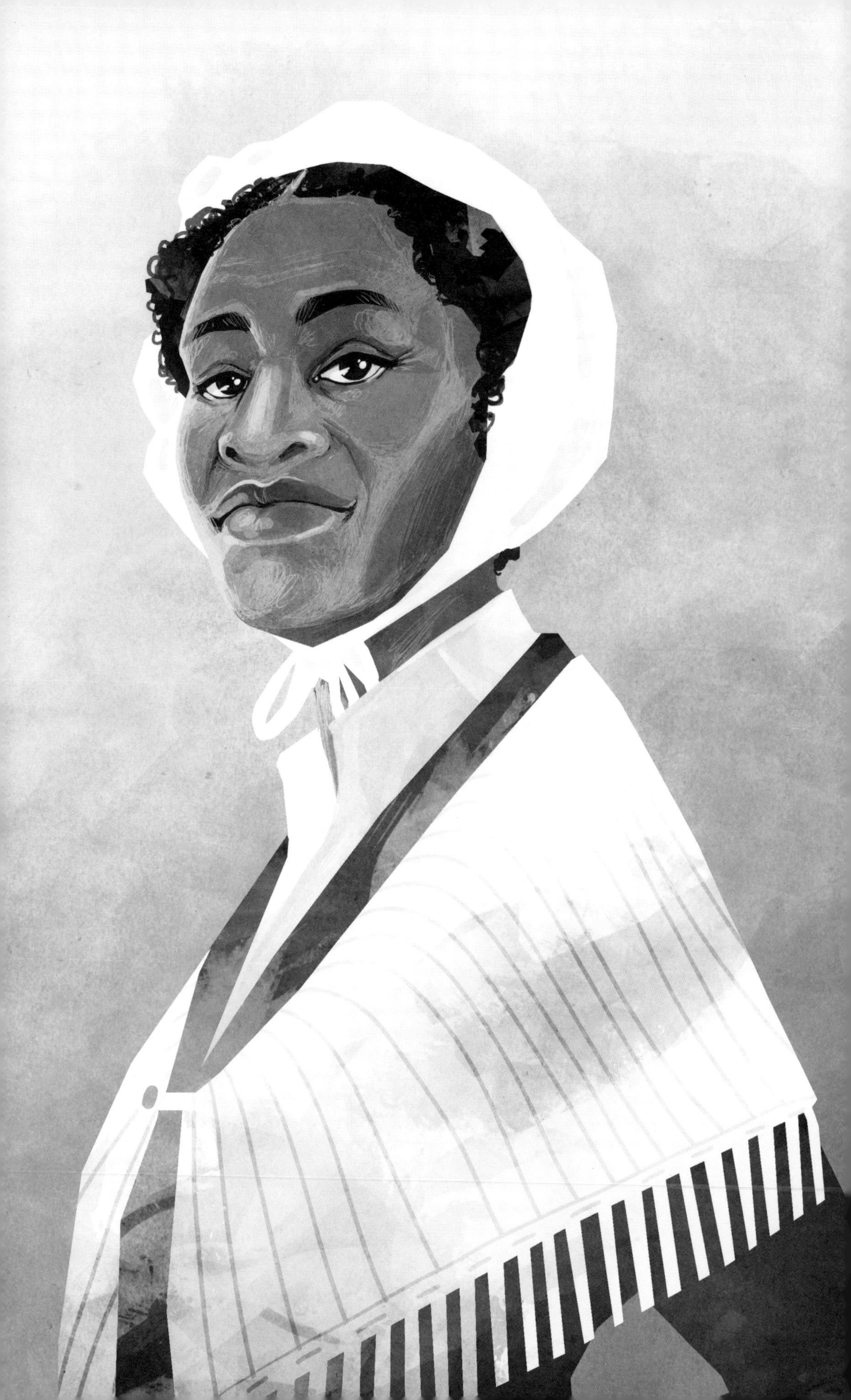

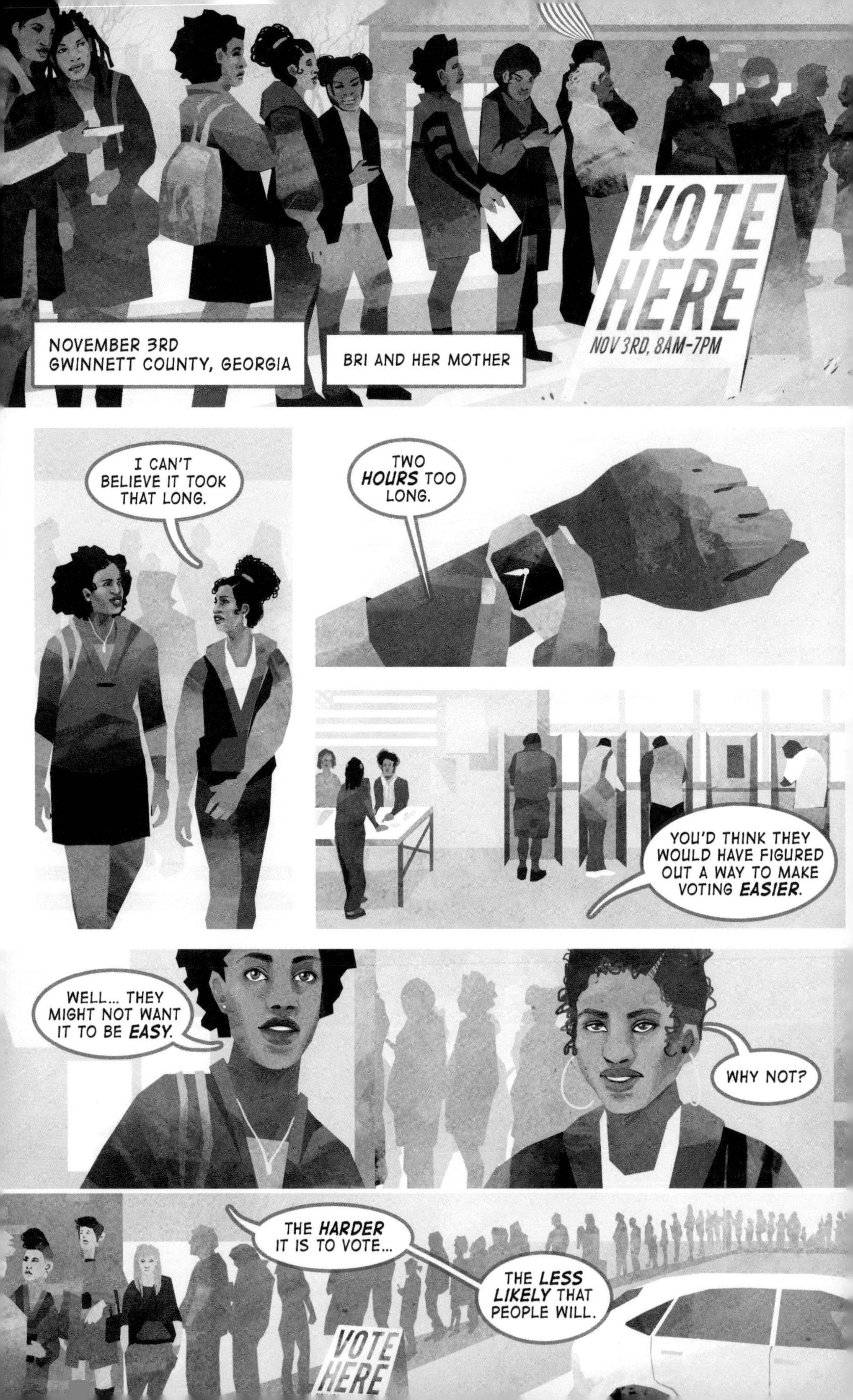

NOVEMBER 3RD
GWINNETT COUNTY, GEORGIA
BRI AND HER MOTHER
VOTE HERE
NOV 3RD, 8AM-7PM
I CAN'T BELIEVE IT TOOK THAT LONG.
TWO HOURS TOO LONG.
YOU'D THINK THEY WOULD HAVE FIGURED OUT A WAY TO MAKE VOTING EASIER.
WELL... THEY MIGHT NOT WANT IT TO BE EASY.
WHY NOT?
THE HARDER IT IS TO VOTE...
THE LESS LIKELY THAT PEOPLE WILL.
VOTE HERE

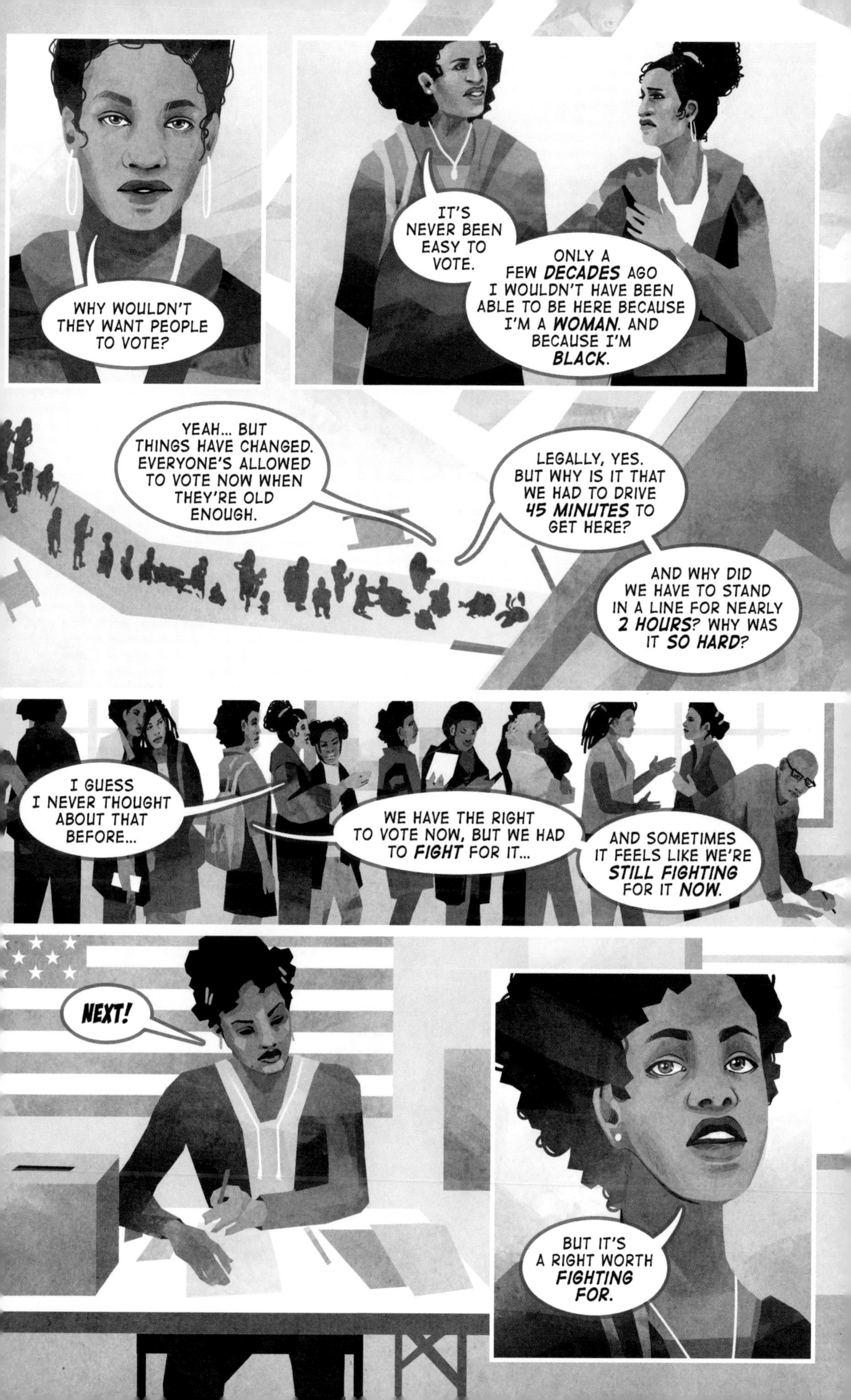
WHY WOULDN'T THEY WANT PEOPLE TO VOTE?
IT'S NEVER BEEN EASY TO VOTE.
ONLY A FEW DECADES AGO I WOULDN'T HAVE BEEN ABLE TO BE HERE BECAUSE I'M A WOMAN. AND BECAUSE I'M BLACK.
YEAH... BUT THINGS HAVE CHANGED. EVERYONE'S ALLOWED TO VOTE NOW WHEN THEY'RE OLD ENOUGH.
LEGALLY, YES. BUT WHY IS IT THAT WE HAD TO DRIVE 45 MINUTES TO GET HERE?
AND WHY DID WE HAVE TO STAND IN A LINE FOR NEARLY 2 HOURS? WHY WAS IT SO HARD?
I GUESS I NEVER THOUGHT ABOUT THAT BEFORE...
WE HAVE THE RIGHT TO VOTE NOW, BUT WE HAD TO FIGHT FOR IT...
AND SOMETIMES IT FEELS LIKE WE'RE STILL FIGHTING FOR IT NOW.
NEXT!
BUT IT'S A RIGHT WORTH FIGHTING FOR.

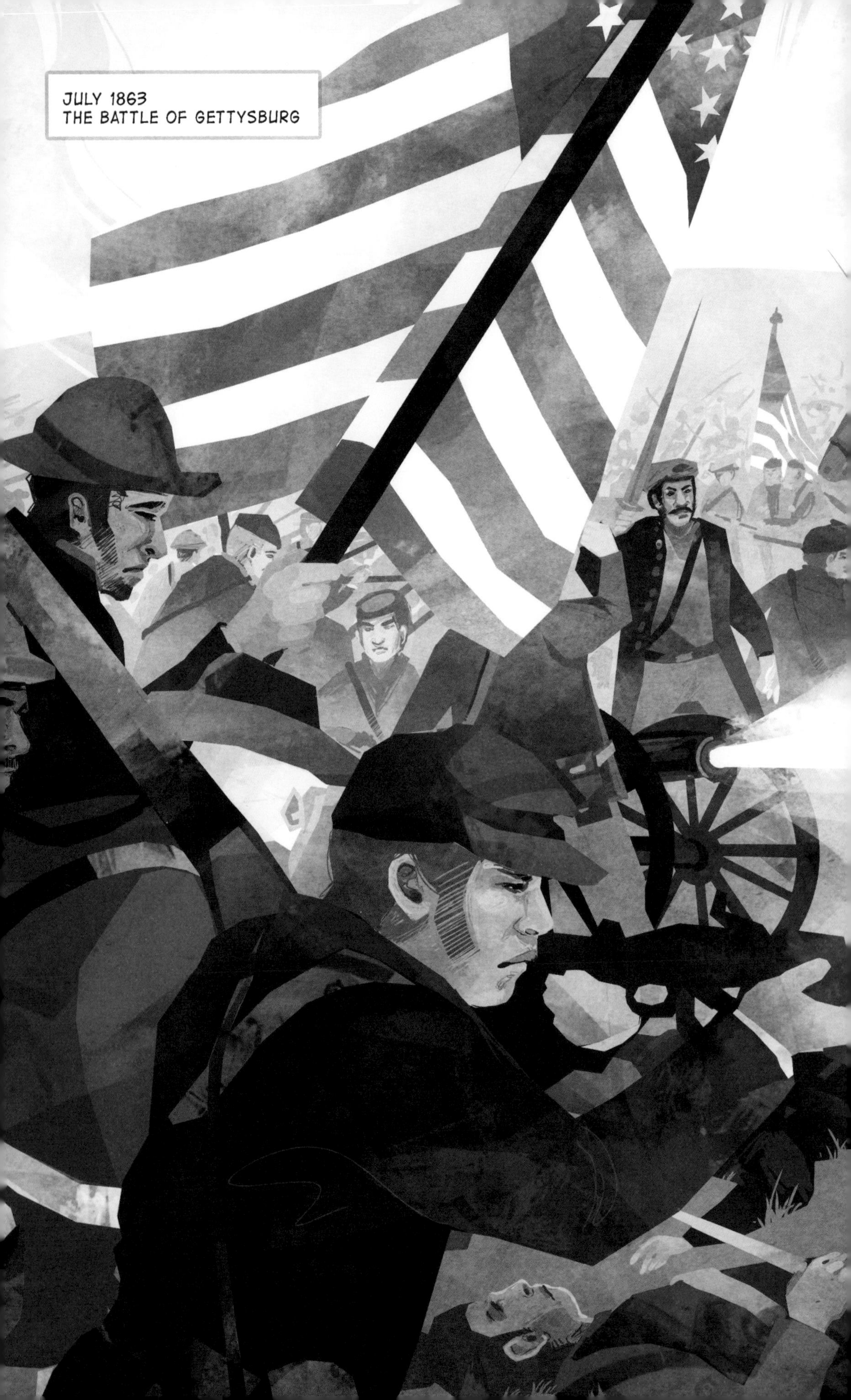
JULY 1863
THE BATTLE OF GETTYSBURG

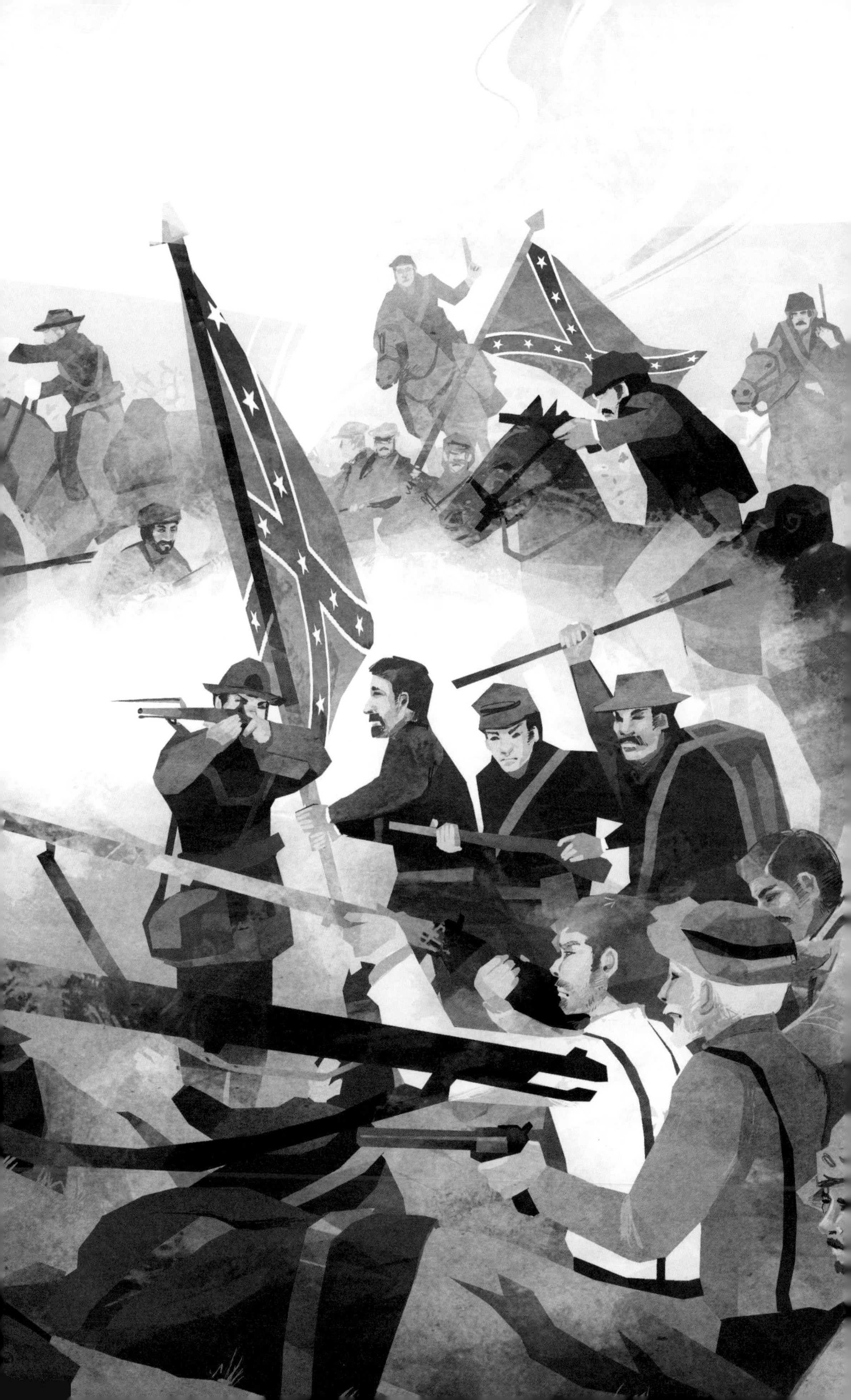

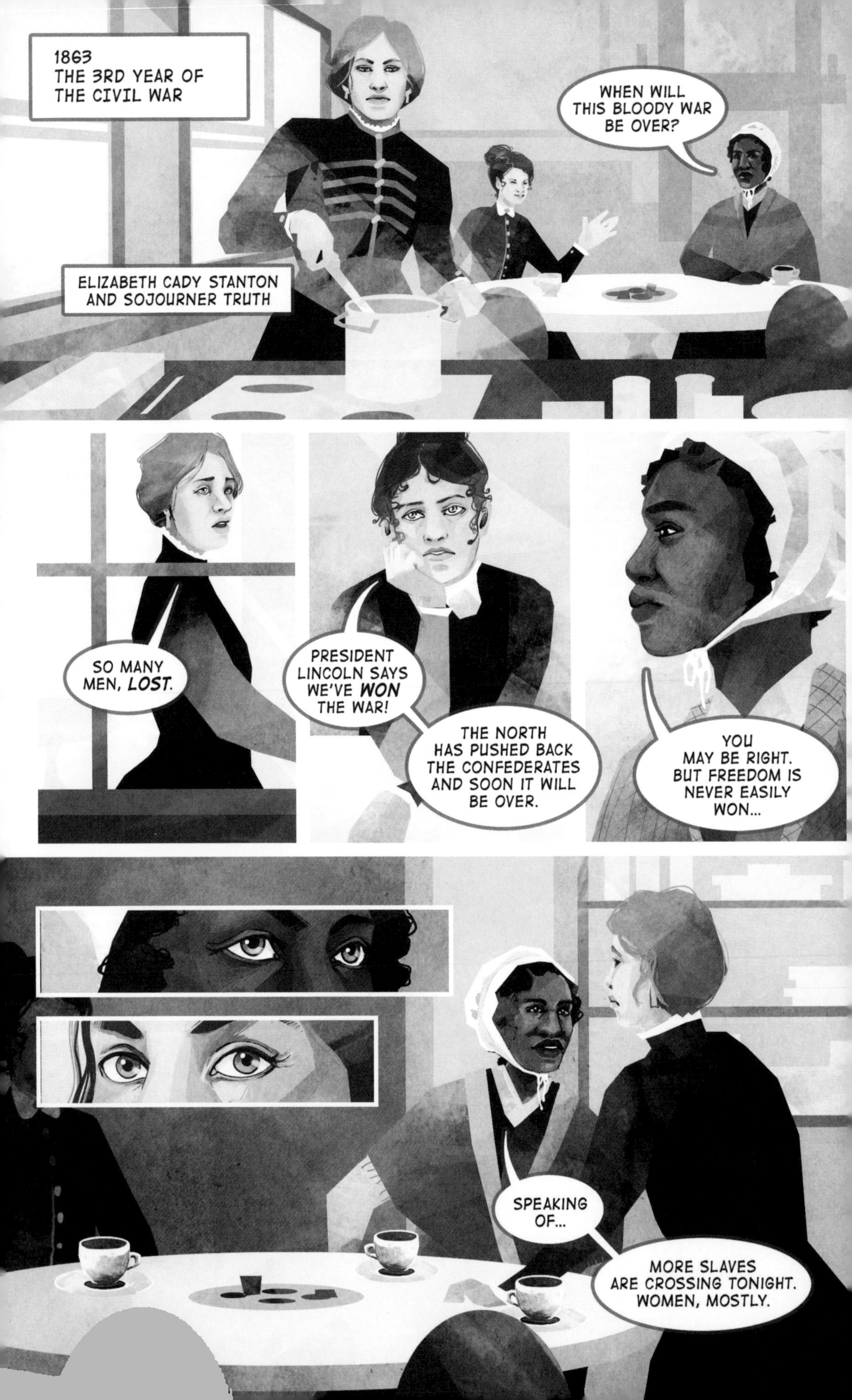
1863
THE 3RD YEAR OF
THE CIVIL WAR
WHEN WILL
THIS BLOODY WAR
BE OVER?
ELIZABETH CADY STANTON
AND SOJOURNER TRUTH
SO MANY
MEN, *LOST*.
PRESIDENT
LINCOLN SAYS
WE'VE *WON*
THE WAR!
THE NORTH
HAS PUSHED BACK
THE CONFEDERATES
AND SOON IT WILL
BE OVER.
YOU
MAY BE RIGHT.
BUT FREEDOM IS
NEVER EASILY
WON...
SPEAKING
OF...
MORE SLAVES
ARE CROSSING TONIGHT.
WOMEN, MOSTLY.

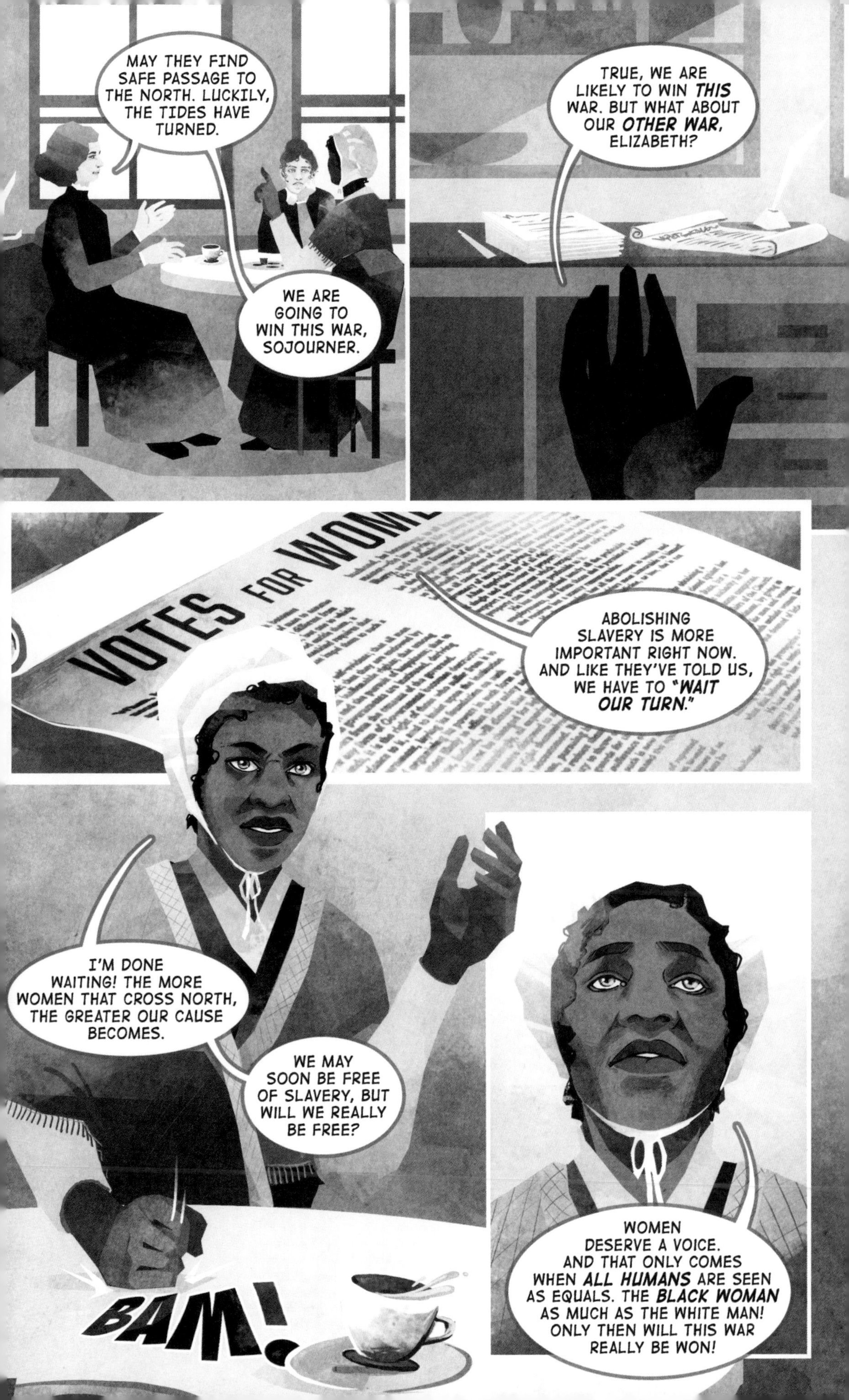
MAY THEY FIND SAFE PASSAGE TO THE NORTH. LUCKILY, THE TIDES HAVE TURNED.
WE ARE GOING TO WIN THIS WAR, SOJOURNER.
TRUE, WE ARE LIKELY TO WIN *THIS* WAR. BUT WHAT ABOUT OUR *OTHER WAR*, ELIZABETH?
VOTES FOR WOM
ABOLISHING SLAVERY IS MORE IMPORTANT RIGHT NOW. AND LIKE THEY'VE TOLD US, WE HAVE TO "*WAIT OUR TURN*."
I'M DONE WAITING! THE MORE WOMEN THAT CROSS NORTH, THE GREATER OUR CAUSE BECOMES.
WE MAY SOON BE FREE OF SLAVERY, BUT WILL WE REALLY BE FREE?
BAM!
WOMEN DESERVE A VOICE. AND THAT ONLY COMES WHEN *ALL HUMANS* ARE SEEN AS EQUALS. THE *BLACK WOMAN* AS MUCH AS THE WHITE MAN! ONLY THEN WILL THIS WAR REALLY BE WON!

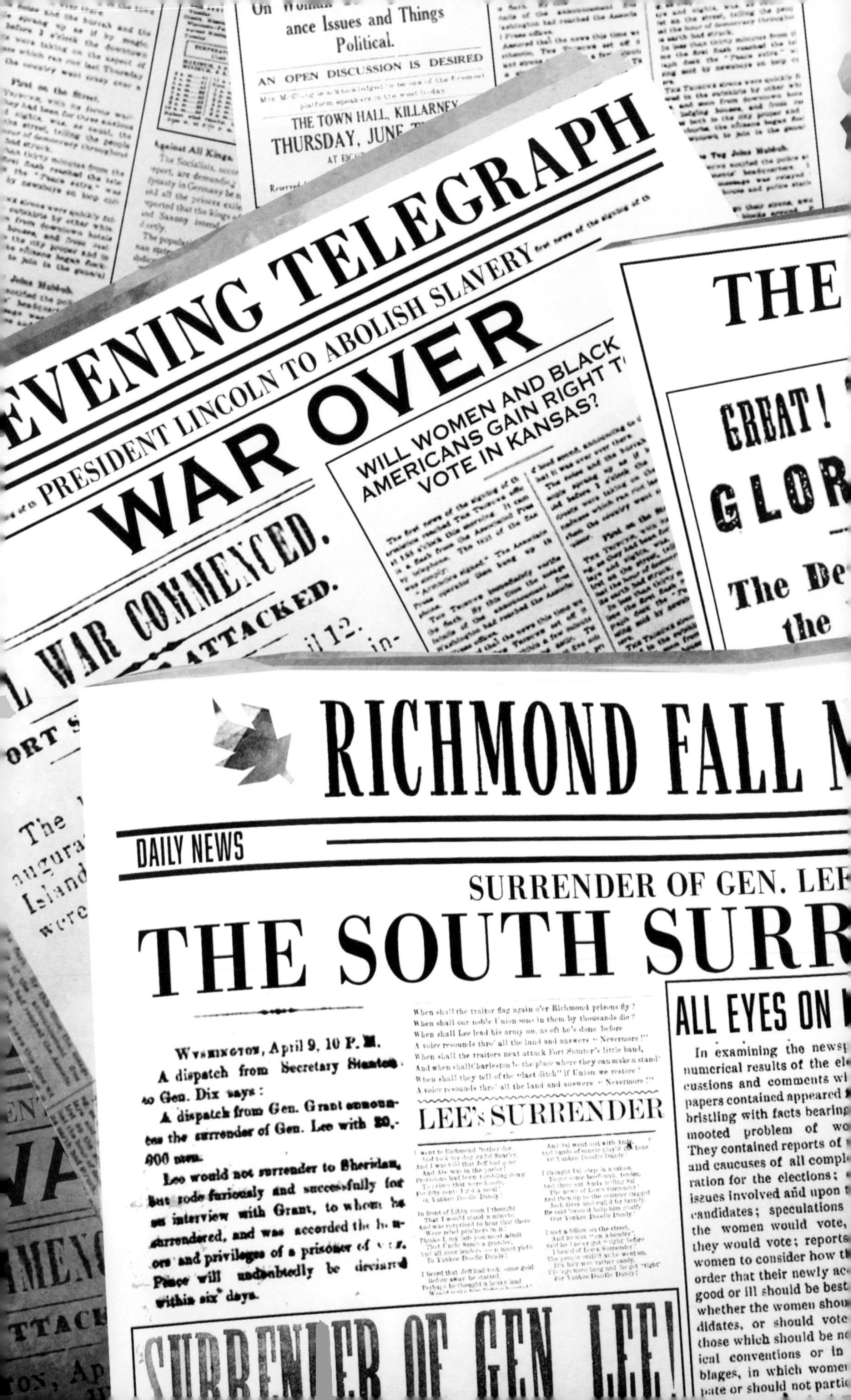

ance Issues and Things Political.
AN OPEN DISCUSSION IS DESIRED
THE TOWN HALL, KILLARNEY
THURSDAY, JUNE
EVENING TELEGRAPH
PRESIDENT LINCOLN TO ABOLISH SLAVERY
WAR OVER
WILL WOMEN AND BLACK AMERICANS GAIN RIGHT TO VOTE IN KANSAS?
WAR COMMENCED.
ATTACKED.
THE
GREAT!
GLOR
The De
the
RICHMOND FALL
DAILY NEWS
SURRENDER OF GEN. LE
THE SOUTH SURR
ALL EYES ON
Washington, April 9, 10 P. M.
A dispatch from Secretary Stanton to Gen. Dix says:
A dispatch from Gen. Grant announces the surrender of Gen. Lee with 20,000 men.
Lee would not surrender to Sheridan, but rode furiously and successfully for an interview with Grant, to whom he surrendered, and was accorded the honors and privileges of a prisoner of war.
Peace will undoubtedly be declared within six days.
When shall the traitor flag again o'er Richmond prisons fly?
When shall our noble Union sons in them by thousands die?
When shall Lee lead his army on, as oft he's done before
A voice resounds thro' all the land and answers "Nevermore!"
When shall the traitors next attack Fort Sumter's little band,
And when shall Charleston be the place where they can make a stand?
When shall they tell of the "last ditch" if Union we restore?
A voice resounds thro' all the land and answers "Nevermore!"
LEE'S SURRENDER
SURRENDER OF GEN. LEE!
In examining the newsp
numerical results of the el
cussions and comments wh
papers contained appeared
bristling with facts bearing
mooted problem of wo
They contained reports of
and caucuses of all comple
ration for the elections;
issues involved and upon t
candidates; speculations
the women would vote,
they would vote; reports
women to consider how th
order that their newly ac
good or ill should be best
whether the women shou
didates, or should vote
those which should be n
ical conventions or in
blages, in which women
pate or should not partic

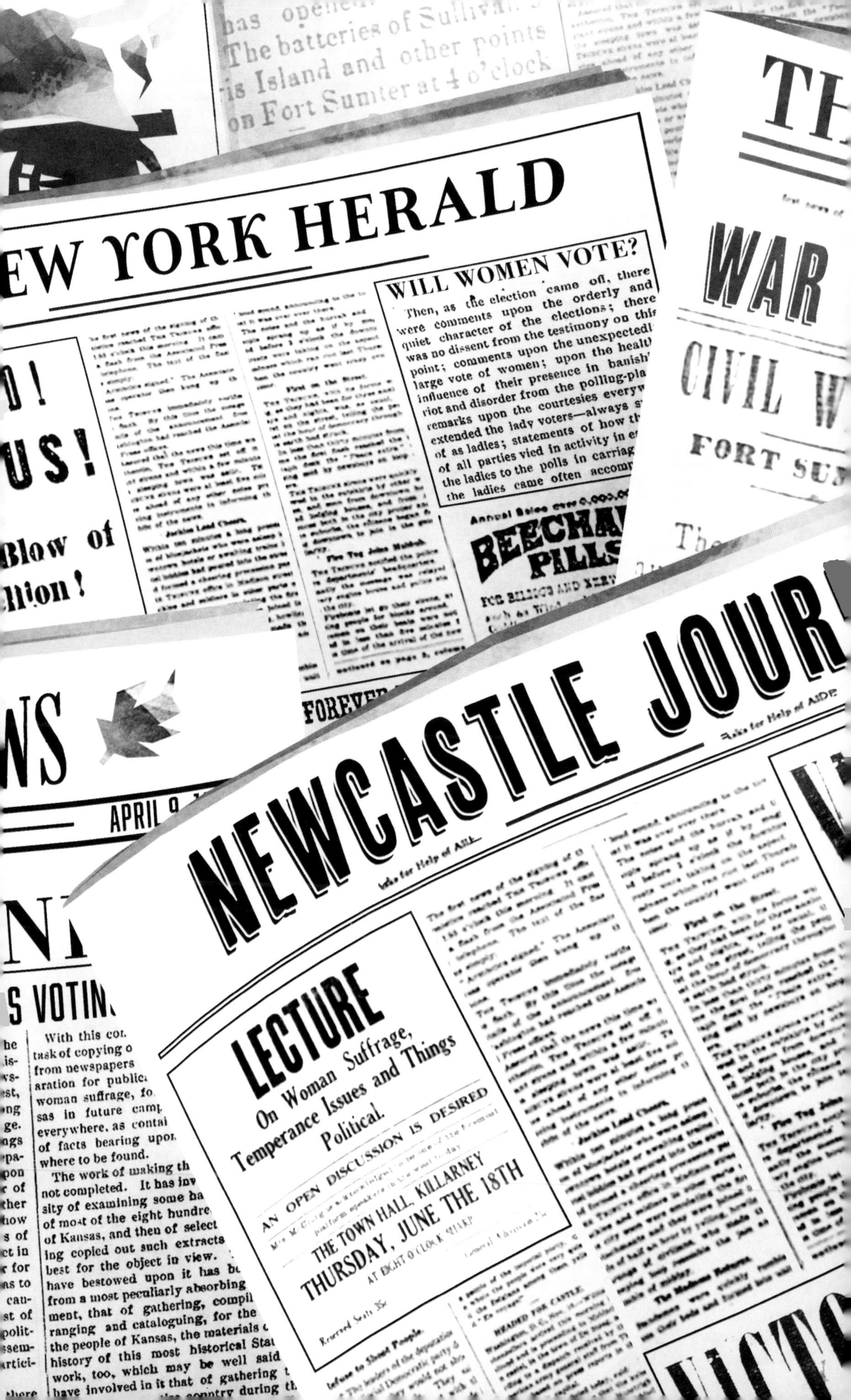

has opened
The batteries of Sullivan's
is Island and other points
on Fort Sumter at 4 o'clock
EW YORK HERALD
WILL WOMEN VOTE?
Then, as the election came off, there were comments upon the orderly and quiet character of the elections; there was no dissent from the testimony on this point; comments upon the unexpectedl large vote of women; upon the healt influence of their presence in banish riot and disorder from the polling-pla remarks upon the courtesies everyw extended the lady voters—always s of as ladies; statements of how th of all parties vied in activity in es the ladies to the polls in carriag the ladies came often accomp
BEECHA
PILLS
WAR
CIVIL W
FORT SU
US!
Blow of
llion!
WS
APRIL 9
FOREVER
NEWCASTLE JOUR
LECTURE
On Woman Suffrage, Temperance Issues and Things Political.
OPEN DISCUSSION IS DESIRED
AN OPEN DISCUSSION
THE TOWN HALL, KILLARNEY
THURSDAY, JUNE THE 18TH
AT EIGHT O'CLOCK SHARP
S VOTIN
With this co task of copying o from newspapers aration for public woman suffrage, fo sas in future camp everywhere, as contai of facts bearing upo where to be found.
The work of making th not completed. It has inv sity of examining some ha of most of the eight hundre of Kansas, and then of select ing copied out such extracts best for the object in view. have bestowed upon it has be from a most peculiarly absorbing ment, that of gathering, compil ranging and cataloguing, for the the people of Kansas, the materials history of this most historical Sta work, too, which may be well said have involved in it that of gathering

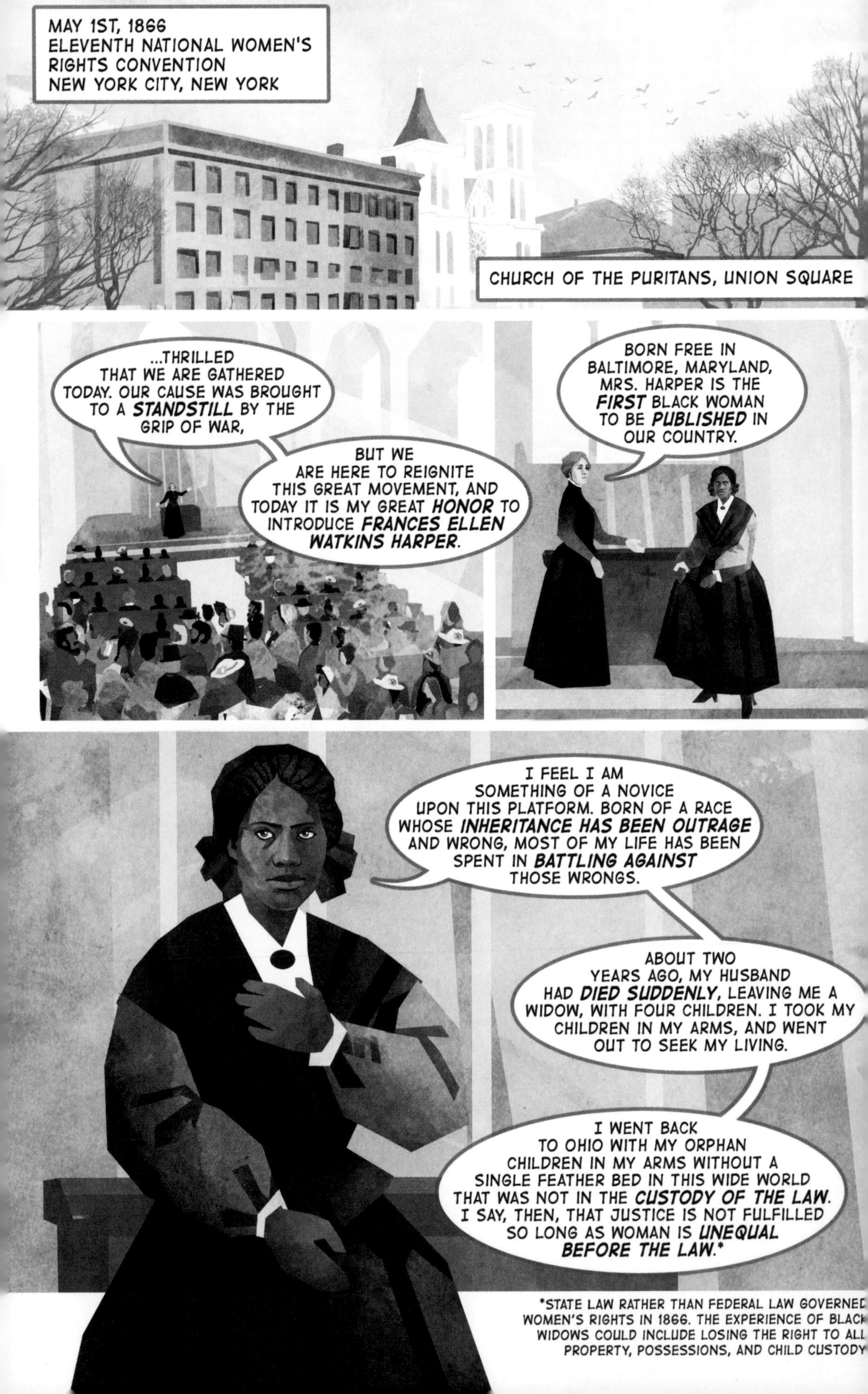
MAY 1ST, 1866
ELEVENTH NATIONAL WOMEN'S RIGHTS CONVENTION
NEW YORK CITY, NEW YORK
CHURCH OF THE PURITANS, UNION SQUARE
...THRILLED THAT WE ARE GATHERED TODAY. OUR CAUSE WAS BROUGHT TO A STANDSTILL BY THE GRIP OF WAR,
BUT WE ARE HERE TO REIGNITE THIS GREAT MOVEMENT, AND TODAY IT IS MY GREAT HONOR TO INTRODUCE FRANCES ELLEN WATKINS HARPER.
BORN FREE IN BALTIMORE, MARYLAND, MRS. HARPER IS THE FIRST BLACK WOMAN TO BE PUBLISHED IN OUR COUNTRY.
I FEEL I AM SOMETHING OF A NOVICE UPON THIS PLATFORM. BORN OF A RACE WHOSE INHERITANCE HAS BEEN OUTRAGE AND WRONG, MOST OF MY LIFE HAS BEEN SPENT IN BATTLING AGAINST THOSE WRONGS.
ABOUT TWO YEARS AGO, MY HUSBAND HAD DIED SUDDENLY, LEAVING ME A WIDOW, WITH FOUR CHILDREN. I TOOK MY CHILDREN IN MY ARMS, AND WENT OUT TO SEEK MY LIVING.
I WENT BACK TO OHIO WITH MY ORPHAN CHILDREN IN MY ARMS WITHOUT A SINGLE FEATHER BED IN THIS WIDE WORLD THAT WAS NOT IN THE CUSTODY OF THE LAW. I SAY, THEN, THAT JUSTICE IS NOT FULFILLED SO LONG AS WOMAN IS UNEQUAL BEFORE THE LAW.*

*STATE LAW RATHER THAN FEDERAL LAW GOVERNED WOMEN'S RIGHTS IN 1866. THE EXPERIENCE OF BLACK WIDOWS COULD INCLUDE LOSING THE RIGHT TO ALL PROPERTY, POSSESSIONS, AND CHILD CUSTODY

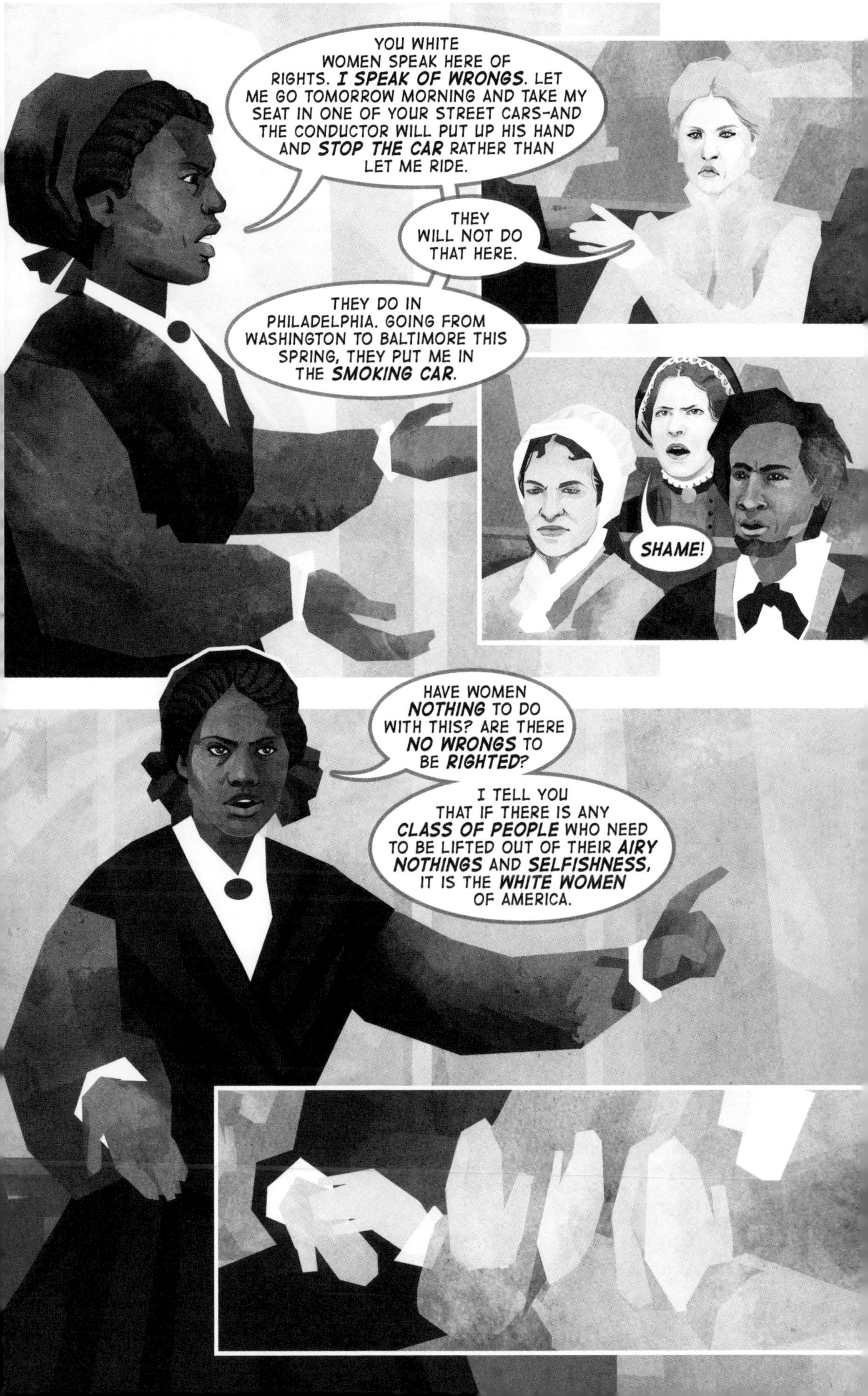
YOU WHITE WOMEN SPEAK HERE OF RIGHTS. I SPEAK OF WRONGS. LET ME GO TOMORROW MORNING AND TAKE MY SEAT IN ONE OF YOUR STREET CARS–AND THE CONDUCTOR WILL PUT UP HIS HAND AND STOP THE CAR RATHER THAN LET ME RIDE.
THEY WILL NOT DO THAT HERE.
THEY DO IN PHILADELPHIA. GOING FROM WASHINGTON TO BALTIMORE THIS SPRING, THEY PUT ME IN THE SMOKING CAR.
SHAME!
HAVE WOMEN NOTHING TO DO WITH THIS? ARE THERE NO WRONGS TO BE RIGHTED?
I TELL YOU THAT IF THERE IS ANY CLASS OF PEOPLE WHO NEED TO BE LIFTED OUT OF THEIR AIRY NOTHINGS AND SELFISHNESS, IT IS THE WHITE WOMEN OF AMERICA.

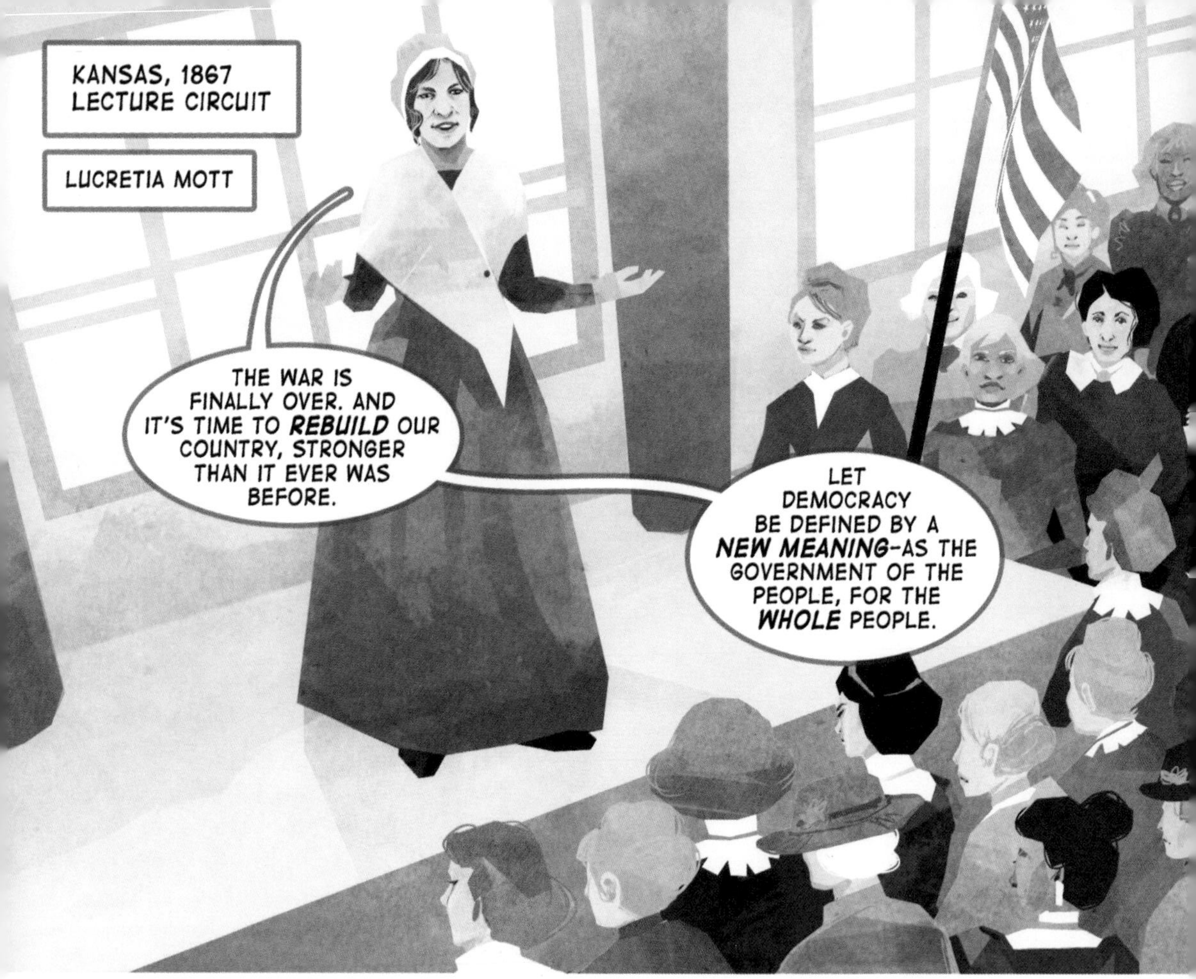
KANSAS, 1867
LECTURE CIRCUIT
LUCRETIA MOTT
THE WAR IS FINALLY OVER. AND IT'S TIME TO ***REBUILD*** OUR COUNTRY, STRONGER THAN IT EVER WAS BEFORE.
LET DEMOCRACY BE DEFINED BY A ***NEW MEANING***–AS THE GOVERNMENT OF THE PEOPLE, FOR THE ***WHOLE*** PEOPLE.

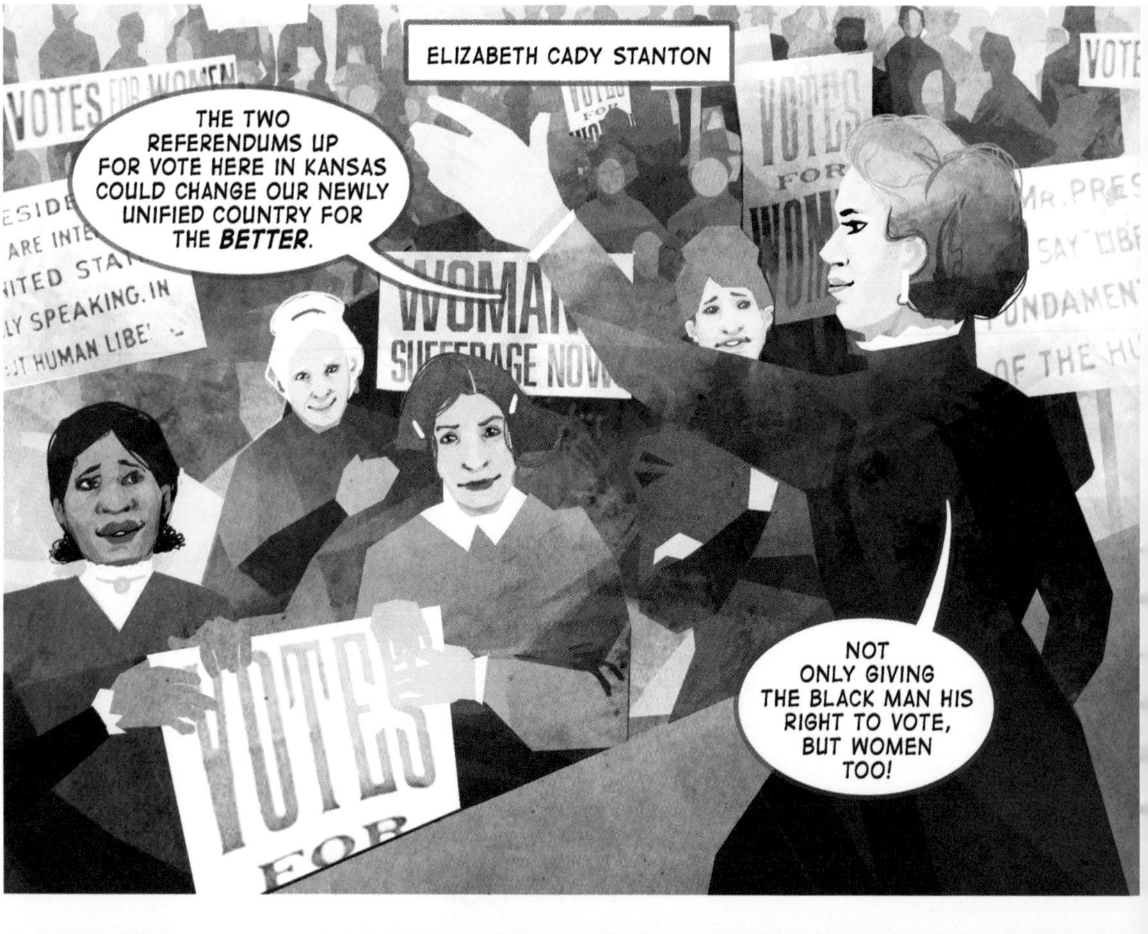
ELIZABETH CADY STANTON
THE TWO REFERENDUMS UP FOR VOTE HERE IN KANSAS COULD CHANGE OUR NEWLY UNIFIED COUNTRY FOR THE ***BETTER***.
NOT ONLY GIVING THE BLACK MAN HIS RIGHT TO VOTE, BUT WOMEN TOO!

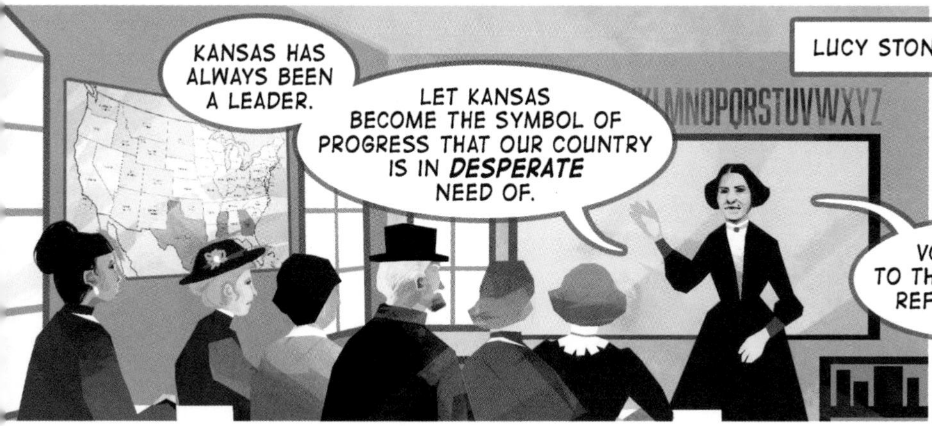
LUCY STONE
KANSAS HAS ALWAYS BEEN A LEADER.
LET KANSAS BECOME THE SYMBOL OF PROGRESS THAT OUR COUNTRY IS IN **DESPERATE** NEED OF.
VOTE **YES** TO THE SUFFRAGE REFERENDUM!

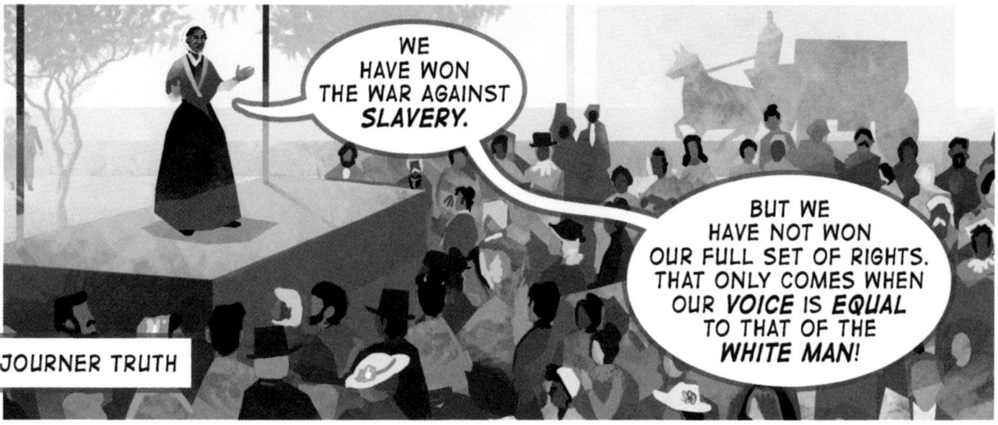
WE HAVE WON THE WAR AGAINST ***SLAVERY.***
BUT WE HAVE NOT WON OUR FULL SET OF RIGHTS. THAT ONLY COMES WHEN OUR ***VOICE*** IS ***EQUAL*** TO THAT OF THE ***WHITE MAN***!
SOJOURNER TRUTH

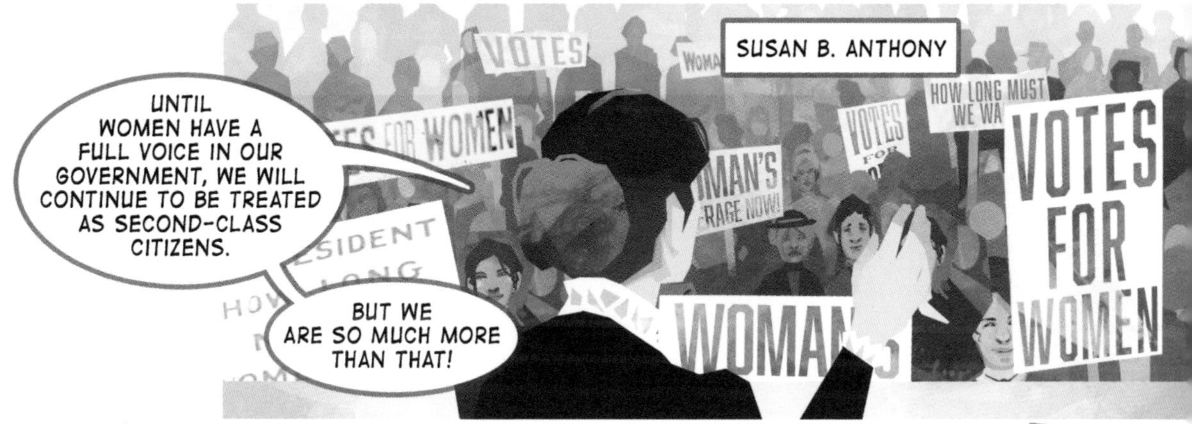
SUSAN B. ANTHONY
UNTIL WOMEN HAVE A FULL VOICE IN OUR GOVERNMENT, WE WILL CONTINUE TO BE TREATED AS SECOND-CLASS CITIZENS.
BUT WE ARE SO MUCH MORE THAN THAT!
VOTES FOR WOMEN

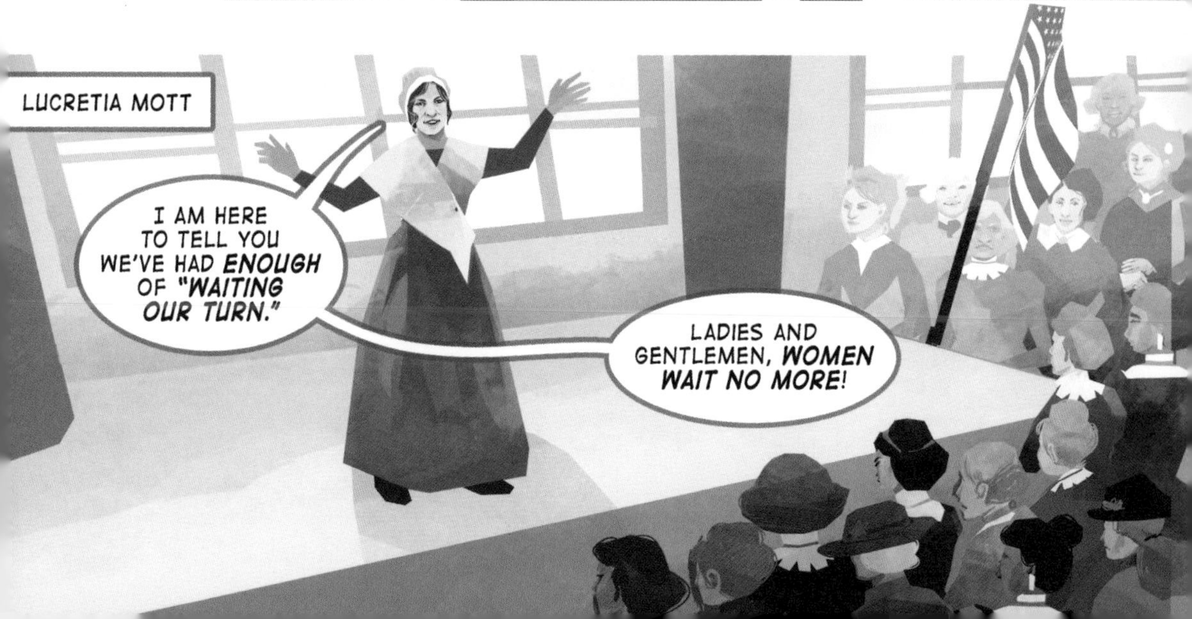
LUCRETIA MOTT
I AM HERE TO TELL YOU WE'VE HAD ***ENOUGH*** OF ***"WAITING OUR TURN."***
LADIES AND GENTLEMEN, ***WOMEN WAIT NO MORE***!

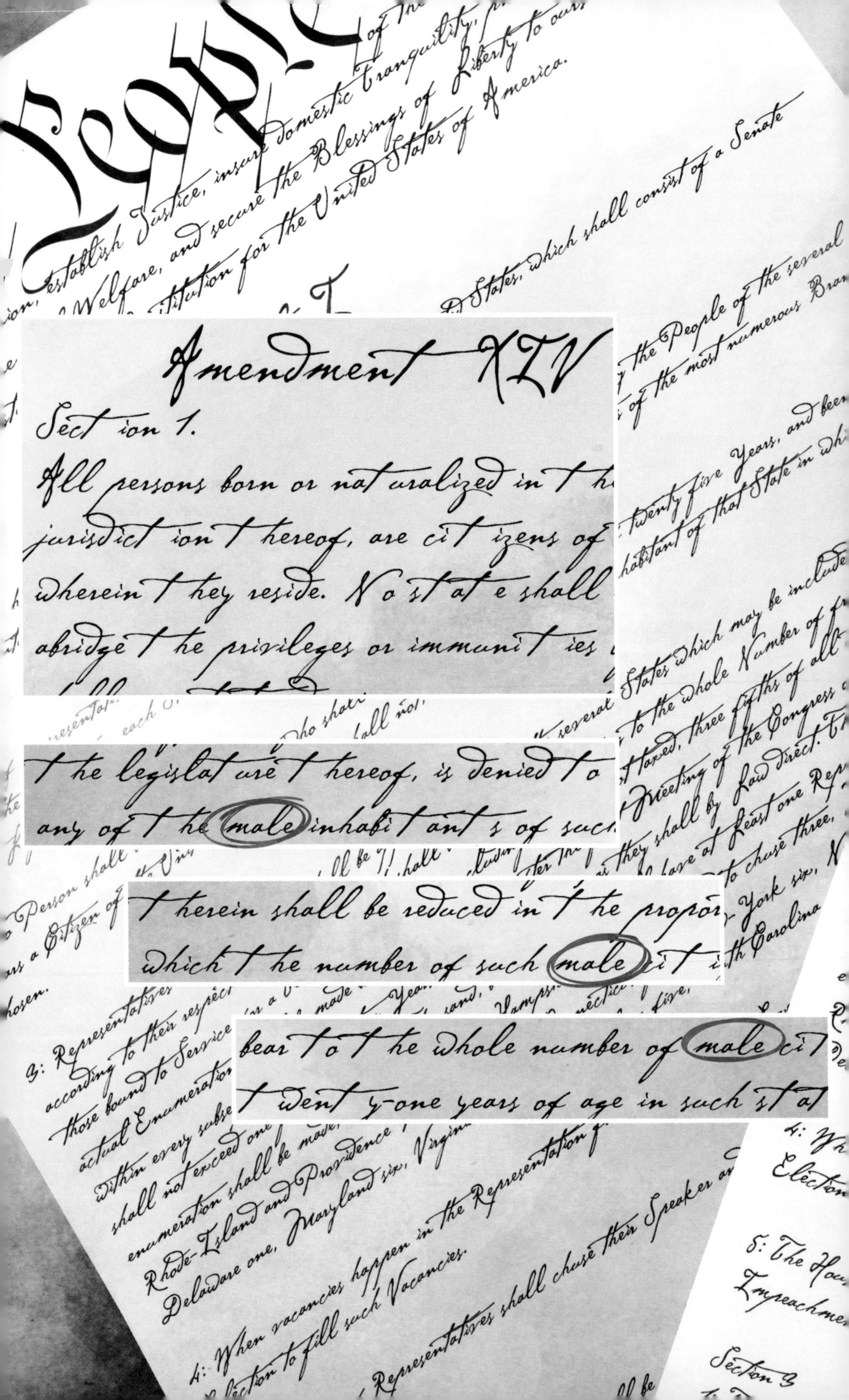
Amendment XIV
Section 1.
All persons born or naturalized in the
jurisdiction thereof, are citizens of
wherein they reside. No state shall
abridge the privileges or immunities
the legislature thereof, is denied to
any of the male inhabitants of such
therein shall be reduced in the propor
which the number of such male cit
bear to the whole number of male cit
twenty-one years of age in such stat

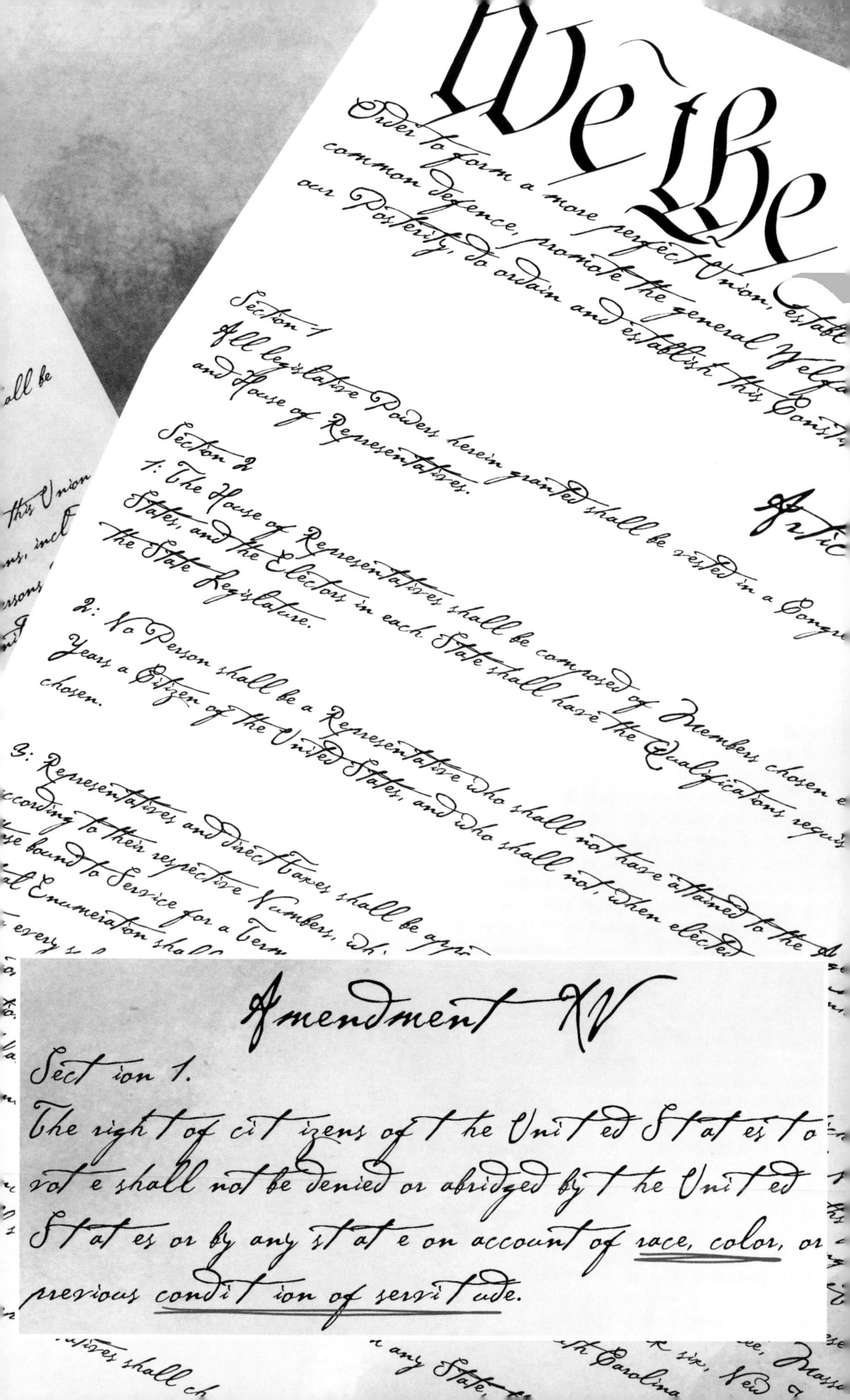

# We the

Order to form a more perfect Union, establ... common defence, promote the general Welfa... our Posterity, do ordain and establish this Consti...

Artic...

Section 1

All legislative Powers herein granted shall be vested in a Congr... and House of Representatives.

Section 2

1. The House of Representatives shall be composed of Members chosen e... States, and the Electors in each State shall have the Qualifications requis... the State Legislature.

2. No Person shall be a Representative who shall not have attained to the ... Years a Citizen of the United States, and who shall not, when elected... chosen.

3. Representatives and Direct Taxes shall be appo... according to their respective Numbers, wh... bound to Service for a Term... Enumeration shall... every...

# Amendment XV

Section 1.

The right of citizens of the United States to vote shall not be denied or abridged by the United States or by any state on account of race, color, or previous condition of servitude.

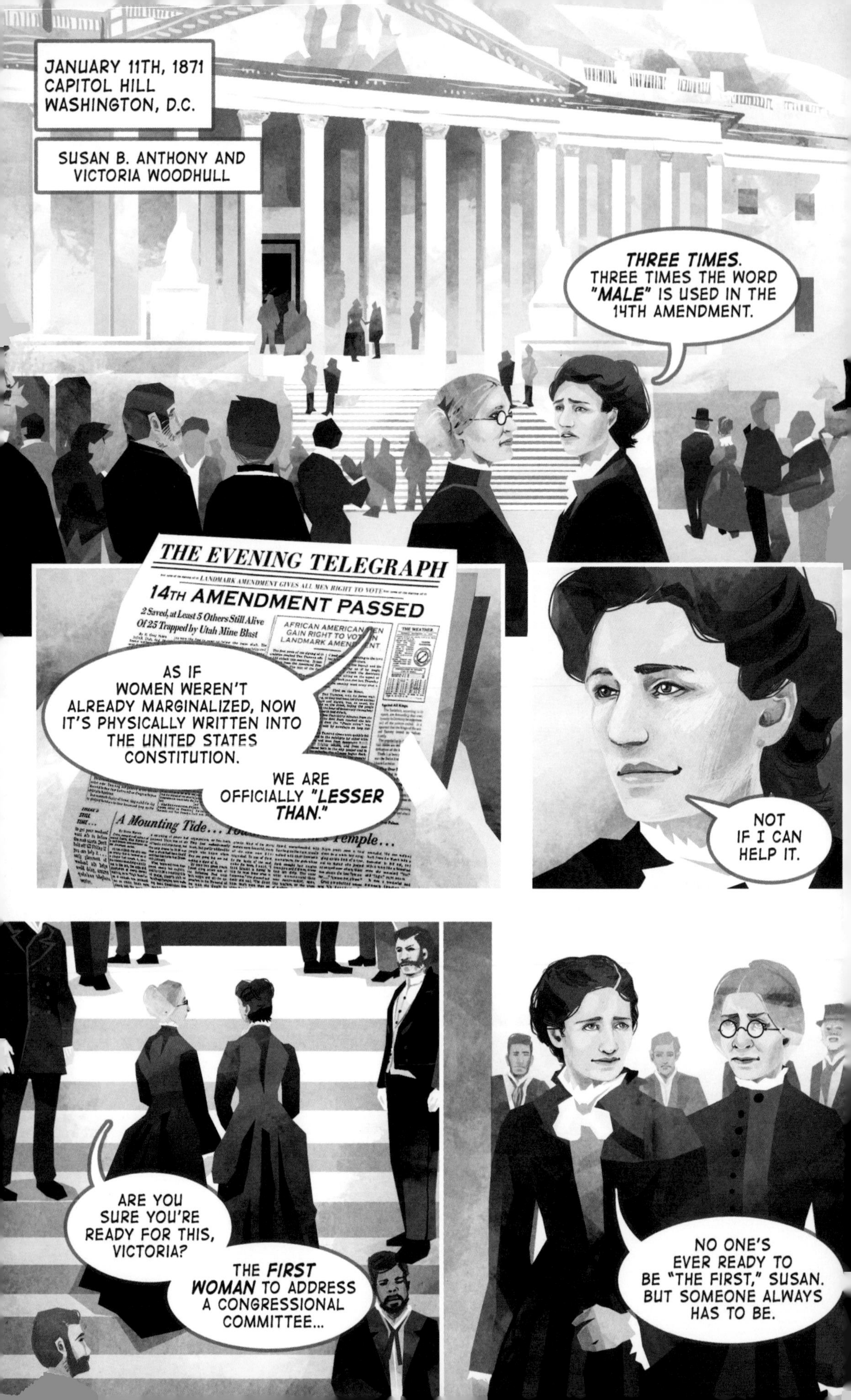
JANUARY 11TH, 1871
CAPITOL HILL
WASHINGTON, D.C.
SUSAN B. ANTHONY AND VICTORIA WOODHULL
THREE TIMES. THREE TIMES THE WORD "MALE" IS USED IN THE 14TH AMENDMENT.
THE EVENING TELEGRAPH
LANDMARK AMENDMENT GIVES ALL MEN RIGHT TO VOTE
14TH AMENDMENT PASSED
2 Saved, at Least 5 Others Still Alive Of 25 Trapped by Utah Mine Blast
A Mounting Tide...
AS IF WOMEN WEREN'T ALREADY MARGINALIZED, NOW IT'S PHYSICALLY WRITTEN INTO THE UNITED STATES CONSTITUTION.
WE ARE OFFICIALLY "LESSER THAN."
NOT IF I CAN HELP IT.
ARE YOU SURE YOU'RE READY FOR THIS, VICTORIA?
THE FIRST WOMAN TO ADDRESS A CONGRESSIONAL COMMITTEE...
NO ONE'S EVER READY TO BE "THE FIRST," SUSAN. BUT SOMEONE ALWAYS HAS TO BE.

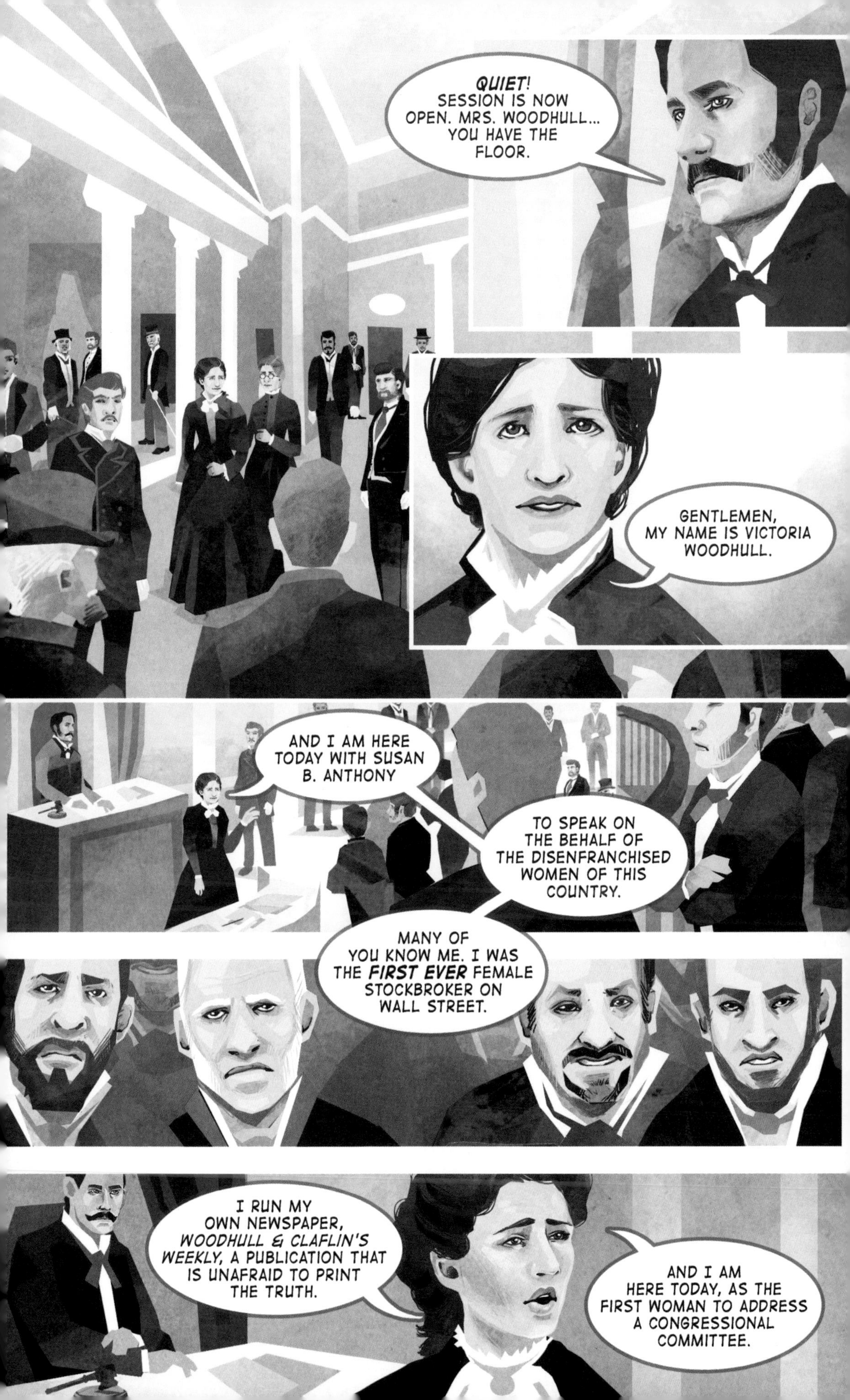
QUIET! SESSION IS NOW OPEN. MRS. WOODHULL... YOU HAVE THE FLOOR.
GENTLEMEN, MY NAME IS VICTORIA WOODHULL.
AND I AM HERE TODAY WITH SUSAN B. ANTHONY
TO SPEAK ON THE BEHALF OF THE DISENFRANCHISED WOMEN OF THIS COUNTRY.
MANY OF YOU KNOW ME. I WAS THE FIRST EVER FEMALE STOCKBROKER ON WALL STREET.
I RUN MY OWN NEWSPAPER, WOODHULL & CLAFLIN'S WEEKLY, A PUBLICATION THAT IS UNAFRAID TO PRINT THE TRUTH.
AND I AM HERE TODAY, AS THE FIRST WOMAN TO ADDRESS A CONGRESSIONAL COMMITTEE.

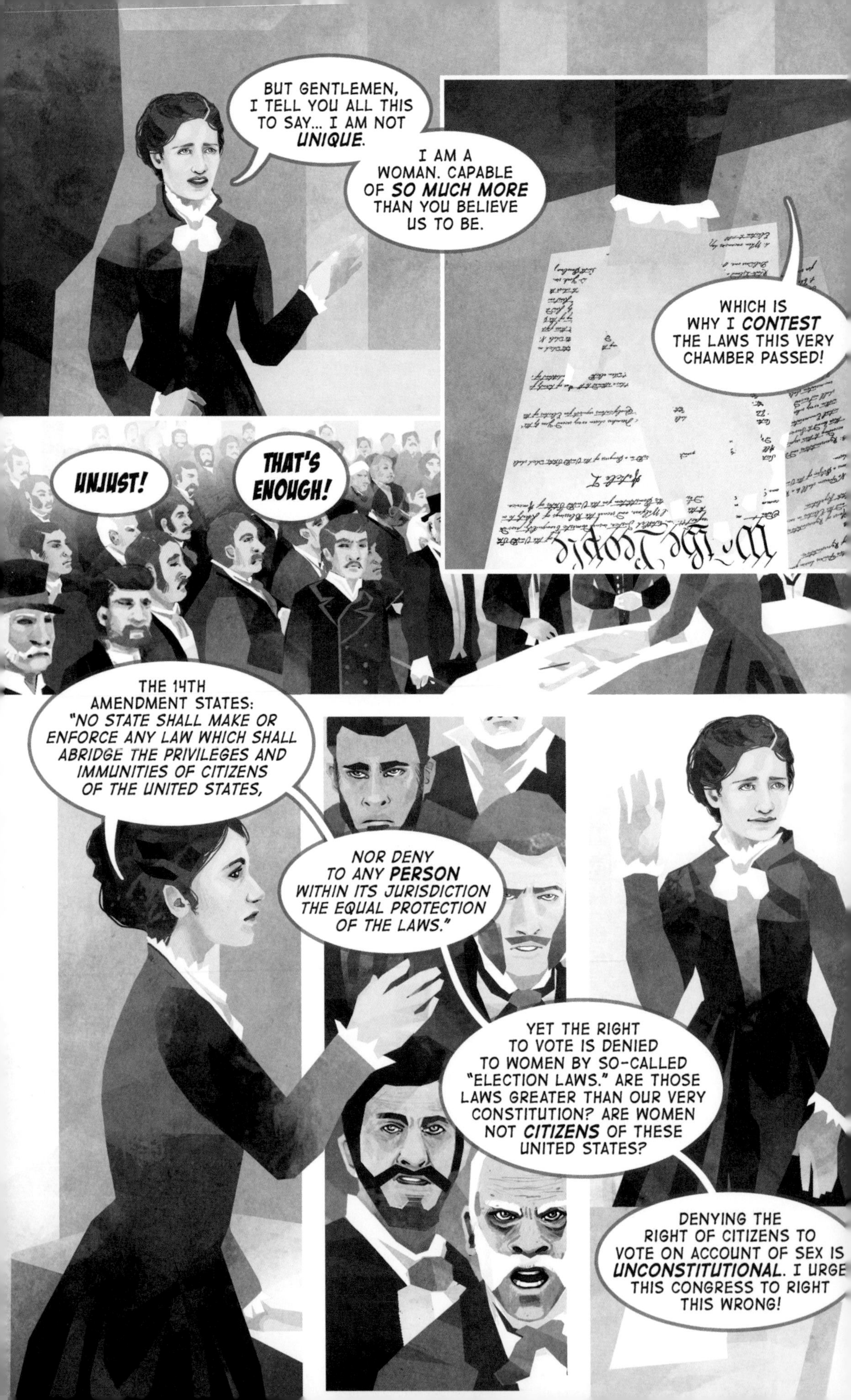
BUT GENTLEMEN, I TELL YOU ALL THIS TO SAY... I AM NOT UNIQUE.
I AM A WOMAN. CAPABLE OF SO MUCH MORE THAN YOU BELIEVE US TO BE.
WHICH IS WHY I CONTEST THE LAWS THIS VERY CHAMBER PASSED!
We the People
UNJUST!
THAT'S ENOUGH!
THE 14TH AMENDMENT STATES: "NO STATE SHALL MAKE OR ENFORCE ANY LAW WHICH SHALL ABRIDGE THE PRIVILEGES AND IMMUNITIES OF CITIZENS OF THE UNITED STATES,
NOR DENY TO ANY PERSON WITHIN ITS JURISDICTION THE EQUAL PROTECTION OF THE LAWS."
YET THE RIGHT TO VOTE IS DENIED TO WOMEN BY SO-CALLED "ELECTION LAWS." ARE THOSE LAWS GREATER THAN OUR VERY CONSTITUTION? ARE WOMEN NOT CITIZENS OF THESE UNITED STATES?
DENYING THE RIGHT OF CITIZENS TO VOTE ON ACCOUNT OF SEX IS UNCONSTITUTIONAL. I URGE THIS CONGRESS TO RIGHT THIS WRONG!

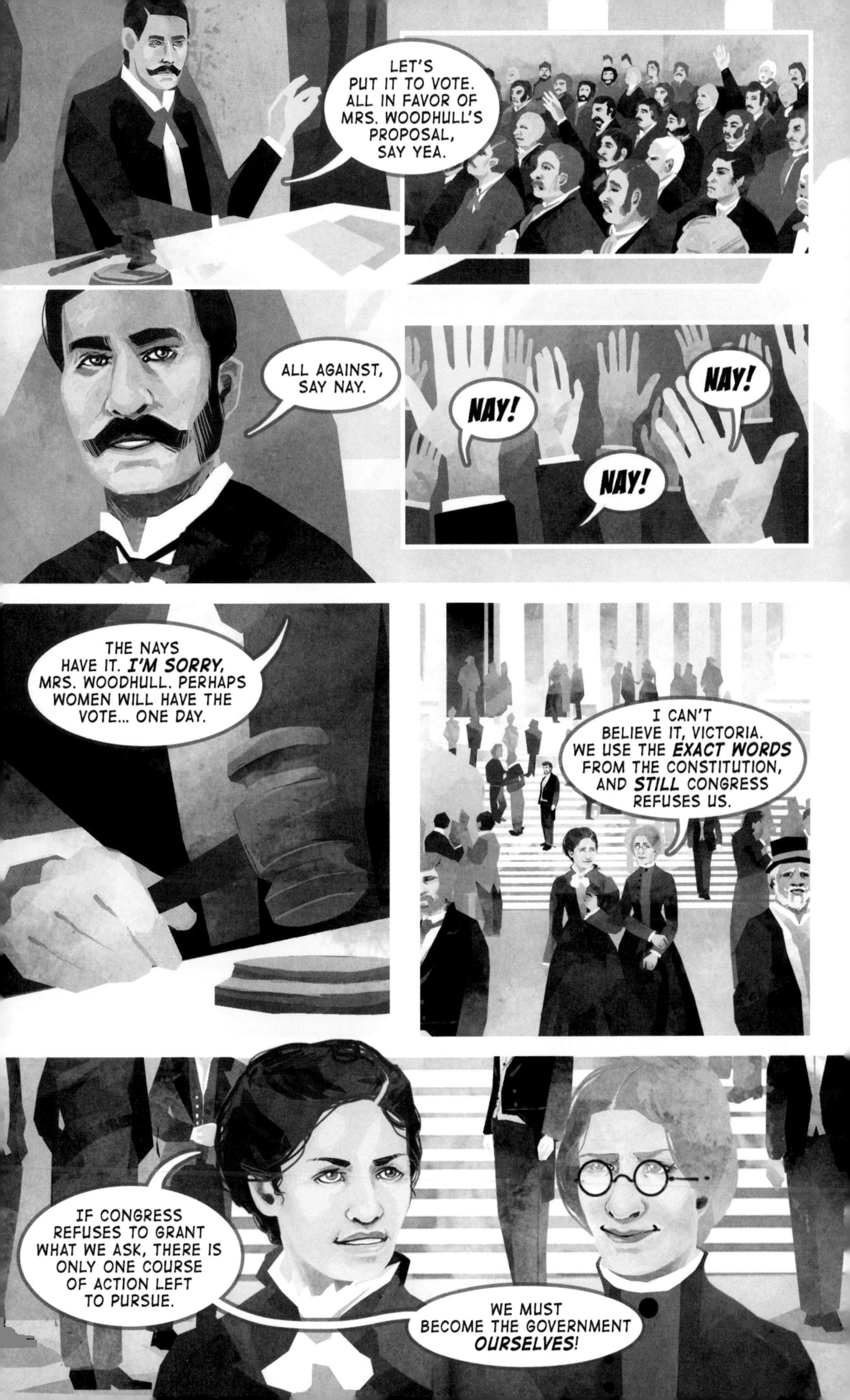
LET'S PUT IT TO VOTE. ALL IN FAVOR OF MRS. WOODHULL'S PROPOSAL, SAY YEA.
ALL AGAINST, SAY NAY.
NAY!
NAY!
NAY!
THE NAYS HAVE IT. I'M SORRY, MRS. WOODHULL. PERHAPS WOMEN WILL HAVE THE VOTE... ONE DAY.
I CAN'T BELIEVE IT, VICTORIA. WE USE THE EXACT WORDS FROM THE CONSTITUTION, AND STILL CONGRESS REFUSES US.
IF CONGRESS REFUSES TO GRANT WHAT WE ASK, THERE IS ONLY ONE COURSE OF ACTION LEFT TO PURSUE.
WE MUST BECOME THE GOVERNMENT OURSELVES!

# COSMO-POLIT[THE]

## NOMINATION FOR PRES[IDENT]

### IN 18[72]

# VICTORIA C.[WOODHULL]

SUBJ[ECT]

RATIFICATION BY TH[E]

## SUFFRAGE MEETING

Addresses — REV. W. J. HINDLEY:
"Women In Public Life"; MRS.
WINONA FLETT DIXON: "Country
Workers for Petitions."

Musical Numbers
MISS WINONA LIGHTCAP, MRS. Mc-
LANDRES and MISS NORRIE
DUTHIE

Reading
MISS M. JONES SMITH

### TUESDAY, Sept. 14

LAURA SECORD SCHOOL
Wolseley Ave.
8.15 P.M.

## Largest Demonstration
On Civil Rights Urges

## BREAKING THE WAY F[OR]
## FUTURE GENERATION[S]

I propose to look at the Woman's Suffrage ques[tion]
legal point of view, and to examine those argum[ents]
are based upon constitutional authority. It is w[ell]
to be told again and again, what rights are po[ssessed by]
women under the laws made by men.

It seems to me that a crisis is approaching, th[at]
has nearly arrived for some decisive measures in[...]
and that with earnest purpose, and a full under[standing of]
all its cl ims; we should go to the root of the [...]
each one of us do our work with a faithful zea[l for]
our cause. I present no new views, but to such as
have not been before discussed. When a body of m[en]
your undivided attention. When a body of [...]
representatives of the needs of a great people,
calmly to deliberate, discuss, and legislate io[...]
thus bringing into a common interest the h[...]
protection; the rights and privileges; the [...]
spe sibilities of all classes who make up the [...]
a country; I am certainly right in assuming [...]
clusions ought to be accepted as of the utm[...]
and authority. Then, when these conclusio[ns]
thus passed by the assembled wisdom of [...]
are sent out to the legislatures of the seve[ral]
again to be discussed, criticised and finall[y]
three-fourths majority so decide) it mus[...]
cepted that by this time the result ought t[o be]
greater prosperity, justice, equality and p[...]
concerned therein.

For, it must be evident to all, that [...]
would not have been called for, but as [...]
grievance, some great wrong that had re[...]
[...]ding legislators, a wrong that had [...]

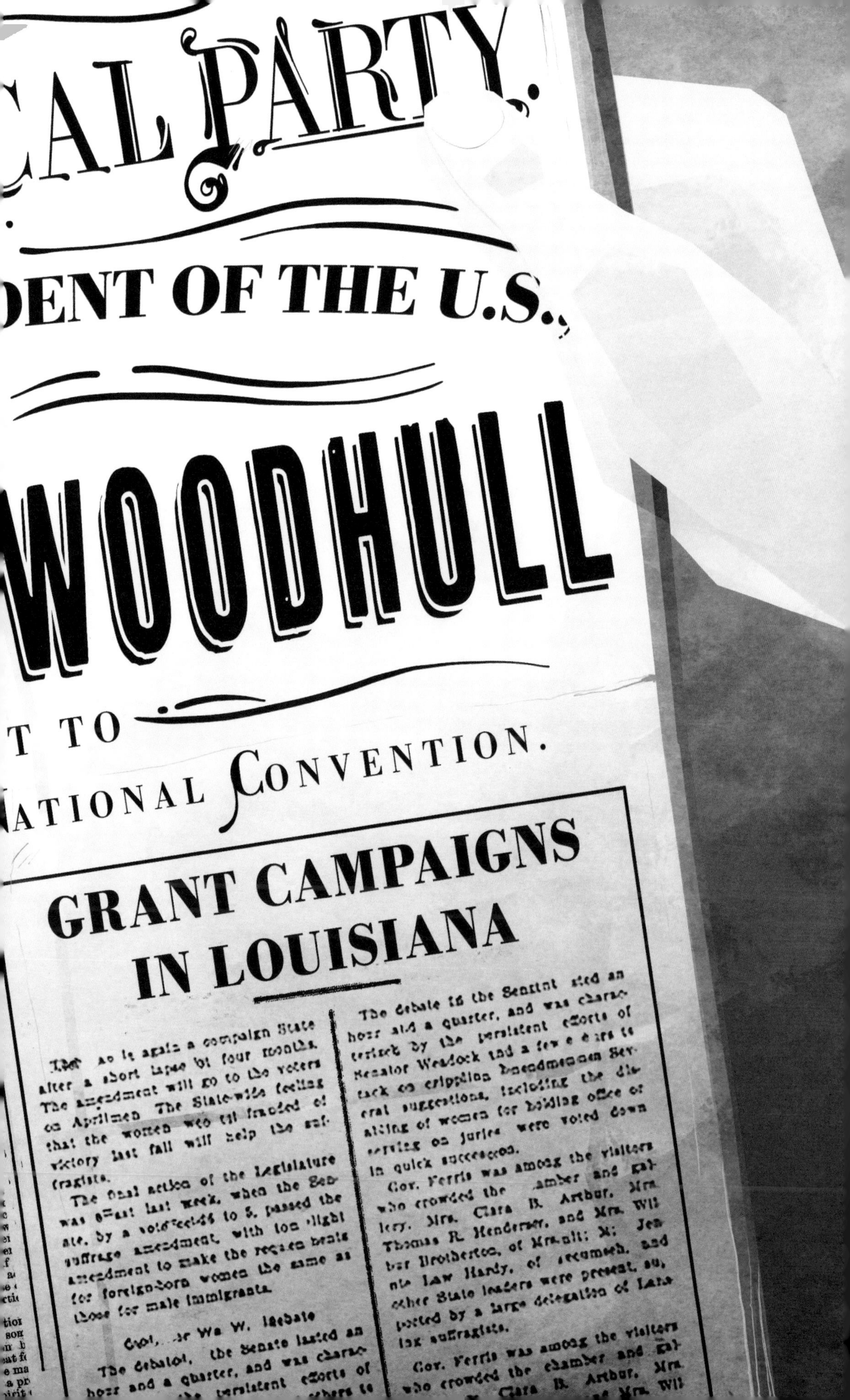

CAL PARTY.

DENT OF THE U.S.

WOODHULL

T TO

NATIONAL CONVENTION.

## GRANT CAMPAIGNS IN LOUISIANA

As it again a campaign State after a short lapse of four months. The amendment will go to the voters on April next. The Statewide feeling that the women who did so much of that victory last fall will help the suffragists.

The final action of the legislature was at last last week, when the Senate, by a vote of 16 to 5, passed the suffrage amendment with but slight amendment to make the requirements for foreign-born women the same as those for male immigrants.

Gov. the Wm W. Iredale

The debate in the Senate lasted an hour and a quarter, and was characterized by the persistent efforts of Senator Weadock and a few others to

The debate in the Senate lasted an hour and a quarter, and was characterized by the persistent efforts of Senator Weadock and a few others to tack on crippling amendments. Several suggestions, including the disabling of women for holding office or serving on juries, were voted down in quick succession.

Gov. Ferris was among the visitors who crowded the chamber and gallery. Mrs. Clara B. Arthur, Mrs. Thomas R. Henderson, and Mrs. Wilbur Brotherton, of Detroit; M. Jennie Law Hardy, of Escanaba, and other State leaders were present, supported by a large delegation of Lansing suffragists.

Gov. Ferris was among the visitors who crowded the chamber and gallery. Mrs. Clara B. Arthur, Mrs.

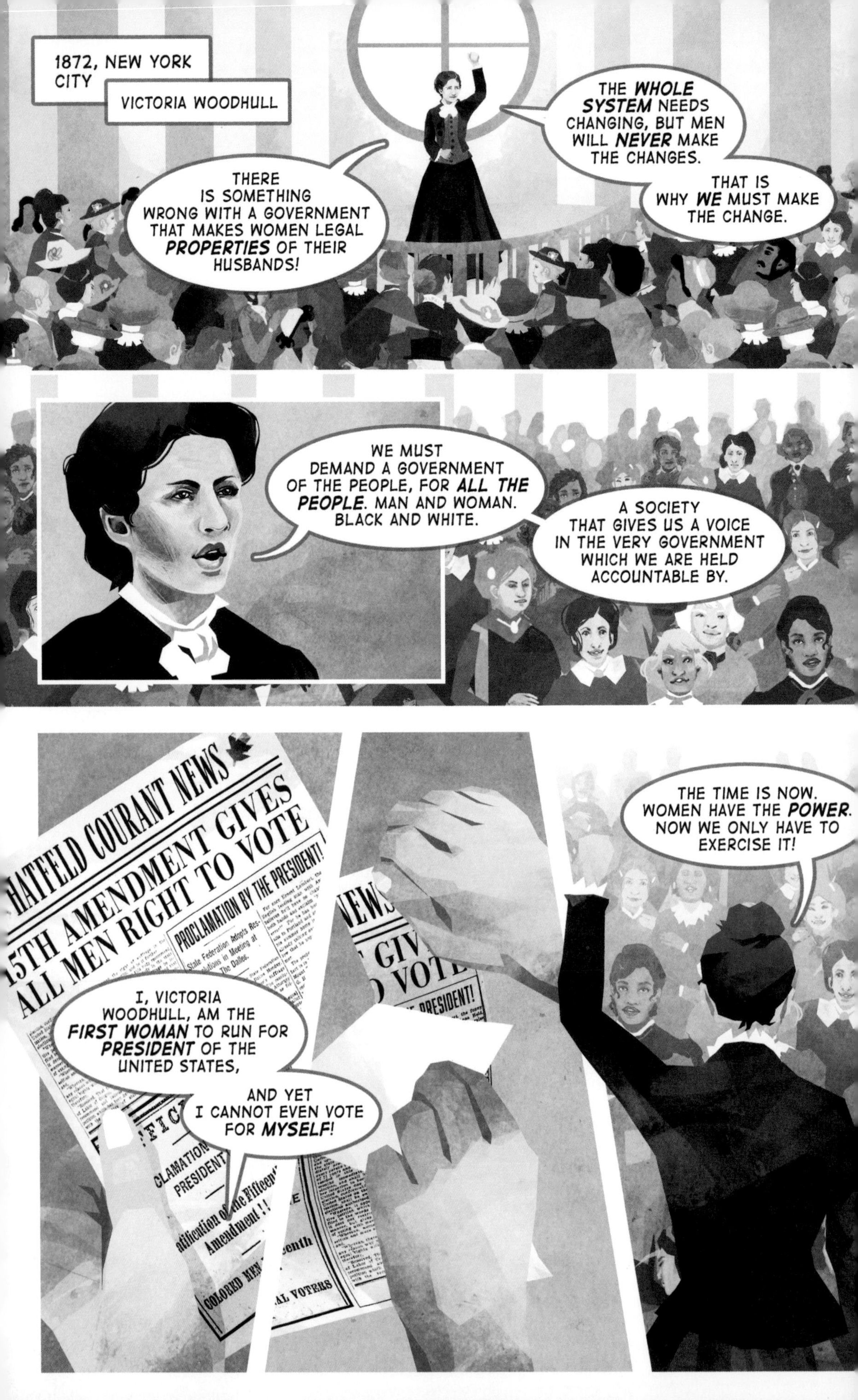
1872, NEW YORK CITY
VICTORIA WOODHULL
THERE IS SOMETHING WRONG WITH A GOVERNMENT THAT MAKES WOMEN LEGAL *PROPERTIES* OF THEIR HUSBANDS!
THE *WHOLE SYSTEM* NEEDS CHANGING, BUT MEN WILL *NEVER* MAKE THE CHANGES.
THAT IS WHY *WE* MUST MAKE THE CHANGE.
WE MUST DEMAND A GOVERNMENT OF THE PEOPLE, FOR *ALL THE PEOPLE*. MAN AND WOMAN. BLACK AND WHITE.
A SOCIETY THAT GIVES US A VOICE IN THE VERY GOVERNMENT WHICH WE ARE HELD ACCOUNTABLE BY.
HATFELD COURANT NEWS
15TH AMENDMENT GIVES ALL MEN RIGHT TO VOTE
PROCLAMATION BY THE PRESIDENT!
I, VICTORIA WOODHULL, AM THE *FIRST WOMAN* TO RUN FOR *PRESIDENT* OF THE UNITED STATES,
AND YET I CANNOT EVEN VOTE FOR *MYSELF*!
THE TIME IS NOW. WOMEN HAVE THE *POWER*. NOW WE ONLY HAVE TO EXERCISE IT!

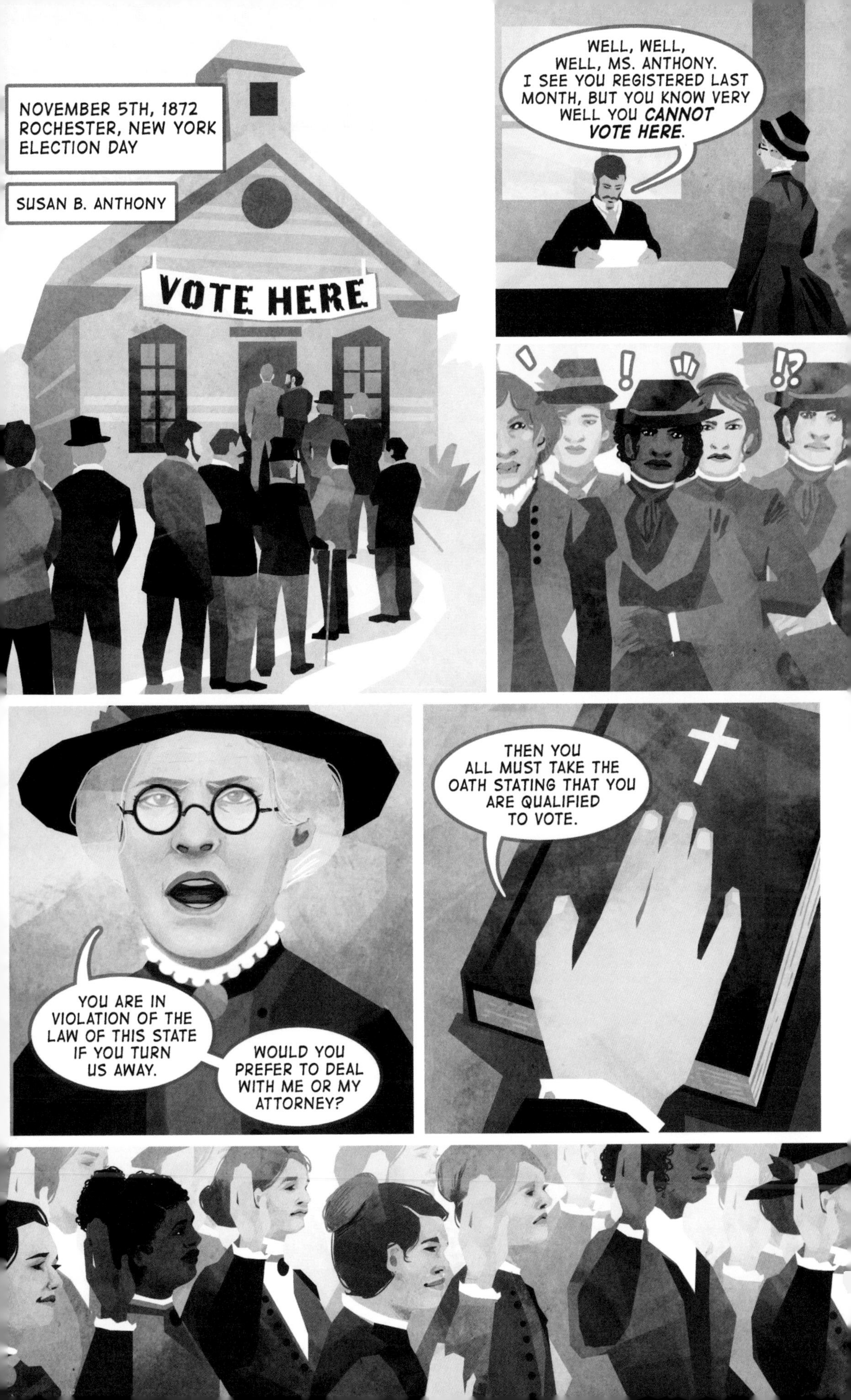
NOVEMBER 5TH, 1872
ROCHESTER, NEW YORK
ELECTION DAY
SUSAN B. ANTHONY
VOTE HERE
WELL, WELL, WELL, MS. ANTHONY. I SEE YOU REGISTERED LAST MONTH, BUT YOU KNOW VERY WELL YOU *CANNOT VOTE HERE*.
!
!
!!
!?
YOU ARE IN VIOLATION OF THE LAW OF THIS STATE IF YOU TURN US AWAY.
WOULD YOU PREFER TO DEAL WITH ME OR MY ATTORNEY?
THEN YOU ALL MUST TAKE THE OATH STATING THAT YOU ARE QUALIFIED TO VOTE.

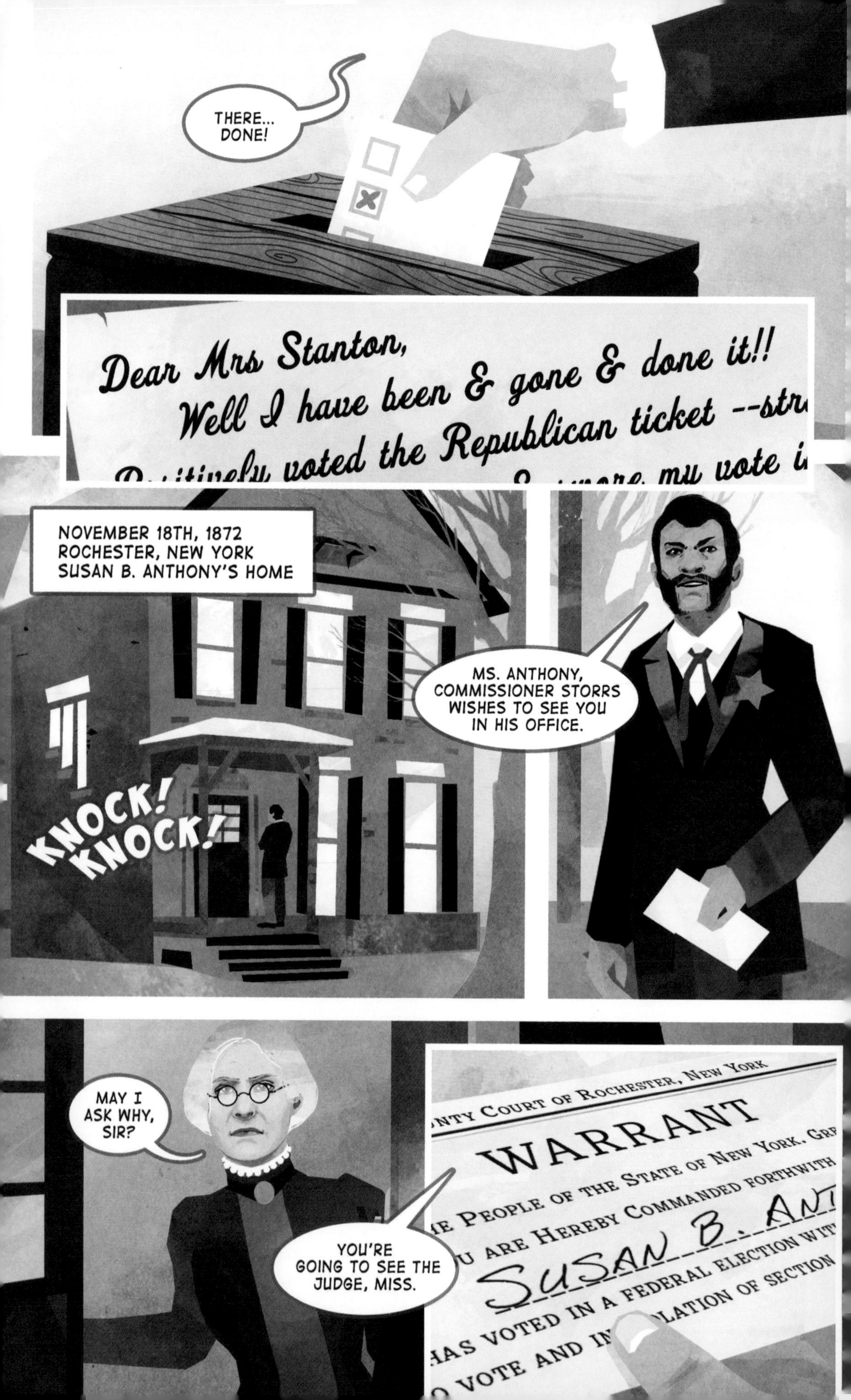
THERE... DONE!
Dear Mrs Stanton,
Well I have been & gone & done it!!
voted the Republican ticket
NOVEMBER 18TH, 1872
ROCHESTER, NEW YORK
SUSAN B. ANTHONY'S HOME
KNOCK! KNOCK!
MS. ANTHONY, COMMISSIONER STORRS WISHES TO SEE YOU IN HIS OFFICE.
MAY I ASK WHY, SIR?
YOU'RE GOING TO SEE THE JUDGE, MISS.
COURT OF ROCHESTER, NEW YORK
WARRANT
PEOPLE OF THE STATE OF NEW YORK,
ARE HEREBY COMMANDED FORTHWITH
SUSAN B.
HAS VOTED IN A FEDERAL ELECTION
VOTE AND IN
OF SECTION

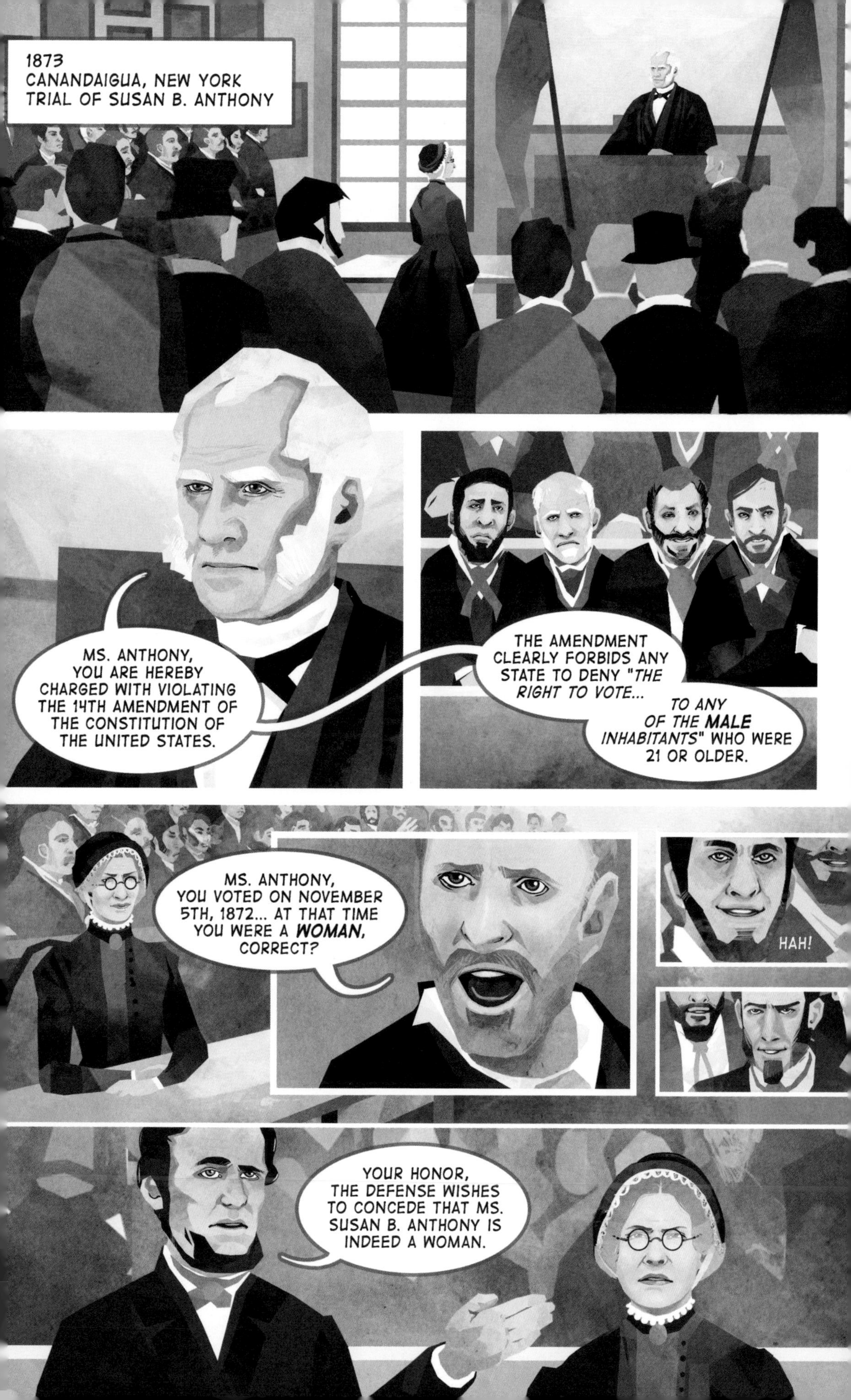
1873
CANANDAIGUA, NEW YORK
TRIAL OF SUSAN B. ANTHONY
MS. ANTHONY, YOU ARE HEREBY CHARGED WITH VIOLATING THE 14TH AMENDMENT OF THE CONSTITUTION OF THE UNITED STATES.
THE AMENDMENT CLEARLY FORBIDS ANY STATE TO DENY "THE RIGHT TO VOTE...
TO ANY OF THE MALE INHABITANTS" WHO WERE 21 OR OLDER.
MS. ANTHONY, YOU VOTED ON NOVEMBER 5TH, 1872... AT THAT TIME YOU WERE A WOMAN, CORRECT?
HAH!
YOUR HONOR, THE DEFENSE WISHES TO CONCEDE THAT MS. SUSAN B. ANTHONY IS INDEED A WOMAN.

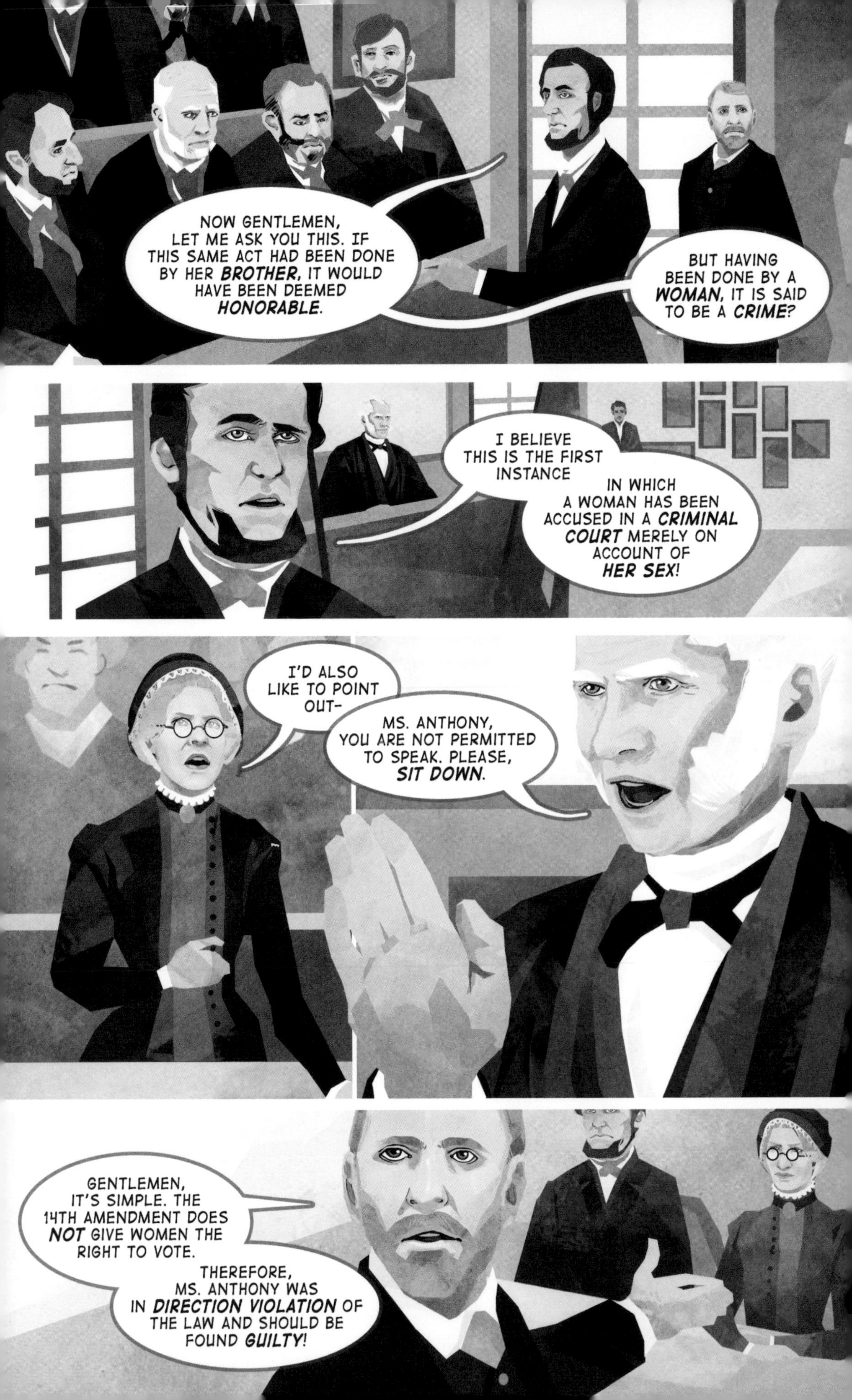
NOW GENTLEMEN, LET ME ASK YOU THIS. IF THIS SAME ACT HAD BEEN DONE BY HER BROTHER, IT WOULD HAVE BEEN DEEMED HONORABLE.
BUT HAVING BEEN DONE BY A WOMAN, IT IS SAID TO BE A CRIME?
I BELIEVE THIS IS THE FIRST INSTANCE
IN WHICH A WOMAN HAS BEEN ACCUSED IN A CRIMINAL COURT MERELY ON ACCOUNT OF HER SEX!
I'D ALSO LIKE TO POINT OUT-
MS. ANTHONY, YOU ARE NOT PERMITTED TO SPEAK. PLEASE, SIT DOWN.
GENTLEMEN, IT'S SIMPLE. THE 14TH AMENDMENT DOES NOT GIVE WOMEN THE RIGHT TO VOTE.
THEREFORE, MS. ANTHONY WAS IN DIRECTION VIOLATION OF THE LAW AND SHOULD BE FOUND GUILTY!

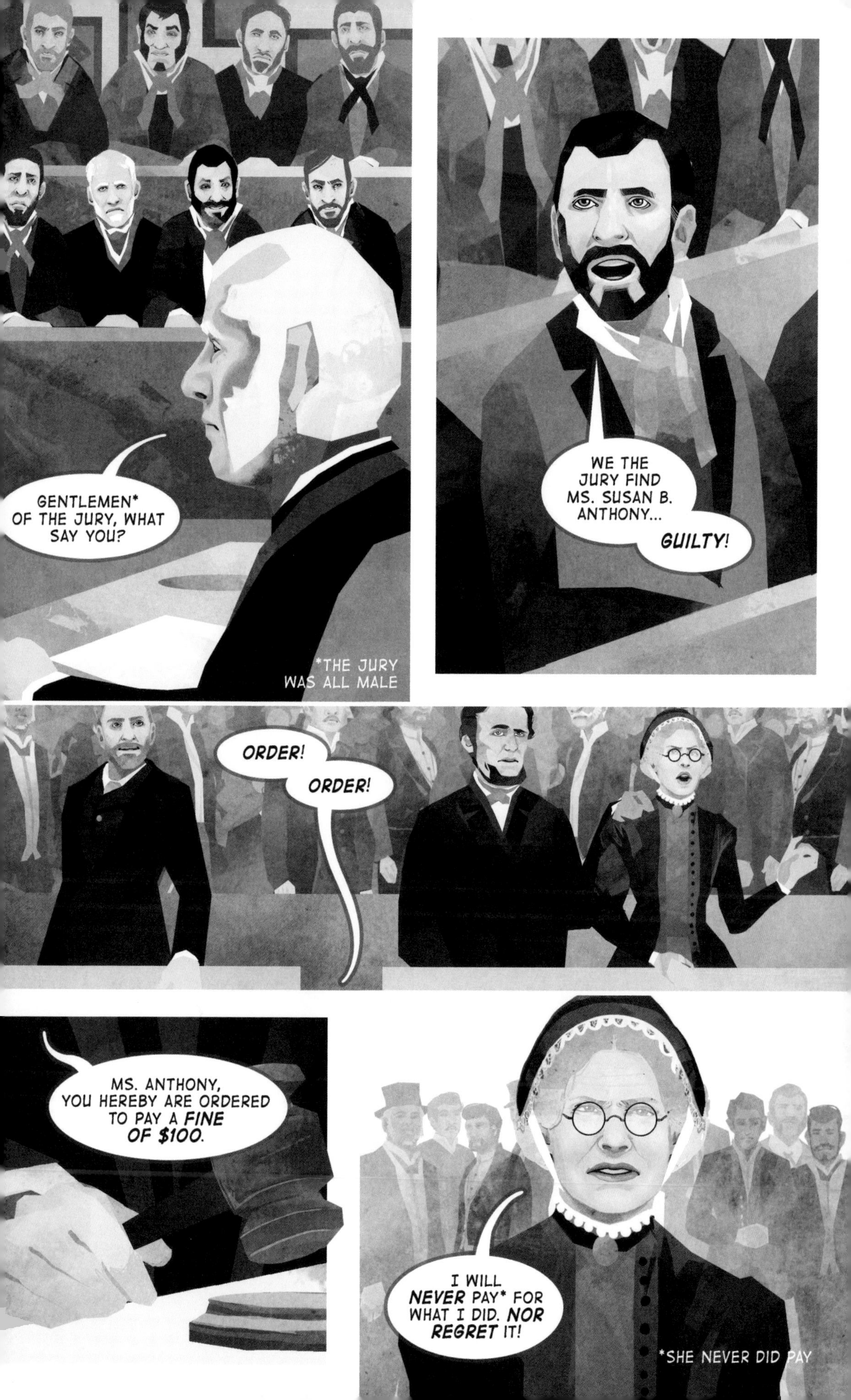
GENTLEMEN* OF THE JURY, WHAT SAY YOU?
*THE JURY WAS ALL MALE
WE THE JURY FIND MS. SUSAN B. ANTHONY...
GUILTY!
ORDER!
ORDER!
MS. ANTHONY, YOU HEREBY ARE ORDERED TO PAY A FINE OF $100.
I WILL NEVER PAY* FOR WHAT I DID. NOR REGRET IT!
*SHE NEVER DID PAY

"YOU HAVE TO MAKE MORE NOISE THAN ANYBODY
ELSE, YOU HAVE TO MAKE YOURSELF MORE OBTRUSIVE
THAN ANYBODY ELSE, YOU HAVE TO FILL ALL THE
PAPERS MORE THAN ANYBODY ELSE, IN FACT YOU HAVE
TO BE THERE ALL THE TIME AND SEE THAT THEY DO
NOT SNOW YOU UNDER, IF YOU ARE REALLY GOING TO
GET YOUR REFORM REALIZED."

EMMELINE PANKHURST
1858–1928

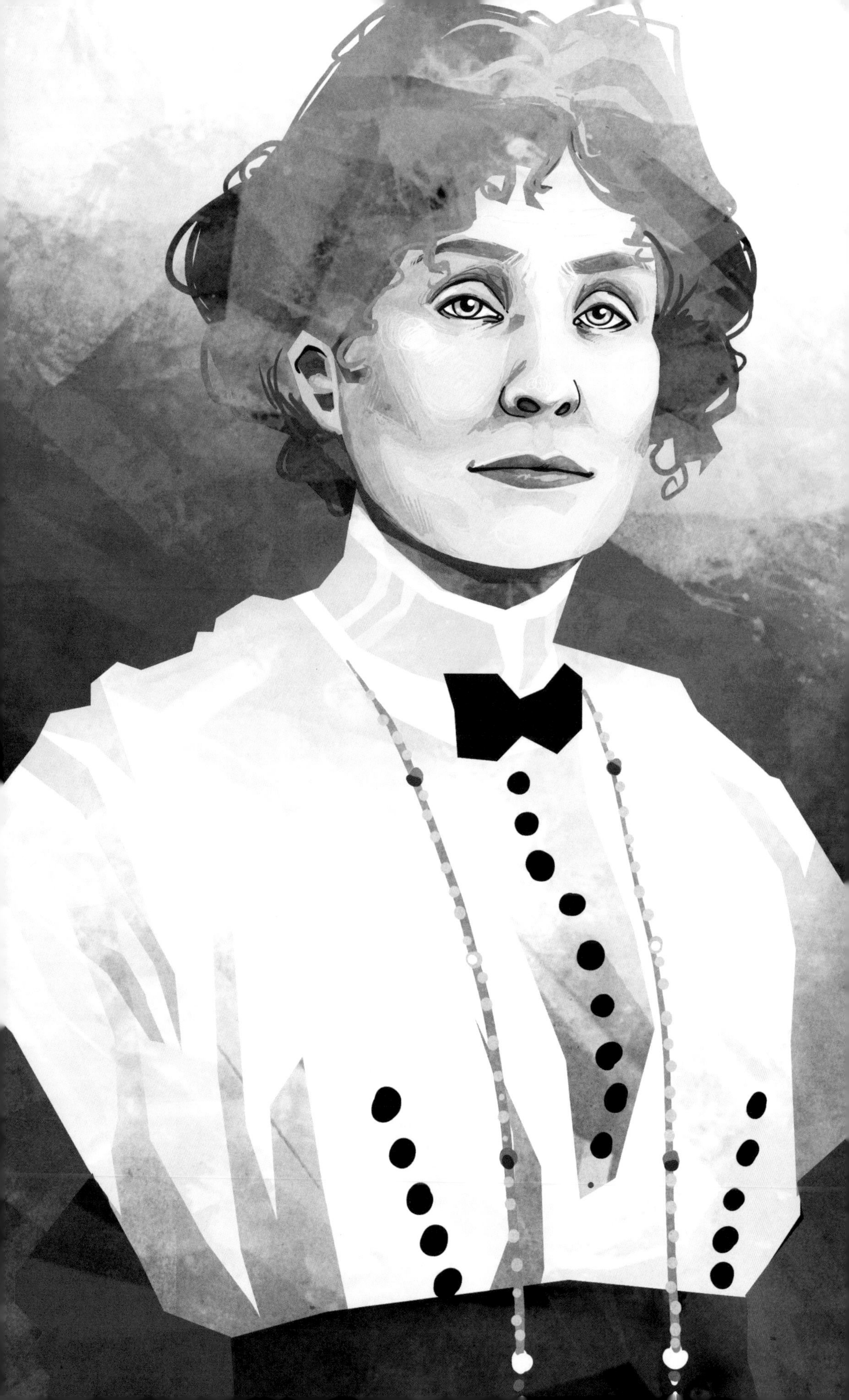

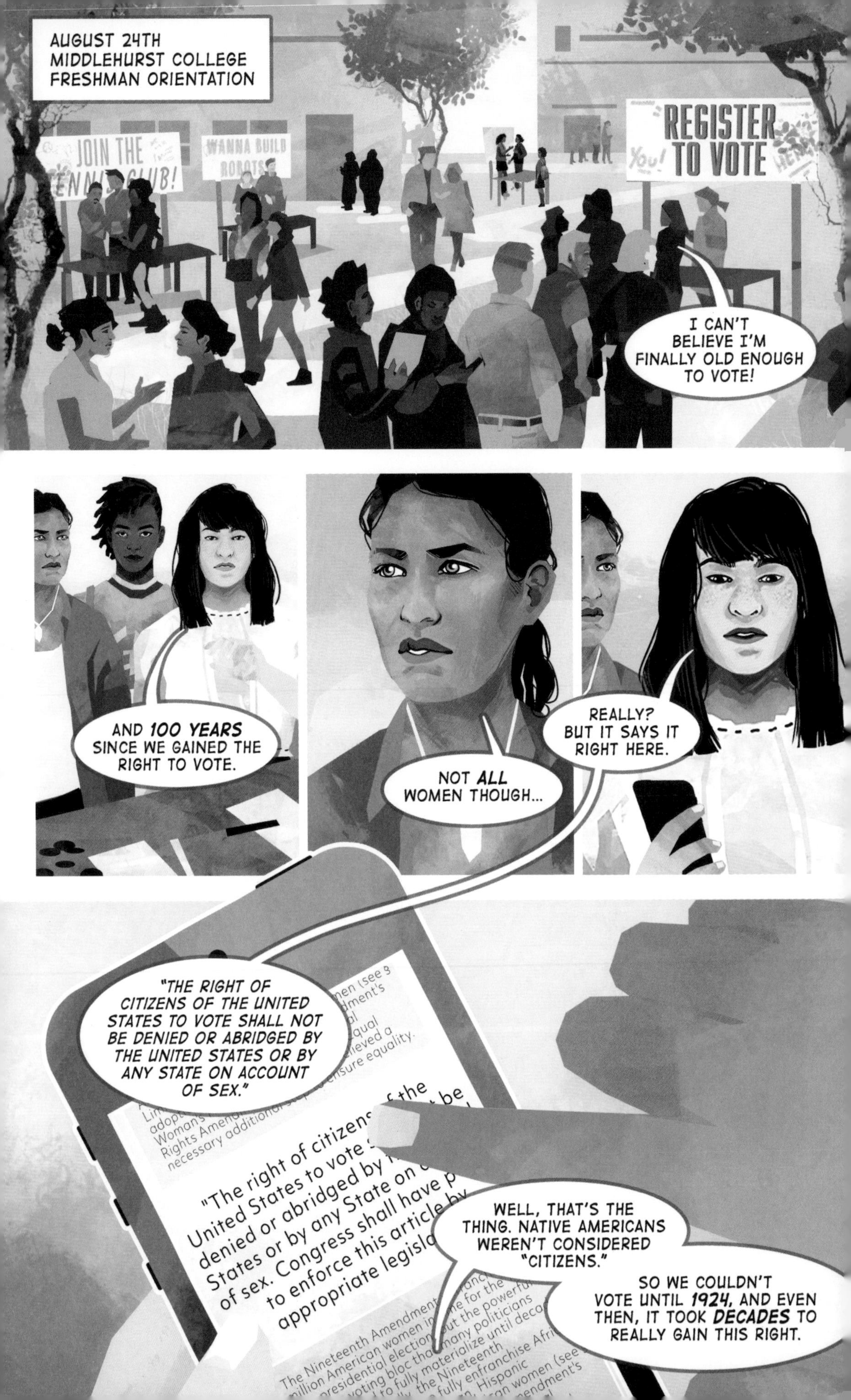
AUGUST 24TH
MIDDLEHURST COLLEGE
FRESHMAN ORIENTATION
JOIN THE
REGISTER TO VOTE
You!
I CAN'T BELIEVE I'M FINALLY OLD ENOUGH TO VOTE!
AND *100 YEARS* SINCE WE GAINED THE RIGHT TO VOTE.
NOT *ALL* WOMEN THOUGH...
REALLY? BUT IT SAYS IT RIGHT HERE.
"THE RIGHT OF CITIZENS OF THE UNITED STATES TO VOTE SHALL NOT BE DENIED OR ABRIDGED BY THE UNITED STATES OR BY ANY STATE ON ACCOUNT OF SEX."
WELL, THAT'S THE THING. NATIVE AMERICANS WEREN'T CONSIDERED "CITIZENS."
SO WE COULDN'T VOTE UNTIL *1924*, AND EVEN THEN, IT TOOK *DECADES* TO REALLY GAIN THIS RIGHT.

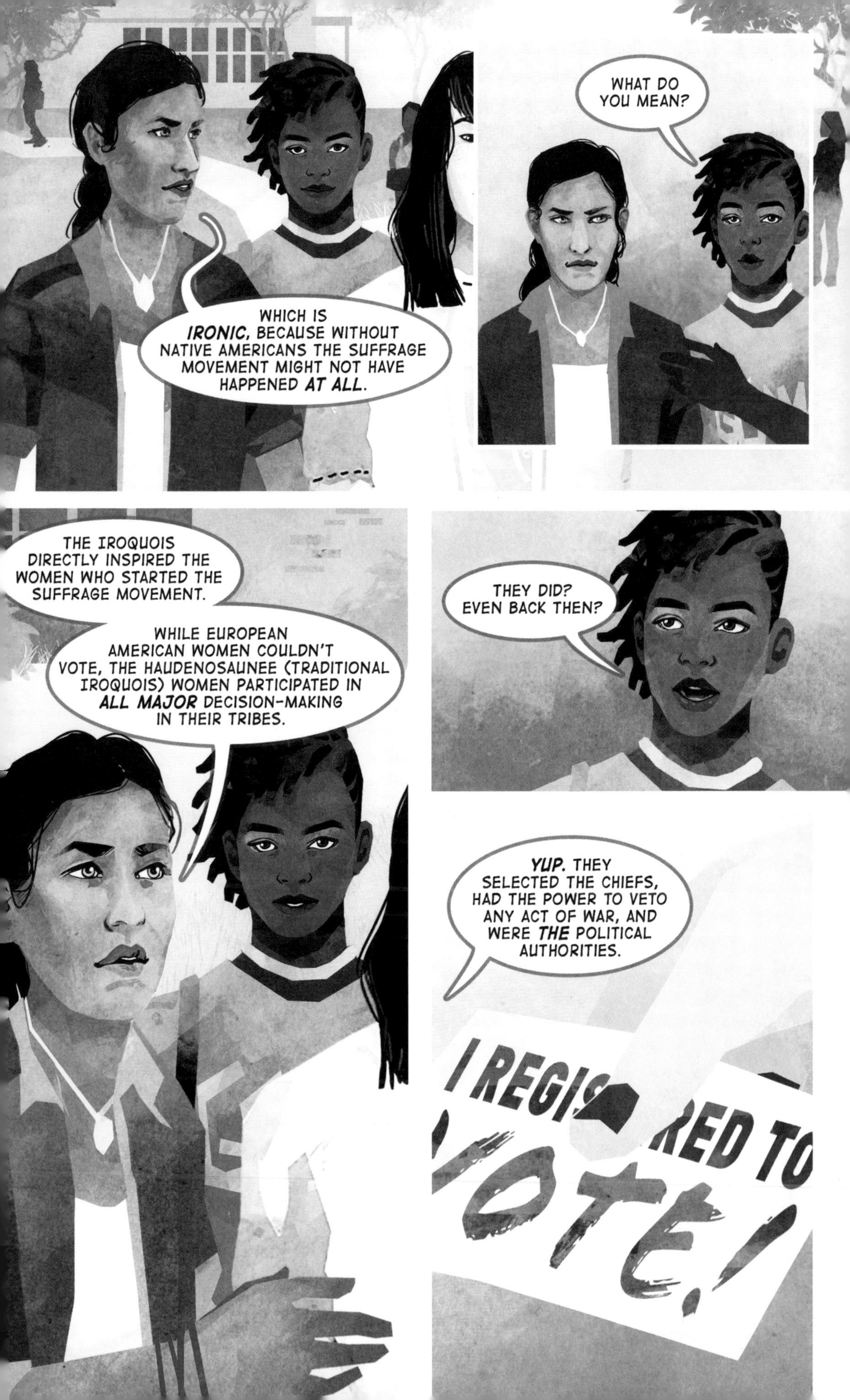
WHICH IS IRONIC, BECAUSE WITHOUT NATIVE AMERICANS THE SUFFRAGE MOVEMENT MIGHT NOT HAVE HAPPENED AT ALL.
WHAT DO YOU MEAN?
THE IROQUOIS DIRECTLY INSPIRED THE WOMEN WHO STARTED THE SUFFRAGE MOVEMENT.
WHILE EUROPEAN AMERICAN WOMEN COULDN'T VOTE, THE HAUDENOSAUNEE (TRADITIONAL IROQUOIS) WOMEN PARTICIPATED IN ALL MAJOR DECISION-MAKING IN THEIR TRIBES.
THEY DID? EVEN BACK THEN?
YUP. THEY SELECTED THE CHIEFS, HAD THE POWER TO VETO ANY ACT OF WAR, AND WERE THE POLITICAL AUTHORITIES.

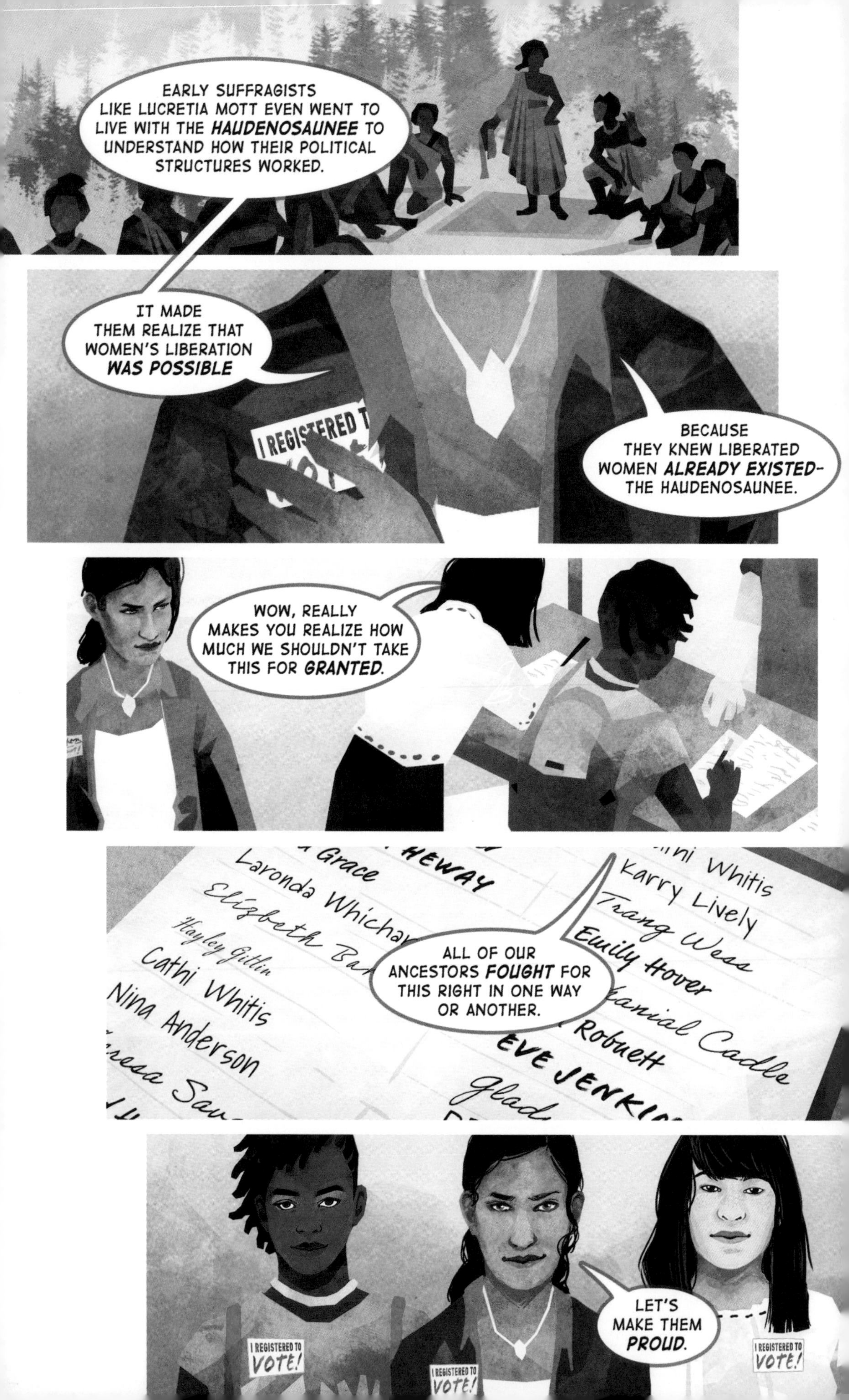
EARLY SUFFRAGISTS LIKE LUCRETIA MOTT EVEN WENT TO LIVE WITH THE ***HAUDENOSAUNEE*** TO UNDERSTAND HOW THEIR POLITICAL STRUCTURES WORKED.
IT MADE THEM REALIZE THAT WOMEN'S LIBERATION ***WAS POSSIBLE***
BECAUSE THEY KNEW LIBERATED WOMEN ***ALREADY EXISTED***– THE HAUDENOSAUNEE.
WOW, REALLY MAKES YOU REALIZE HOW MUCH WE SHOULDN'T TAKE THIS FOR ***GRANTED***.
Karry Lively
Trang Wess
Emily Hover
Hayley Gitlin
Cathi Whitis
Nina Anderson
ALL OF OUR ANCESTORS ***FOUGHT*** FOR THIS RIGHT IN ONE WAY OR ANOTHER.
I REGISTERED TO VOTE!
I REGISTERED TO VOTE!
LET'S MAKE THEM ***PROUD***.
I REGISTERED TO VOTE!

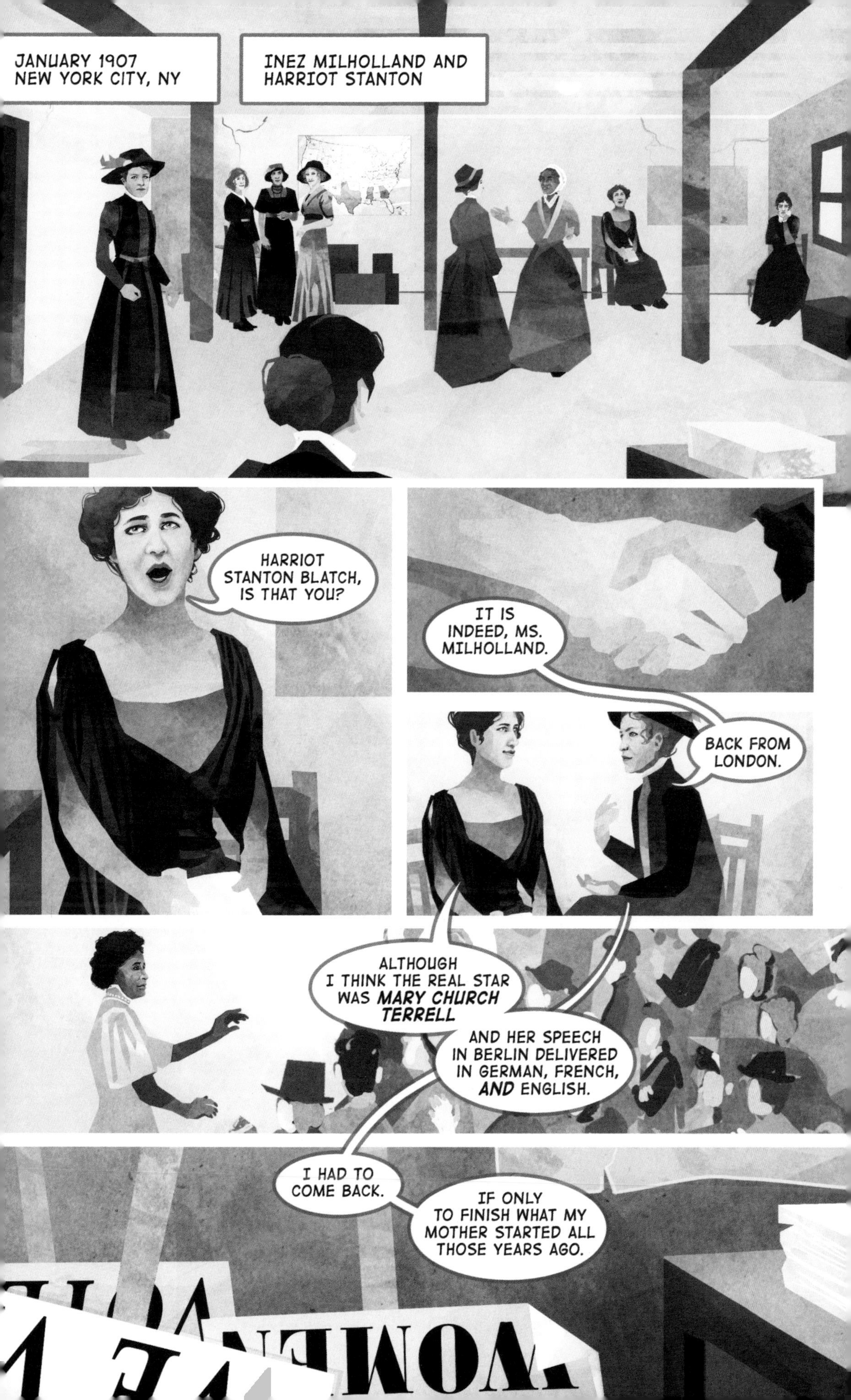
JANUARY 1907
NEW YORK CITY, NY
INEZ MILHOLLAND AND HARRIOT STANTON
HARRIOT STANTON BLATCH, IS THAT YOU?
IT IS INDEED, MS. MILHOLLAND.
BACK FROM LONDON.
ALTHOUGH I THINK THE REAL STAR WAS MARY CHURCH TERRELL
AND HER SPEECH IN BERLIN DELIVERED IN GERMAN, FRENCH, AND ENGLISH.
I HAD TO COME BACK.
IF ONLY TO FINISH WHAT MY MOTHER STARTED ALL THOSE YEARS AGO.

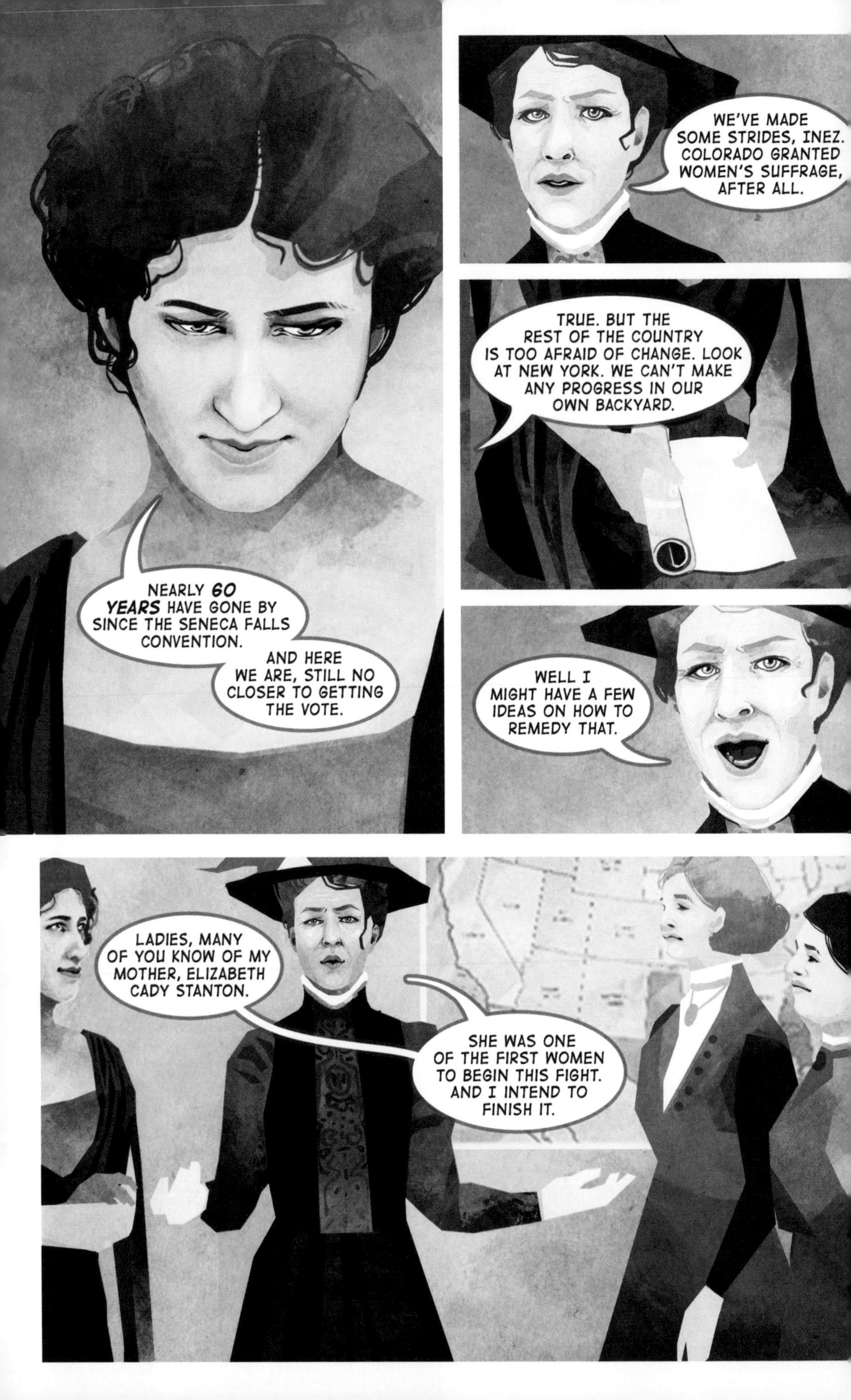
NEARLY 60 YEARS HAVE GONE BY SINCE THE SENECA FALLS CONVENTION.
AND HERE WE ARE, STILL NO CLOSER TO GETTING THE VOTE.
WE'VE MADE SOME STRIDES, INEZ. COLORADO GRANTED WOMEN'S SUFFRAGE, AFTER ALL.
TRUE. BUT THE REST OF THE COUNTRY IS TOO AFRAID OF CHANGE. LOOK AT NEW YORK. WE CAN'T MAKE ANY PROGRESS IN OUR OWN BACKYARD.
WELL I MIGHT HAVE A FEW IDEAS ON HOW TO REMEDY THAT.
LADIES, MANY OF YOU KNOW OF MY MOTHER, ELIZABETH CADY STANTON.
SHE WAS ONE OF THE FIRST WOMEN TO BEGIN THIS FIGHT. AND I INTEND TO FINISH IT.

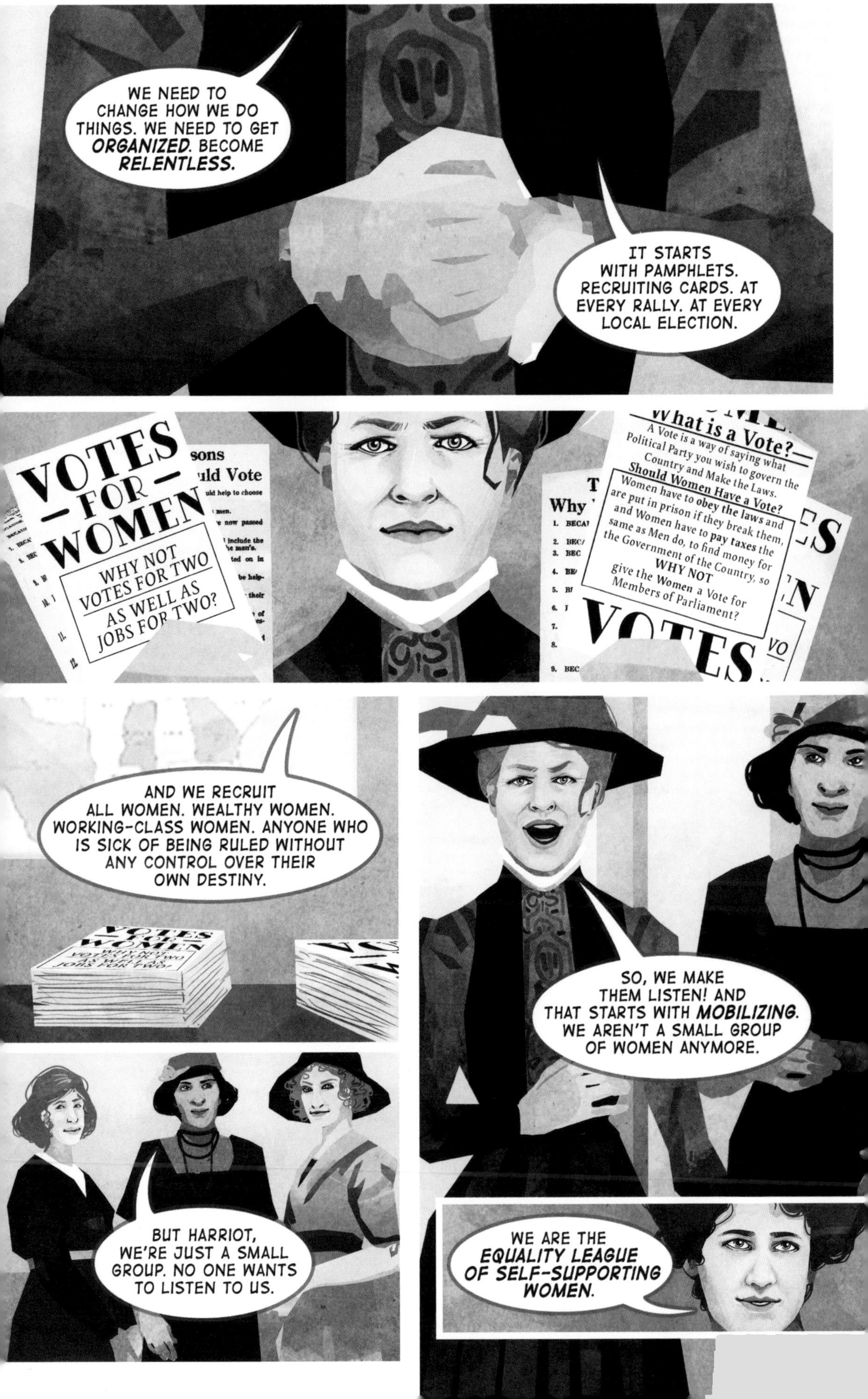
WE NEED TO CHANGE HOW WE DO THINGS. WE NEED TO GET ORGANIZED. BECOME RELENTLESS.
IT STARTS WITH PAMPHLETS. RECRUITING CARDS. AT EVERY RALLY. AT EVERY LOCAL ELECTION.
VOTES FOR WOMEN
WHY NOT VOTES FOR TWO AS WELL AS JOBS FOR TWO?
What is a Vote?
A Vote is a way of saying what Political Party you wish to govern the Country and Make the Laws.
Should Women Have a Vote?
Women have to obey the laws and are put in prison if they break them, and Women have to pay taxes the same as Men do, to find money for the Government of the Country, so WHY NOT give the Women a Vote for Members of Parliament?
VOTES
AND WE RECRUIT ALL WOMEN. WEALTHY WOMEN. WORKING-CLASS WOMEN. ANYONE WHO IS SICK OF BEING RULED WITHOUT ANY CONTROL OVER THEIR OWN DESTINY.
BUT HARRIOT, WE'RE JUST A SMALL GROUP. NO ONE WANTS TO LISTEN TO US.
SO, WE MAKE THEM LISTEN! AND THAT STARTS WITH MOBILIZING. WE AREN'T A SMALL GROUP OF WOMEN ANYMORE.
WE ARE THE EQUALITY LEAGUE OF SELF-SUPPORTING WOMEN.

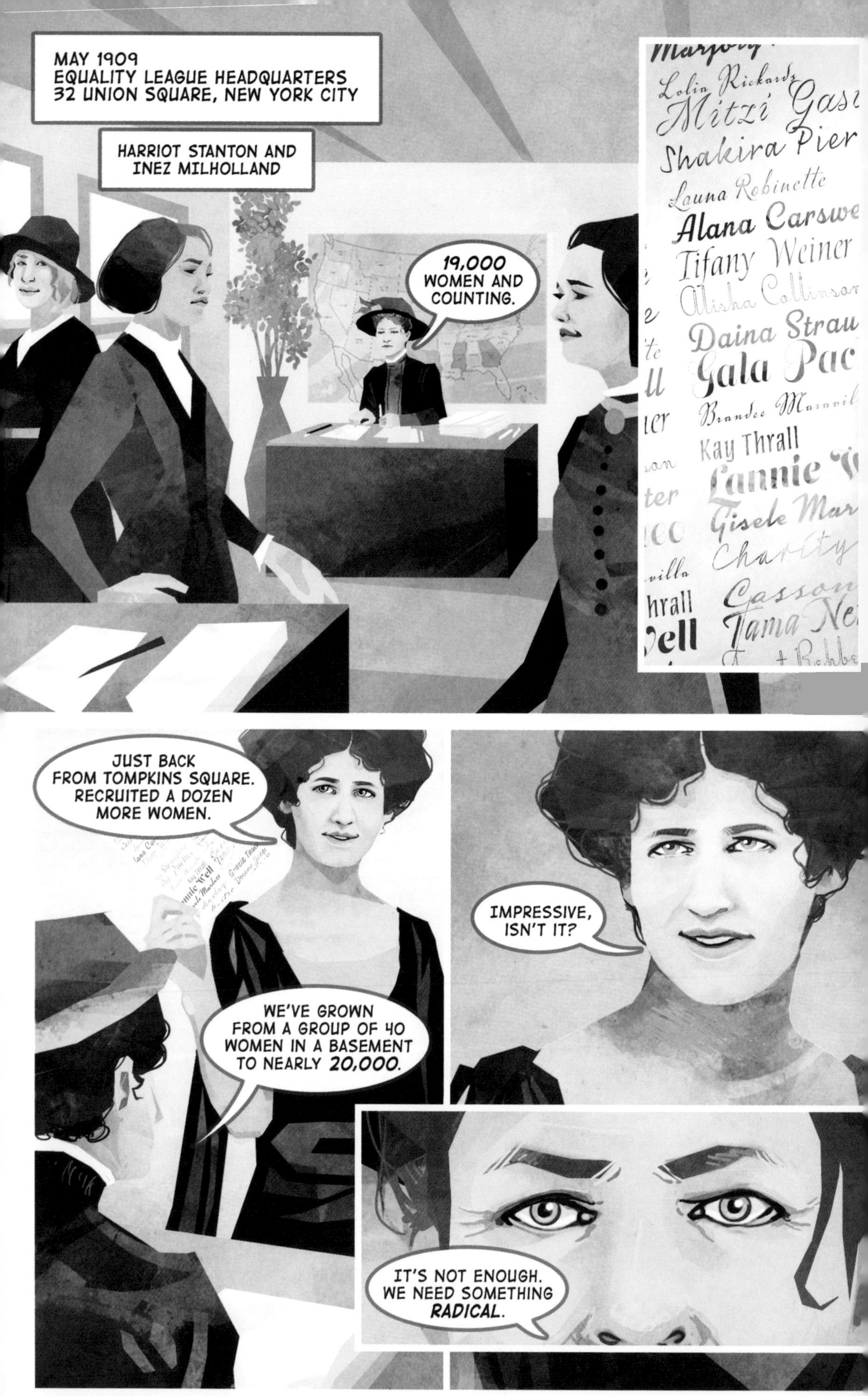
MAY 1909
EQUALITY LEAGUE HEADQUARTERS
32 UNION SQUARE, NEW YORK CITY
HARRIOT STANTON AND
INEZ MILHOLLAND
19,000 WOMEN AND COUNTING.
Lolia Rickards
Launa Robinette
Tifany Weiner
Kay Thrall
JUST BACK FROM TOMPKINS SQUARE. RECRUITED A DOZEN MORE WOMEN.
IMPRESSIVE, ISN'T IT?
WE'VE GROWN FROM A GROUP OF 40 WOMEN IN A BASEMENT TO NEARLY 20,000.
IT'S NOT ENOUGH. WE NEED SOMETHING RADICAL.

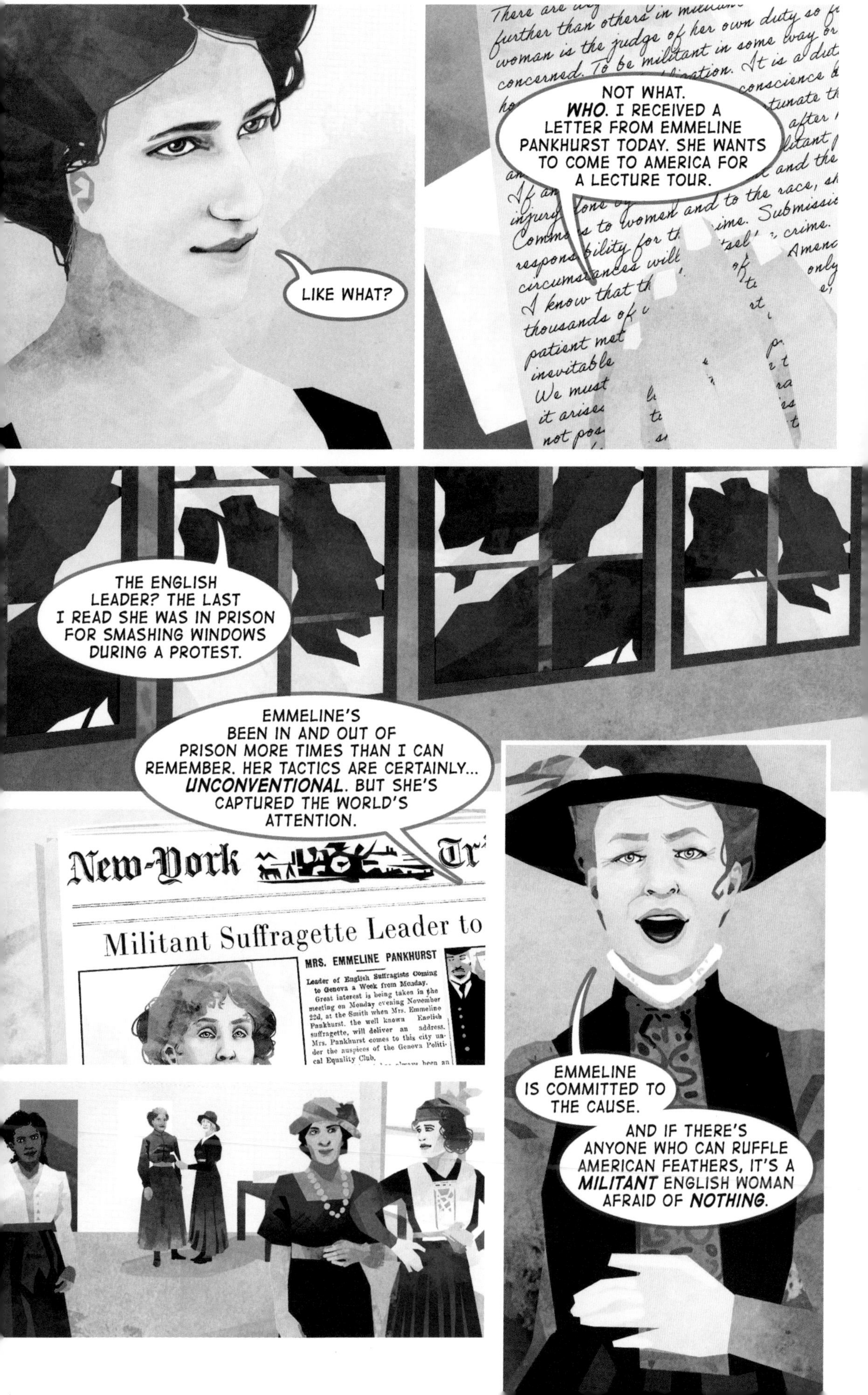
LIKE WHAT?
NOT WHAT. **WHO**. I RECEIVED A LETTER FROM EMMELINE PANKHURST TODAY. SHE WANTS TO COME TO AMERICA FOR A LECTURE TOUR.
THE ENGLISH LEADER? THE LAST I READ SHE WAS IN PRISON FOR SMASHING WINDOWS DURING A PROTEST.
EMMELINE'S BEEN IN AND OUT OF PRISON MORE TIMES THAN I CAN REMEMBER. HER TACTICS ARE CERTAINLY... ***UNCONVENTIONAL***. BUT SHE'S CAPTURED THE WORLD'S ATTENTION.
New-York
Militant Suffragette Leader to
MRS. EMMELINE PANKHURST
Leader of English Suffragists Coming to Geneva a Week from Monday.
Great interest is being taken in the meeting on Monday evening November 22d, at the Smith when Mrs. Emmeline Pankhurst, the well known English suffragette, will deliver an address. Mrs. Pankhurst comes to this city under the auspices of the Geneva Political Equality Club.
EMMELINE IS COMMITTED TO THE CAUSE.
AND IF THERE'S ANYONE WHO CAN RUFFLE AMERICAN FEATHERS, IT'S A ***MILITANT*** ENGLISH WOMAN AFRAID OF ***NOTHING***.

# Militant Suffragette

## MRS. EM

Leader of E
to Geneva
Great inte
meeting on
22nd, at the
Pankhurst-
suffragett
Mrs. Par
der the
cal Equ
Mrs.
active
to vot
about
don
in a
of P
fro
to

The
hon
trite
Seam
tack
era
a
in

### ANXIOUS TO HEAR MRS. PANKHURST

Mrs. Emmeline Pankhurst, the cele-
brated militant suffragette of England,
who is touring this country and at present this section of the state, passed
through this city Monday en route
from Rochester where she spoke Sunday
evening, to Auburn, where she delivered
an address Monday evening. On
Friday Mrs. Pankhurst will be in Buf-
falo, and will speak in the afternoon
Theater. While in Buf-
guest of Mrs.

US TO HEAR
PANKHURST

DISPOSED OF
BR SEATS
THE LEO
AY.
, the cele-
of England,
and at pres-
, passed
route
Sunday
vered
On
Buf-
noon
s.
George H
Pankhurst
city, where
Mrs. Elizabeth
Anne F. Miller
evening she deli
the Smith Opera H
piece of the Geneva
Club.
Mrs. Emmeline Pank
brated militant suffragett
who is touring this count
ent this section of th
through this
from Ro

# Tribune.

One Halfpenny.

# Leader to Visit U.S.

## E PANKHURST

Suffragists Coming
k from Monday.

being taken in the
y evening November
when Mrs. Emmeline
ell known English
deliver an address.
comes to this city un-
s of the Geneva Politi-

ub.

rst has always been an
e for the right of women
this country heard little
il she was sent to a Lon-
leading a suffragette band
on members of the House
nt. When she was released
she sailed for the U.S.
nds for the cause abroad.

Gov. Ferris was among the visitors
who crowded the chamber and gallery. Mrs. Clara R. Arthur, Mrs
Thomas R. Henderson and Mrs. Wil
ber Brotherton, of Detroit; Mrs. Jen
nie Law Hardy, of P onsed, and
other State leaders were prominent, sup
ported by a large delegation of Lans
ing suffragists.

The final stand of the opposition
was made by Senator Murtha in the
hope of putting off the submission till
November, 1914, and this also failed.

Of the five who opposed the measure on the c end mreccit, three were
from Detroit.

## MRS. PANKHURST BEING GRILLED

### ENGLISH SUFFRAGETTE WHO IS TO APPEAR HERE DRAWS ADVERSE COMMENT.

### HER PUBLIC UTTERANCES REVIEWED

Rochester Herald in an Editorial
Today, Sharply Comments on
Some Statements Visitor
Has Made.

Mrs. Pankhurst arriv.d in America
last month for a five weeks' lectur
tour. Editorial pens have been bu
since her arrival with comments
her remarks.

Perhaps the one most adverse
ment on the woman's movemen
supported by Mrs. Pankhurst, v
appeared in the editorial colum
has been published in this se
the Rochester Herald of today
Flower City's comment was
lows:

We have Mrs. Pankhurst,
lish suffragette, with us
during the past few days
given us a good opportuni
her measure. The other d
welcomed in Philadelphia
Century club, the Colleg
the Mother's Congress,
speech she made thi
statement: "The acid
England is merely an
reat civil war. I ne
such

November

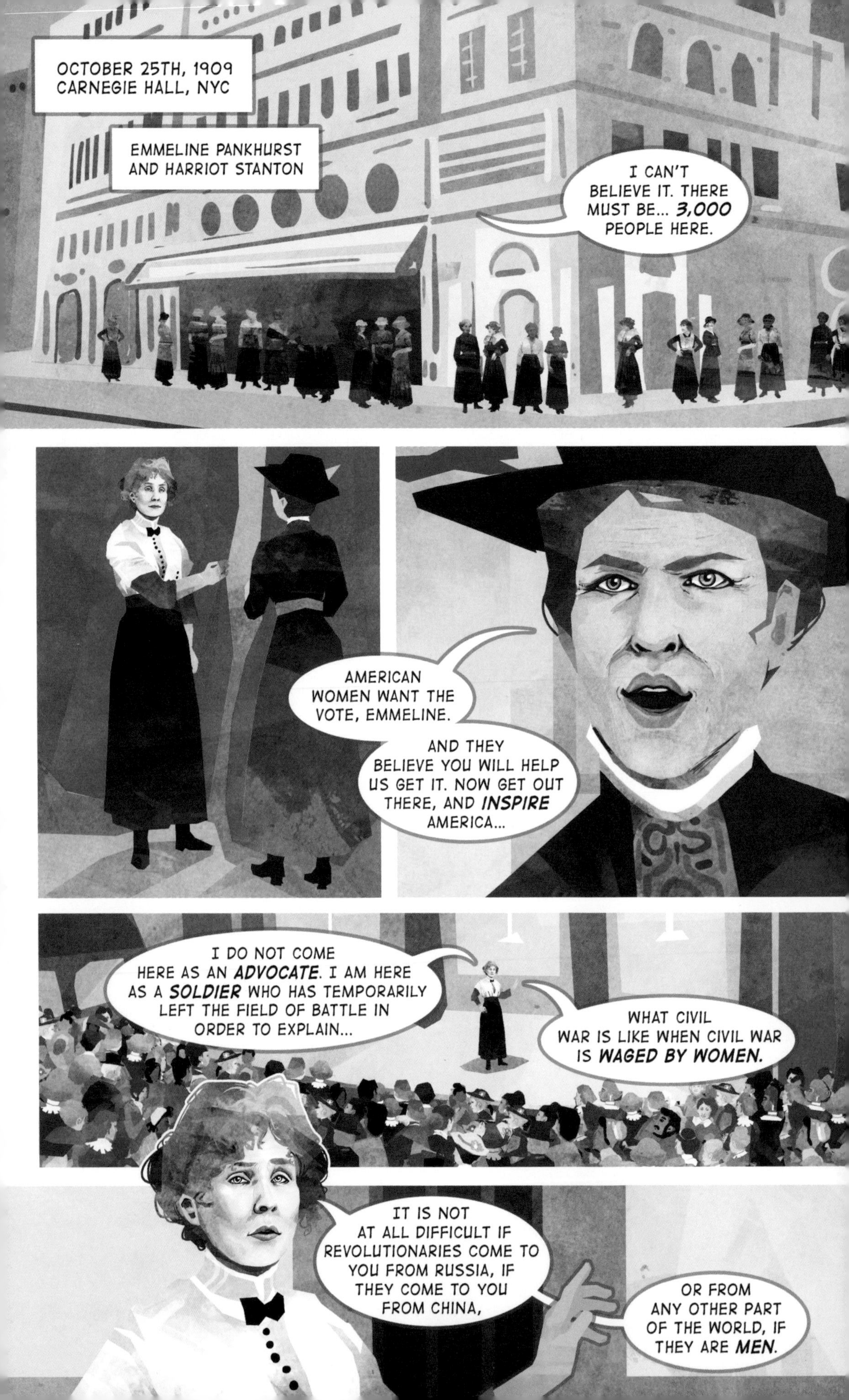

OCTOBER 25TH, 1909
CARNEGIE HALL, NYC
EMMELINE PANKHURST AND HARRIOT STANTON
I CAN'T BELIEVE IT. THERE MUST BE... *3,000* PEOPLE HERE.
AMERICAN WOMEN WANT THE VOTE, EMMELINE.
AND THEY BELIEVE YOU WILL HELP US GET IT. NOW GET OUT THERE, AND *INSPIRE* AMERICA...
I DO NOT COME HERE AS AN *ADVOCATE*. I AM HERE AS A *SOLDIER* WHO HAS TEMPORARILY LEFT THE FIELD OF BATTLE IN ORDER TO EXPLAIN...
WHAT CIVIL WAR IS LIKE WHEN CIVIL WAR IS *WAGED BY WOMEN.*
IT IS NOT AT ALL DIFFICULT IF REVOLUTIONARIES COME TO YOU FROM RUSSIA, IF THEY COME TO YOU FROM CHINA,
OR FROM ANY OTHER PART OF THE WORLD, IF THEY ARE *MEN*.

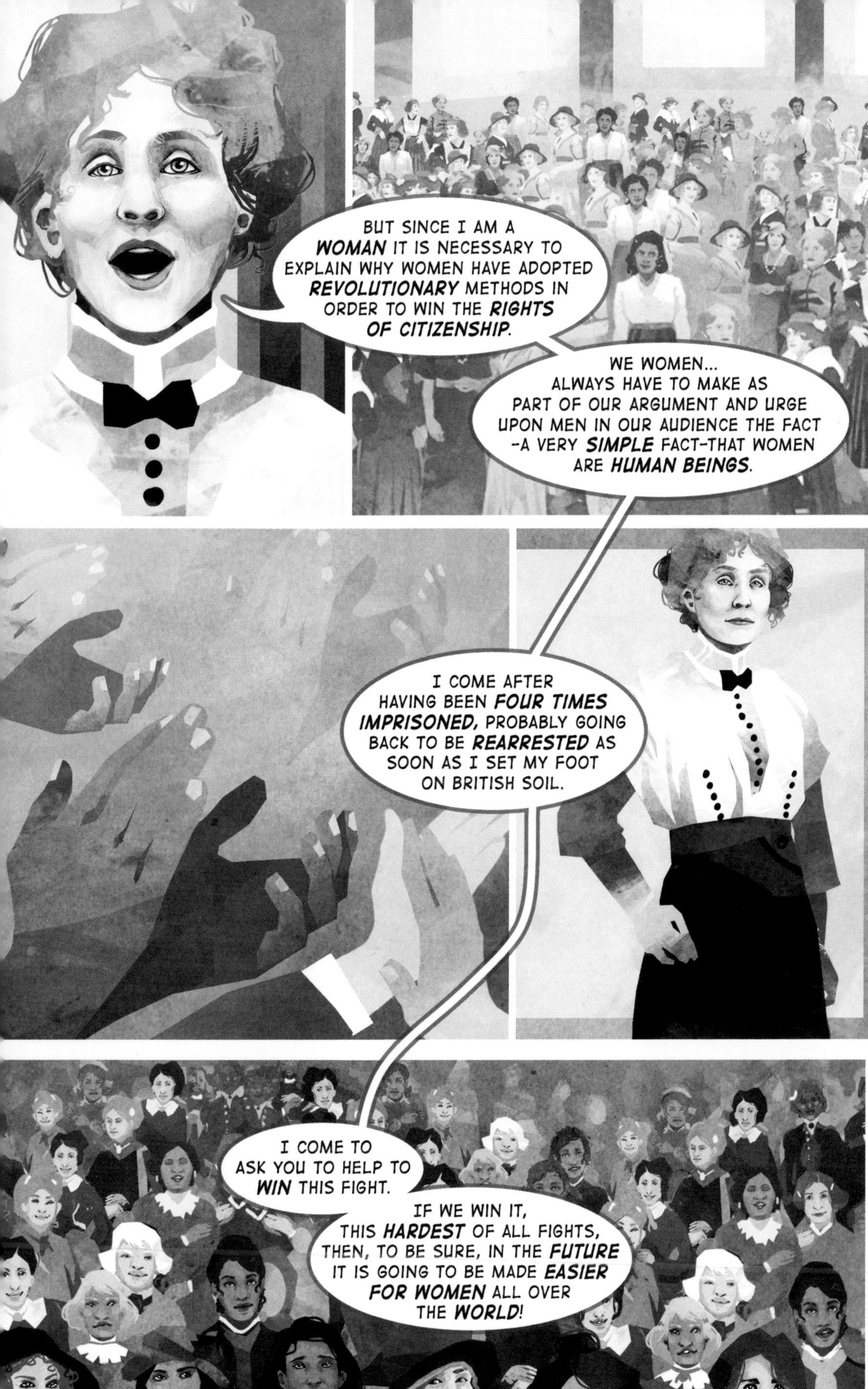
BUT SINCE I AM A WOMAN IT IS NECESSARY TO EXPLAIN WHY WOMEN HAVE ADOPTED REVOLUTIONARY METHODS IN ORDER TO WIN THE RIGHTS OF CITIZENSHIP.
WE WOMEN... ALWAYS HAVE TO MAKE AS PART OF OUR ARGUMENT AND URGE UPON MEN IN OUR AUDIENCE THE FACT -A VERY SIMPLE FACT-THAT WOMEN ARE HUMAN BEINGS.
I COME AFTER HAVING BEEN FOUR TIMES IMPRISONED, PROBABLY GOING BACK TO BE REARRESTED AS SOON AS I SET MY FOOT ON BRITISH SOIL.
I COME TO ASK YOU TO HELP TO WIN THIS FIGHT.
IF WE WIN IT, THIS HARDEST OF ALL FIGHTS, THEN, TO BE SURE, IN THE FUTURE IT IS GOING TO BE MADE EASIER FOR WOMEN ALL OVER THE WORLD!

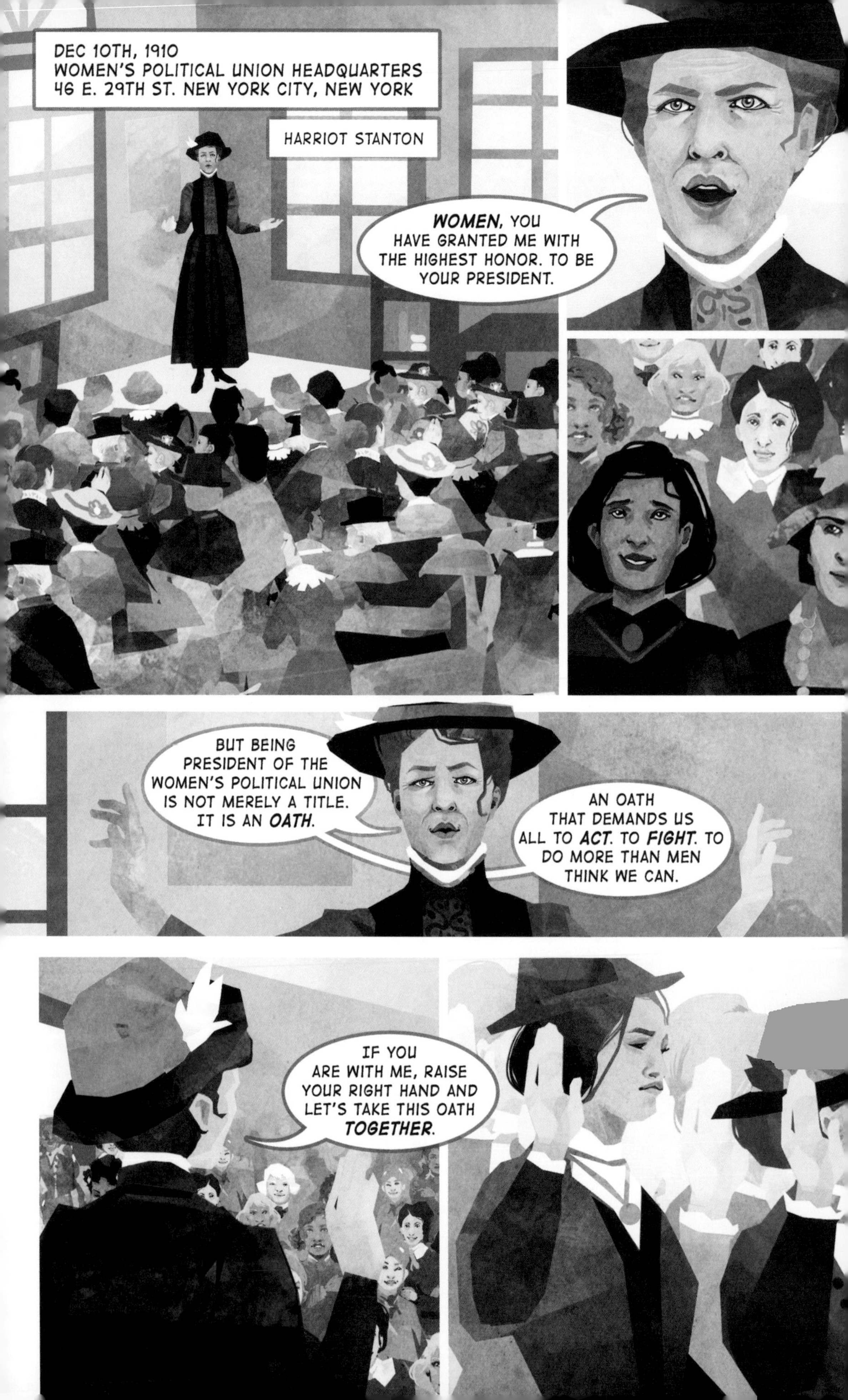
DEC 10TH, 1910
WOMEN'S POLITICAL UNION HEADQUARTERS
46 E. 29TH ST. NEW YORK CITY, NEW YORK
HARRIOT STANTON
WOMEN, YOU HAVE GRANTED ME WITH THE HIGHEST HONOR. TO BE YOUR PRESIDENT.
BUT BEING PRESIDENT OF THE WOMEN'S POLITICAL UNION IS NOT MERELY A TITLE. IT IS AN OATH.
AN OATH THAT DEMANDS US ALL TO ACT. TO FIGHT. TO DO MORE THAN MEN THINK WE CAN.
IF YOU ARE WITH ME, RAISE YOUR RIGHT HAND AND LET'S TAKE THIS OATH TOGETHER.

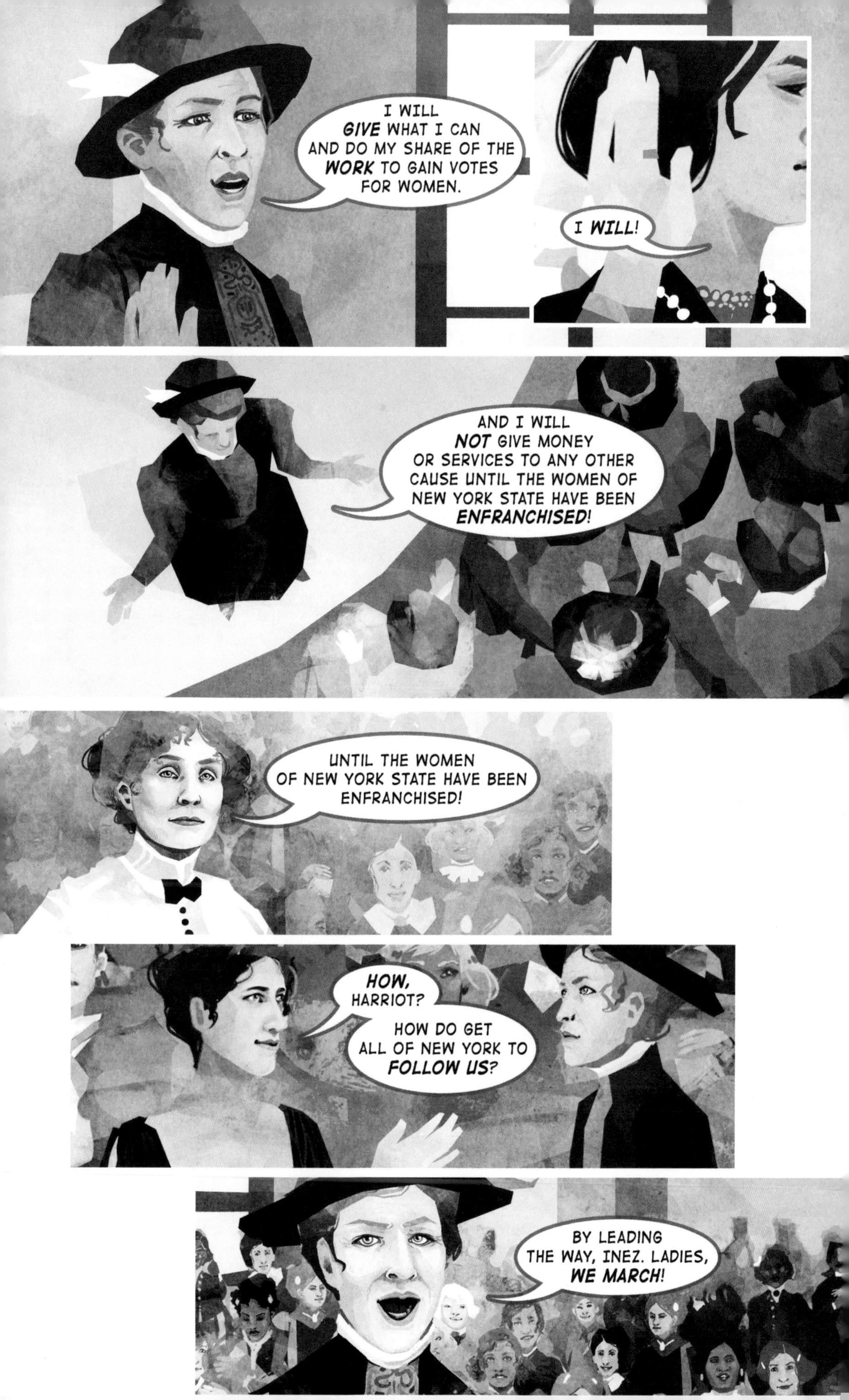
I WILL GIVE WHAT I CAN AND DO MY SHARE OF THE WORK TO GAIN VOTES FOR WOMEN.
I WILL!
AND I WILL NOT GIVE MONEY OR SERVICES TO ANY OTHER CAUSE UNTIL THE WOMEN OF NEW YORK STATE HAVE BEEN ENFRANCHISED!
UNTIL THE WOMEN OF NEW YORK STATE HAVE BEEN ENFRANCHISED!
HOW, HARRIOT?
HOW DO GET ALL OF NEW YORK TO FOLLOW US?
BY LEADING THE WAY, INEZ. LADIES, WE MARCH!

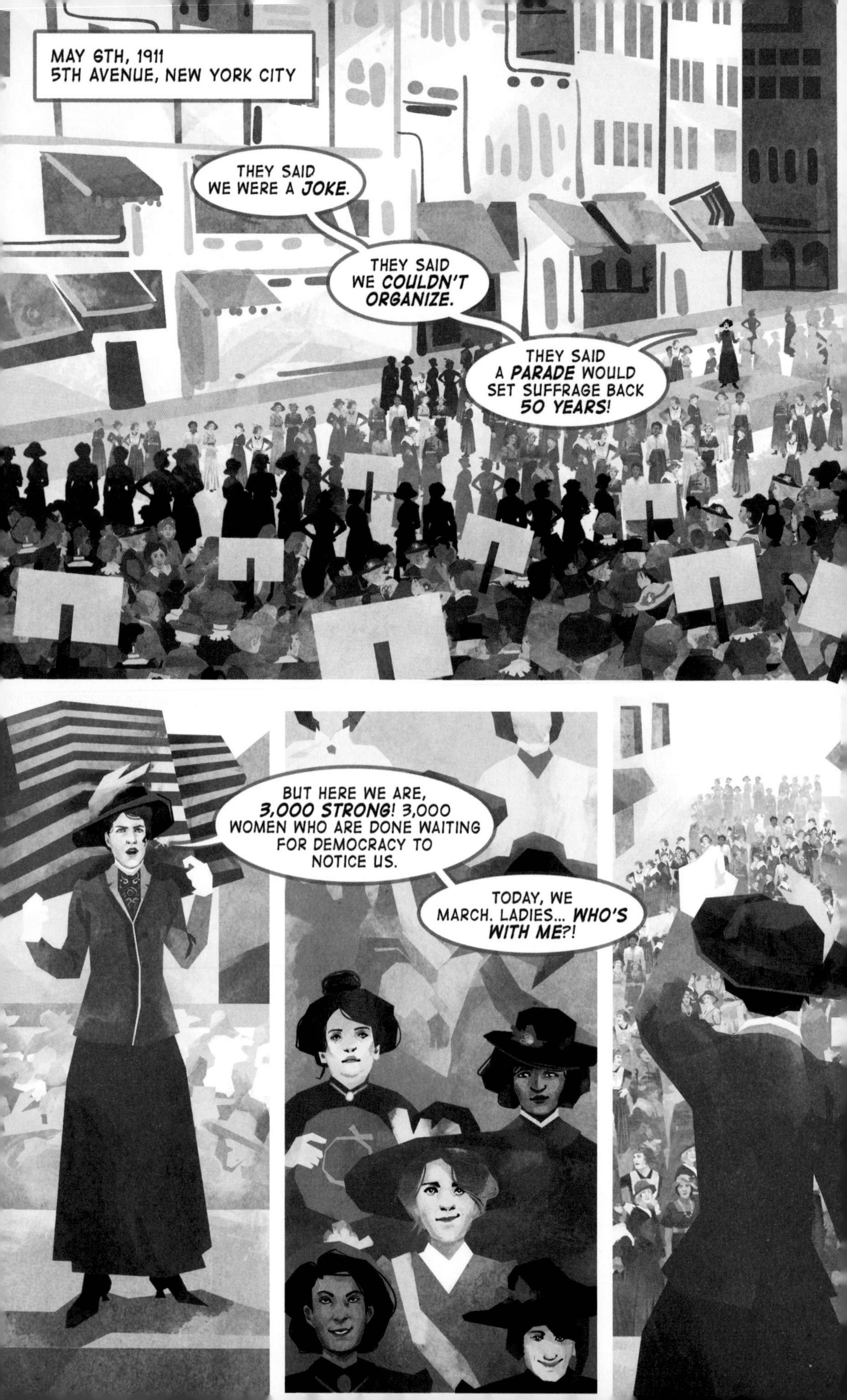
MAY 6TH, 1911
5TH AVENUE, NEW YORK CITY
THEY SAID WE WERE A JOKE.
THEY SAID WE COULDN'T ORGANIZE.
THEY SAID A PARADE WOULD SET SUFFRAGE BACK 50 YEARS!
BUT HERE WE ARE, 3,000 STRONG! 3,000 WOMEN WHO ARE DONE WAITING FOR DEMOCRACY TO NOTICE US.
TODAY, WE MARCH. LADIES... WHO'S WITH ME?!

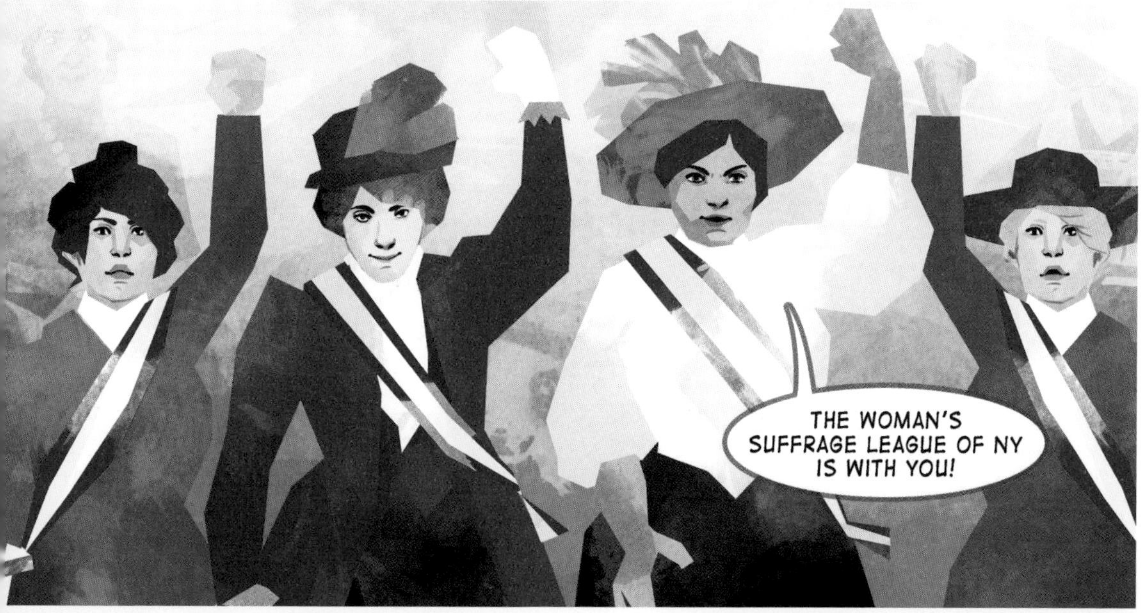
THE WOMAN'S SUFFRAGE LEAGUE OF NY IS WITH YOU!

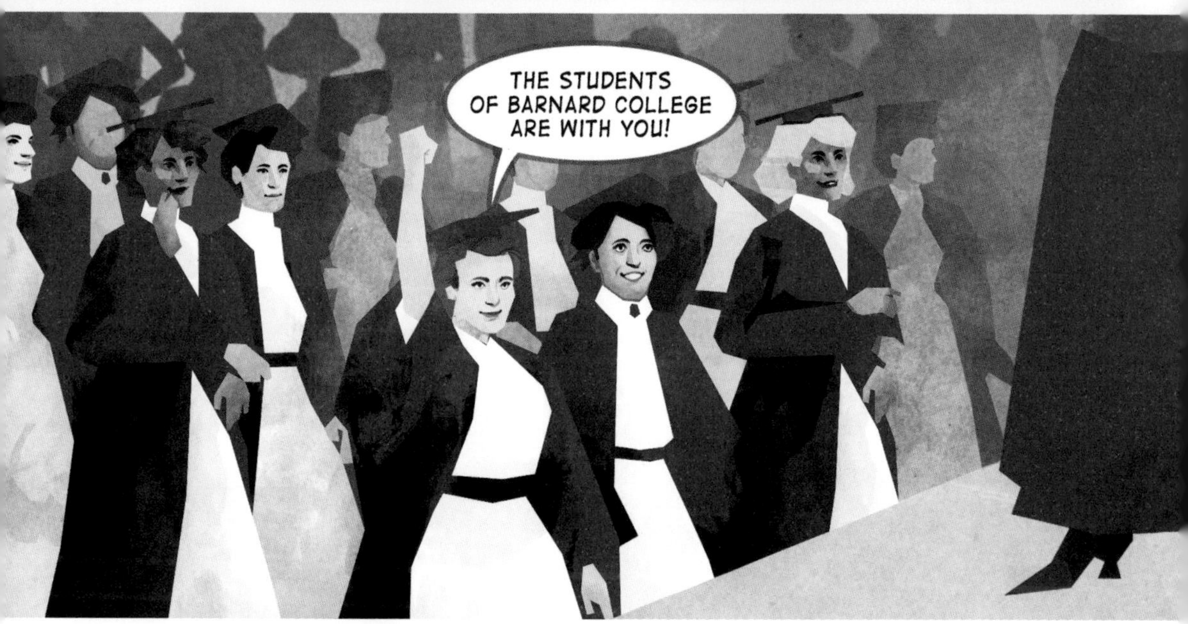
THE STUDENTS OF BARNARD COLLEGE ARE WITH YOU!

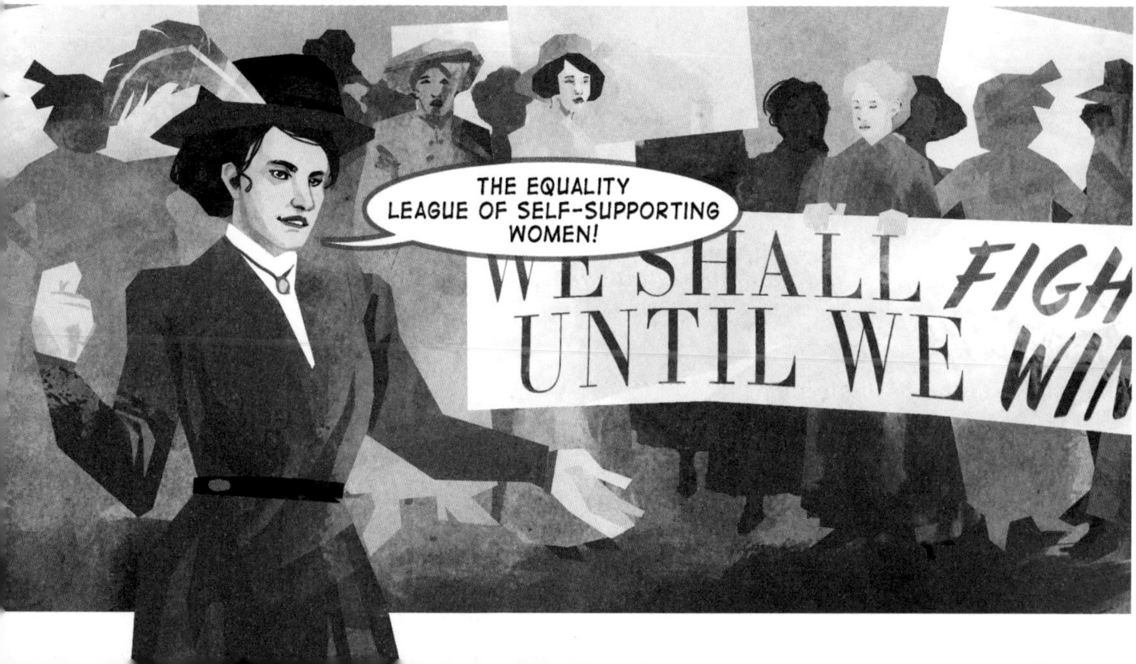
THE EQUALITY LEAGUE OF SELF-SUPPORTING WOMEN!
WE SHALL FIGH
UNTIL WE WI

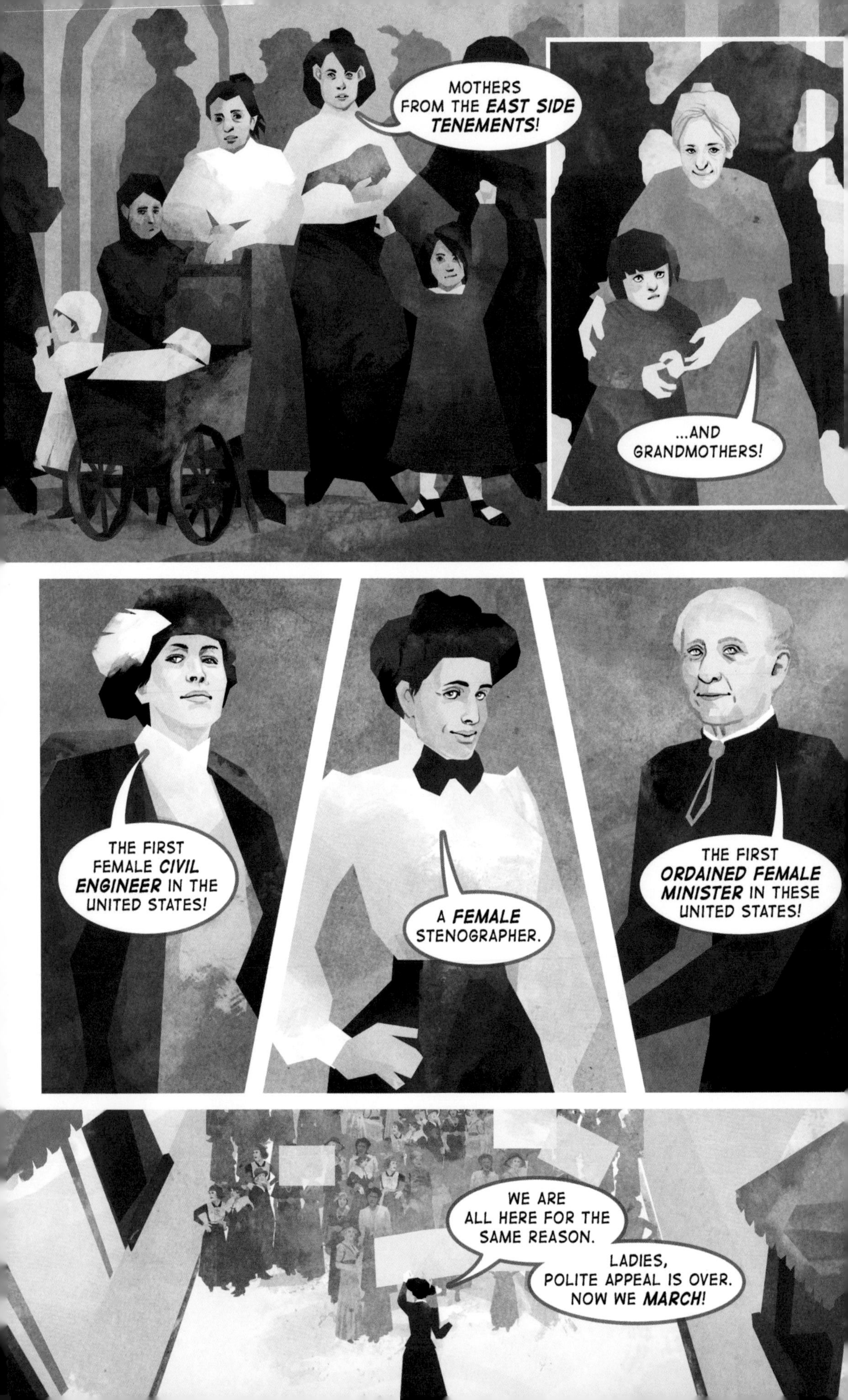
MOTHERS FROM THE EAST SIDE TENEMENTS!
...AND GRANDMOTHERS!
THE FIRST FEMALE CIVIL ENGINEER IN THE UNITED STATES!
A FEMALE STENOGRAPHER.
THE FIRST ORDAINED FEMALE MINISTER IN THESE UNITED STATES!
WE ARE ALL HERE FOR THE SAME REASON.
LADIES, POLITE APPEAL IS OVER. NOW WE MARCH!

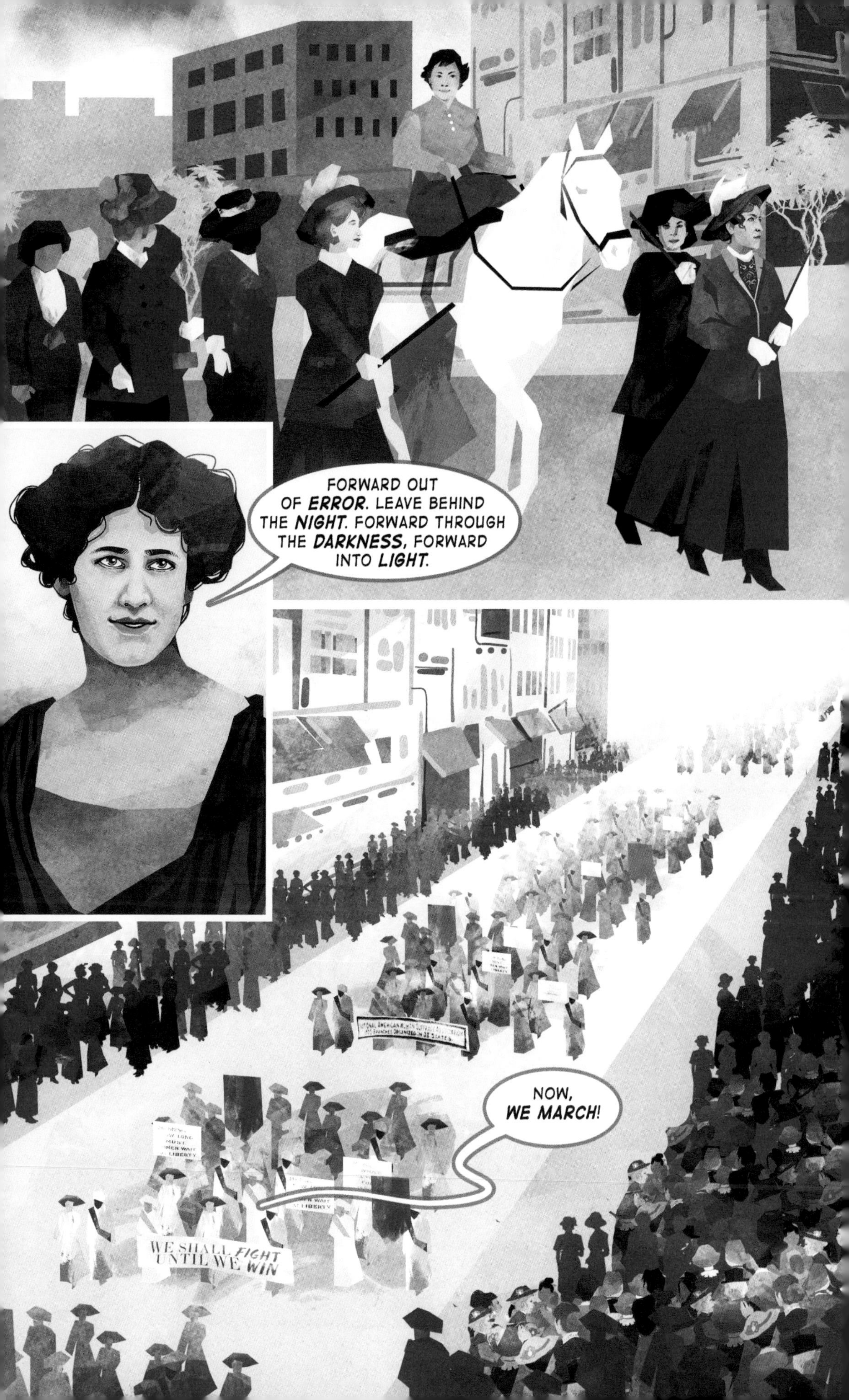
FORWARD OUT OF **ERROR**. LEAVE BEHIND THE **NIGHT**. FORWARD THROUGH THE **DARKNESS**, FORWARD INTO **LIGHT**.
NOW, **WE MARCH!**
WE SHALL *FIGHT* UNTIL WE *WIN*

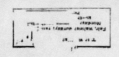
# NEW YORK SUFFRAGE
# BILL PUT TO VO

Was anything been disgraced.
victory. I cause of indifferent wo
men are in need another allied Sta
of the treason at given one sove gists

Ten thousand women from all over
the country had planned a magnifi
cent parade and pageant which place
in Washington on Ma nth d tions,
pageant leaders, designers, women of
influence and renown were ready to
give a wonderful and beautiful piece
of suffrage work to the public that

# York Times.

Fair, warmer sunday; rain
Monday

1911—W Price. In Eight Lines.

# SUFFRAGISTS BUSY IN ALBANY
## SENATOR STILWELL PUTS IN A BILL GIVING WOMEN THE VOTE

Got, the Wa Wal, ed.

The debate, the debate a after an
hour and a quarter, and was charac
terized by the persistent efforts of
Senator Weafock and a few others to
tack on crippling amendments. Sev
eral suggestions for a ctenight dis
alling cuck a ator Weaf9n notice of
resting answer on chmwwa down
in quick a c Brota B.

Gov. Ferris was among the visitors
who crowded the chamber ann wal
lery. Mrs. Clara B. Arthur, Mrs
Thomas R. Henderson and Mrs. Wil
ber Brotherton, of Del Wa Mrs. Jen
nte Law Hardy, of Tecumseh, and
other State leaders were present, sup
ported by a large delegation of Lans
ing suffragists.

The final stand of the opposition
was made by Senator Murtha in the
hope of putting off the submission till
November, 1914. tho failed.

Of the fe ge of some meas
ure on the na ciation three were
from Detroit.

A complete campaign of organiza
tion and education has been mapped
out by the State As ciation The
on ed osmed on

nte Law Hardy, of ecumseh, and
other State leaders were present, su,
ported by a large delegation of Lans
ing suffragists.

Gov. Ferris was among the visitors
who crowded the chamber and gal
lery. Mrs. Clara B. Arthur, Mrs.
Thomas R. Henderson and Mrs. Wil
ber Brotherton of Detroit; Mrs. Jen
nte Law Sta R of Tecumseh, and
other State leaders were present, sup
ported by a large delegation of Lans
ing suffragists.

The final stand of the opposition
was made by Senator Murtha in the
hope of putting off the submission till
November, 1914, and then oc 1.

Of the fire mf some 1 mf act pas
ure on the tn Lan till) Lan were
from Detroit i

A complete campaign of organiza
tion and education has been mapped

The final stand of the opposition
was made by Senator Murtha in the
hope of putting at the submission till
November, 191 further, is also pas ted
Of the fire asole fire e the Se e t
ure on the cnd map woc three woc th
from Detroit

A complete campaign of organiza
tion and education has been mapped
out by the Stat Sinociin,

# NEWS

Trio adtadeir gooe
*longer* and *stroenr stro*
in any other woman's ma
of similar circulation. T
*stronger* good because
confidence of our reade

---

# York Times.

THE WEATHER.
Fair, warmer Sunday; rain probably
Monday

PRICE FIVE CENTS.

In Eight

---

# Should Women Vote in New York State?

...led as it again a campaign State
after a short lapse of four months.
The amendment will go to the voters
on April next. The State-wide feeling
that the women who till fraoded of
victory last fall will help the suffragists.

The final action of the Legislature
was that last week, when the Senate, by a vote of 46 to 5, passed the
suffrage amendment, with ten slight
attendment to make the requan heals
for foreign-born women the same as
those for male immigrants.

### Col. the Wm W. isebate

The debate, the Senate lasted an
hour and a quarter, and was characterized by the persistent efforts of
Senator Wadfock and a few others to
tack on crippling amendments Several suggestions, including the dis-
alling of women for holding office or
serving on juries, were voted down
in quick succession.

Gov. Ferris was among the visitors
who crowded the chamber ann wal-
lery. Mrs. Clara B. Arthur, xra
Thomas R. Henderson Wo Mrs. Wilbur Brotherton, of Detroit, Mrs. Jennie Law Hardy, of Tecumseh, and
other State leaders were present, supported by a large delegation of Lansing suffragists.

The final stand of the opposition
was made by Senator Murtha in the
hope of putting off the submission till
November, 1914, and this too failed.

Of the five who opposed the measure on the final rollcall, three were
from Detroit.

A complete campaign of organization and education has been mapped
out by the State Association The

The debate in the Senate sted an
hour and a quarter, and was characterized by the persistent efforts of
Senator Wadfock and a few e ers to
tack on crippling amendments Several suggestions, including the dis-
alling of women for holding office or
serving on juries were voted down
in quick succession.

Gov. Ferris was among the visitors
who crowded the amber and gallery. Mrs. Clara B. Arthur, Mrs.
Thomas R. Henderson, and Mrs. Wilbur Brotherton, of Mranli; M. Jennie Law Hardy, of Tecumseh, and
other State leaders were present, su-
ported by a large delegation of Lansing suffragists.

Gov. Ferris was among the visitors
who crowded the chamber and gallery. Mrs. Clara B. Arthur, Mrs.
Thomas R. Henderson and Mrs. Wilbur Brotherton, of Detroit; Mrs. Jennie Law Hardy, of Tecumseh, and
other State leaders weppresent, supported by a large delegation of Lansing suffragists.

The final stand of the opposition
was made by Senator Murtha in the
hope of putting off the submission till
November, 1914, and this also failed.

Of the five who opposed the measure on the end rollcall, three were
from Detroit.

A complete campaign of organization and education has been mapped
out by the State Association

---

ijuns should stray
s, you can bet we'd
m have what they
re plentiful than
er friends should
halls, we'd throw
earts and pocket
ake the ladies of
ke them a present

ned. The news of
an had asked for
elled slowly west-
Pacific, until it
nd the Legislature
not the Western

solemnly, when he
of suffrage should
s territory. Why,
don't know as just
ooced we can't see
l clear water-hole.

he said, "to the re-
gret that the great
een so long remiss
is a selfish motive
in need of woman's
ll means let us ex-
pliments and our
t of franchise"

hings better in Newport."

he reflection of our English friends
the charming manner in which Mrs.
l for the "rally" in favor of woman
rble house.

ob of women with student voices
to jail, or throwing bricks or seeking
n his bedroom by having themselves
parcels through the mails.

Belmont's function enjoyed a view
magnificent dwelling, or on the lawn
Julia Ward Howe's plea for giving
Howe, who dates back to the Seneca
d at the time of the civil war wrote
epublic."

and very beautiful, but as to practical
er. *The hearing before a joint legis-*
adt winger developed the fact that the
an suffrage are to be found among

the subject jocularly, to declare sar-
the ground that if it were established
ntly present bills for millinery or
not desire to see his wife, his sisters
bloom by being mixed up in the
with which even men are disgusted.
ablished in Wyoming fifty years ago,
ago and in Utah and Idaho thirteen
n those four States does not substan-
woman suffragists as to the alleged
lation and administration that would
allot.

and other institutions for the protec-
en and children flourish in a higher

New York and been arrested and fined. The news of
all this agitation because a woman had asked for
something and been refused, had travelled slowly west-
ward, along the line of the Union Pacific, until it
reached the Wyoming cattle ranges and the Legislature
in session in Cheyenne. That was not the Western
way of dealing with a woman

"I believe," said Mr. Foglesong, solemnly, when he
introduced his bill, "that the right of suffrage should
no longer be denied the ladies of this territory. Why,
even a sheep-herder can vote! I don't know as just
because we're men we need get so loooed we can't see
anybody unless we look in a good clear water-hole.
We act like a lot of baked skunks.

"If a bunch of road agents or Injuns should stray
in here and make any polite requests, you can bet we'd
all throw up our hands and let them have what they
wanted. And they're a heap more plentiful than
ladies. If this Miss Anthony and her friends should
suddenly walk into these legislative halls, we'd throw
up our hands and our hats and hearts and pocket-
books. I say we don't wait to make the ladies of
Wyoming ask favors of us. Let's make them a present
of the ballot.

"They don't have much fun, anyhow. They can't
punch cows or wrangle horses or shoot Indians. I say
let them vote and have a little pleasure."

He sat down amid shouts of laughter and much
applause, and Col. William R. Steele rose quietly
and seriously. He was an attorney, one of the silver-
tongued orators of that day and generation. At one
time he represented Wyoming in Congress.

Man is inclined to treat the sub-
castically that he favors it on the gr
women could not consistently p
alimony. At heart he does not des
or his daughters lose their bloom
vulgar political controversies with v

---

Fair, walnut surway, raw

Trse of
*longacation.*
in sim s to

---

ong fee's electsir di-
ator Wedfock anfice or
co chwed down
Brota B.

was among the visitors
the chamber ann wal-
lara B. Arthur, xra
lenderson Wo Mrs. Wil-
n, of Det Wa Mrs. Jen-
dly, W Tecumseh, and
aders were present, sup-
large delegation of Lans-

tand of the opposition
Senator Murtha in the
ng of the submission till
4, tho failed.
Se of those meas-
n. ballot three were

campaign of organiza-
tion has been mapped
tate As ciation The
ned on

---

lery. Mrs. Clara B. Arthur, Mrs.
Thomas R. Henderson and Mrs. Wilbur Brotherton of Detroit; Mrs. Jennie Law Sta R of oresh, and
other State leaders wepondtement, supported by a large delegation of Lansing suffragists.

The final stand of the opposition
was made by Senator Murtha in the
hope of putting off the submission till
November, 1914, and this of s.

Of the five who opposed the measure on the n law till law were
from Detroit

A complete campaign of organization and education has been mapped

The final stand of the opposition
was made by Senator Murtha in the
hope of putting off the submission till
November, 191 ember, is also pas er

Of the five who opposed the measure on the end map woe three woe
from Detroit.

A complete campaign of organization and education has been mapped
out in the State. Siaocell

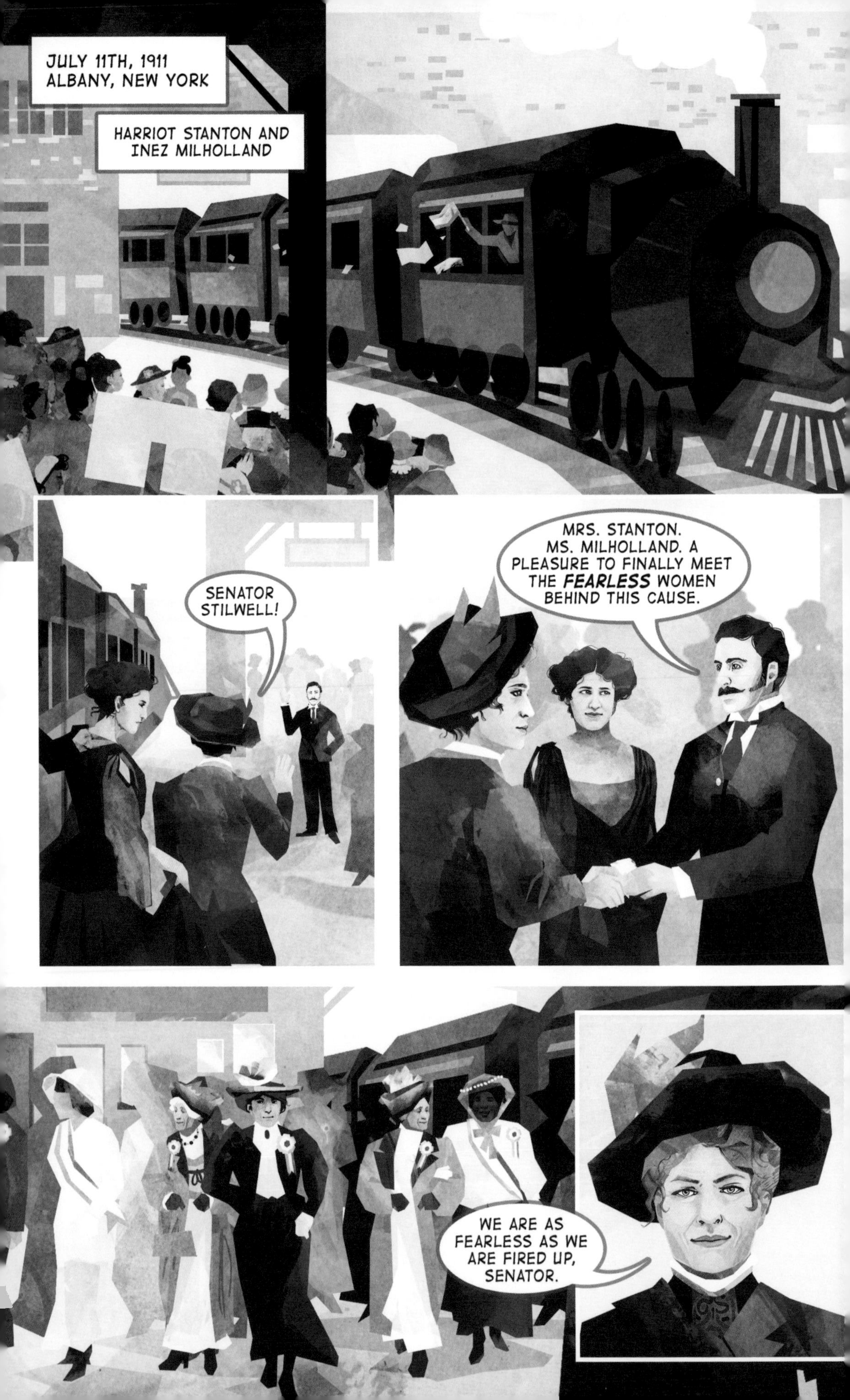
JULY 11TH, 1911
ALBANY, NEW YORK
HARRIOT STANTON AND INEZ MILHOLLAND
SENATOR STILWELL!
MRS. STANTON. MS. MILHOLLAND. A PLEASURE TO FINALLY MEET THE *FEARLESS* WOMEN BEHIND THIS CAUSE.
WE ARE AS FEARLESS AS WE ARE FIRED UP, SENATOR.

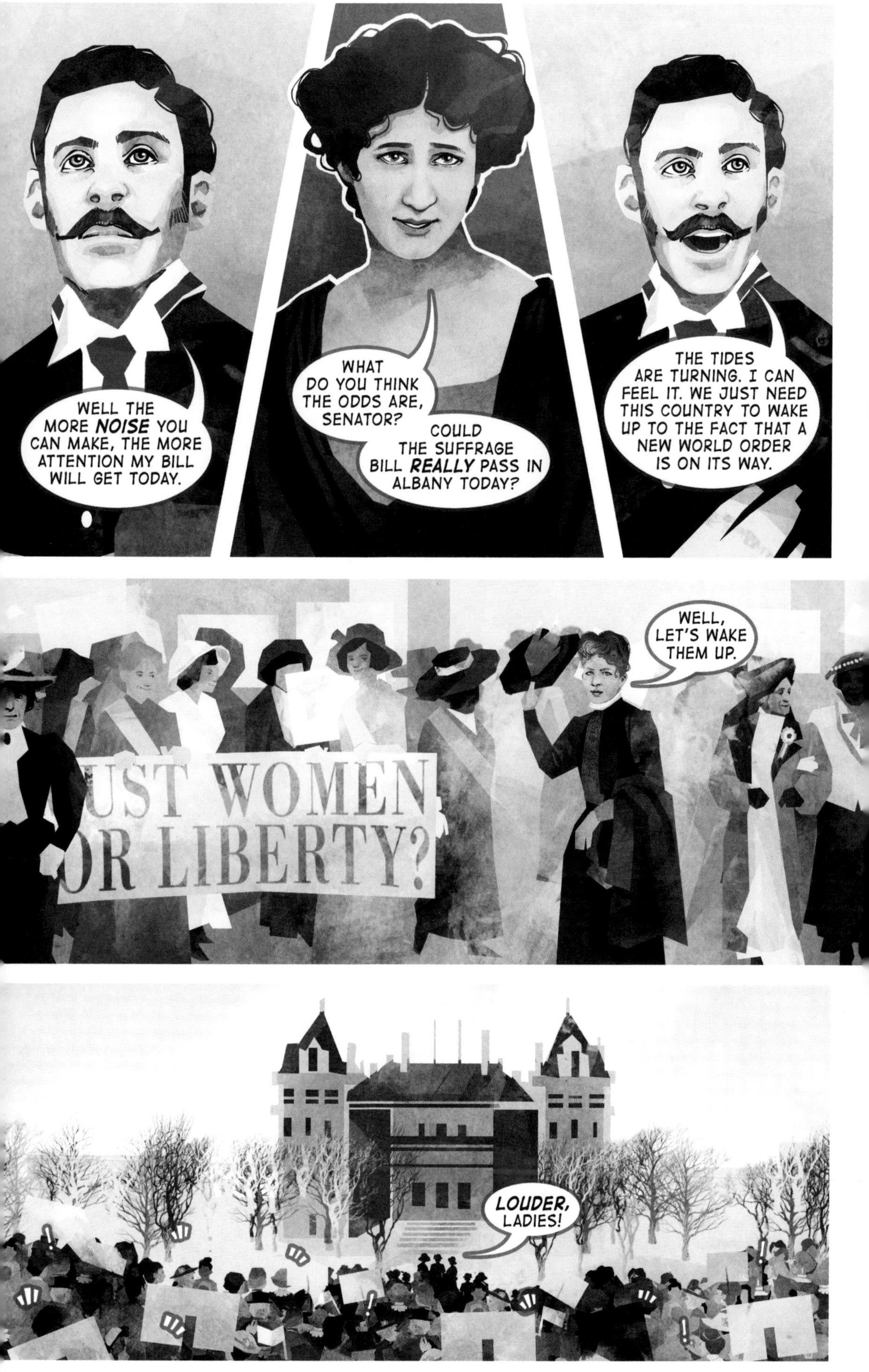
WELL THE MORE NOISE YOU CAN MAKE, THE MORE ATTENTION MY BILL WILL GET TODAY.
WHAT DO YOU THINK THE ODDS ARE, SENATOR?
COULD THE SUFFRAGE BILL REALLY PASS IN ALBANY TODAY?
THE TIDES ARE TURNING. I CAN FEEL IT. WE JUST NEED THIS COUNTRY TO WAKE UP TO THE FACT THAT A NEW WORLD ORDER IS ON ITS WAY.
UST WOMEN
OR LIBERTY?
WELL, LET'S WAKE THEM UP.
LOUDER, LADIES!

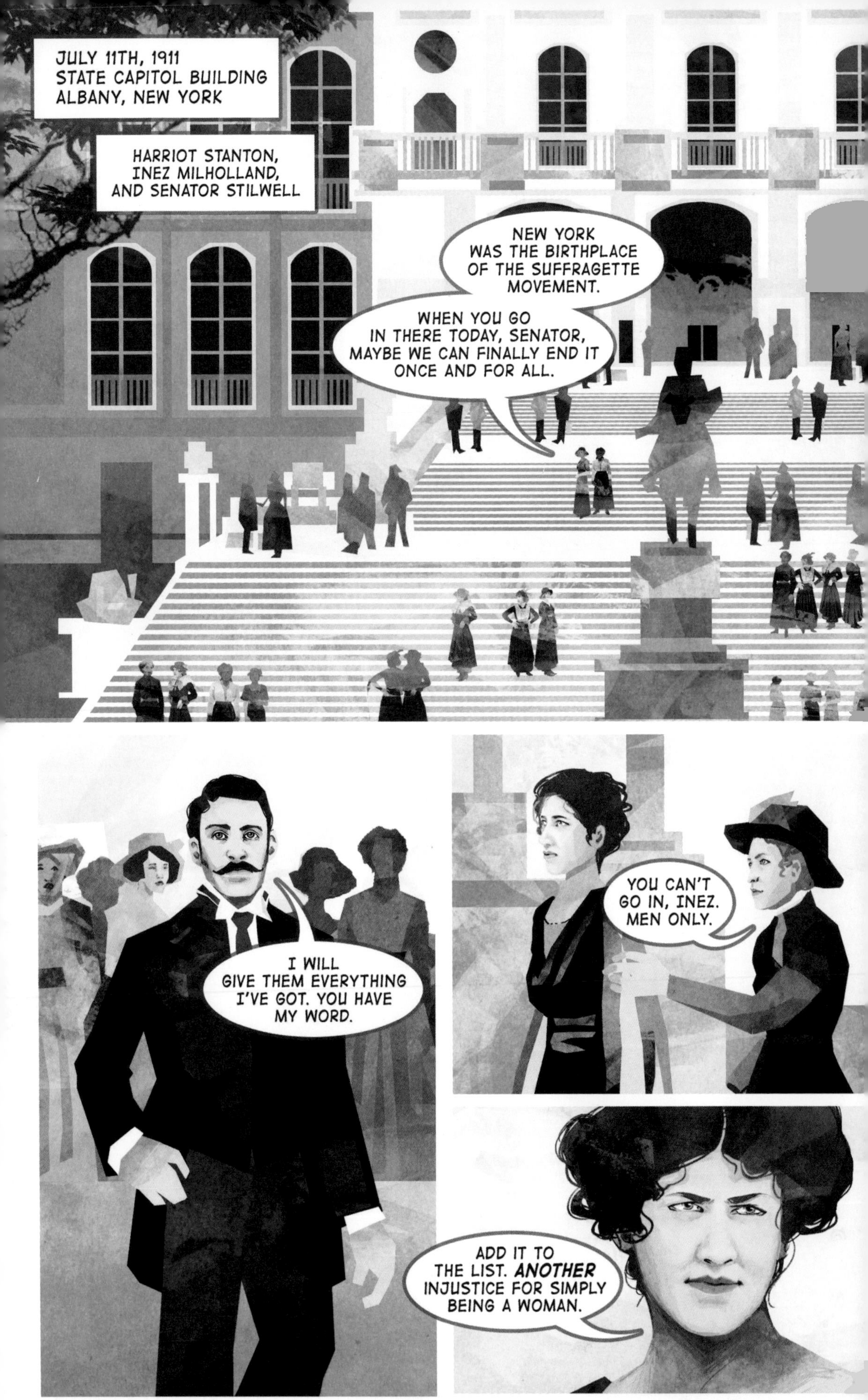

JULY 11TH, 1911
STATE CAPITOL BUILDING
ALBANY, NEW YORK
HARRIOT STANTON, INEZ MILHOLLAND, AND SENATOR STILWELL
NEW YORK WAS THE BIRTHPLACE OF THE SUFFRAGETTE MOVEMENT.
WHEN YOU GO IN THERE TODAY, SENATOR, MAYBE WE CAN FINALLY END IT ONCE AND FOR ALL.
I WILL GIVE THEM EVERYTHING I'VE GOT. YOU HAVE MY WORD.
YOU CAN'T GO IN, INEZ. MEN ONLY.
ADD IT TO THE LIST. ***ANOTHER*** INJUSTICE FOR SIMPLY BEING A WOMAN.

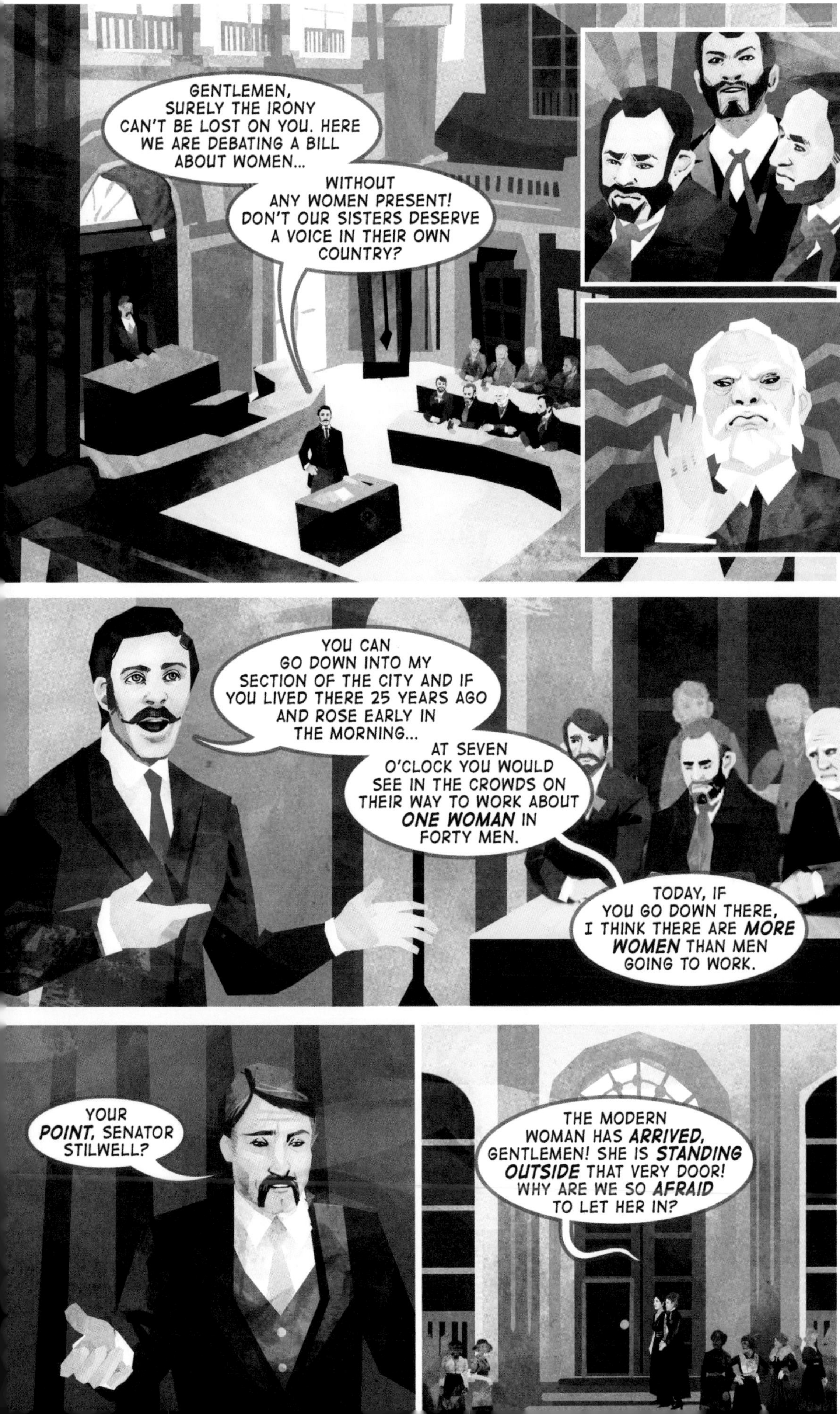
GENTLEMEN, SURELY THE IRONY CAN'T BE LOST ON YOU. HERE WE ARE DEBATING A BILL ABOUT WOMEN...
WITHOUT ANY WOMEN PRESENT! DON'T OUR SISTERS DESERVE A VOICE IN THEIR OWN COUNTRY?
YOU CAN GO DOWN INTO MY SECTION OF THE CITY AND IF YOU LIVED THERE 25 YEARS AGO AND ROSE EARLY IN THE MORNING...
AT SEVEN O'CLOCK YOU WOULD SEE IN THE CROWDS ON THEIR WAY TO WORK ABOUT ONE WOMAN IN FORTY MEN.
TODAY, IF YOU GO DOWN THERE, I THINK THERE ARE MORE WOMEN THAN MEN GOING TO WORK.
YOUR POINT, SENATOR STILWELL?
THE MODERN WOMAN HAS ARRIVED, GENTLEMEN! SHE IS STANDING OUTSIDE THAT VERY DOOR! WHY ARE WE SO AFRAID TO LET HER IN?

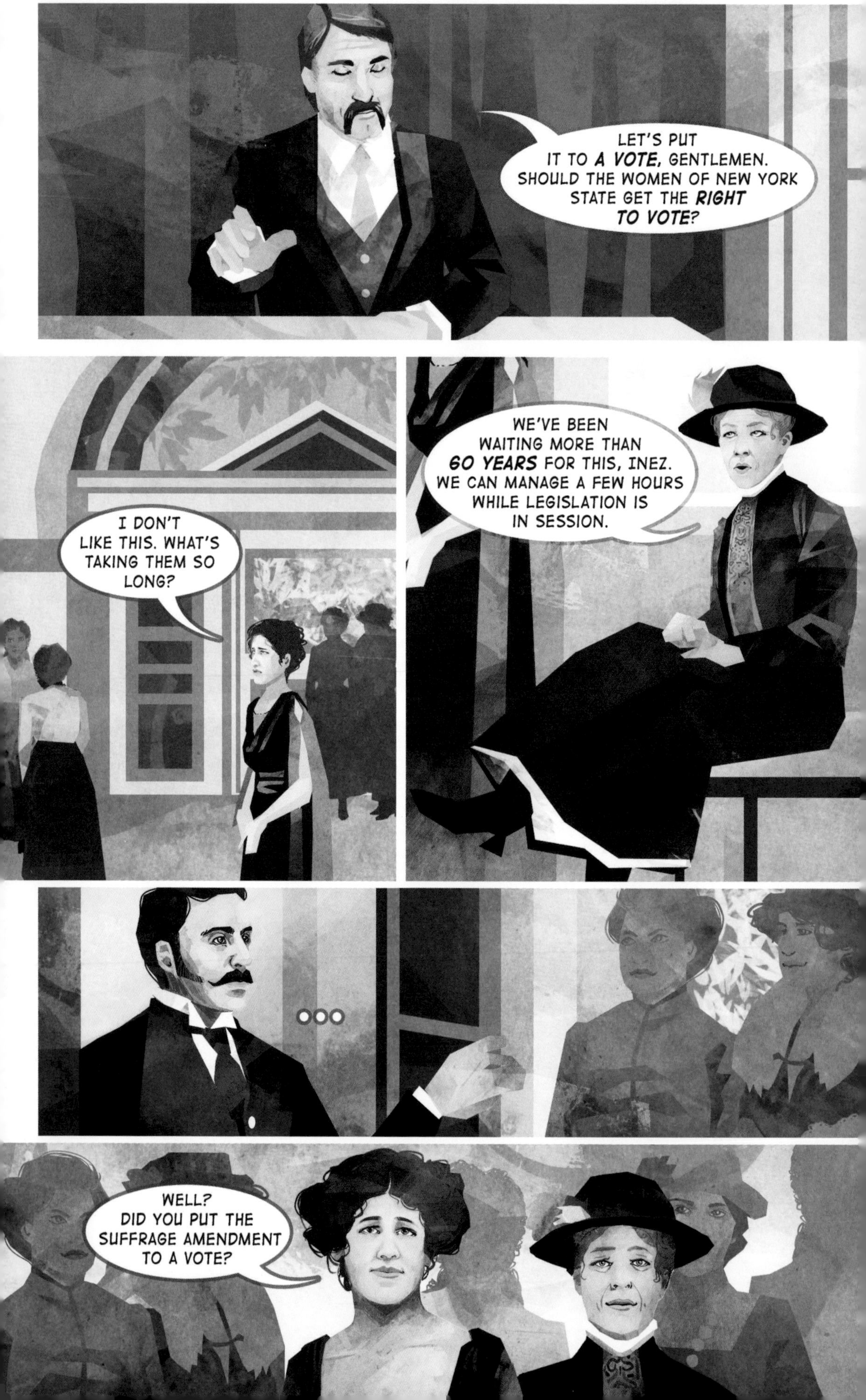
LET'S PUT IT TO A VOTE, GENTLEMEN. SHOULD THE WOMEN OF NEW YORK STATE GET THE RIGHT TO VOTE?
I DON'T LIKE THIS. WHAT'S TAKING THEM SO LONG?
WE'VE BEEN WAITING MORE THAN 60 YEARS FOR THIS, INEZ. WE CAN MANAGE A FEW HOURS WHILE LEGISLATION IS IN SESSION.
WELL? DID YOU PUT THE SUFFRAGE AMENDMENT TO A VOTE?

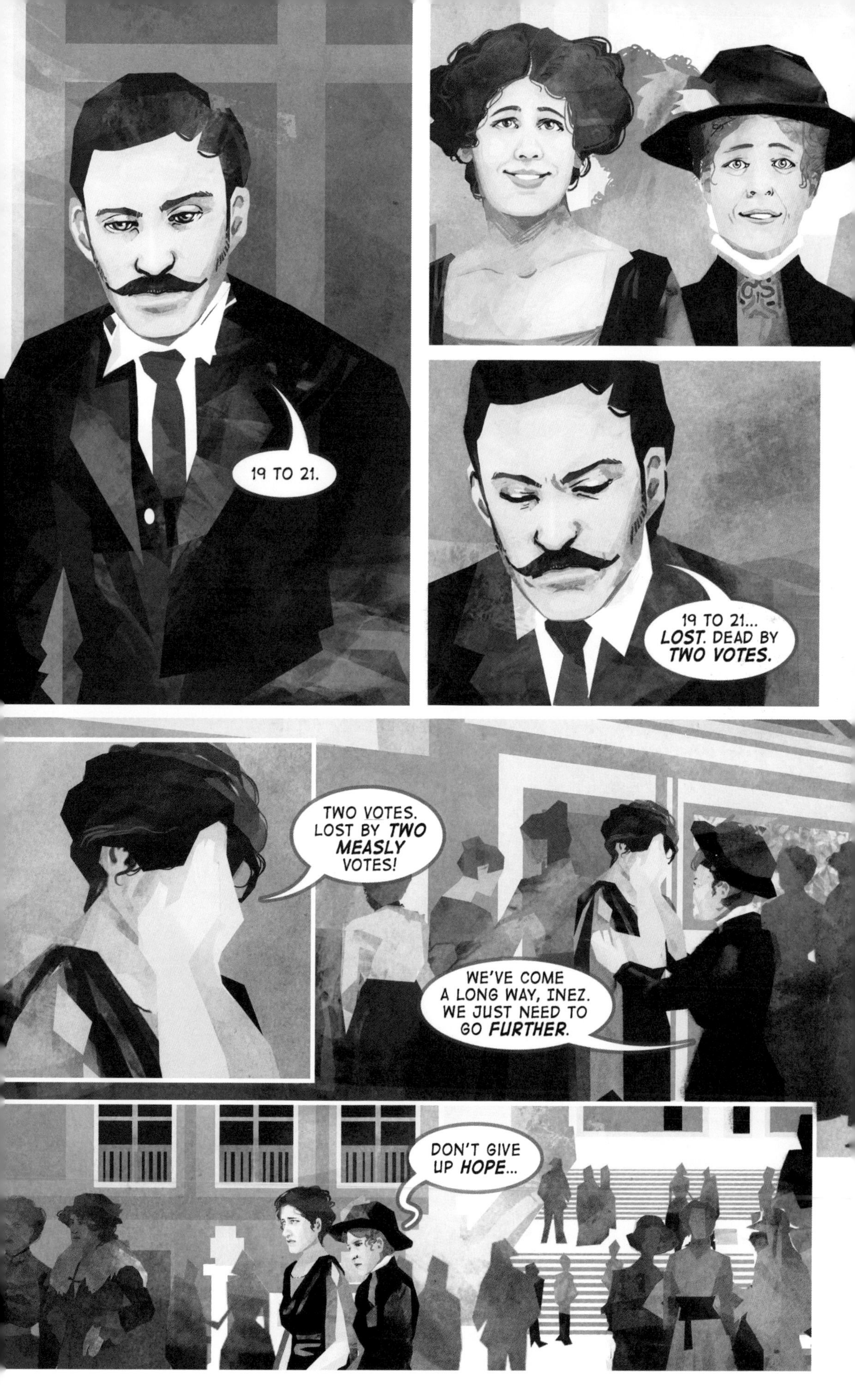
19 TO 21.
19 TO 21... LOST. DEAD BY TWO VOTES.
TWO VOTES. LOST BY TWO MEASLY VOTES!
WE'VE COME A LONG WAY, INEZ. WE JUST NEED TO GO FURTHER.
DON'T GIVE UP HOPE...

"I AM PREPARED TO SACRIFICE EVERY
SO-CALLED PRIVILEGE I POSSESS IN
ORDER TO HAVE A FEW RIGHTS."

INEZ MILHOLLAND
1886–1916

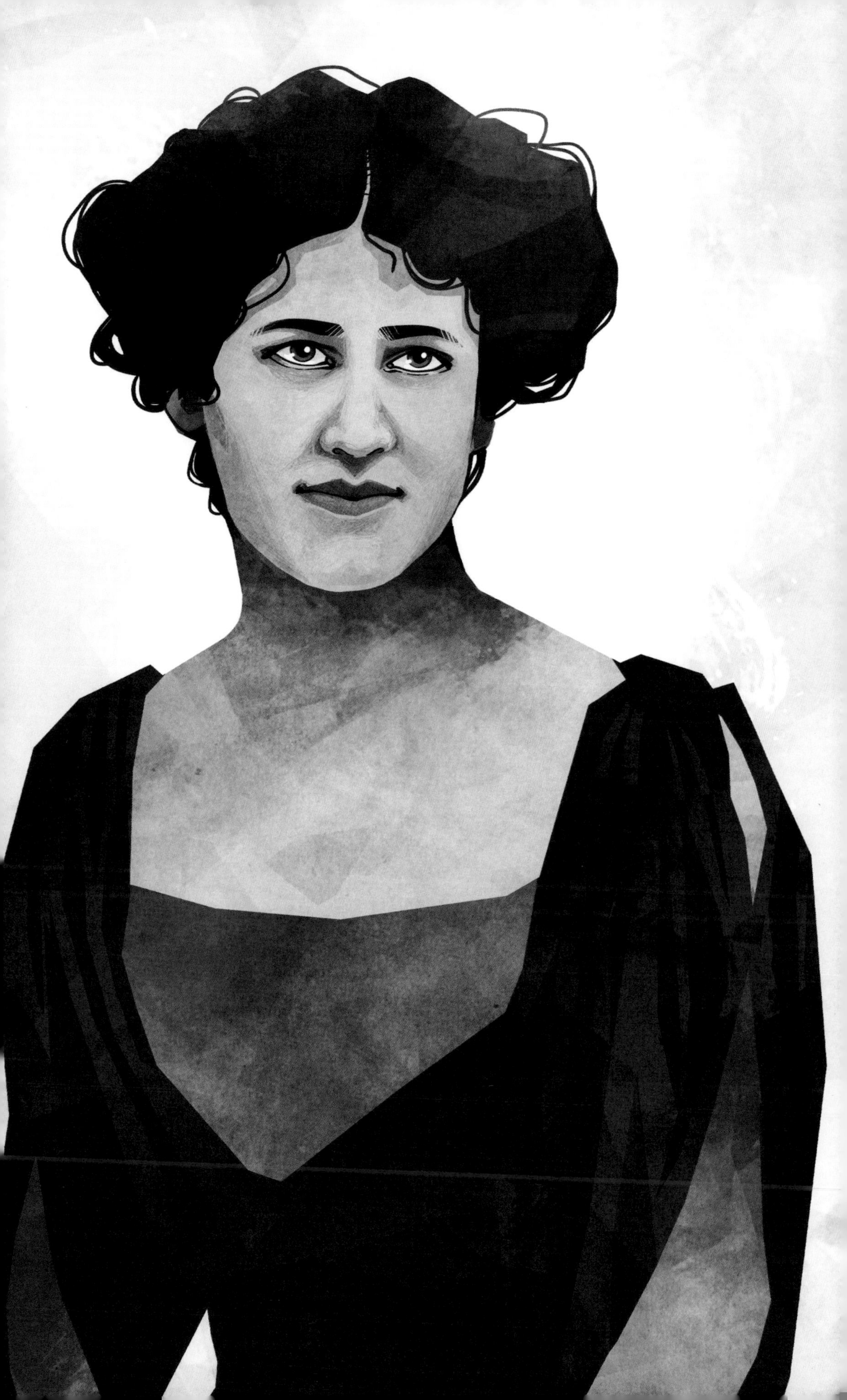

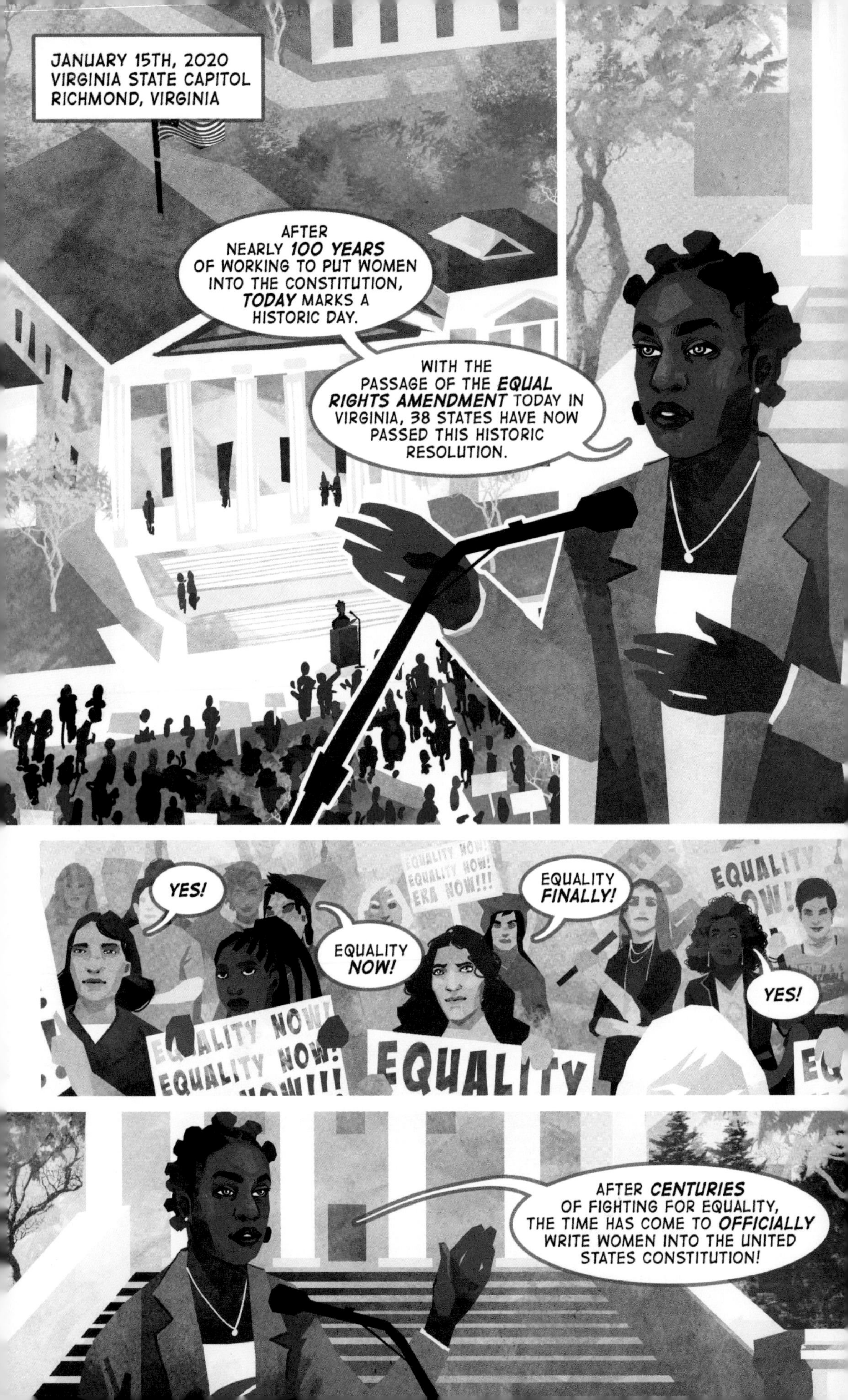
JANUARY 15TH, 2020
VIRGINIA STATE CAPITOL
RICHMOND, VIRGINIA
AFTER NEARLY 100 YEARS OF WORKING TO PUT WOMEN INTO THE CONSTITUTION, TODAY MARKS A HISTORIC DAY.
WITH THE PASSAGE OF THE EQUAL RIGHTS AMENDMENT TODAY IN VIRGINIA, 38 STATES HAVE NOW PASSED THIS HISTORIC RESOLUTION.
YES!
EQUALITY NOW!
EQUALITY FINALLY!
YES!
EQUALITY
AFTER CENTURIES OF FIGHTING FOR EQUALITY, THE TIME HAS COME TO OFFICIALLY WRITE WOMEN INTO THE UNITED STATES CONSTITUTION!

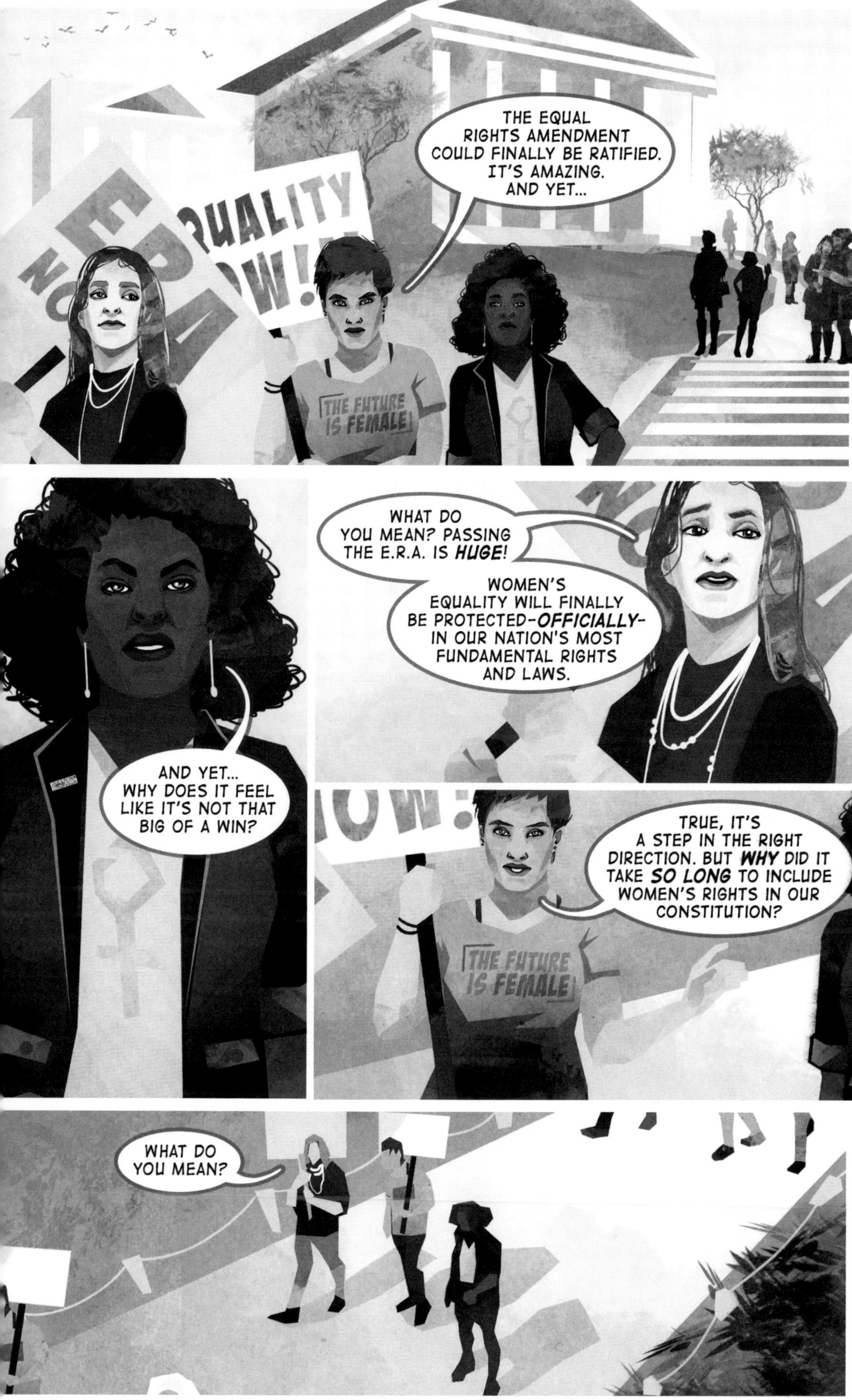
THE EQUAL RIGHTS AMENDMENT COULD FINALLY BE RATIFIED. IT'S AMAZING. AND YET...
EQUALITY NOW!!
ERA NOW
THE FUTURE IS FEMALE
WHAT DO YOU MEAN? PASSING THE E.R.A. IS HUGE!
WOMEN'S EQUALITY WILL FINALLY BE PROTECTED-OFFICIALLY- IN OUR NATION'S MOST FUNDAMENTAL RIGHTS AND LAWS.
AND YET... WHY DOES IT FEEL LIKE IT'S NOT THAT BIG OF A WIN?
TRUE, IT'S A STEP IN THE RIGHT DIRECTION. BUT WHY DID IT TAKE SO LONG TO INCLUDE WOMEN'S RIGHTS IN OUR CONSTITUTION?
WHAT DO YOU MEAN?

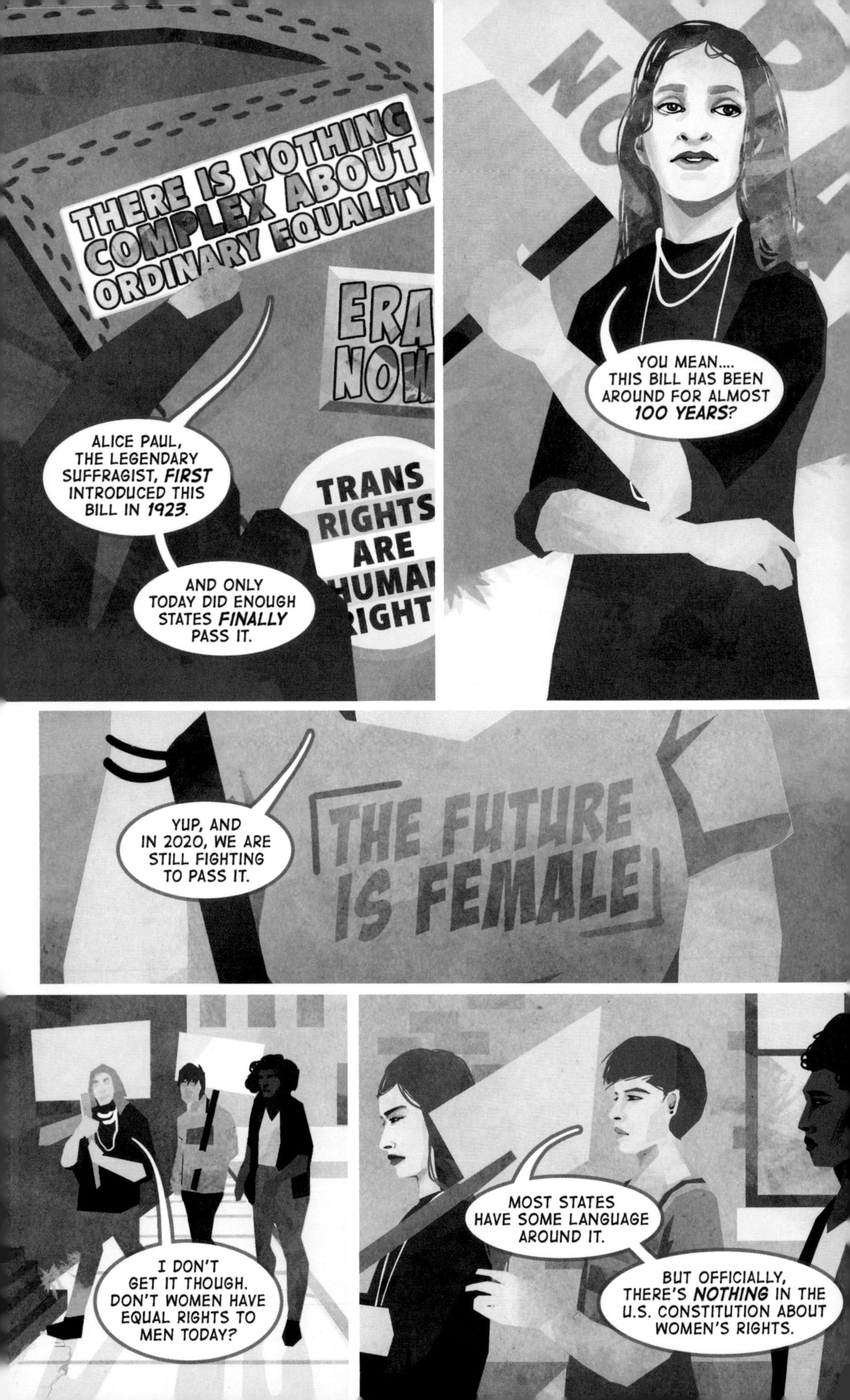
THERE IS NOTHING COMPLEX ABOUT ORDINARY EQUALITY
ERA NOW
TRANS RIGHTS ARE HUMAN RIGHTS
ALICE PAUL, THE LEGENDARY SUFFRAGIST, *FIRST* INTRODUCED THIS BILL IN *1923*.
AND ONLY TODAY DID ENOUGH STATES *FINALLY* PASS IT.
YOU MEAN.... THIS BILL HAS BEEN AROUND FOR ALMOST *100 YEARS*?
THE FUTURE IS FEMALE
YUP, AND IN 2020, WE ARE STILL FIGHTING TO PASS IT.
I DON'T GET IT THOUGH. DON'T WOMEN HAVE EQUAL RIGHTS TO MEN TODAY?
MOST STATES HAVE SOME LANGUAGE AROUND IT.
BUT OFFICIALLY, THERE'S *NOTHING* IN THE U.S. CONSTITUTION ABOUT WOMEN'S RIGHTS.

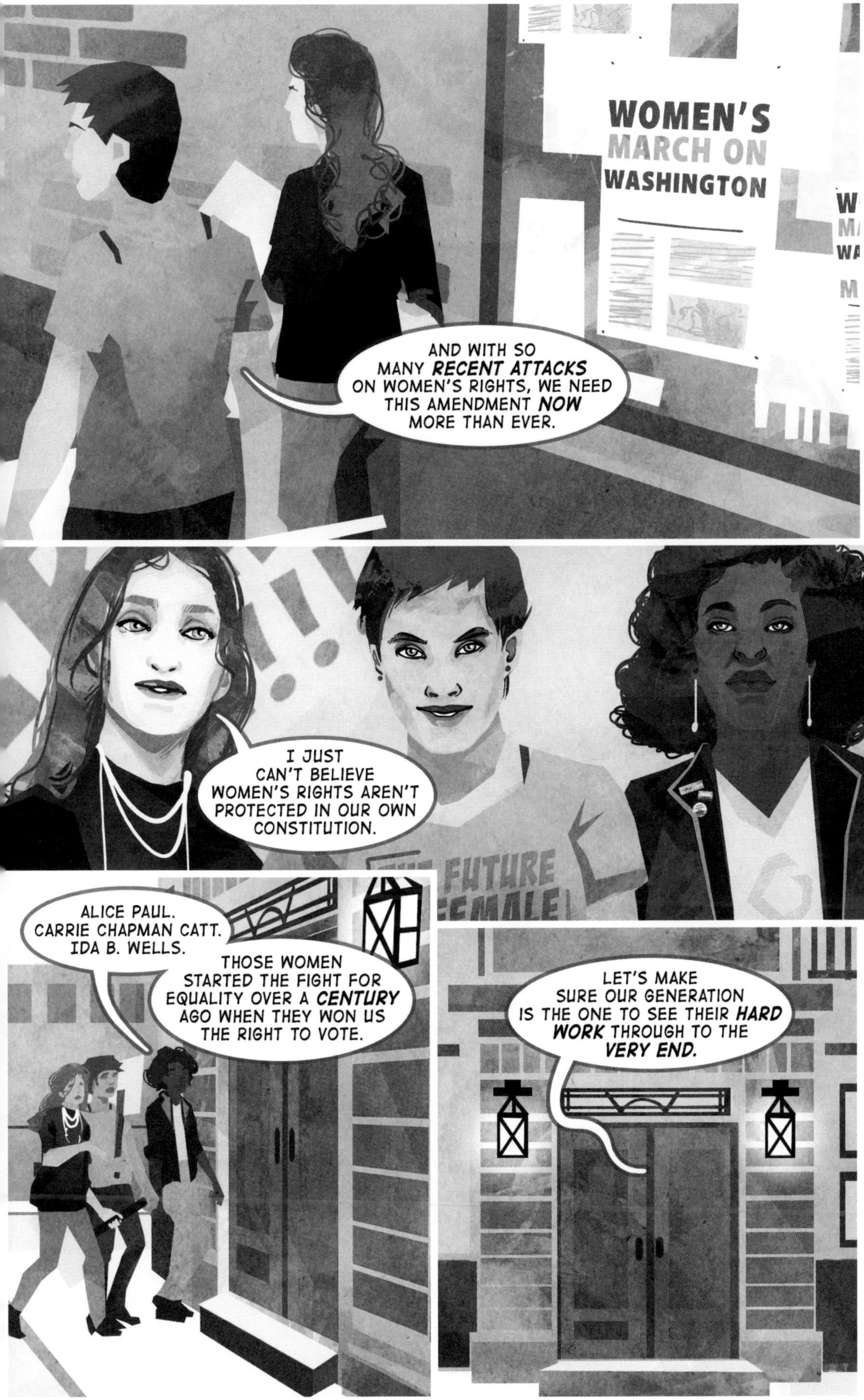
WOMEN'S MARCH ON WASHINGTON
AND WITH SO MANY RECENT ATTACKS ON WOMEN'S RIGHTS, WE NEED THIS AMENDMENT NOW MORE THAN EVER.
I JUST CAN'T BELIEVE WOMEN'S RIGHTS AREN'T PROTECTED IN OUR OWN CONSTITUTION.
ALICE PAUL. CARRIE CHAPMAN CATT. IDA B. WELLS.
THOSE WOMEN STARTED THE FIGHT FOR EQUALITY OVER A CENTURY AGO WHEN THEY WON US THE RIGHT TO VOTE.
LET'S MAKE SURE OUR GENERATION IS THE ONE TO SEE THEIR HARD WORK THROUGH TO THE VERY END.

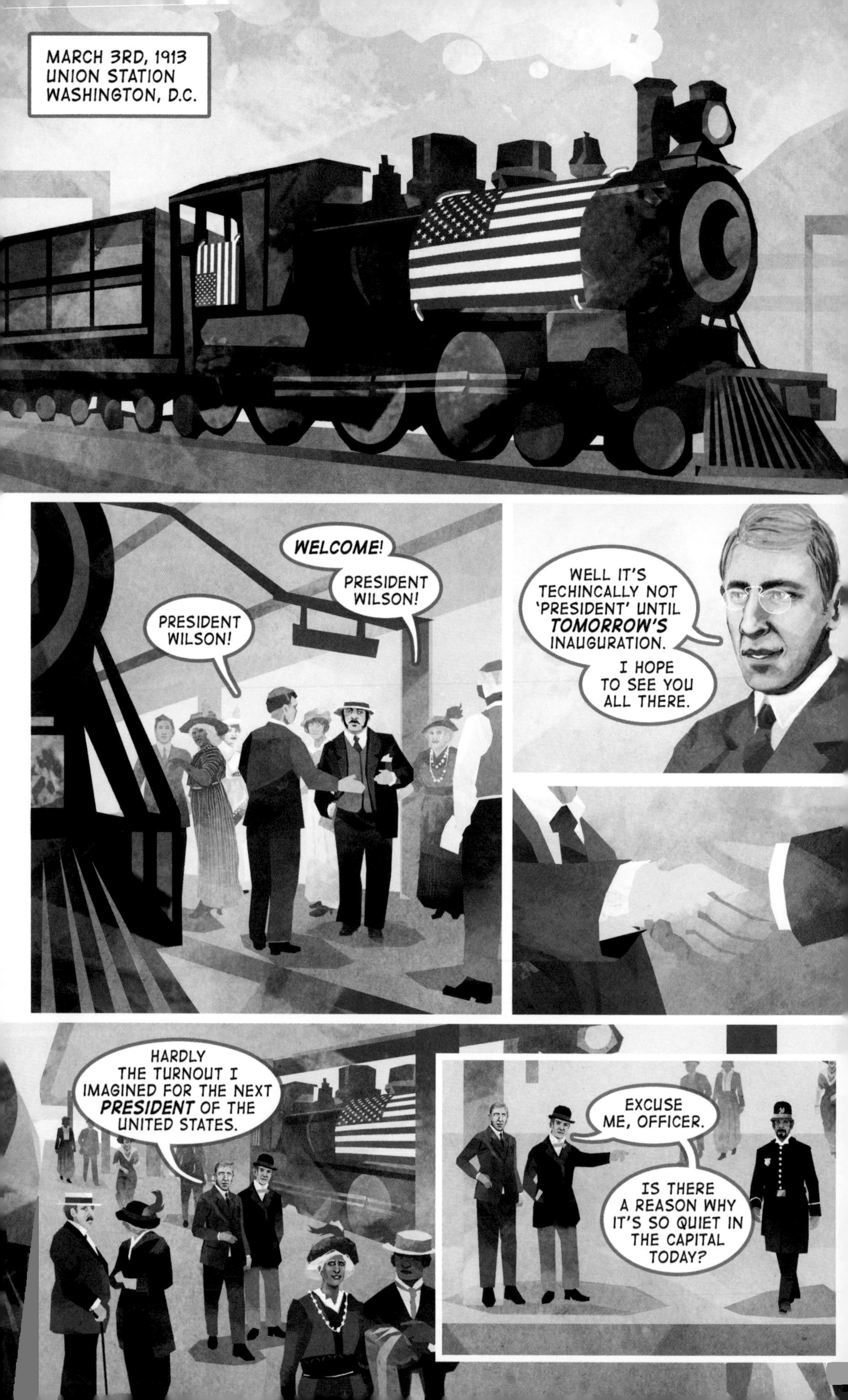
MARCH 3RD, 1913
UNION STATION
WASHINGTON, D.C.
WELCOME!
PRESIDENT WILSON!
PRESIDENT WILSON!
WELL IT'S TECHINCALLY NOT 'PRESIDENT' UNTIL TOMORROW'S INAUGURATION.
I HOPE TO SEE YOU ALL THERE.
HARDLY THE TURNOUT I IMAGINED FOR THE NEXT PRESIDENT OF THE UNITED STATES.
EXCUSE ME, OFFICER.
IS THERE A REASON WHY IT'S SO QUIET IN THE CAPITAL TODAY?

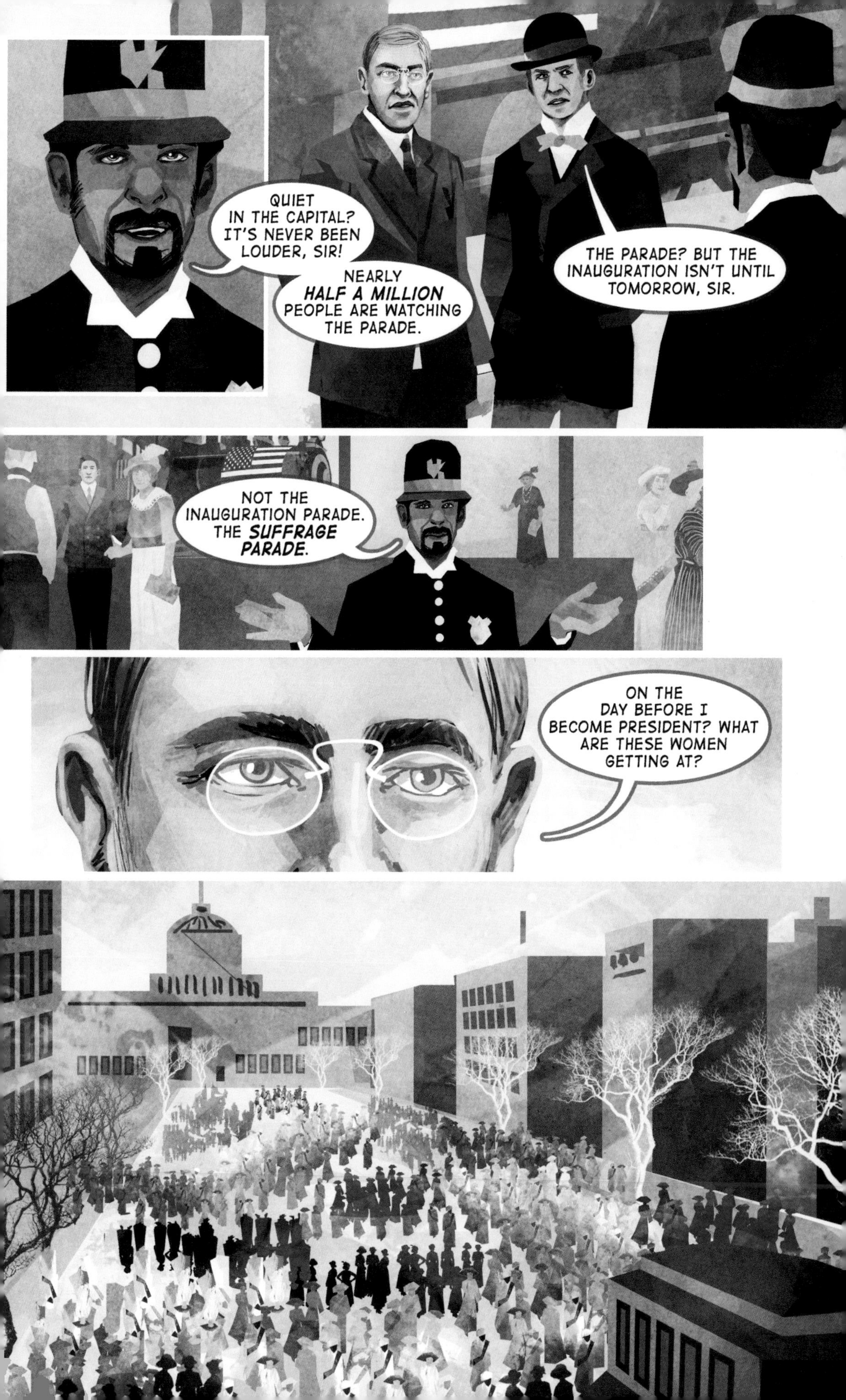
QUIET IN THE CAPITAL? IT'S NEVER BEEN LOUDER, SIR!
NEARLY *HALF A MILLION* PEOPLE ARE WATCHING THE PARADE.
THE PARADE? BUT THE INAUGURATION ISN'T UNTIL TOMORROW, SIR.
NOT THE INAUGURATION PARADE. THE *SUFFRAGE PARADE*.
ON THE DAY BEFORE I BECOME PRESIDENT? WHAT ARE THESE WOMEN GETTING AT?

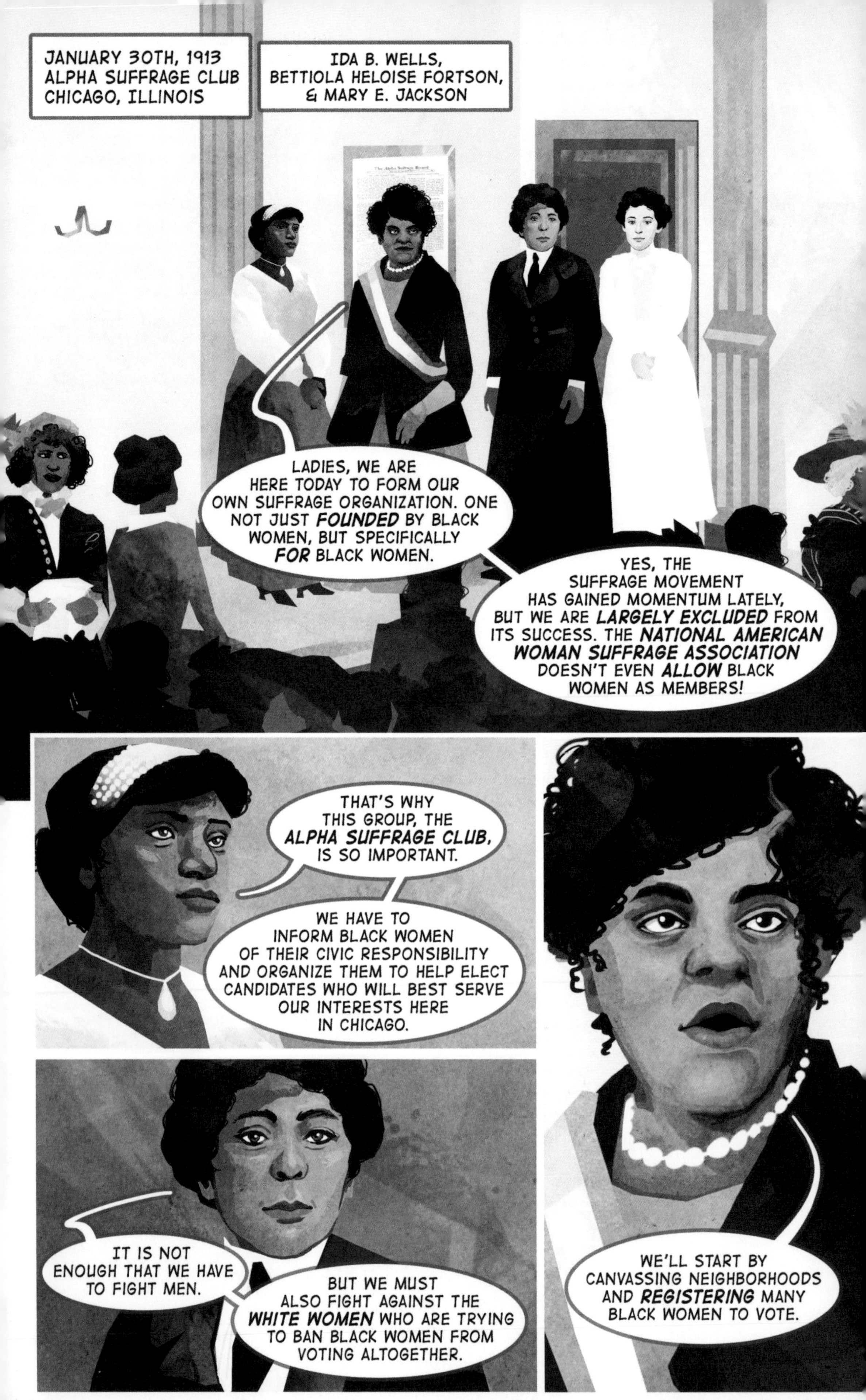

JANUARY 30TH, 1913
ALPHA SUFFRAGE CLUB
CHICAGO, ILLINOIS
IDA B. WELLS,
BETTIOLA HELOISE FORTSON,
& MARY E. JACKSON
LADIES, WE ARE HERE TODAY TO FORM OUR OWN SUFFRAGE ORGANIZATION. ONE NOT JUST FOUNDED BY BLACK WOMEN, BUT SPECIFICALLY FOR BLACK WOMEN.
YES, THE SUFFRAGE MOVEMENT HAS GAINED MOMENTUM LATELY, BUT WE ARE LARGELY EXCLUDED FROM ITS SUCCESS. THE NATIONAL AMERICAN WOMAN SUFFRAGE ASSOCIATION DOESN'T EVEN ALLOW BLACK WOMEN AS MEMBERS!
THAT'S WHY THIS GROUP, THE ALPHA SUFFRAGE CLUB, IS SO IMPORTANT.
WE HAVE TO INFORM BLACK WOMEN OF THEIR CIVIC RESPONSIBILITY AND ORGANIZE THEM TO HELP ELECT CANDIDATES WHO WILL BEST SERVE OUR INTERESTS HERE IN CHICAGO.
IT IS NOT ENOUGH THAT WE HAVE TO FIGHT MEN.
BUT WE MUST ALSO FIGHT AGAINST THE WHITE WOMEN WHO ARE TRYING TO BAN BLACK WOMEN FROM VOTING ALTOGETHER.
WE'LL START BY CANVASSING NEIGHBORHOODS AND REGISTERING MANY BLACK WOMEN TO VOTE.

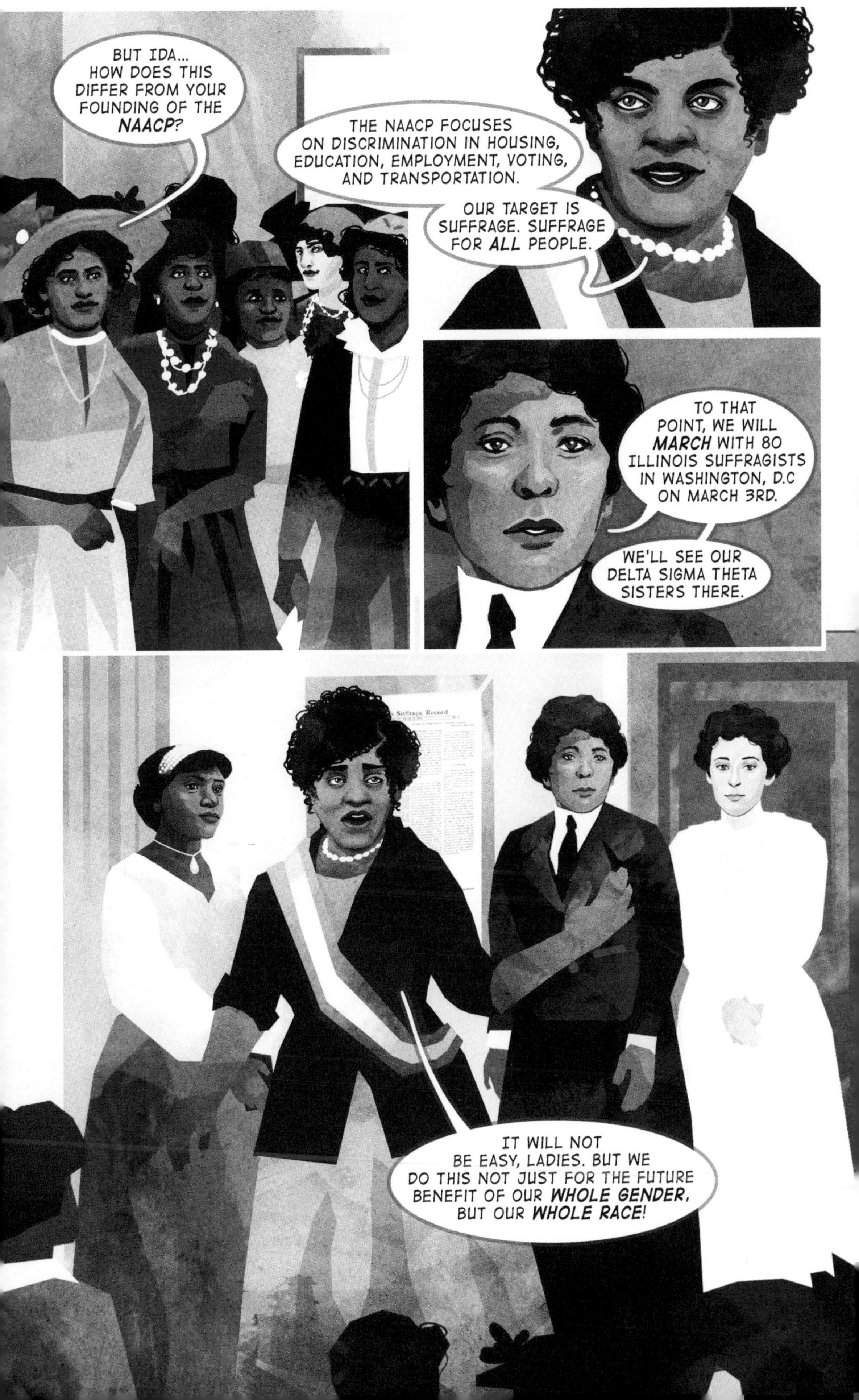
BUT IDA... HOW DOES THIS DIFFER FROM YOUR FOUNDING OF THE NAACP?
THE NAACP FOCUSES ON DISCRIMINATION IN HOUSING, EDUCATION, EMPLOYMENT, VOTING, AND TRANSPORTATION.
OUR TARGET IS SUFFRAGE. SUFFRAGE FOR ALL PEOPLE.
TO THAT POINT, WE WILL MARCH WITH 80 ILLINOIS SUFFRAGISTS IN WASHINGTON, D.C ON MARCH 3RD.
WE'LL SEE OUR DELTA SIGMA THETA SISTERS THERE.
IT WILL NOT BE EASY, LADIES. BUT WE DO THIS NOT JUST FOR THE FUTURE BENEFIT OF OUR WHOLE GENDER, BUT OUR WHOLE RACE!

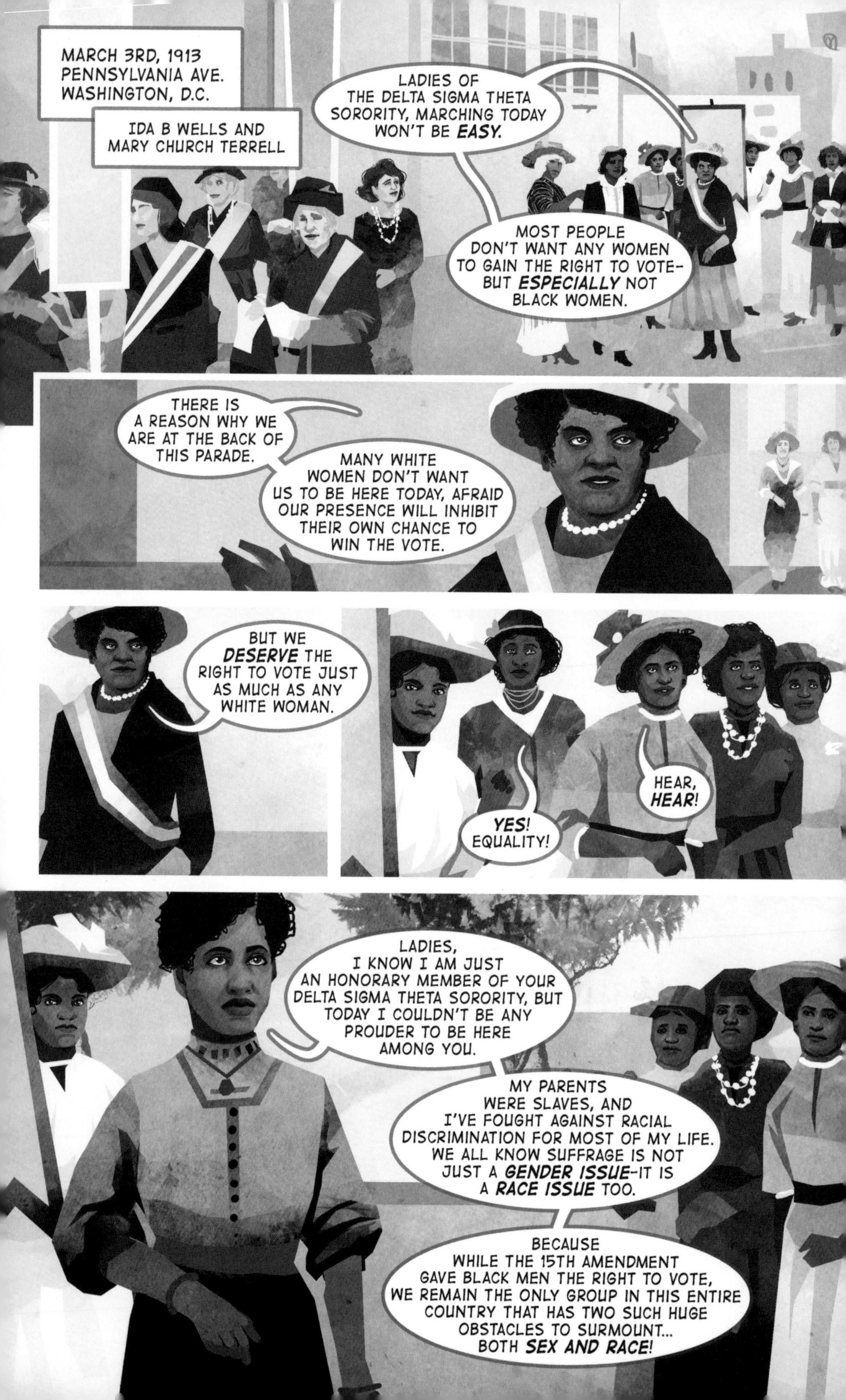
MARCH 3RD, 1913 PENNSYLVANIA AVE. WASHINGTON, D.C.
IDA B WELLS AND MARY CHURCH TERRELL
LADIES OF THE DELTA SIGMA THETA SORORITY, MARCHING TODAY WON'T BE EASY.
MOST PEOPLE DON'T WANT ANY WOMEN TO GAIN THE RIGHT TO VOTE- BUT ESPECIALLY NOT BLACK WOMEN.
THERE IS A REASON WHY WE ARE AT THE BACK OF THIS PARADE.
MANY WHITE WOMEN DON'T WANT US TO BE HERE TODAY, AFRAID OUR PRESENCE WILL INHIBIT THEIR OWN CHANCE TO WIN THE VOTE.
BUT WE DESERVE THE RIGHT TO VOTE JUST AS MUCH AS ANY WHITE WOMAN.
HEAR, HEAR!
YES! EQUALITY!
LADIES, I KNOW I AM JUST AN HONORARY MEMBER OF YOUR DELTA SIGMA THETA SORORITY, BUT TODAY I COULDN'T BE ANY PROUDER TO BE HERE AMONG YOU.
MY PARENTS WERE SLAVES, AND I'VE FOUGHT AGAINST RACIAL DISCRIMINATION FOR MOST OF MY LIFE. WE ALL KNOW SUFFRAGE IS NOT JUST A GENDER ISSUE-IT IS A RACE ISSUE TOO.
BECAUSE WHILE THE 15TH AMENDMENT GAVE BLACK MEN THE RIGHT TO VOTE, WE REMAIN THE ONLY GROUP IN THIS ENTIRE COUNTRY THAT HAS TWO SUCH HUGE OBSTACLES TO SURMOUNT... BOTH SEX AND RACE!

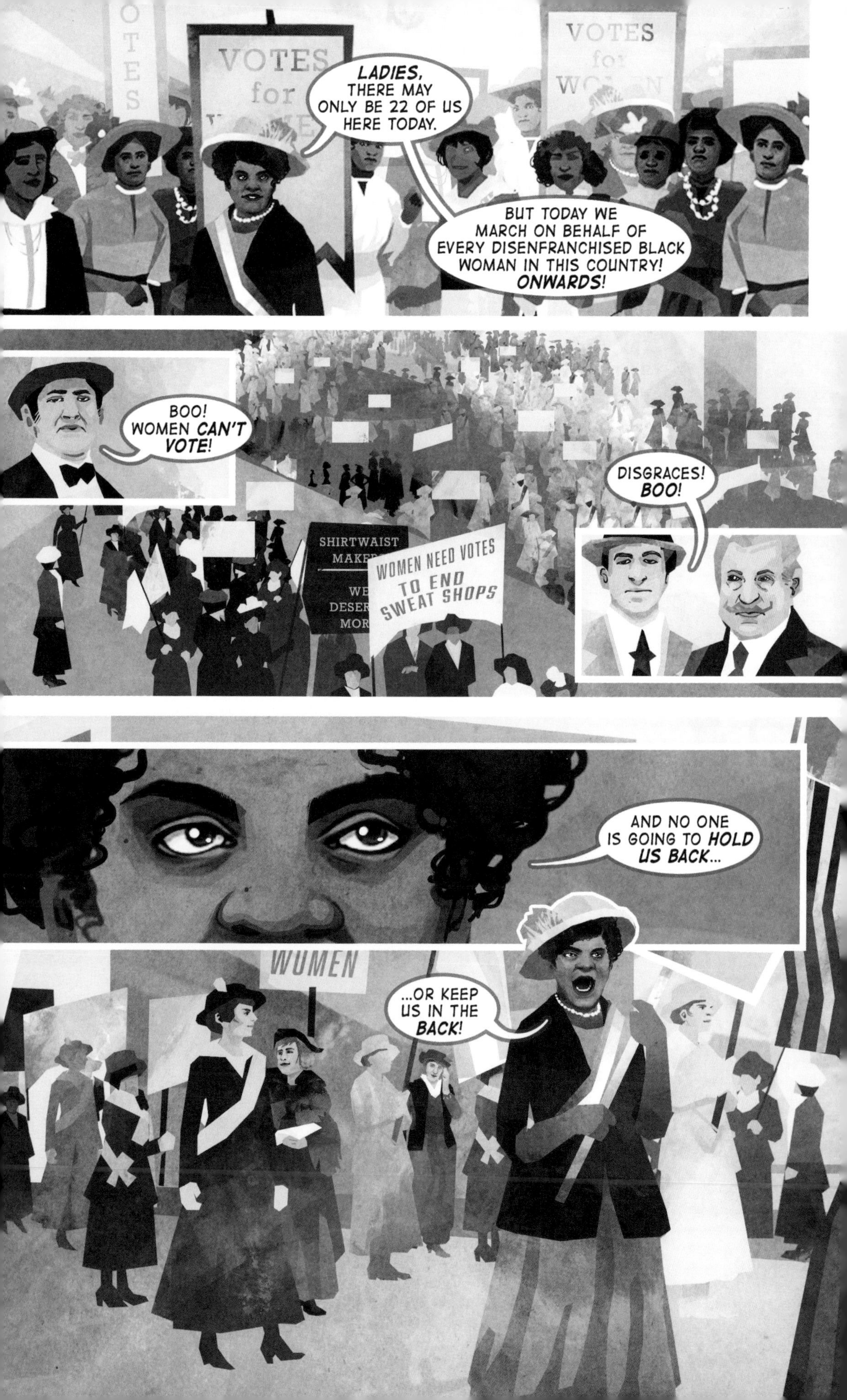
VOTES
VOTES for
VOTES for
LADIES, THERE MAY ONLY BE 22 OF US HERE TODAY.
BUT TODAY WE MARCH ON BEHALF OF EVERY DISENFRANCHISED BLACK WOMAN IN THIS COUNTRY! ONWARDS!
BOO! WOMEN CAN'T VOTE!
DISGRACES! BOO!
SHIRTWAIST MAKER
WOMEN NEED VOTES TO END SWEAT SHOPS
AND NO ONE IS GOING TO HOLD US BACK...
WOMEN
...OR KEEP US IN THE BACK!

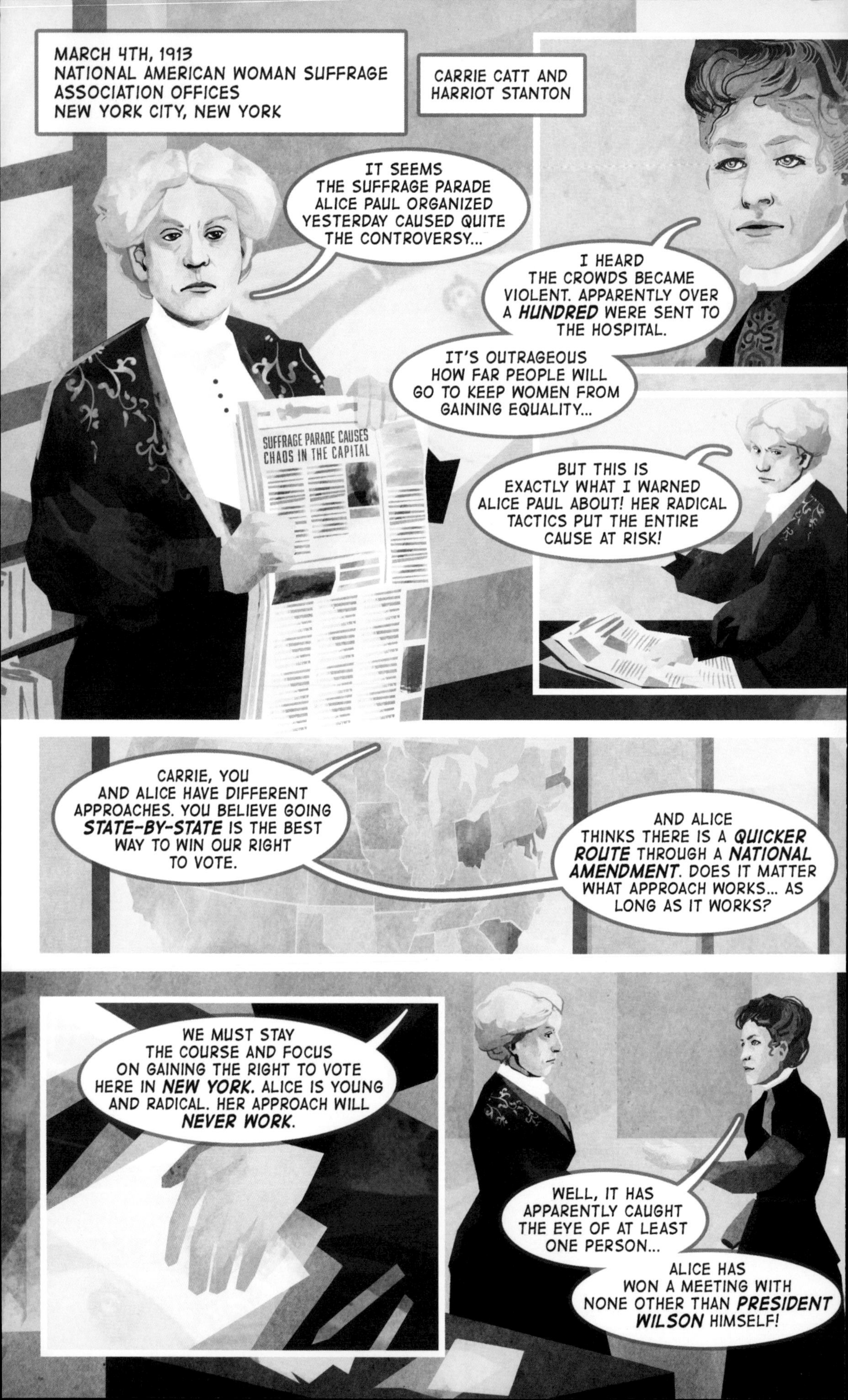
MARCH 4TH, 1913
NATIONAL AMERICAN WOMAN SUFFRAGE ASSOCIATION OFFICES
NEW YORK CITY, NEW YORK
CARRIE CATT AND HARRIOT STANTON
IT SEEMS THE SUFFRAGE PARADE ALICE PAUL ORGANIZED YESTERDAY CAUSED QUITE THE CONTROVERSY...
SUFFRAGE PARADE CAUSES CHAOS IN THE CAPITAL
I HEARD THE CROWDS BECAME VIOLENT. APPARENTLY OVER A *HUNDRED* WERE SENT TO THE HOSPITAL.
IT'S OUTRAGEOUS HOW FAR PEOPLE WILL GO TO KEEP WOMEN FROM GAINING EQUALITY...
BUT THIS IS EXACTLY WHAT I WARNED ALICE PAUL ABOUT! HER RADICAL TACTICS PUT THE ENTIRE CAUSE AT RISK!
CARRIE, YOU AND ALICE HAVE DIFFERENT APPROACHES. YOU BELIEVE GOING *STATE-BY-STATE* IS THE BEST WAY TO WIN OUR RIGHT TO VOTE.
AND ALICE THINKS THERE IS A *QUICKER ROUTE* THROUGH A *NATIONAL AMENDMENT*. DOES IT MATTER WHAT APPROACH WORKS... AS LONG AS IT WORKS?
WE MUST STAY THE COURSE AND FOCUS ON GAINING THE RIGHT TO VOTE HERE IN *NEW YORK.* ALICE IS YOUNG AND RADICAL. HER APPROACH WILL *NEVER WORK*.
WELL, IT HAS APPARENTLY CAUGHT THE EYE OF AT LEAST ONE PERSON...
ALICE HAS WON A MEETING WITH NONE OTHER THAN *PRESIDENT WILSON* HIMSELF!

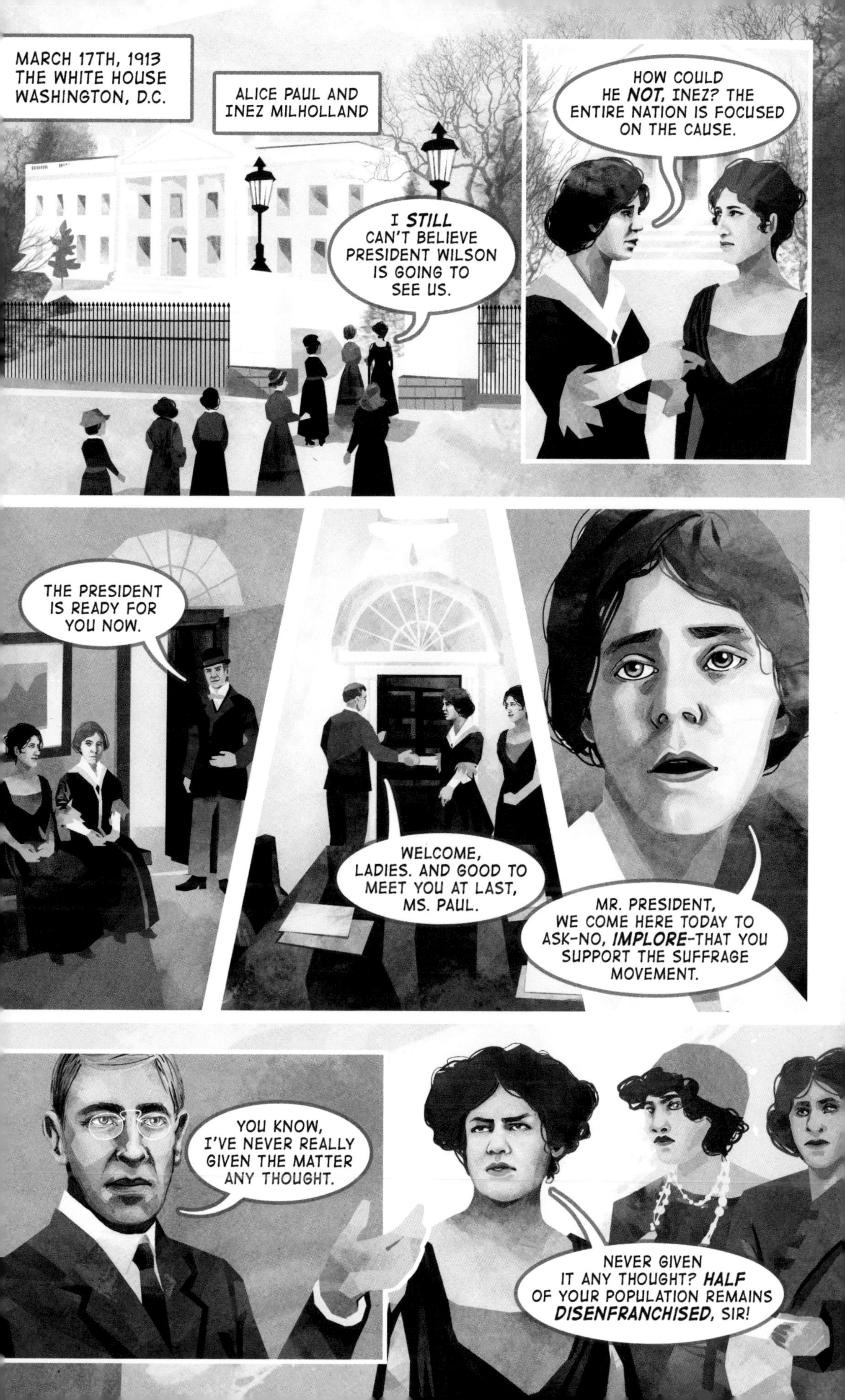
MARCH 17TH, 1913 THE WHITE HOUSE WASHINGTON, D.C.
ALICE PAUL AND INEZ MILHOLLAND
I STILL CAN'T BELIEVE PRESIDENT WILSON IS GOING TO SEE US.
HOW COULD HE NOT, INEZ? THE ENTIRE NATION IS FOCUSED ON THE CAUSE.
THE PRESIDENT IS READY FOR YOU NOW.
WELCOME, LADIES. AND GOOD TO MEET YOU AT LAST, MS. PAUL.
MR. PRESIDENT, WE COME HERE TODAY TO ASK-NO, IMPLORE-THAT YOU SUPPORT THE SUFFRAGE MOVEMENT.
YOU KNOW, I'VE NEVER REALLY GIVEN THE MATTER ANY THOUGHT.
NEVER GIVEN IT ANY THOUGHT? HALF OF YOUR POPULATION REMAINS DISENFRANCHISED, SIR!

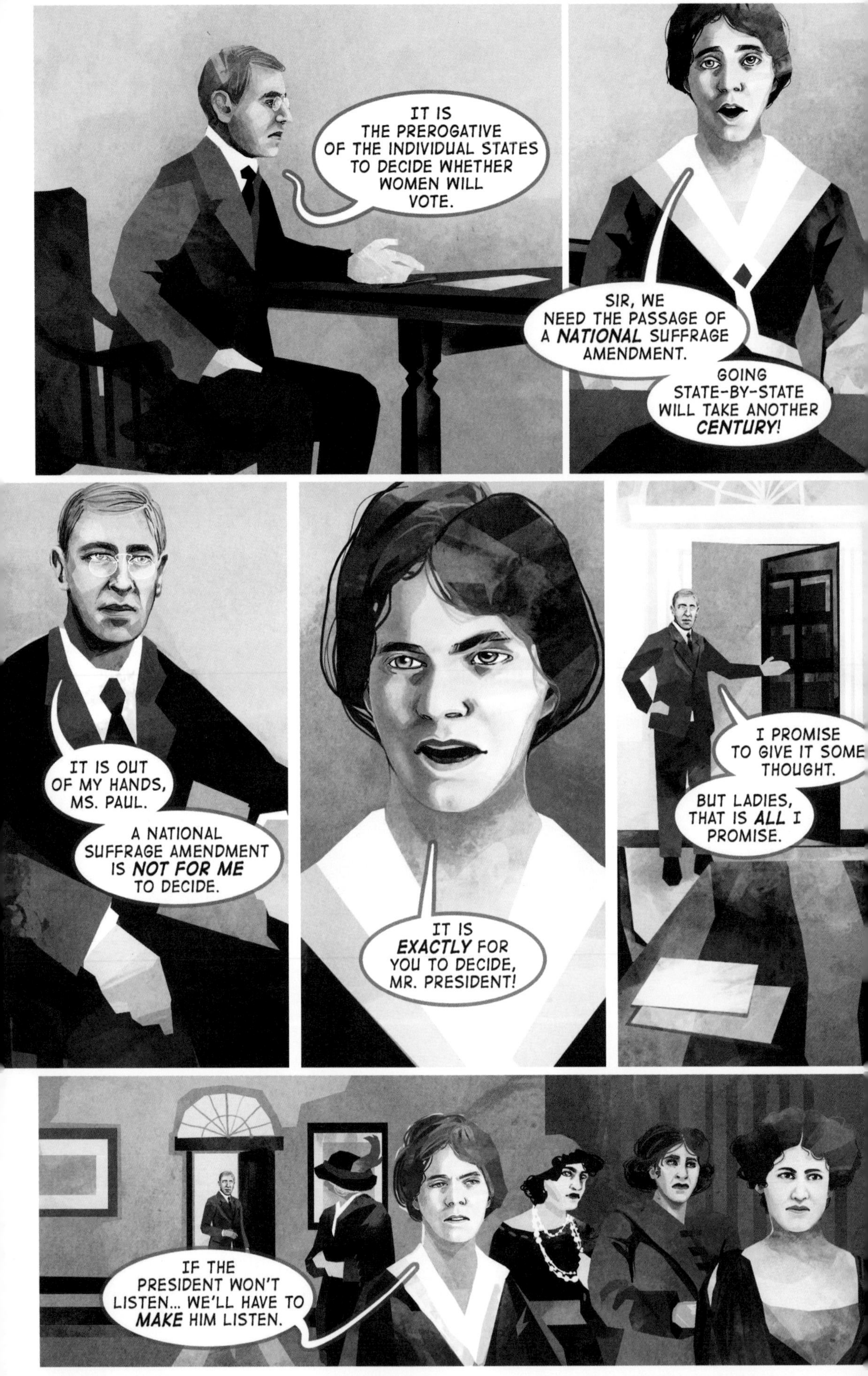
IT IS THE PREROGATIVE OF THE INDIVIDUAL STATES TO DECIDE WHETHER WOMEN WILL VOTE.
SIR, WE NEED THE PASSAGE OF A ***NATIONAL*** SUFFRAGE AMENDMENT.
GOING STATE-BY-STATE WILL TAKE ANOTHER ***CENTURY***!
IT IS OUT OF MY HANDS, MS. PAUL.
A NATIONAL SUFFRAGE AMENDMENT IS ***NOT FOR ME*** TO DECIDE.
IT IS ***EXACTLY*** FOR YOU TO DECIDE, MR. PRESIDENT!
I PROMISE TO GIVE IT SOME THOUGHT.
BUT LADIES, THAT IS ***ALL*** I PROMISE.
IF THE PRESIDENT WON'T LISTEN... WE'LL HAVE TO ***MAKE*** HIM LISTEN.

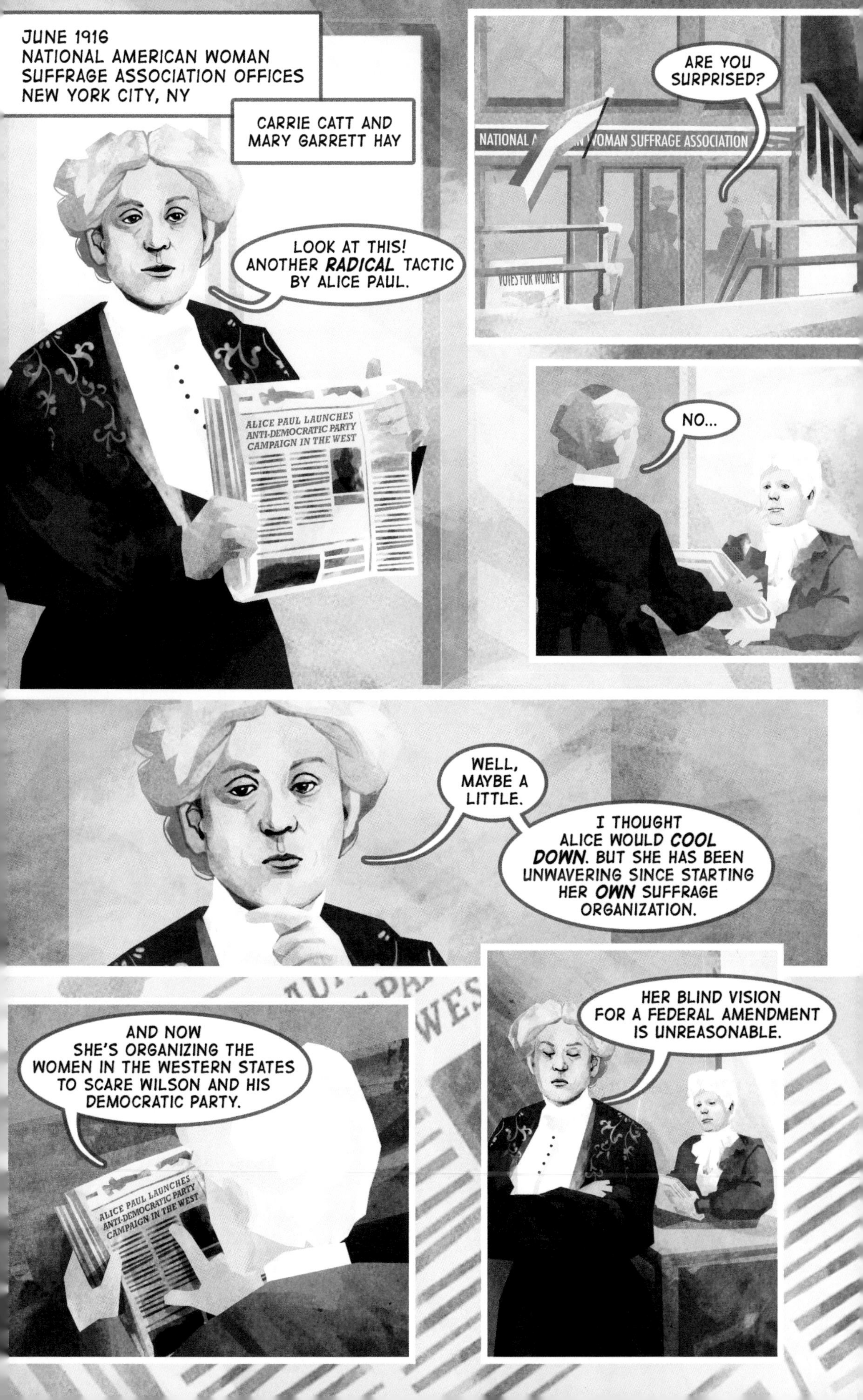
JUNE 1916
NATIONAL AMERICAN WOMAN SUFFRAGE ASSOCIATION OFFICES
NEW YORK CITY, NY
CARRIE CATT AND MARY GARRETT HAY
NATIONAL A... WOMAN SUFFRAGE ASSOCIATION
VOTES FOR WOMEN
ARE YOU SURPRISED?
LOOK AT THIS! ANOTHER *RADICAL* TACTIC BY ALICE PAUL.
ALICE PAUL LAUNCHES ANTI-DEMOCRATIC PARTY CAMPAIGN IN THE WEST
NO...
WELL, MAYBE A LITTLE.
I THOUGHT ALICE WOULD *COOL DOWN*. BUT SHE HAS BEEN UNWAVERING SINCE STARTING HER *OWN* SUFFRAGE ORGANIZATION.
AND NOW SHE'S ORGANIZING THE WOMEN IN THE WESTERN STATES TO SCARE WILSON AND HIS DEMOCRATIC PARTY.
ALICE PAUL LAUNCHES ANTI-DEMOCRATIC PARTY CAMPAIGN IN THE WEST
HER BLIND VISION FOR A FEDERAL AMENDMENT IS UNREASONABLE.

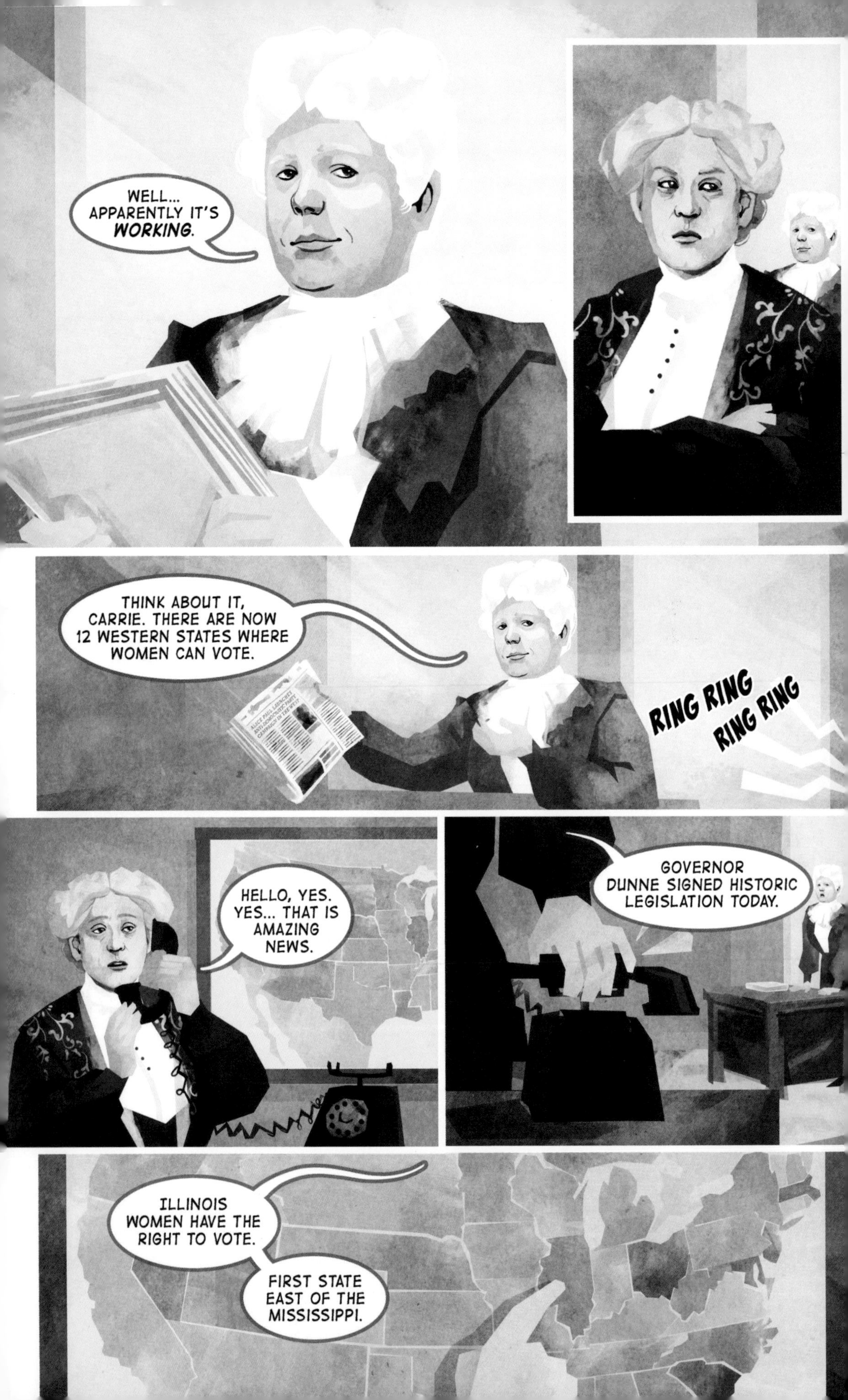
WELL... APPARENTLY IT'S *WORKING*.
THINK ABOUT IT, CARRIE. THERE ARE NOW 12 WESTERN STATES WHERE WOMEN CAN VOTE.
RING RING
RING RING
HELLO, YES. YES... THAT IS AMAZING NEWS.
GOVERNOR DUNNE SIGNED HISTORIC LEGISLATION TODAY.
ILLINOIS WOMEN HAVE THE RIGHT TO VOTE.
FIRST STATE EAST OF THE MISSISSIPPI.

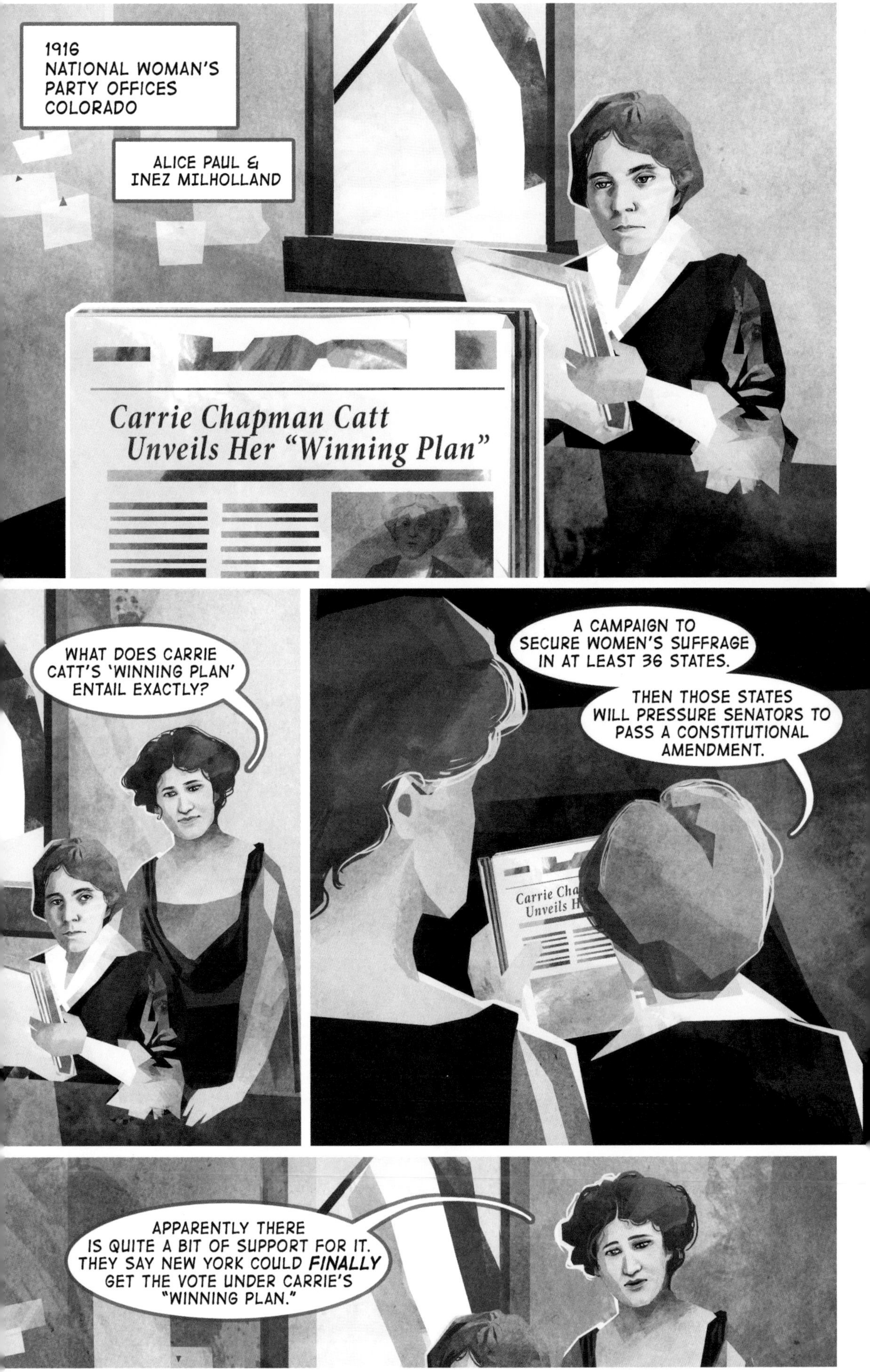
1916
NATIONAL WOMAN'S PARTY OFFICES
COLORADO
ALICE PAUL & INEZ MILHOLLAND
Carrie Chapman Catt Unveils Her "Winning Plan"
WHAT DOES CARRIE CATT'S 'WINNING PLAN' ENTAIL EXACTLY?
A CAMPAIGN TO SECURE WOMEN'S SUFFRAGE IN AT LEAST 36 STATES.
THEN THOSE STATES WILL PRESSURE SENATORS TO PASS A CONSTITUTIONAL AMENDMENT.
APPARENTLY THERE IS QUITE A BIT OF SUPPORT FOR IT. THEY SAY NEW YORK COULD *FINALLY* GET THE VOTE UNDER CARRIE'S "WINNING PLAN."

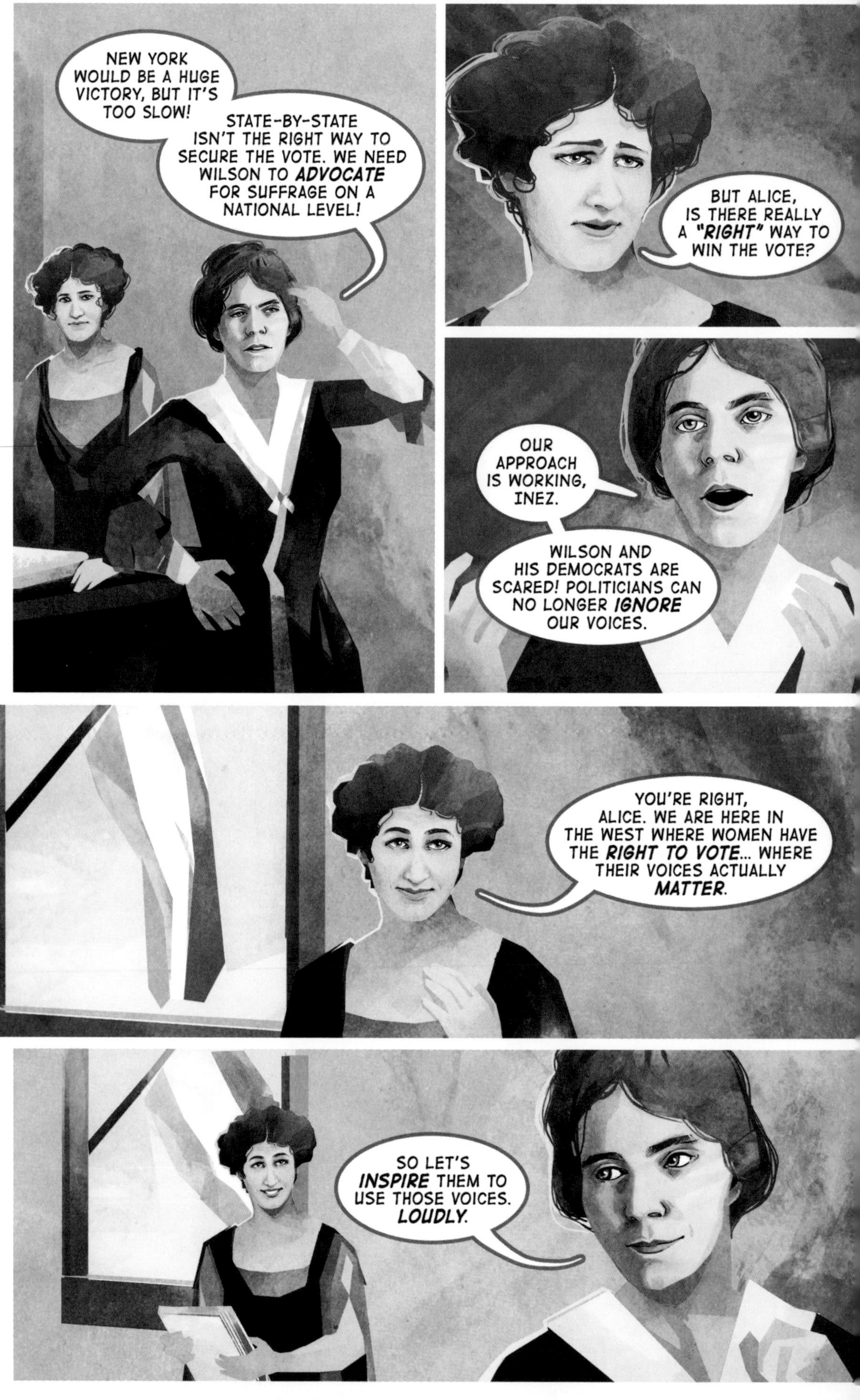
NEW YORK WOULD BE A HUGE VICTORY, BUT IT'S TOO SLOW!
STATE-BY-STATE ISN'T THE RIGHT WAY TO SECURE THE VOTE. WE NEED WILSON TO *ADVOCATE* FOR SUFFRAGE ON A NATIONAL LEVEL!
BUT ALICE, IS THERE REALLY A *"RIGHT"* WAY TO WIN THE VOTE?
OUR APPROACH IS WORKING, INEZ.
WILSON AND HIS DEMOCRATS ARE SCARED! POLITICIANS CAN NO LONGER *IGNORE* OUR VOICES.
YOU'RE RIGHT, ALICE. WE ARE HERE IN THE WEST WHERE WOMEN HAVE THE *RIGHT TO VOTE*... WHERE THEIR VOICES ACTUALLY *MATTER*.
SO LET'S *INSPIRE* THEM TO USE THOSE VOICES. *LOUDLY*.

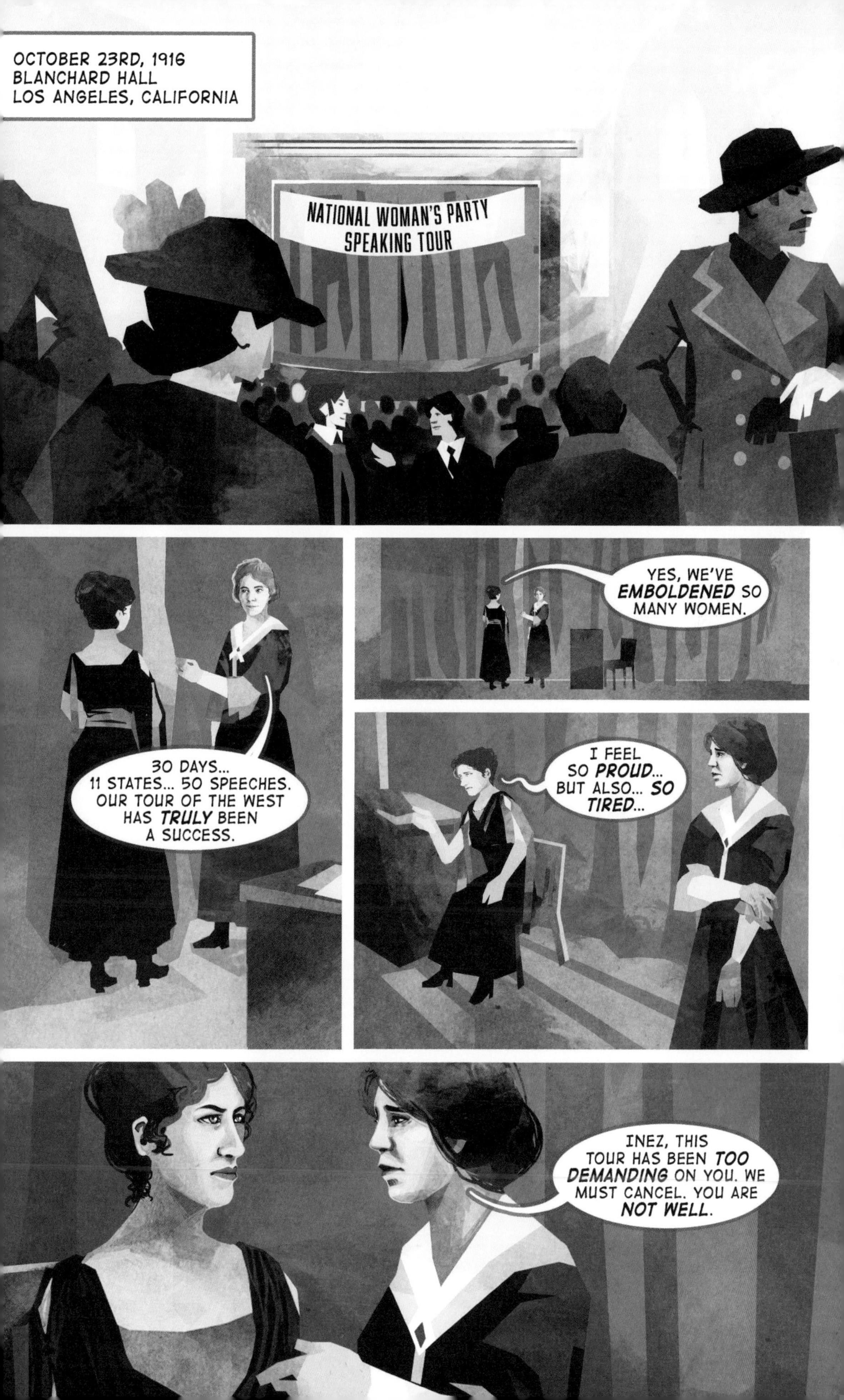
OCTOBER 23RD, 1916
BLANCHARD HALL
LOS ANGELES, CALIFORNIA
NATIONAL WOMAN'S PARTY SPEAKING TOUR
30 DAYS... 11 STATES... 50 SPEECHES. OUR TOUR OF THE WEST HAS TRULY BEEN A SUCCESS.
YES, WE'VE EMBOLDENED SO MANY WOMEN.
I FEEL SO PROUD... BUT ALSO... SO TIRED...
INEZ, THIS TOUR HAS BEEN TOO DEMANDING ON YOU. WE MUST CANCEL. YOU ARE NOT WELL.

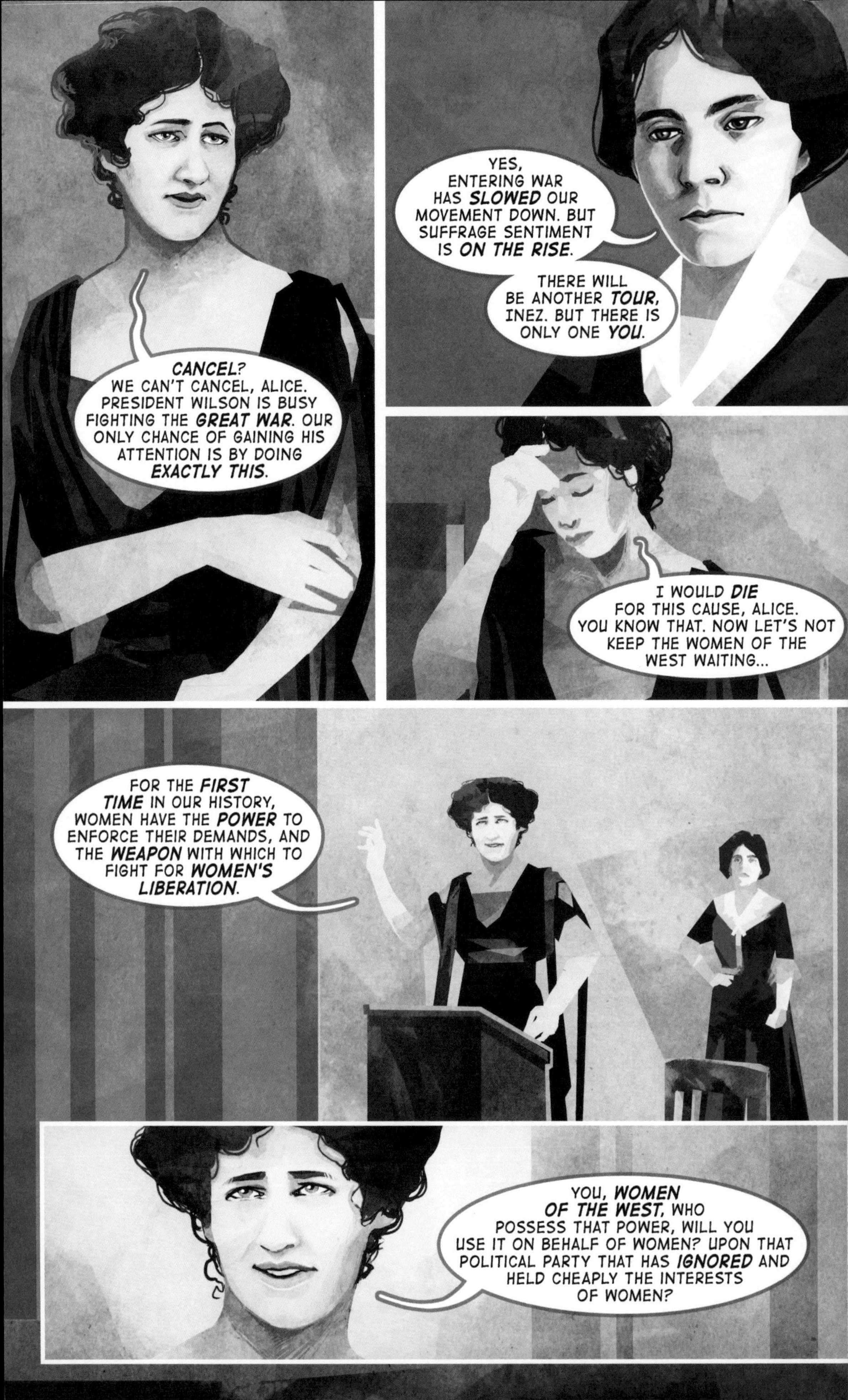
CANCEL? WE CAN'T CANCEL, ALICE. PRESIDENT WILSON IS BUSY FIGHTING THE GREAT WAR. OUR ONLY CHANCE OF GAINING HIS ATTENTION IS BY DOING EXACTLY THIS.
YES, ENTERING WAR HAS SLOWED OUR MOVEMENT DOWN. BUT SUFFRAGE SENTIMENT IS ON THE RISE.
THERE WILL BE ANOTHER TOUR, INEZ. BUT THERE IS ONLY ONE YOU.
I WOULD DIE FOR THIS CAUSE, ALICE. YOU KNOW THAT. NOW LET'S NOT KEEP THE WOMEN OF THE WEST WAITING...
FOR THE FIRST TIME IN OUR HISTORY, WOMEN HAVE THE POWER TO ENFORCE THEIR DEMANDS, AND THE WEAPON WITH WHICH TO FIGHT FOR WOMEN'S LIBERATION.
YOU, WOMEN OF THE WEST, WHO POSSESS THAT POWER, WILL YOU USE IT ON BEHALF OF WOMEN? UPON THAT POLITICAL PARTY THAT HAS IGNORED AND HELD CHEAPLY THE INTERESTS OF WOMEN?

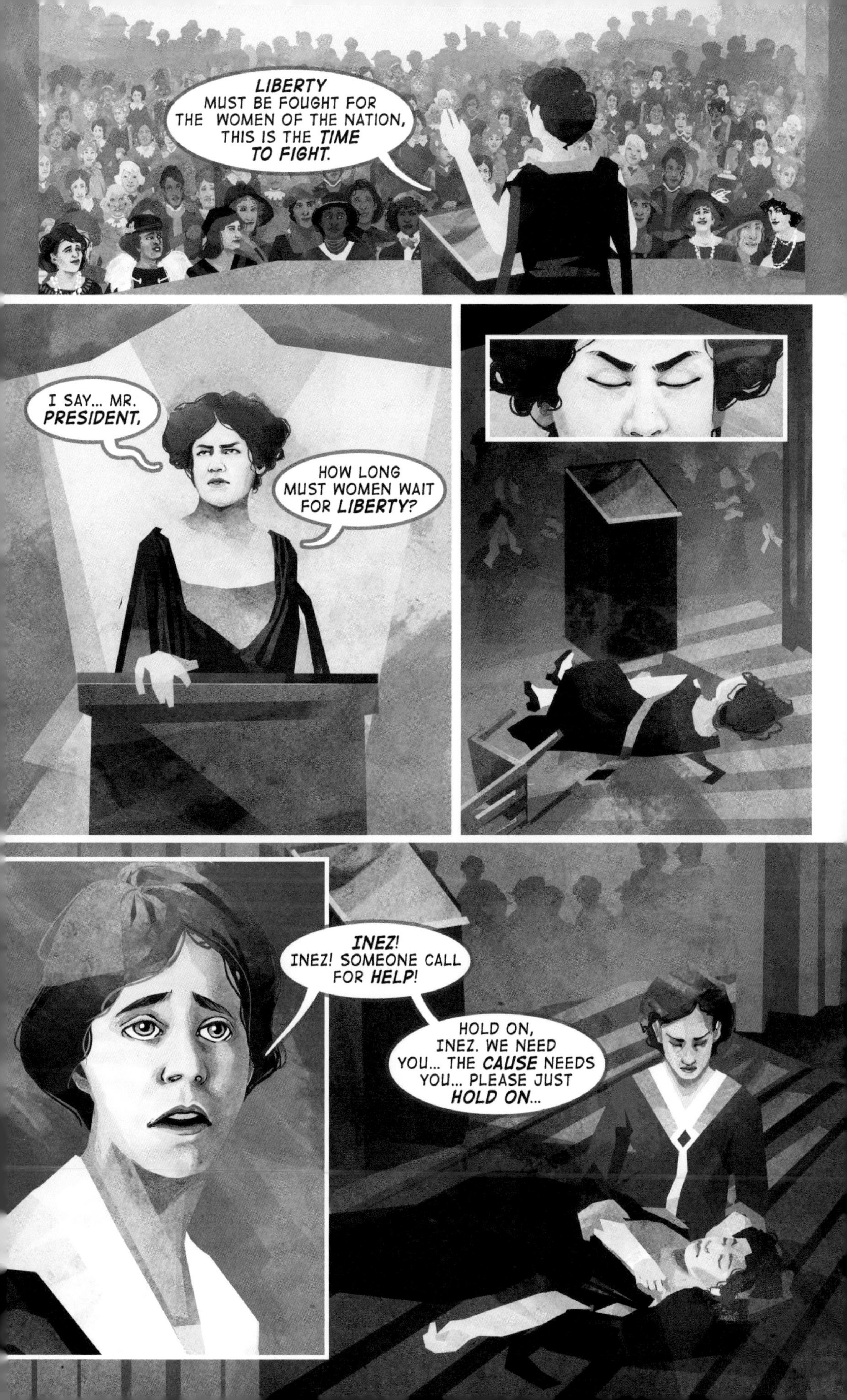
LIBERTY MUST BE FOUGHT FOR THE WOMEN OF THE NATION, THIS IS THE TIME TO FIGHT.
I SAY... MR. PRESIDENT,
HOW LONG MUST WOMEN WAIT FOR LIBERTY?
INEZ! INEZ! SOMEONE CALL FOR HELP!
HOLD ON, INEZ. WE NEED YOU... THE CAUSE NEEDS YOU... PLEASE JUST HOLD ON...

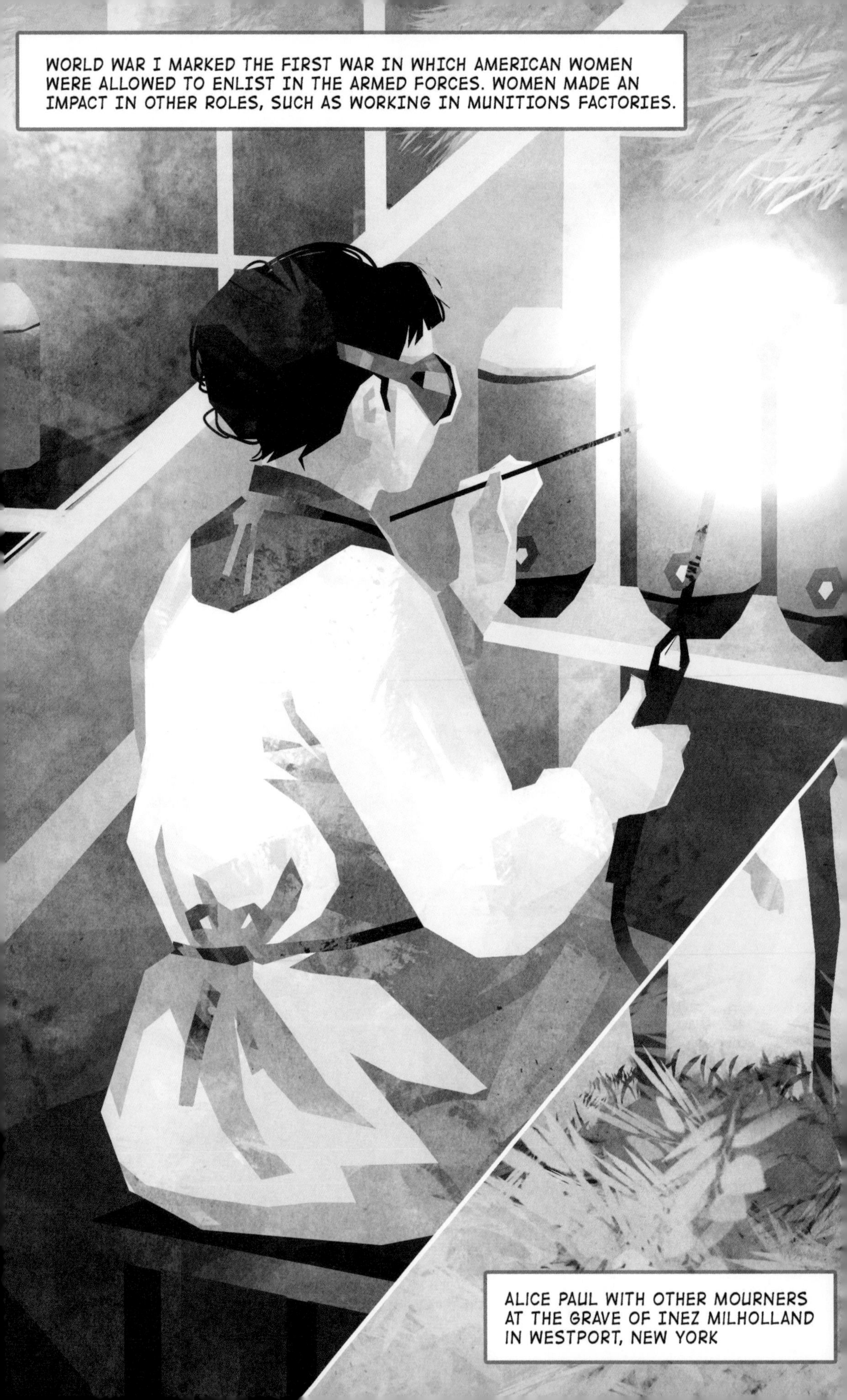
WORLD WAR I MARKED THE FIRST WAR IN WHICH AMERICAN WOMEN WERE ALLOWED TO ENLIST IN THE ARMED FORCES. WOMEN MADE AN IMPACT IN OTHER ROLES, SUCH AS WORKING IN MUNITIONS FACTORIES.
ALICE PAUL WITH OTHER MOURNERS AT THE GRAVE OF INEZ MILHOLLAND IN WESTPORT, NEW YORK

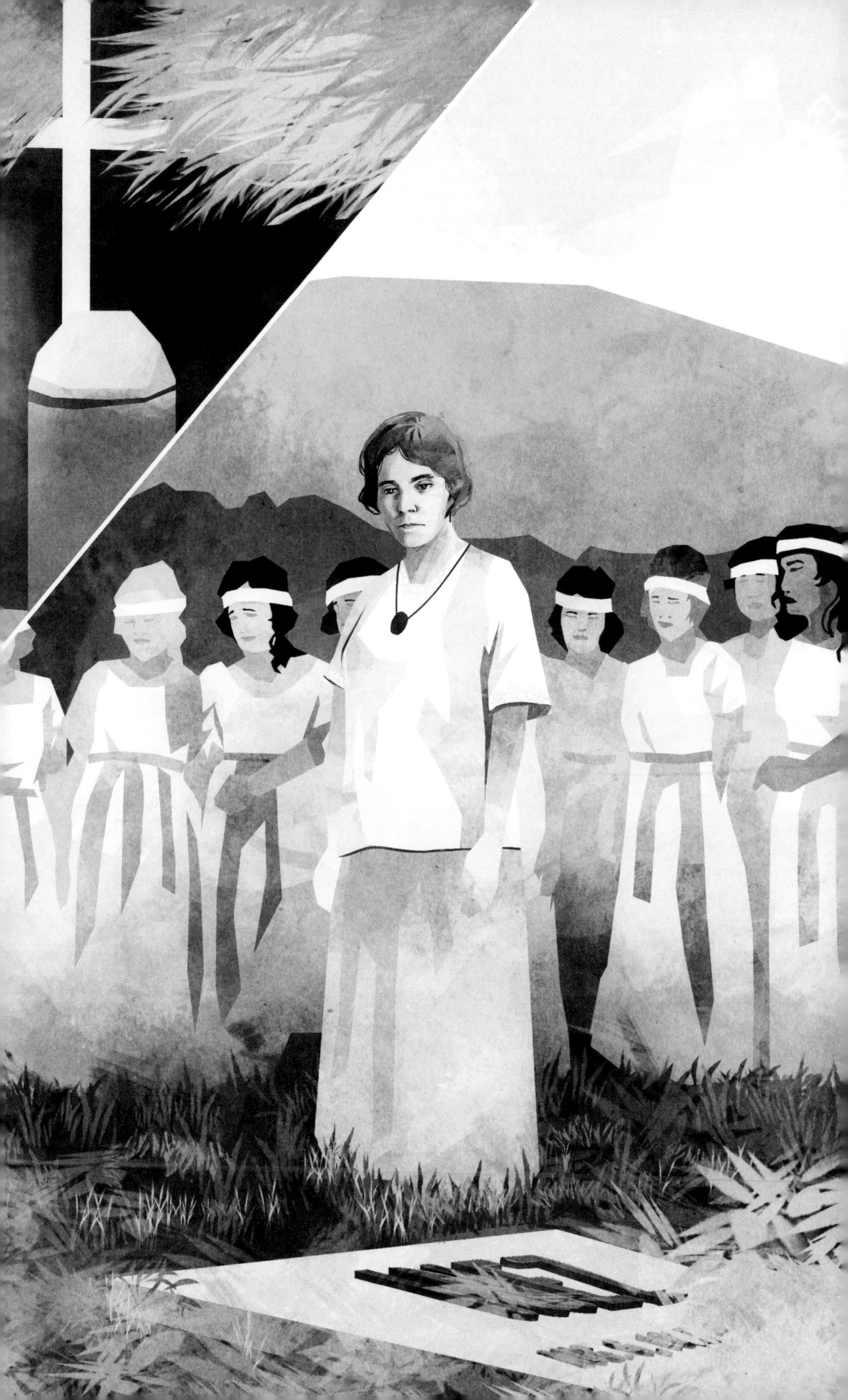

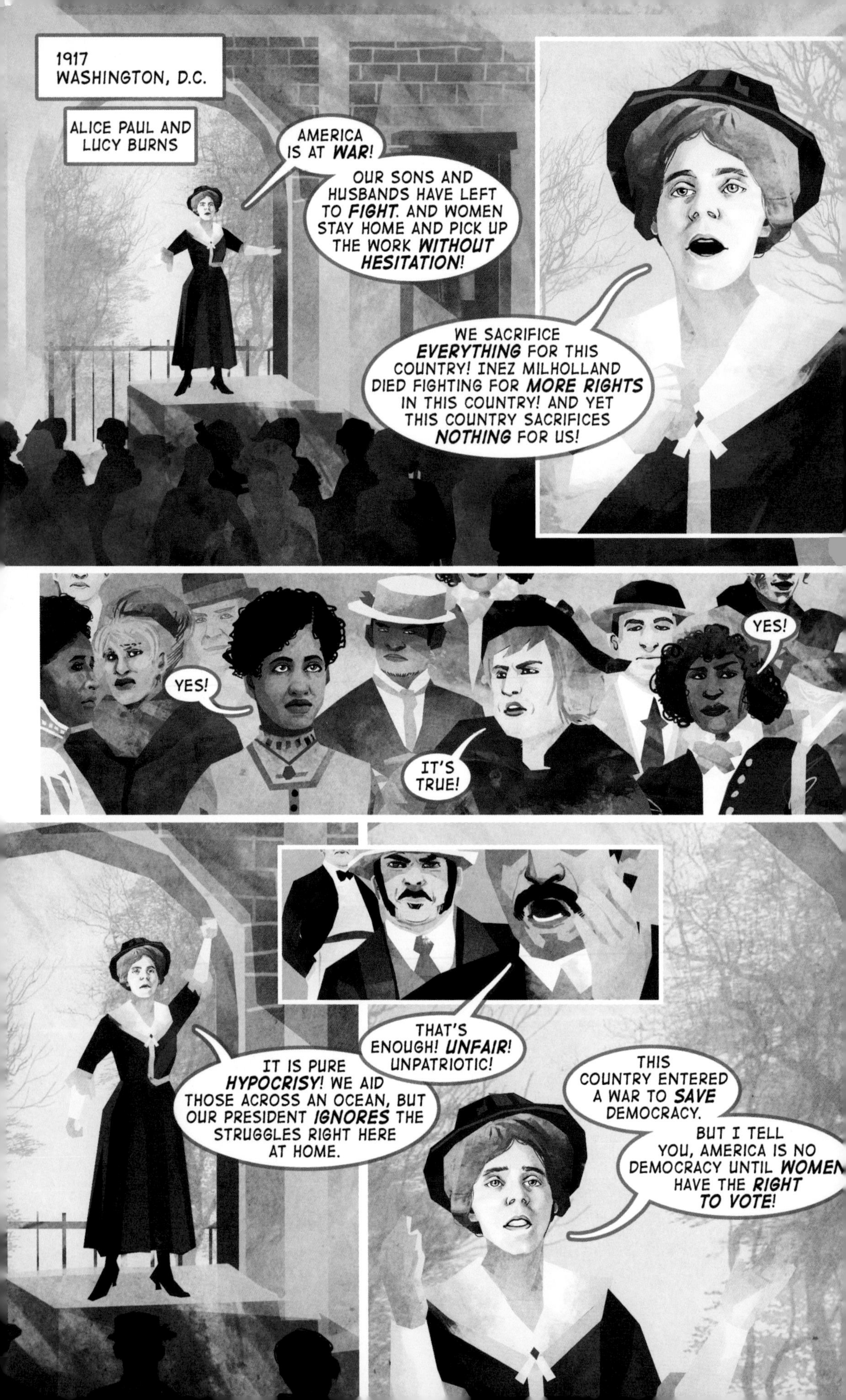

1917
WASHINGTON, D.C.
ALICE PAUL AND LUCY BURNS
AMERICA IS AT WAR!
OUR SONS AND HUSBANDS HAVE LEFT TO FIGHT. AND WOMEN STAY HOME AND PICK UP THE WORK WITHOUT HESITATION!
WE SACRIFICE EVERYTHING FOR THIS COUNTRY! INEZ MILHOLLAND DIED FIGHTING FOR MORE RIGHTS IN THIS COUNTRY! AND YET THIS COUNTRY SACRIFICES NOTHING FOR US!
YES!
IT'S TRUE!
YES!
THAT'S ENOUGH! UNFAIR! UNPATRIOTIC!
IT IS PURE HYPOCRISY! WE AID THOSE ACROSS AN OCEAN, BUT OUR PRESIDENT IGNORES THE STRUGGLES RIGHT HERE AT HOME.
THIS COUNTRY ENTERED A WAR TO SAVE DEMOCRACY.
BUT I TELL YOU, AMERICA IS NO DEMOCRACY UNTIL WOMEN HAVE THE RIGHT TO VOTE!

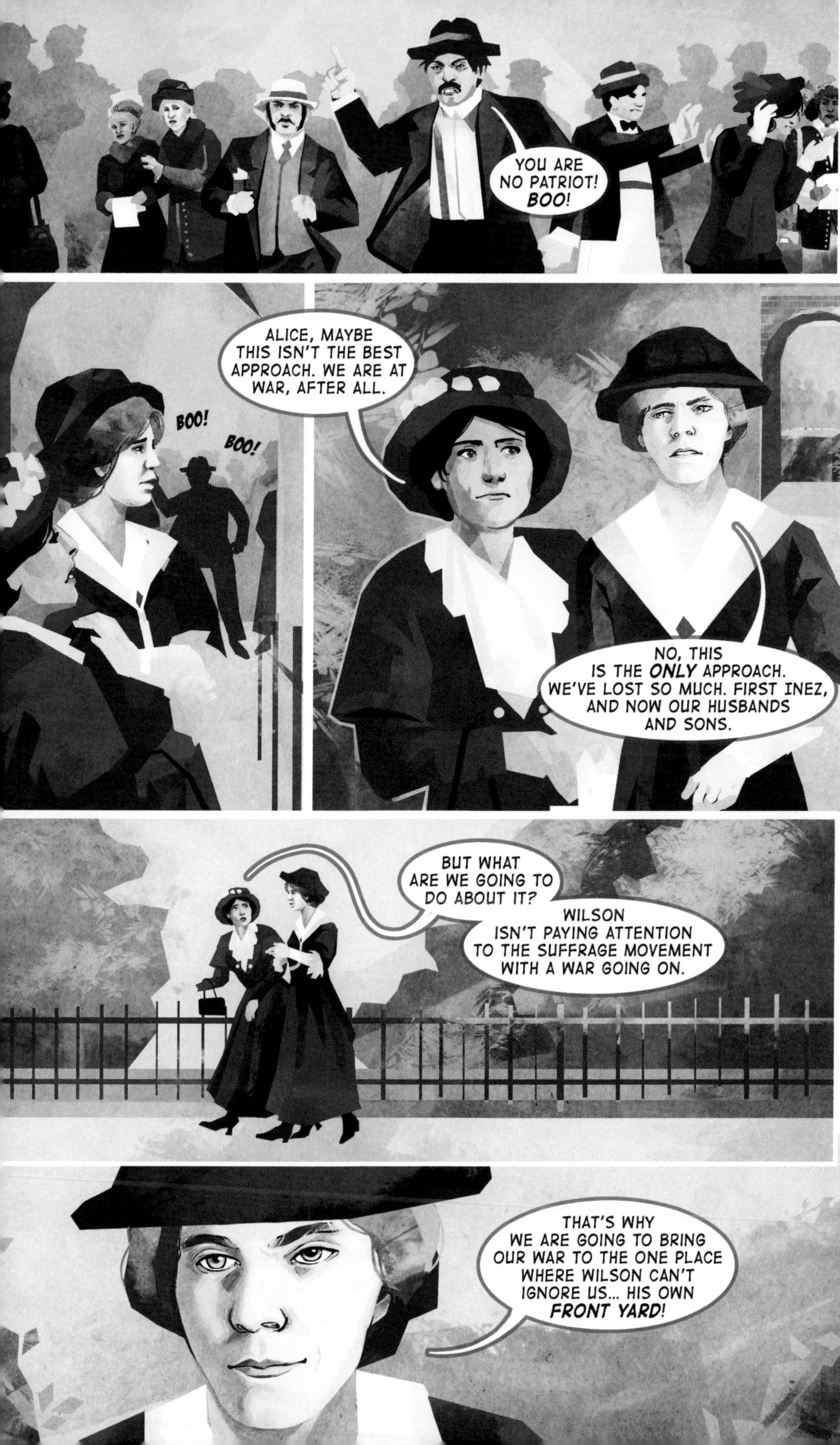
YOU ARE NO PATRIOT! BOO!
ALICE, MAYBE THIS ISN'T THE BEST APPROACH. WE ARE AT WAR, AFTER ALL.
BOO!
BOO!
NO, THIS IS THE ONLY APPROACH. WE'VE LOST SO MUCH. FIRST INEZ, AND NOW OUR HUSBANDS AND SONS.
BUT WHAT ARE WE GOING TO DO ABOUT IT?
WILSON ISN'T PAYING ATTENTION TO THE SUFFRAGE MOVEMENT WITH A WAR GOING ON.
THAT'S WHY WE ARE GOING TO BRING OUR WAR TO THE ONE PLACE WHERE WILSON CAN'T IGNORE US... HIS OWN FRONT YARD!

"I NEVER DOUBTED THAT EQUAL RIGHTS WAS THE RIGHT DIRECTION. MOST REFORMS, MOST PROBLEMS ARE COMPLICATED. BUT TO ME THERE IS NOTHING COMPLICATED ABOUT ORDINARY EQUALITY."

ALICE PAUL
1885–1977

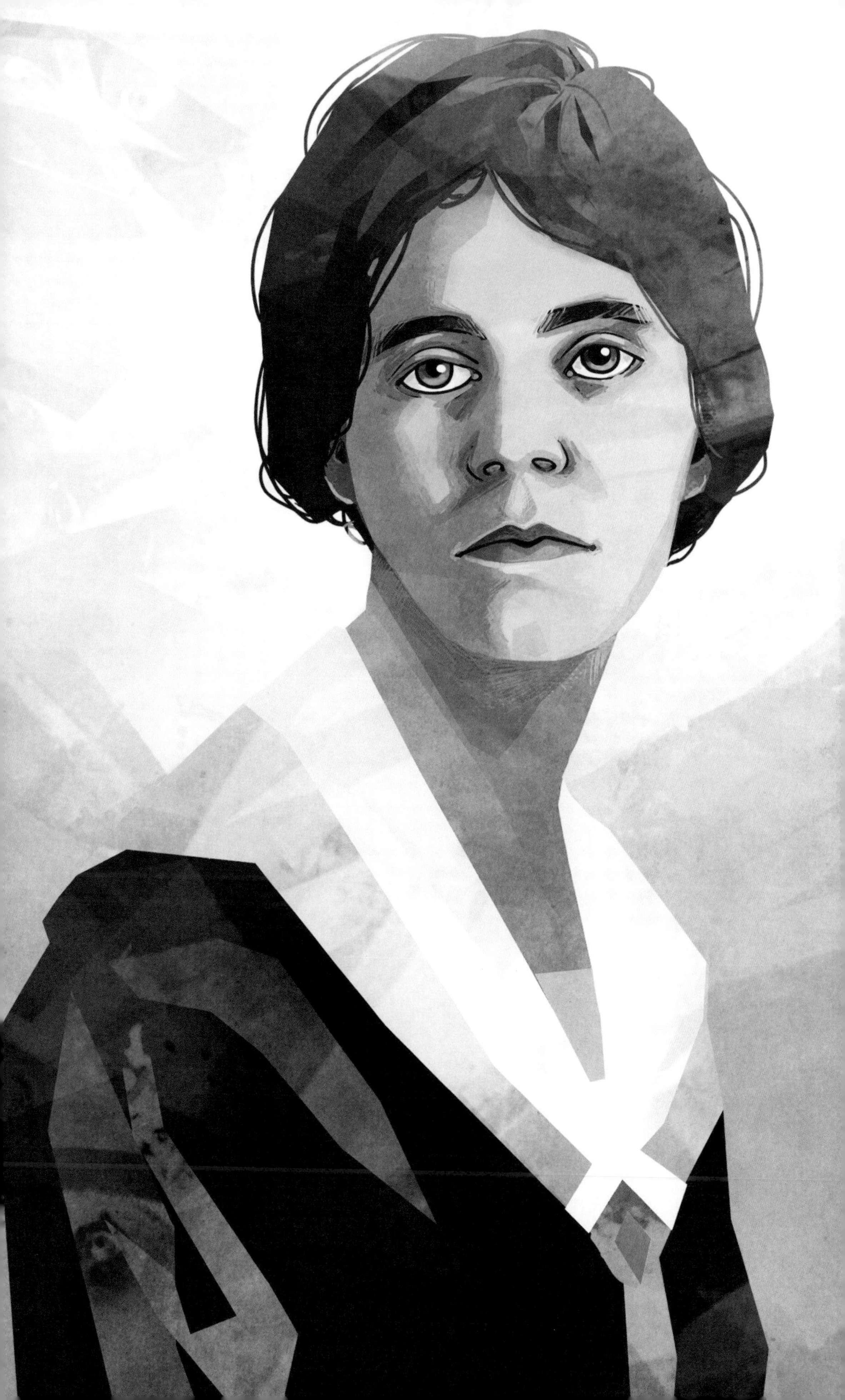

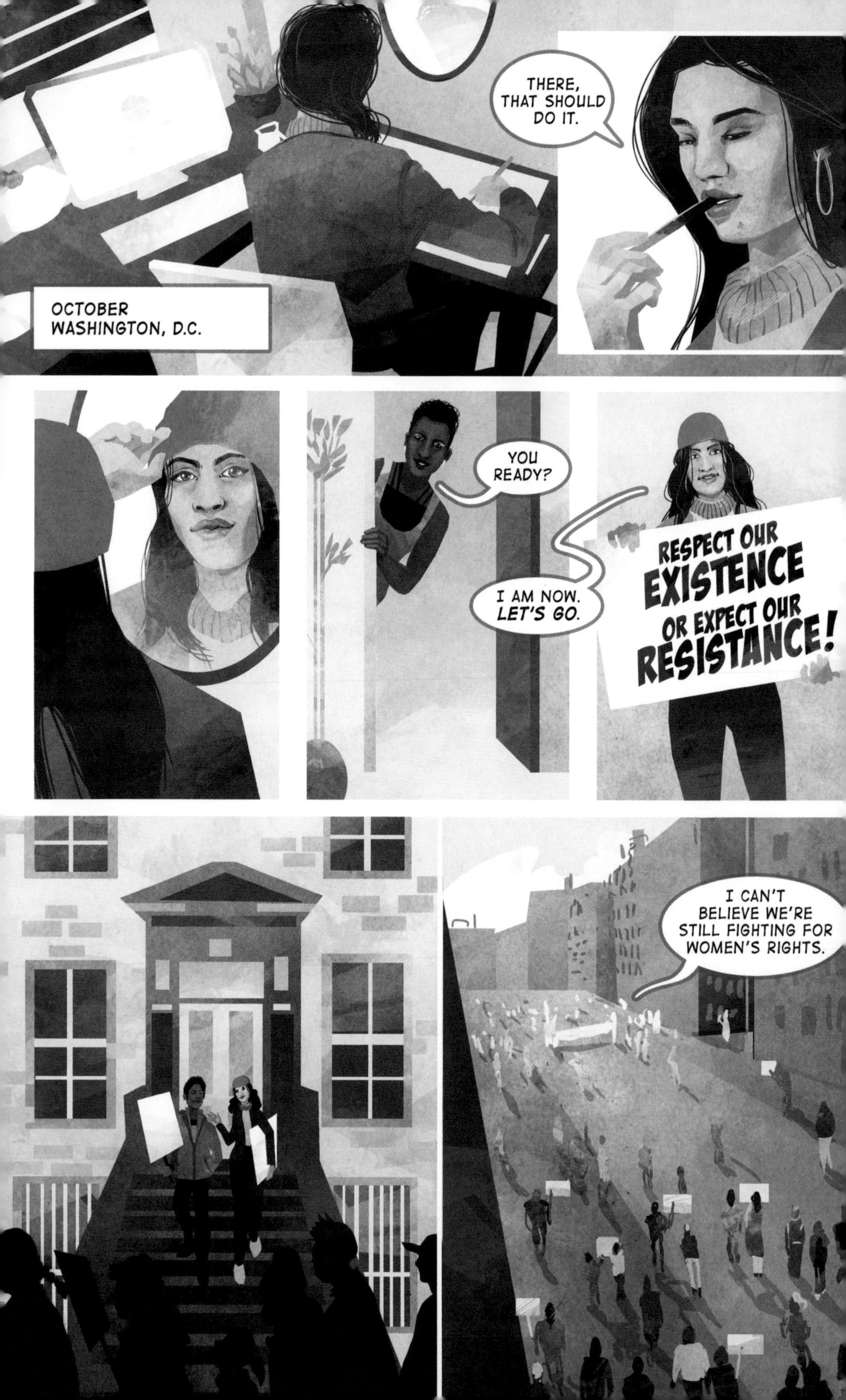
OCTOBER
WASHINGTON, D.C.
THERE, THAT SHOULD DO IT.
YOU READY?
I AM NOW. *LET'S GO.*
RESPECT OUR EXISTENCE OR EXPECT OUR RESISTANCE!
I CAN'T BELIEVE WE'RE STILL FIGHTING FOR WOMEN'S RIGHTS.

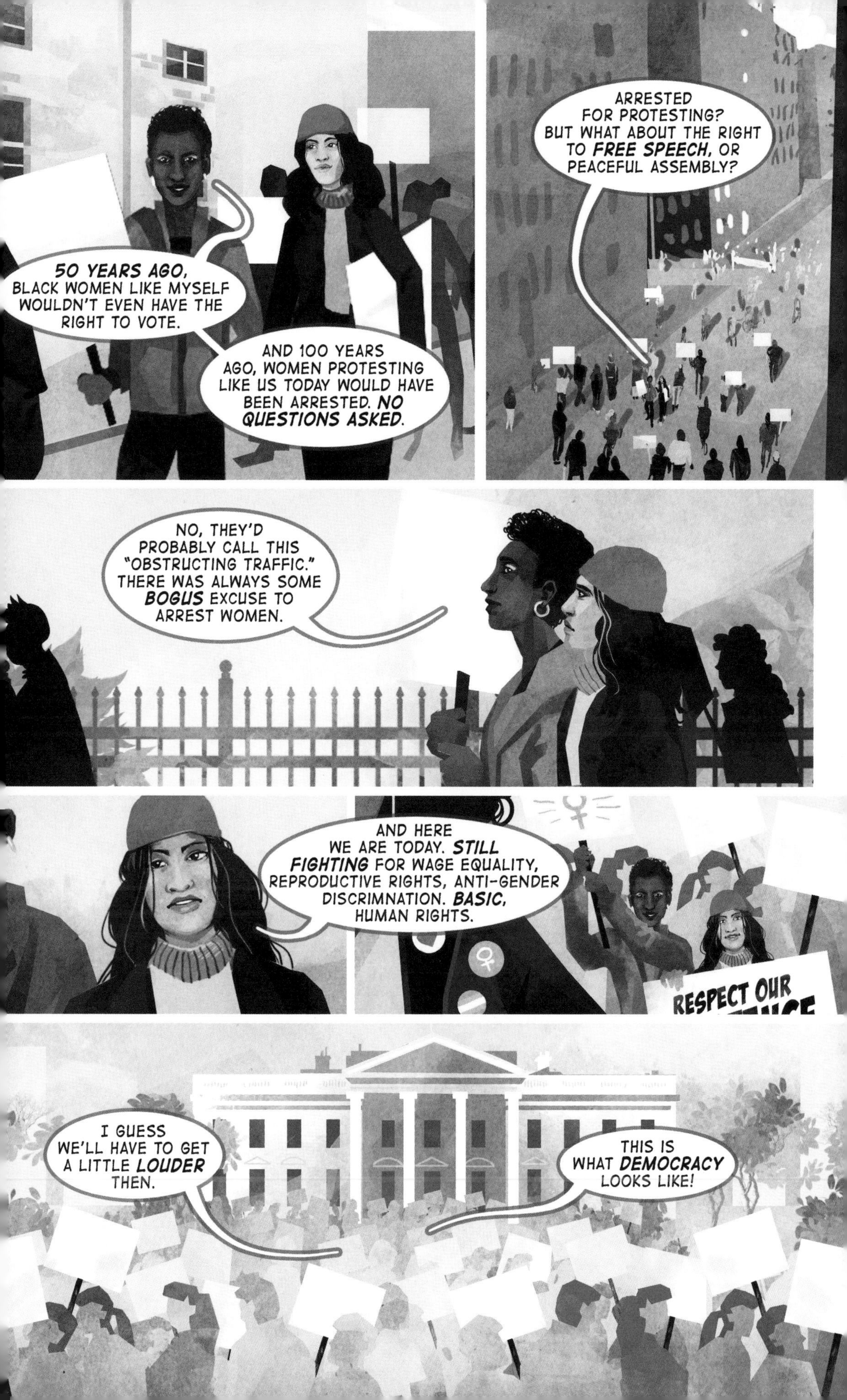

50 YEARS AGO, BLACK WOMEN LIKE MYSELF WOULDN'T EVEN HAVE THE RIGHT TO VOTE.
AND 100 YEARS AGO, WOMEN PROTESTING LIKE US TODAY WOULD HAVE BEEN ARRESTED. NO QUESTIONS ASKED.
ARRESTED FOR PROTESTING? BUT WHAT ABOUT THE RIGHT TO FREE SPEECH, OR PEACEFUL ASSEMBLY?
NO, THEY'D PROBABLY CALL THIS "OBSTRUCTING TRAFFIC." THERE WAS ALWAYS SOME BOGUS EXCUSE TO ARREST WOMEN.
AND HERE WE ARE TODAY. STILL FIGHTING FOR WAGE EQUALITY, REPRODUCTIVE RIGHTS, ANTI-GENDER DISCRIMNATION. BASIC, HUMAN RIGHTS.
RESPECT OUR
I GUESS WE'LL HAVE TO GET A LITTLE LOUDER THEN.
THIS IS WHAT DEMOCRACY LOOKS LIKE!

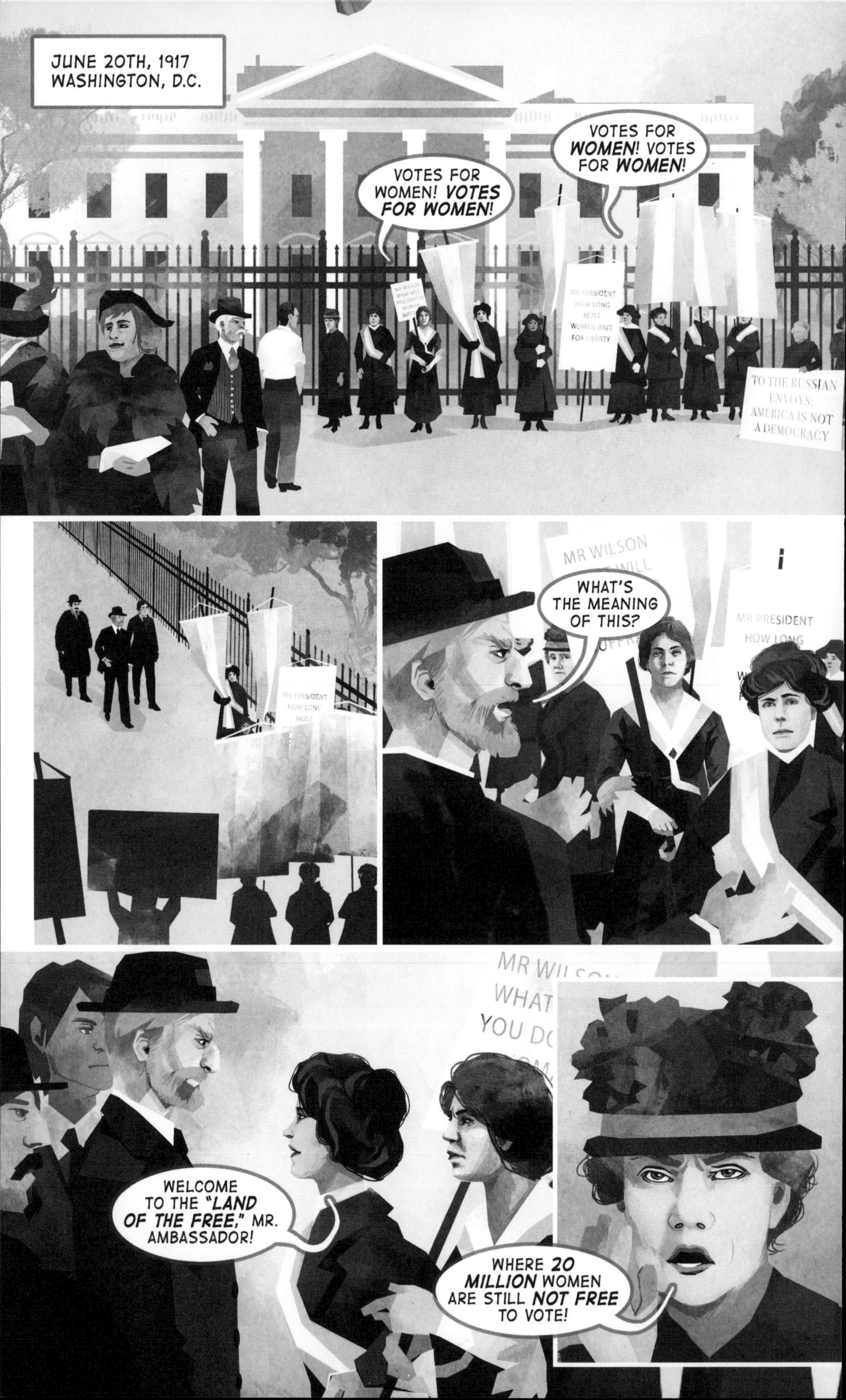
JUNE 20TH, 1917
WASHINGTON, D.C.
VOTES FOR WOMEN! VOTES FOR WOMEN!
VOTES FOR WOMEN! VOTES FOR WOMEN!
MR PRESIDENT HOW LONG MUST WOMEN WAIT FOR LIBERTY
TO THE RUSSIAN ENVOYS: AMERICA IS NOT A DEMOCRACY
WHAT'S THE MEANING OF THIS?
WELCOME TO THE "LAND OF THE FREE," MR. AMBASSADOR!
WHERE 20 MILLION WOMEN ARE STILL NOT FREE TO VOTE!

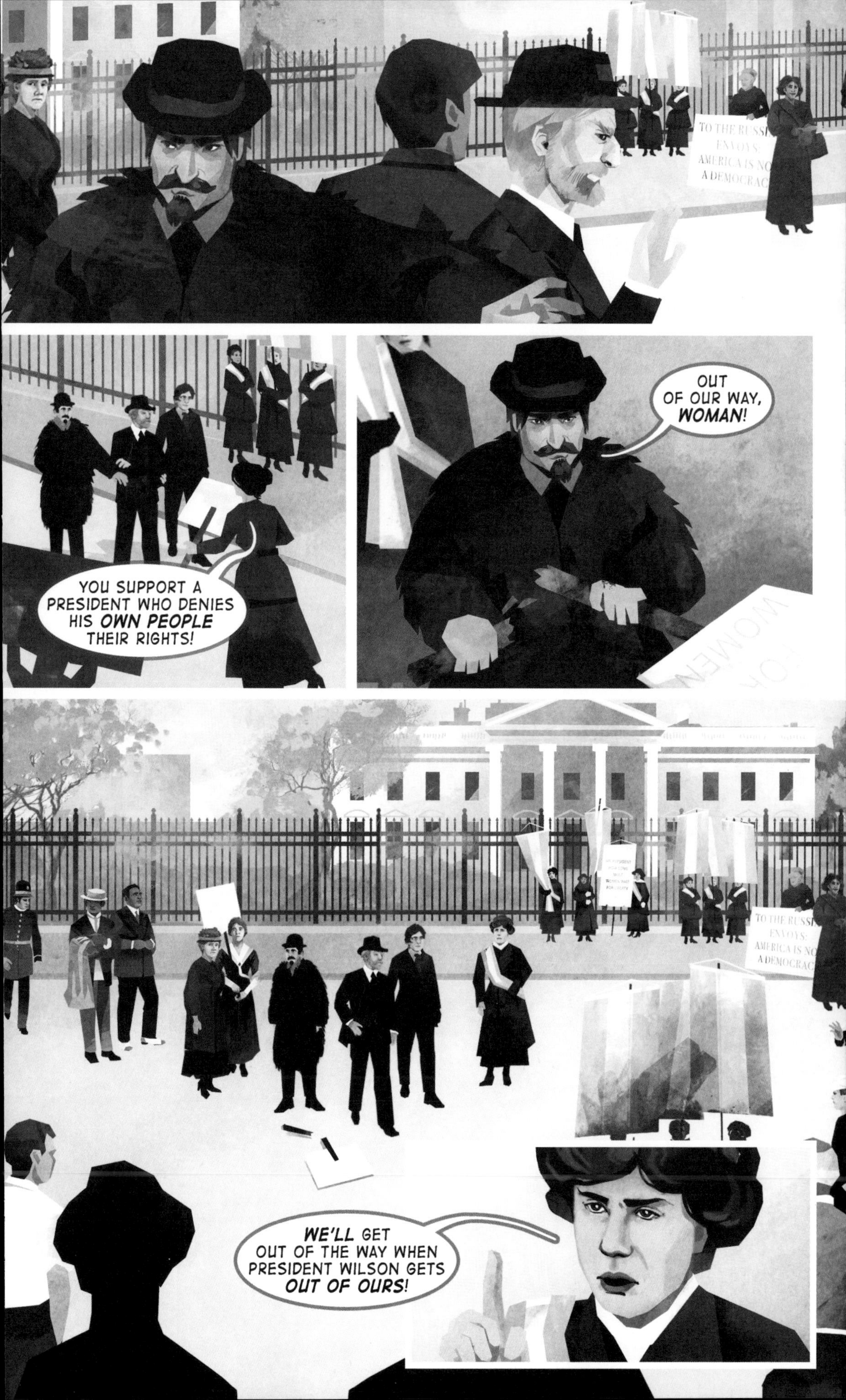
YOU SUPPORT A PRESIDENT WHO DENIES HIS *OWN PEOPLE* THEIR RIGHTS!
OUT OF OUR WAY, ***WOMAN***!
***WE'LL*** GET OUT OF THE WAY WHEN PRESIDENT WILSON GETS ***OUT OF OURS***!

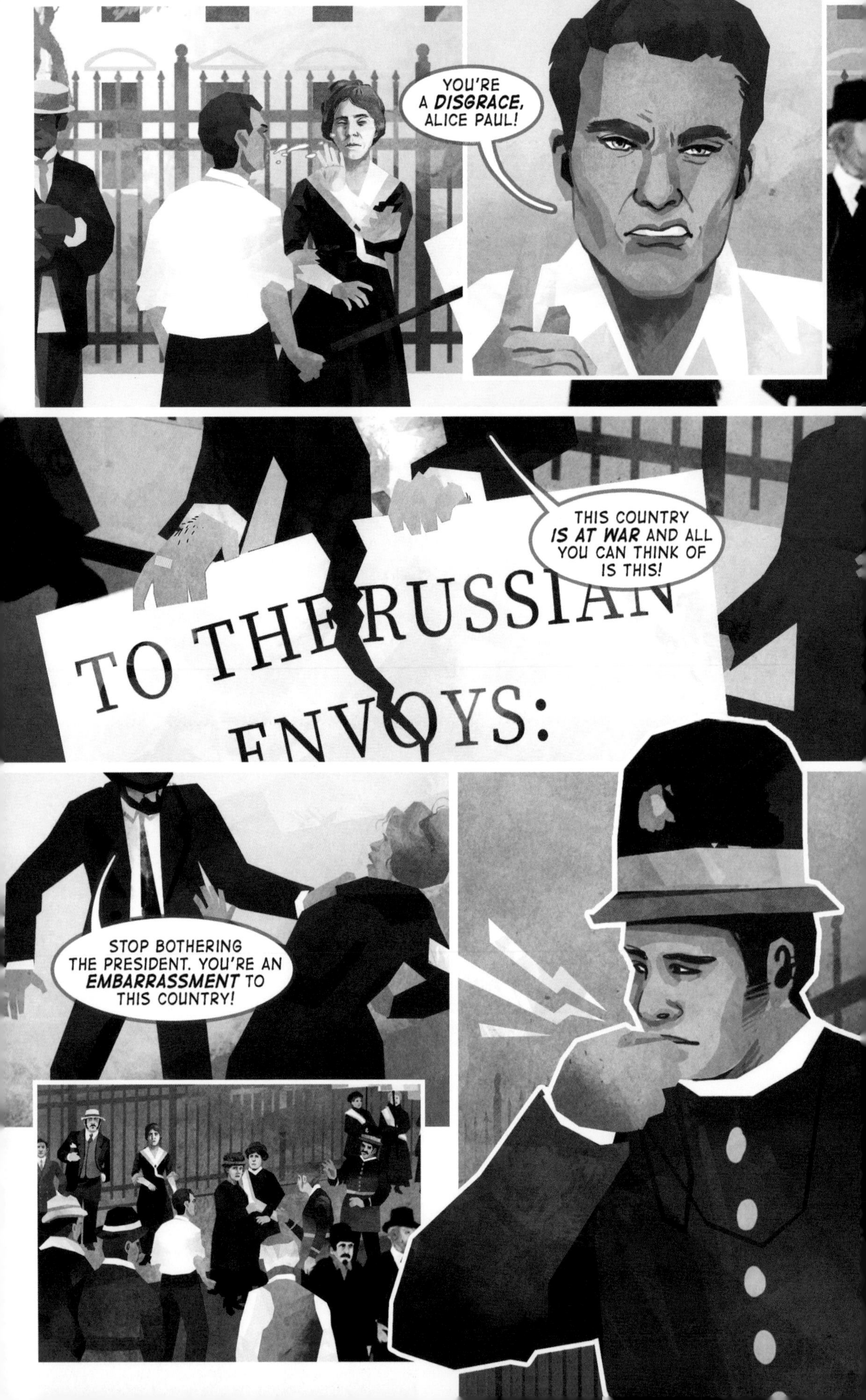
YOU'RE A **DISGRACE,** ALICE PAUL!
THIS COUNTRY **IS AT WAR** AND ALL YOU CAN THINK OF IS THIS!
TO THE RUSSIAN ENVOYS:
STOP BOTHERING THE PRESIDENT. YOU'RE AN **EMBARRASSMENT** TO THIS COUNTRY!

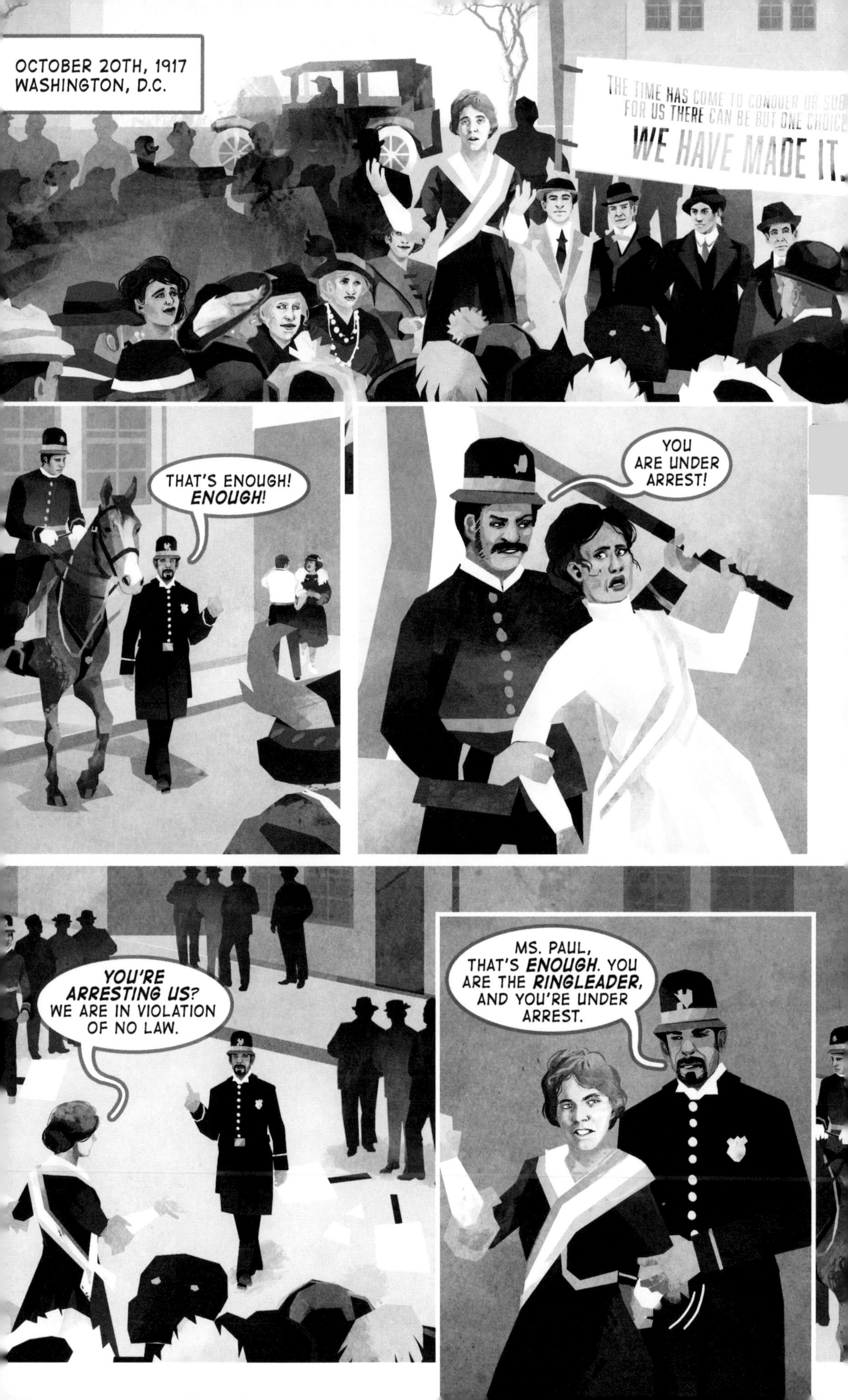
OCTOBER 20TH, 1917
WASHINGTON, D.C.
THE TIME HAS COME TO CONQUER OR SUB
FOR US THERE CAN BE BUT ONE CHOICE
WE HAVE MADE IT.
THAT'S ENOUGH! ENOUGH!
YOU ARE UNDER ARREST!
YOU'RE ARRESTING US? WE ARE IN VIOLATION OF NO LAW.
MS. PAUL, THAT'S ENOUGH. YOU ARE THE RINGLEADER, AND YOU'RE UNDER ARREST.

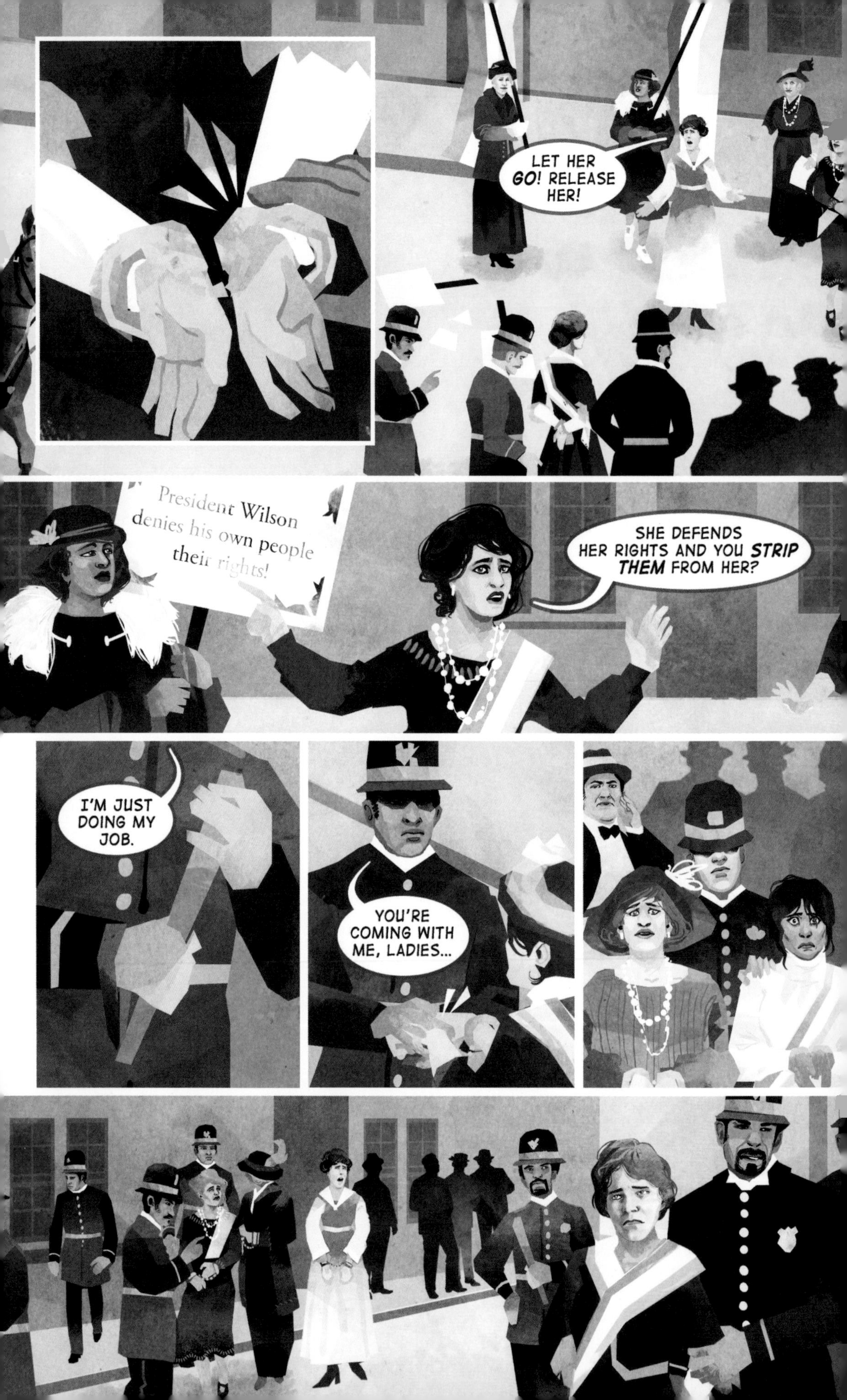
LET HER GO! RELEASE HER!
President Wilson denies his own people their rights!
SHE DEFENDS HER RIGHTS AND YOU STRIP THEM FROM HER?
I'M JUST DOING MY JOB.
YOU'RE COMING WITH ME, LADIES...

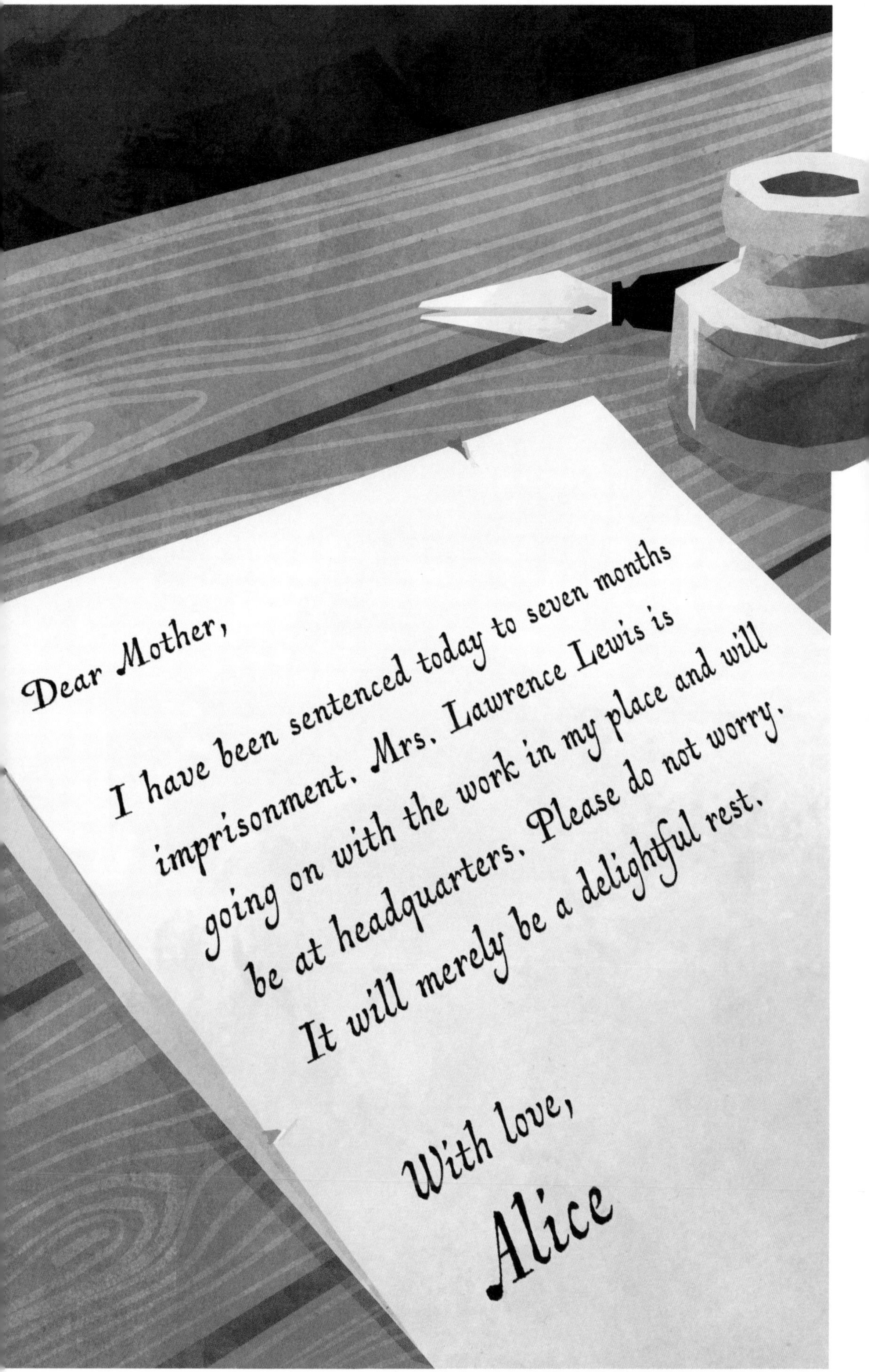
Dear Mother,

I have been sentenced today to seven months imprisonment. Mrs. Lawrence Lewis is going on with the work in my place and will be at headquarters. Please do not worry. It will merely be a delightful rest.

With love,

Alice

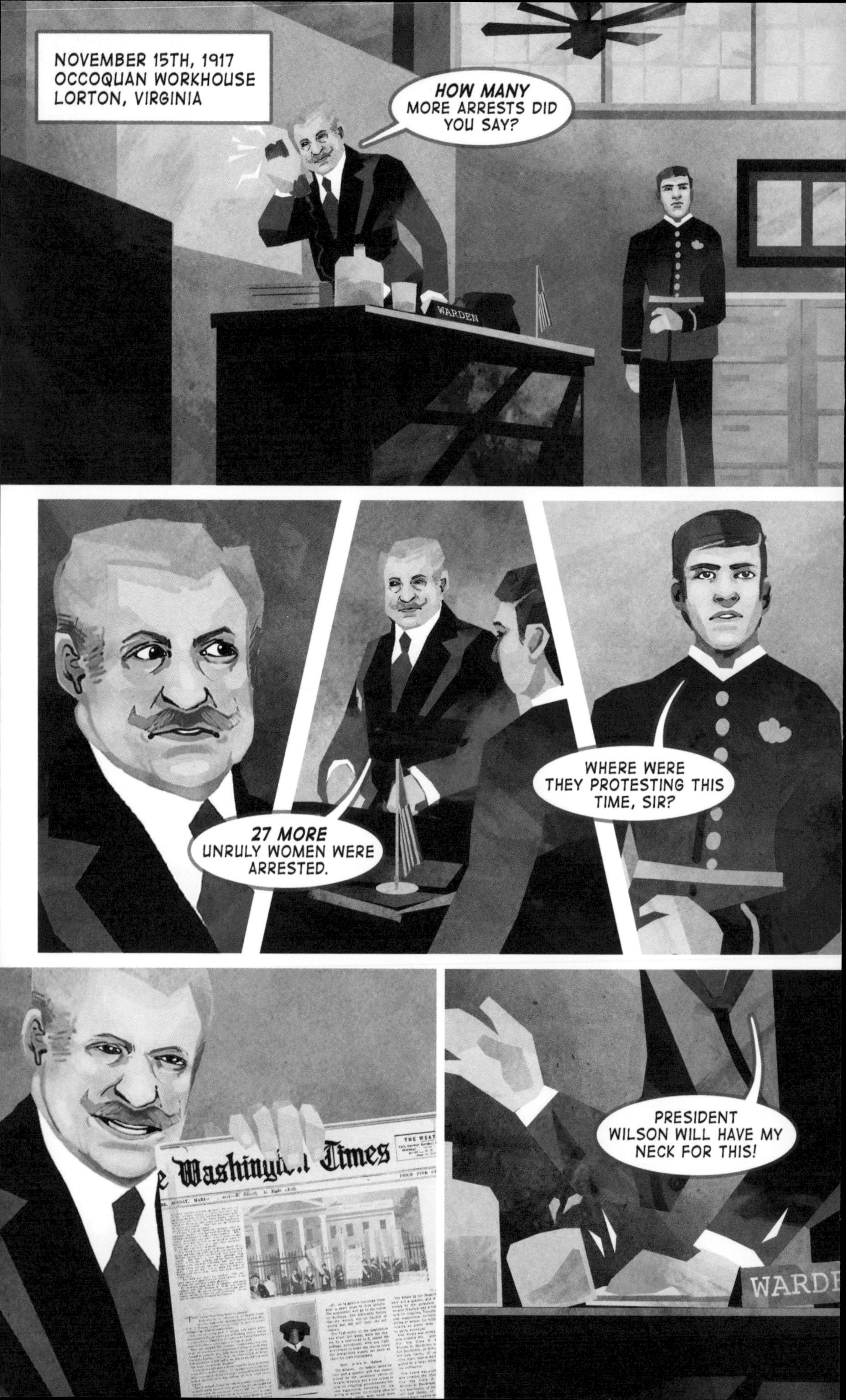
NOVEMBER 15TH, 1917
OCCOQUAN WORKHOUSE
LORTON, VIRGINIA
HOW MANY MORE ARRESTS DID YOU SAY?
WARDEN
27 MORE UNRULY WOMEN WERE ARRESTED.
WHERE WERE THEY PROTESTING THIS TIME, SIR?
Washingt..l Times
PRESIDENT WILSON WILL HAVE MY NECK FOR THIS!
WARDE

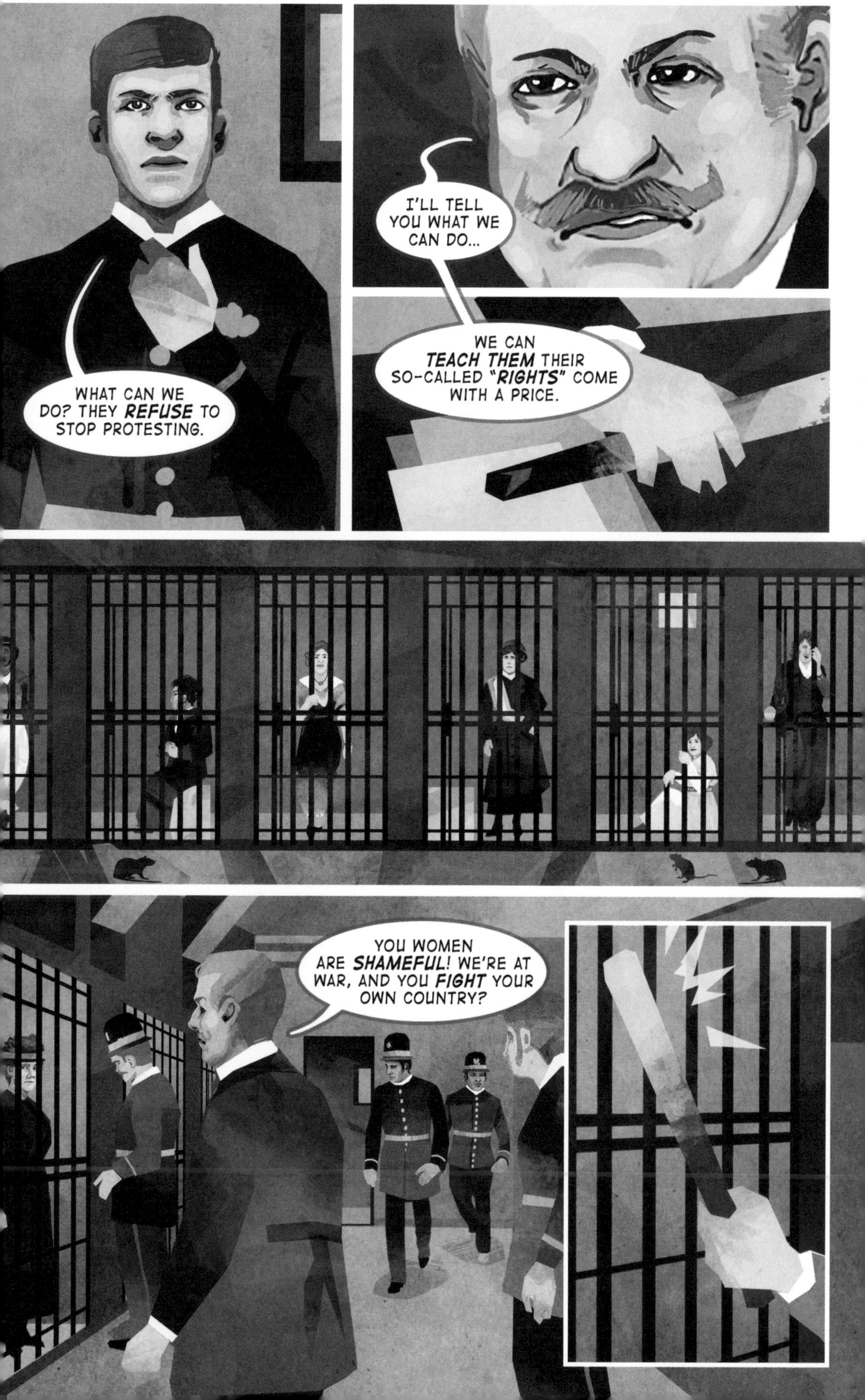
WHAT CAN WE DO? THEY REFUSE TO STOP PROTESTING.
I'LL TELL YOU WHAT WE CAN DO...
WE CAN TEACH THEM THEIR SO-CALLED "RIGHTS" COME WITH A PRICE.
YOU WOMEN ARE SHAMEFUL! WE'RE AT WAR, AND YOU FIGHT YOUR OWN COUNTRY?

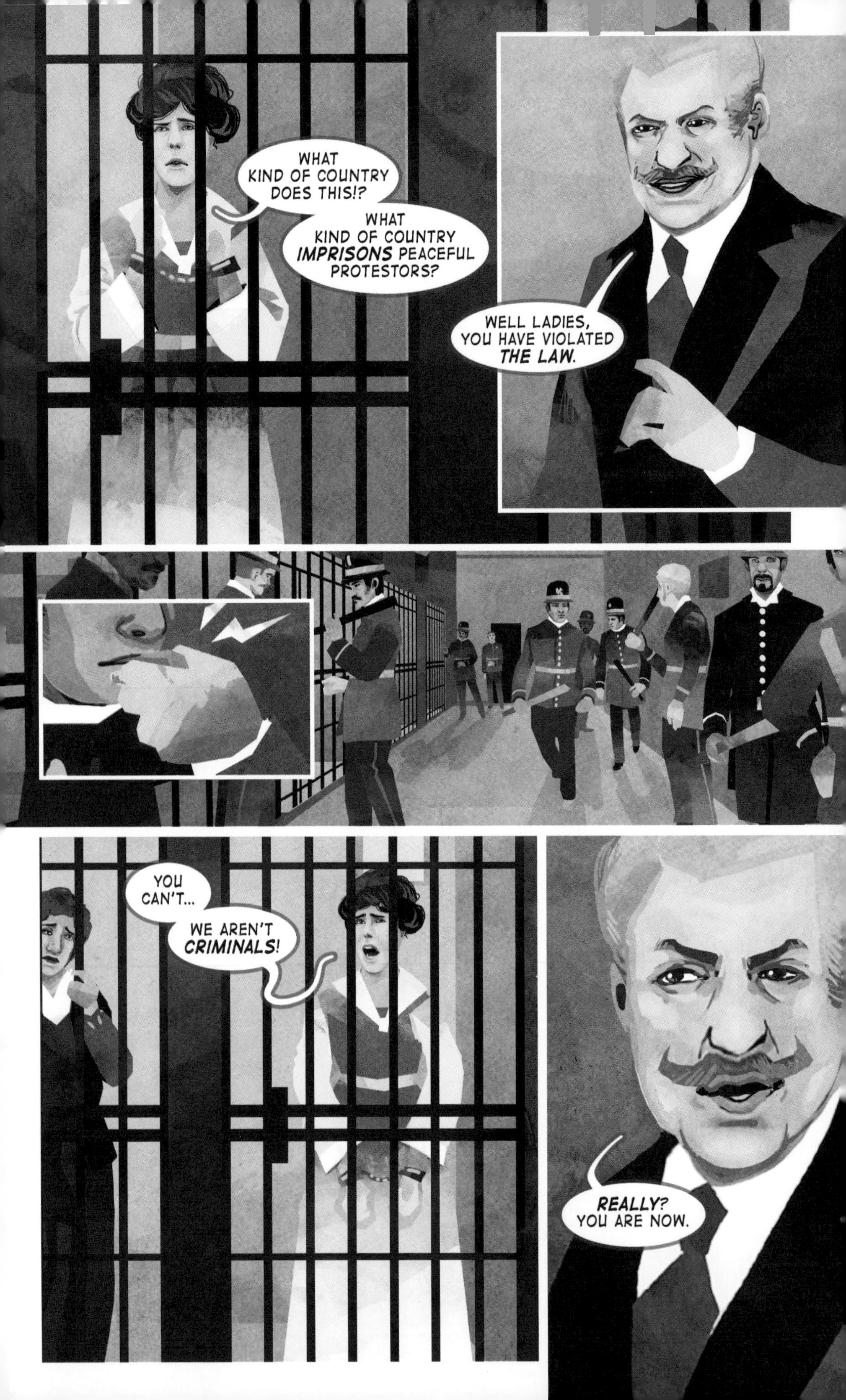
WHAT KIND OF COUNTRY DOES THIS!?
WHAT KIND OF COUNTRY *IMPRISONS* PEACEFUL PROTESTORS?
WELL LADIES, YOU HAVE VIOLATED *THE LAW*.
YOU CAN'T...
WE AREN'T *CRIMINALS*!
*REALLY?* YOU ARE NOW.

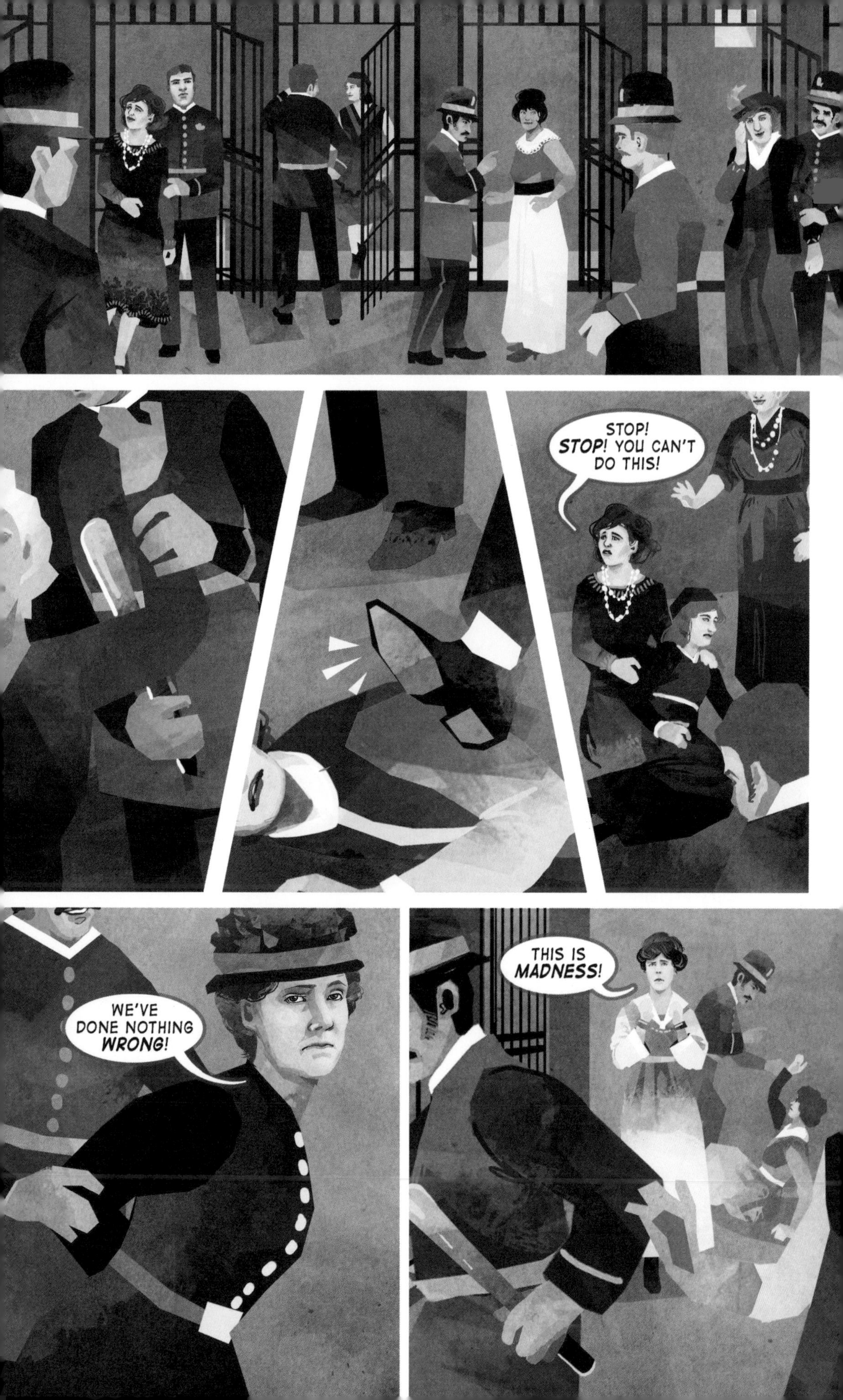
STOP! STOP! YOU CAN'T DO THIS!
WE'VE DONE NOTHING WRONG!
THIS IS MADNESS!

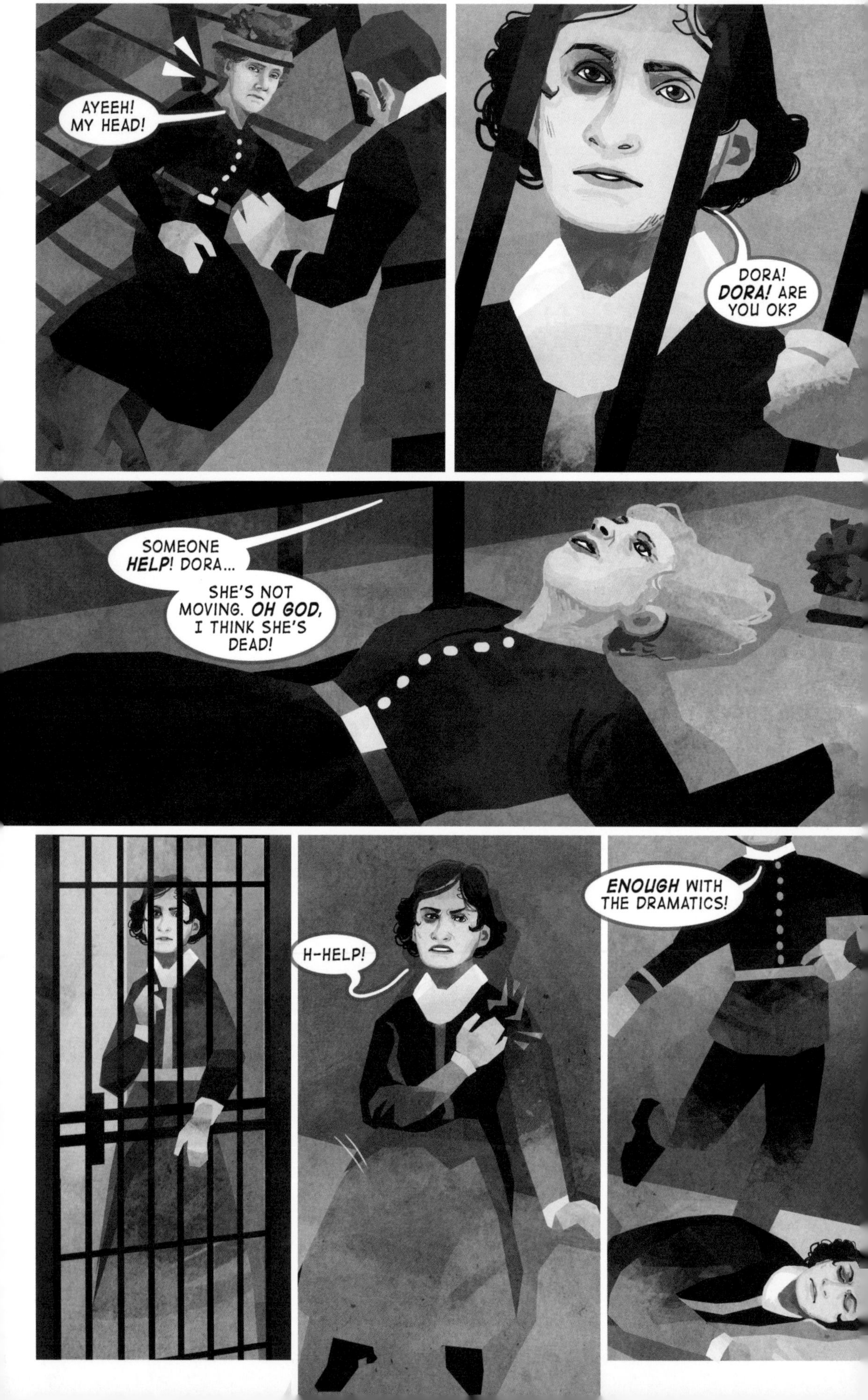
AYEEH! MY HEAD!
DORA! DORA! ARE YOU OK?
SOMEONE HELP! DORA...
SHE'S NOT MOVING. OH GOD, I THINK SHE'S DEAD!
H-HELP!
ENOUGH WITH THE DRAMATICS!

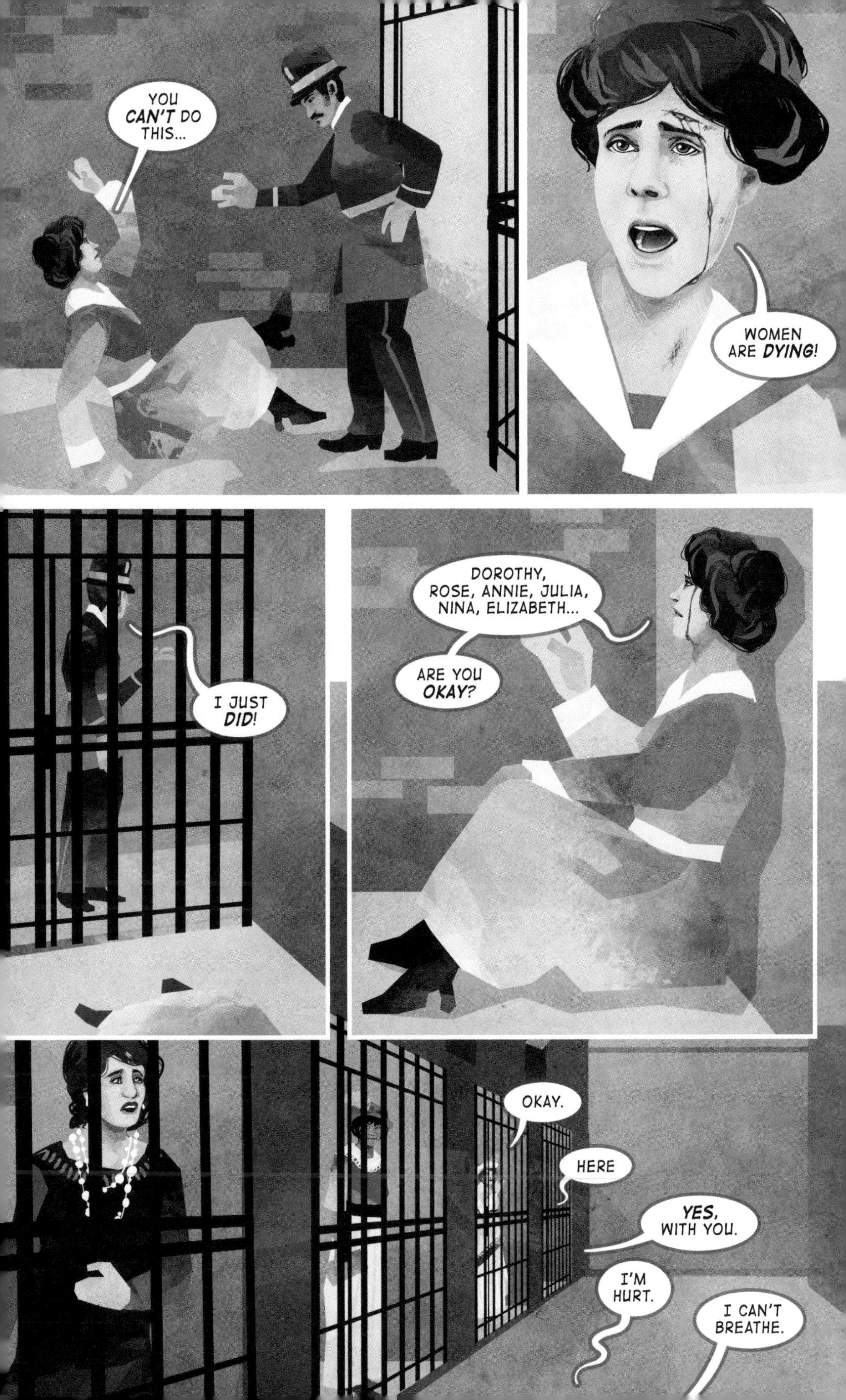
YOU CAN'T DO THIS...
WOMEN ARE DYING!
I JUST DID!
DOROTHY, ROSE, ANNIE, JULIA, NINA, ELIZABETH...
ARE YOU OKAY?
OKAY.
HERE
YES, WITH YOU.
I'M HURT.
I CAN'T BREATHE.

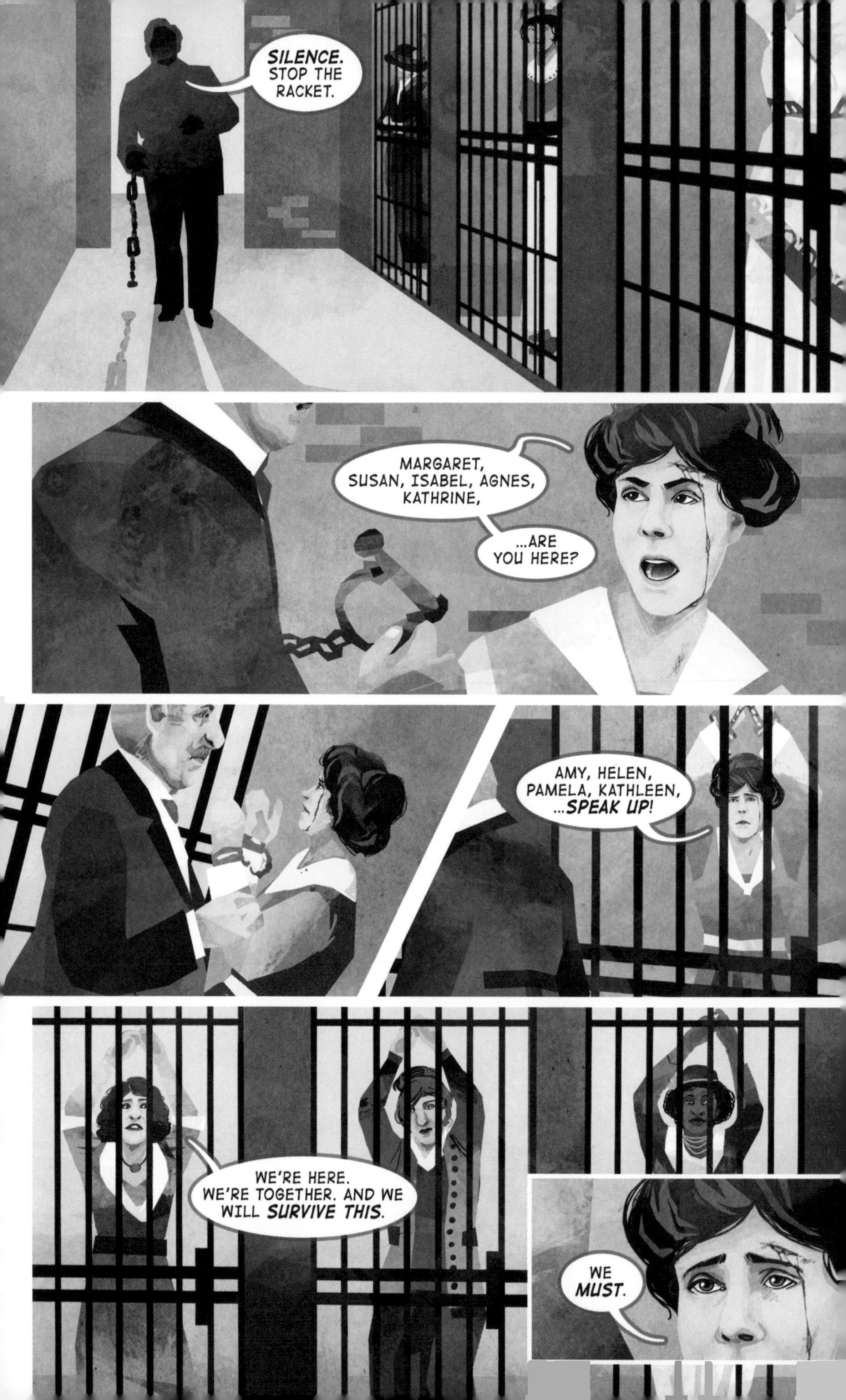
SILENCE. STOP THE RACKET.
MARGARET, SUSAN, ISABEL, AGNES, KATHRINE,
...ARE YOU HERE?
AMY, HELEN, PAMELA, KATHLEEN, ...SPEAK UP!
WE'RE HERE. WE'RE TOGETHER. AND WE WILL SURVIVE THIS.
WE MUST.

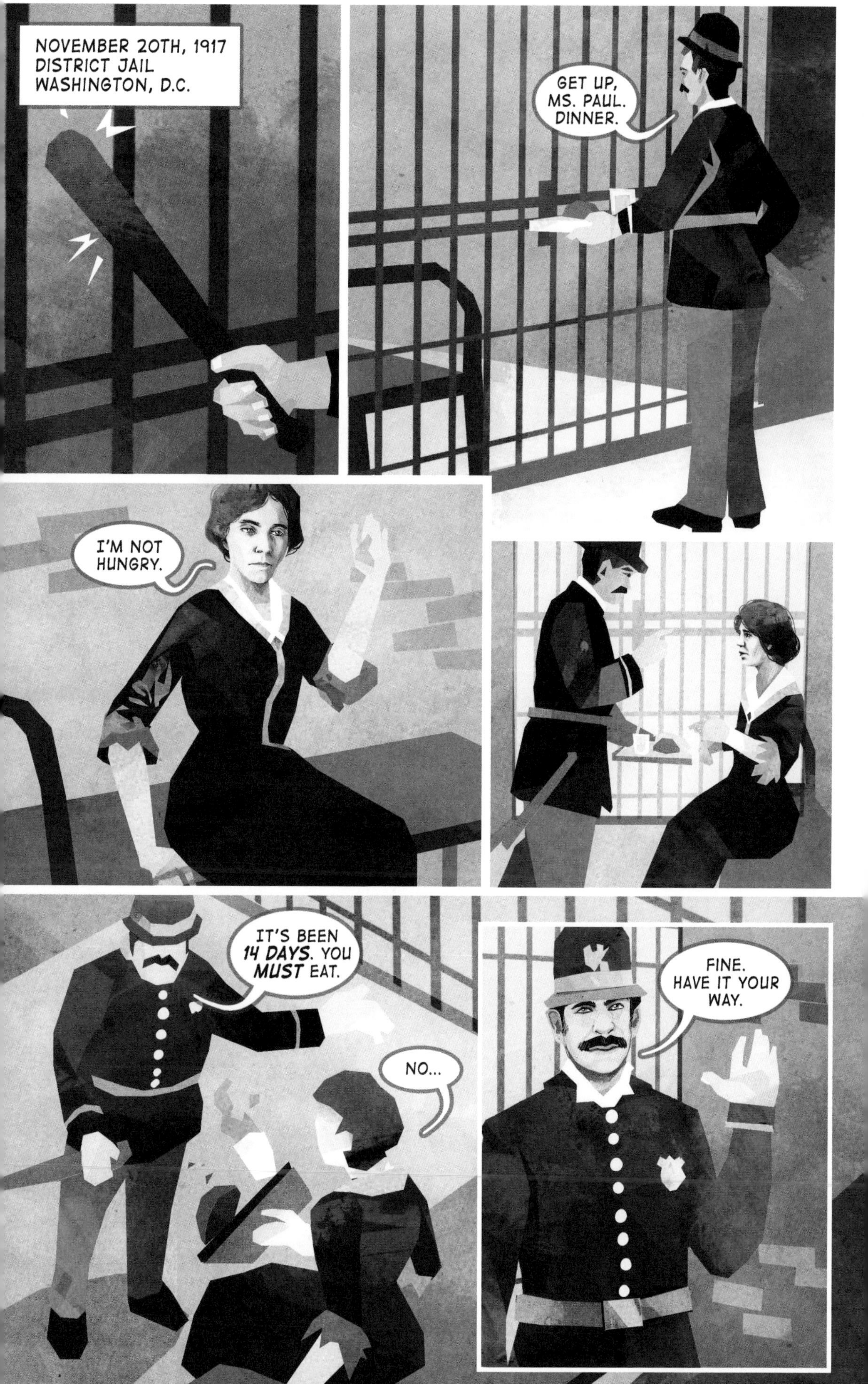
NOVEMBER 20TH, 1917
DISTRICT JAIL
WASHINGTON, D.C.
GET UP, MS. PAUL. DINNER.
I'M NOT HUNGRY.
IT'S BEEN *14 DAYS*. YOU *MUST* EAT.
NO...
FINE. HAVE IT YOUR WAY.

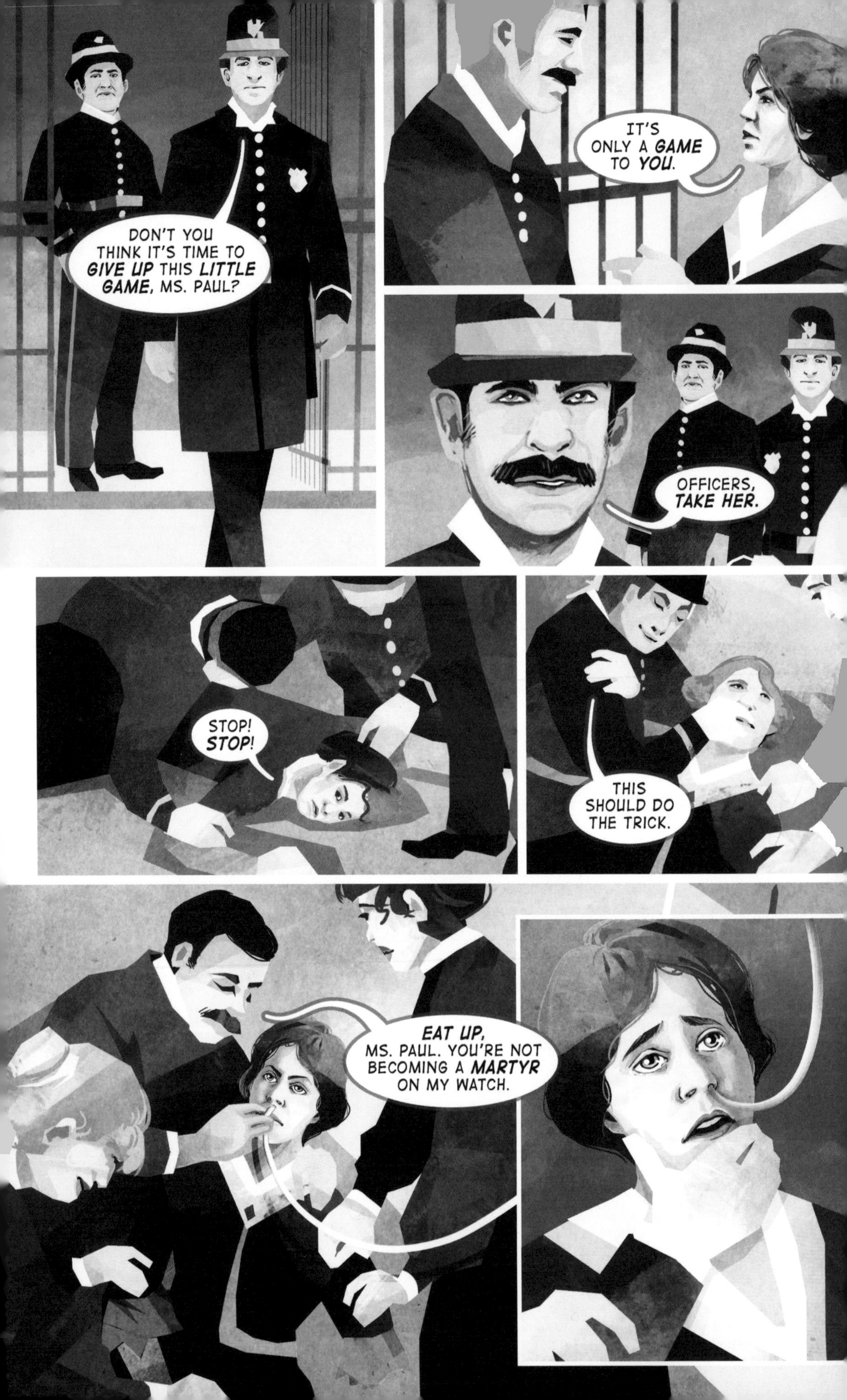
DON'T YOU THINK IT'S TIME TO GIVE UP THIS LITTLE GAME, MS. PAUL?
IT'S ONLY A GAME TO YOU.
OFFICERS, TAKE HER.
STOP! STOP!
THIS SHOULD DO THE TRICK.
EAT UP, MS. PAUL. YOU'RE NOT BECOMING A MARTYR ON MY WATCH.

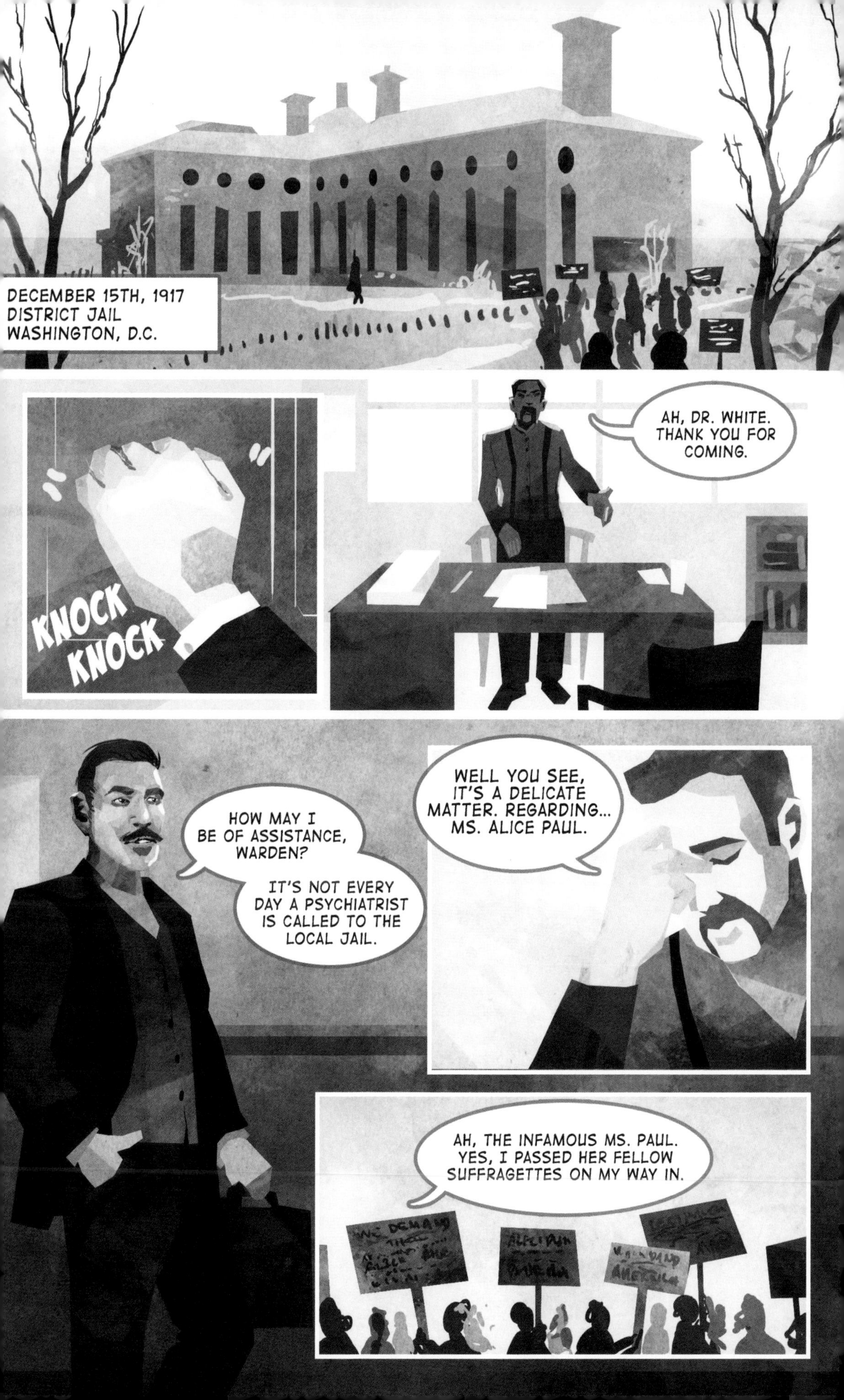
DECEMBER 15TH, 1917
DISTRICT JAIL
WASHINGTON, D.C.
KNOCK
KNOCK
AH, DR. WHITE. THANK YOU FOR COMING.
HOW MAY I BE OF ASSISTANCE, WARDEN?
IT'S NOT EVERY DAY A PSYCHIATRIST IS CALLED TO THE LOCAL JAIL.
WELL YOU SEE, IT'S A DELICATE MATTER. REGARDING... MS. ALICE PAUL.
AH, THE INFAMOUS MS. PAUL. YES, I PASSED HER FELLOW SUFFRAGETTES ON MY WAY IN.

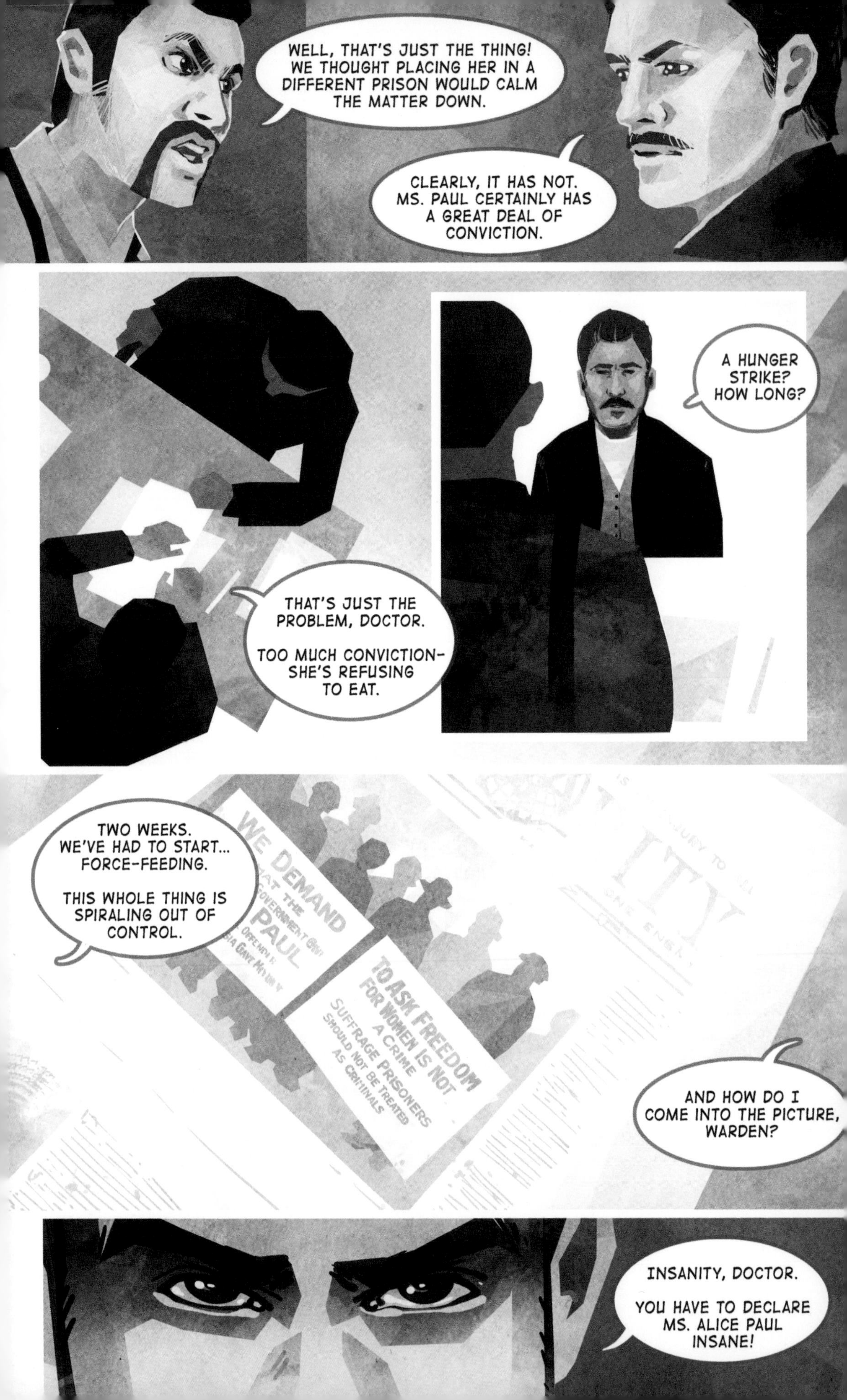
WELL, THAT'S JUST THE THING! WE THOUGHT PLACING HER IN A DIFFERENT PRISON WOULD CALM THE MATTER DOWN.
CLEARLY, IT HAS NOT. MS. PAUL CERTAINLY HAS A GREAT DEAL OF CONVICTION.
A HUNGER STRIKE? HOW LONG?
THAT'S JUST THE PROBLEM, DOCTOR.
TOO MUCH CONVICTION- SHE'S REFUSING TO EAT.
TWO WEEKS. WE'VE HAD TO START... FORCE-FEEDING.
THIS WHOLE THING IS SPIRALING OUT OF CONTROL.
WE DEMAND
PAUL
TO ASK FREEDOM FOR WOMEN IS NOT A CRIME
SUFFRAGE PRISONERS SHOULD NOT BE TREATED AS CRIMINALS
AND HOW DO I COME INTO THE PICTURE, WARDEN?
INSANITY, DOCTOR.
YOU HAVE TO DECLARE MS. ALICE PAUL INSANE!

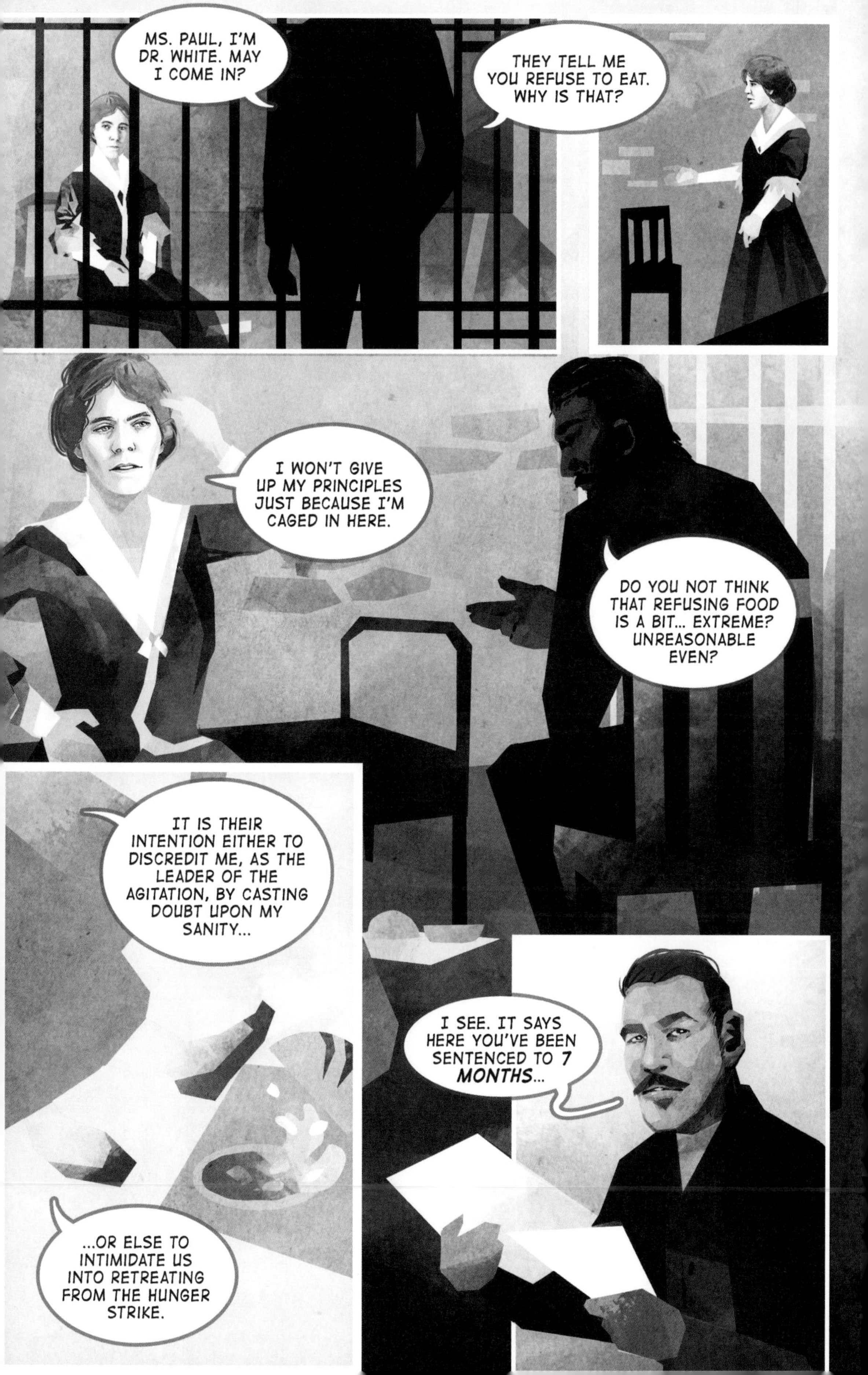
MS. PAUL, I'M DR. WHITE. MAY I COME IN?
THEY TELL ME YOU REFUSE TO EAT. WHY IS THAT?
I WON'T GIVE UP MY PRINCIPLES JUST BECAUSE I'M CAGED IN HERE.
DO YOU NOT THINK THAT REFUSING FOOD IS A BIT... EXTREME? UNREASONABLE EVEN?
IT IS THEIR INTENTION EITHER TO DISCREDIT ME, AS THE LEADER OF THE AGITATION, BY CASTING DOUBT UPON MY SANITY...
...OR ELSE TO INTIMIDATE US INTO RETREATING FROM THE HUNGER STRIKE.
I SEE. IT SAYS HERE YOU'VE BEEN SENTENCED TO 7 *MONTHS*...

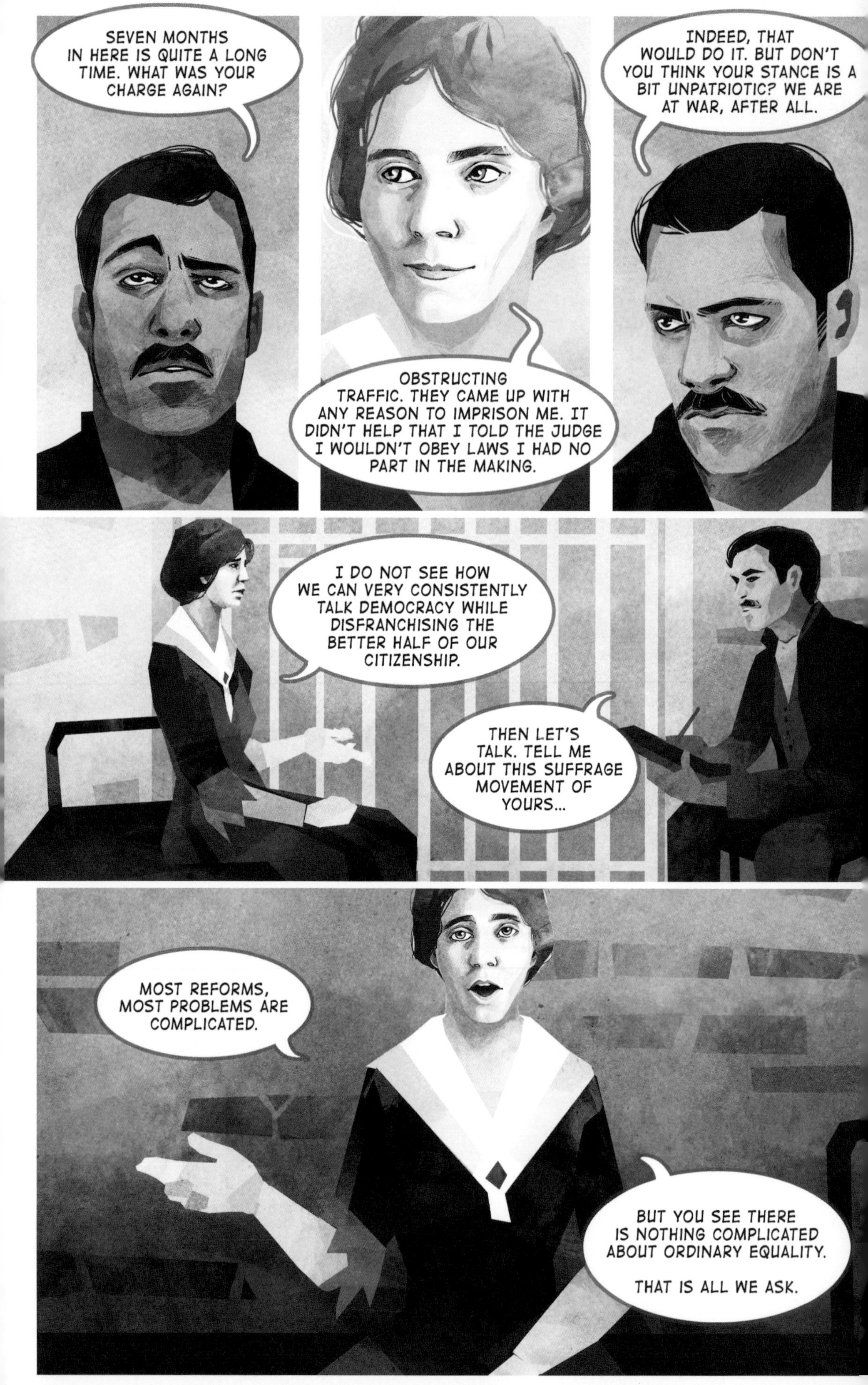
SEVEN MONTHS IN HERE IS QUITE A LONG TIME. WHAT WAS YOUR CHARGE AGAIN?
OBSTRUCTING TRAFFIC. THEY CAME UP WITH ANY REASON TO IMPRISON ME. IT DIDN'T HELP THAT I TOLD THE JUDGE I WOULDN'T OBEY LAWS I HAD NO PART IN THE MAKING.
INDEED, THAT WOULD DO IT. BUT DON'T YOU THINK YOUR STANCE IS A BIT UNPATRIOTIC? WE ARE AT WAR, AFTER ALL.
I DO NOT SEE HOW WE CAN VERY CONSISTENTLY TALK DEMOCRACY WHILE DISFRANCHISING THE BETTER HALF OF OUR CITIZENSHIP.
THEN LET'S TALK. TELL ME ABOUT THIS SUFFRAGE MOVEMENT OF YOURS...
MOST REFORMS, MOST PROBLEMS ARE COMPLICATED.
BUT YOU SEE THERE IS NOTHING COMPLICATED ABOUT ORDINARY EQUALITY.
THAT IS ALL WE ASK.

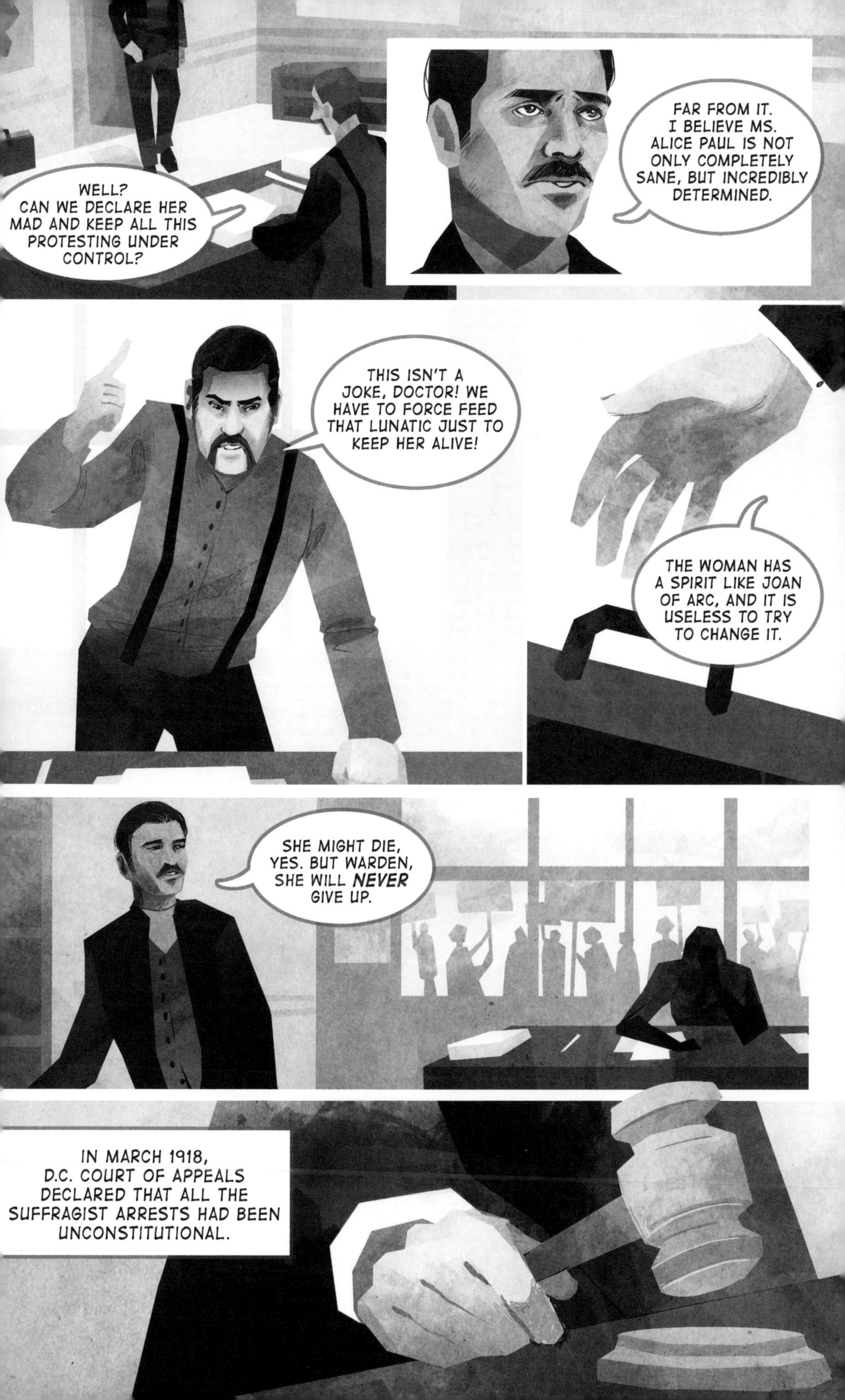
WELL? CAN WE DECLARE HER MAD AND KEEP ALL THIS PROTESTING UNDER CONTROL?
FAR FROM IT. I BELIEVE MS. ALICE PAUL IS NOT ONLY COMPLETELY SANE, BUT INCREDIBLY DETERMINED.
THIS ISN'T A JOKE, DOCTOR! WE HAVE TO FORCE FEED THAT LUNATIC JUST TO KEEP HER ALIVE!
THE WOMAN HAS A SPIRIT LIKE JOAN OF ARC, AND IT IS USELESS TO TRY TO CHANGE IT.
SHE MIGHT DIE, YES. BUT WARDEN, SHE WILL ***NEVER*** GIVE UP.
IN MARCH 1918, D.C. COURT OF APPEALS DECLARED THAT ALL THE SUFFRAGIST ARRESTS HAD BEEN UNCONSTITUTIONAL.

"TO THE WRONGS THAT NEED RESISTANCE, TO THE RIGHT THAT NEEDS ASSISTANCE, TO THE FUTURE IN THE DISTANCE, GIVE YOURSELVES."

CARRIE CHAPMAN CATT
1859–1947

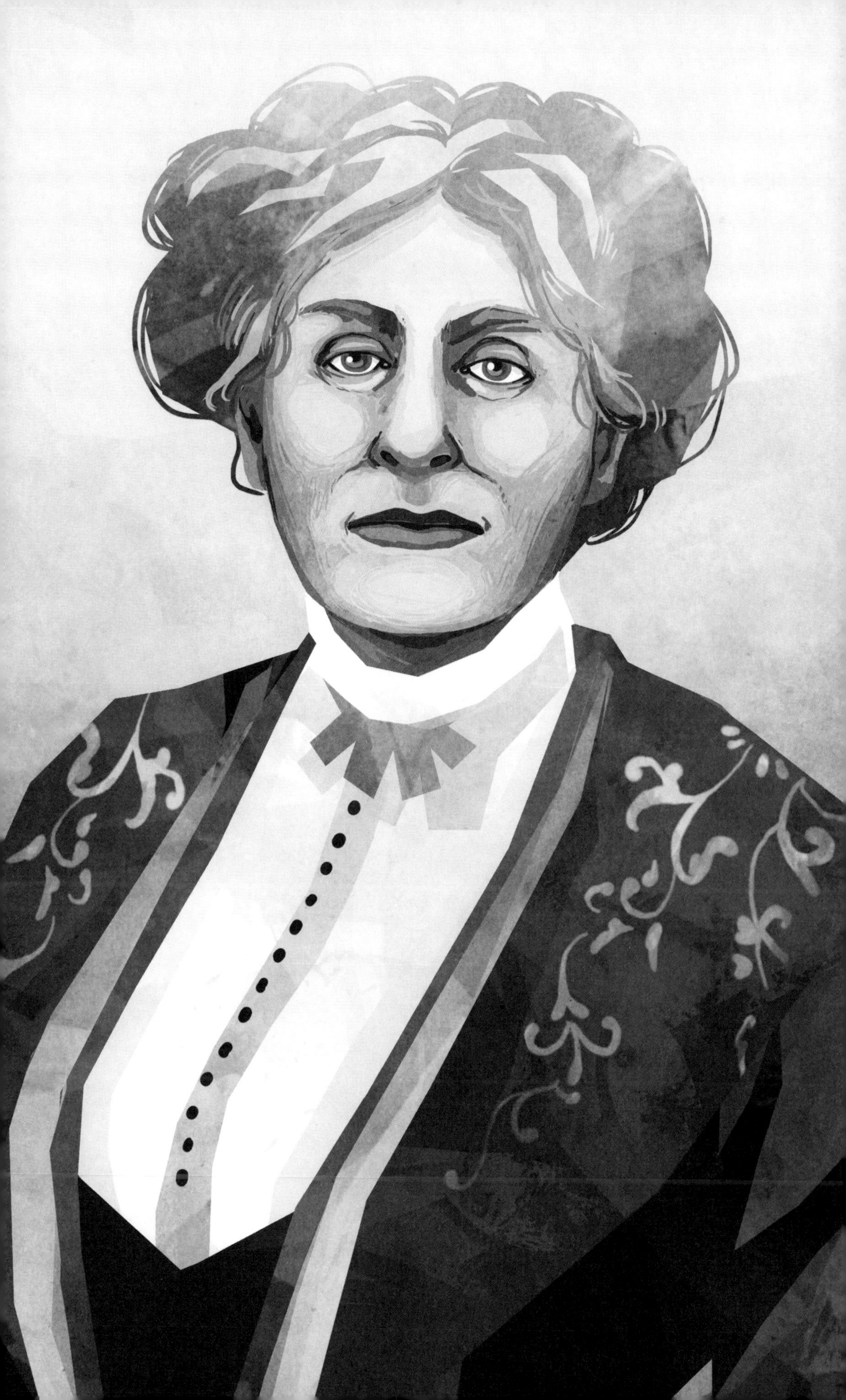

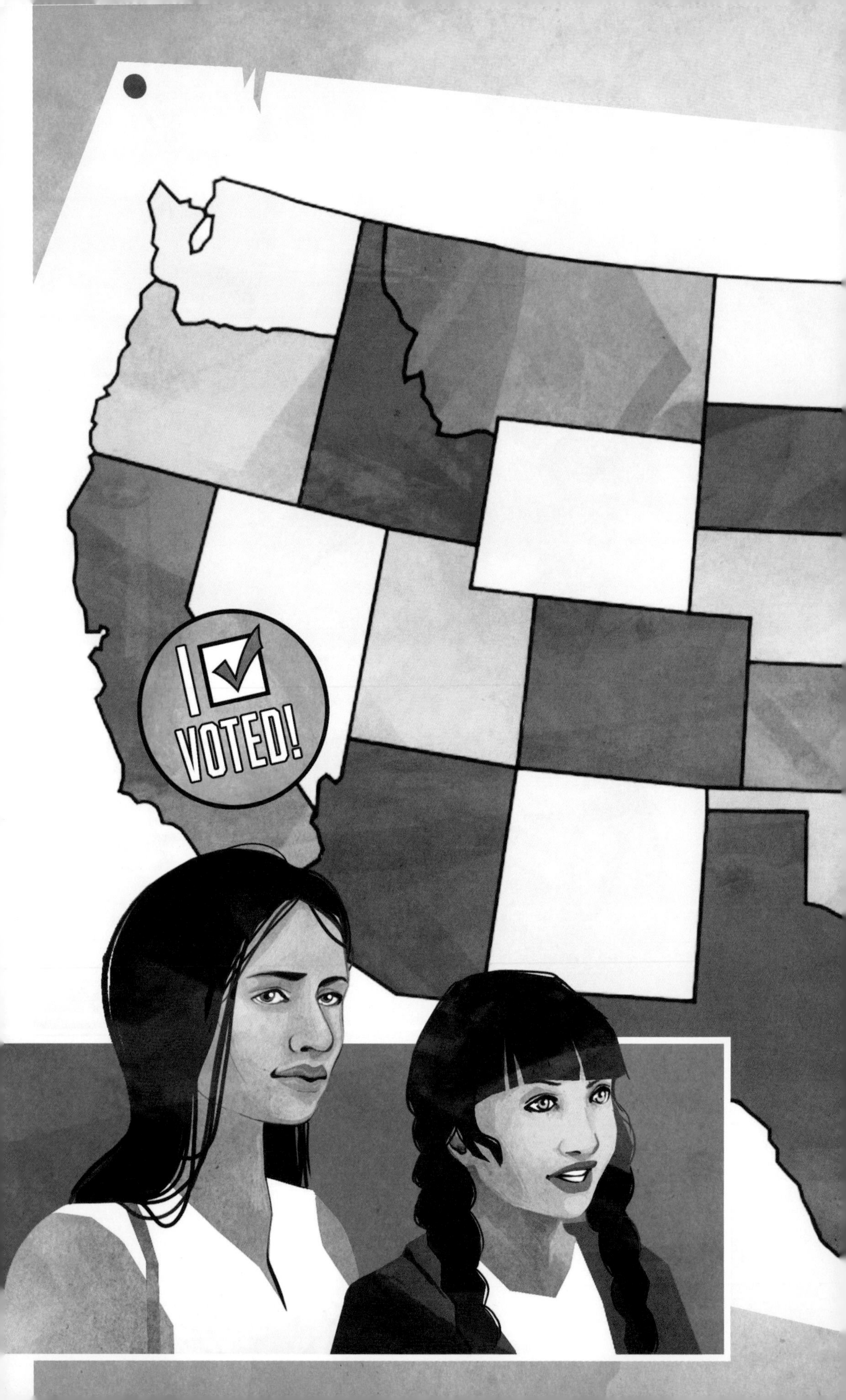
I
VOTED!

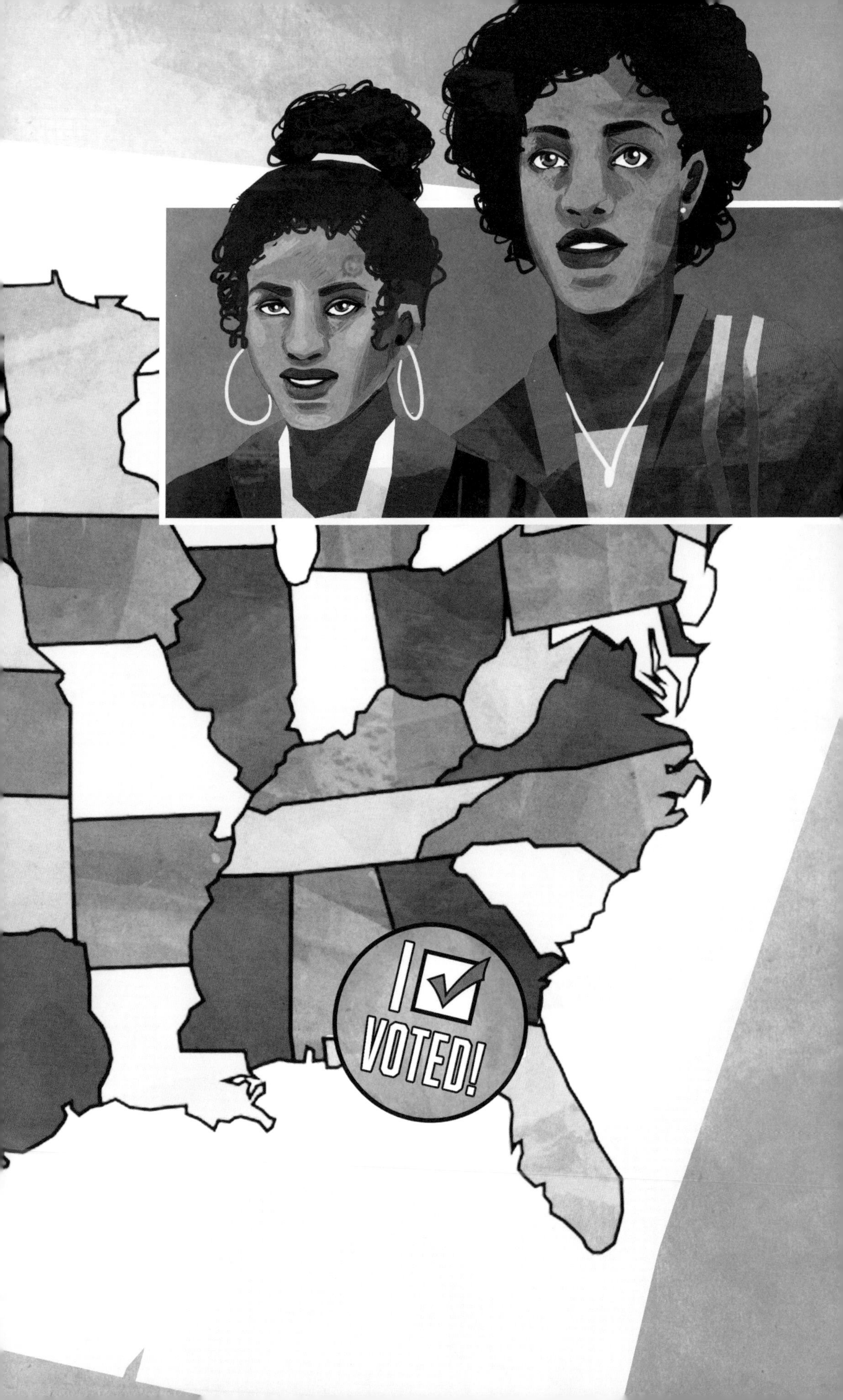

I VOTED!

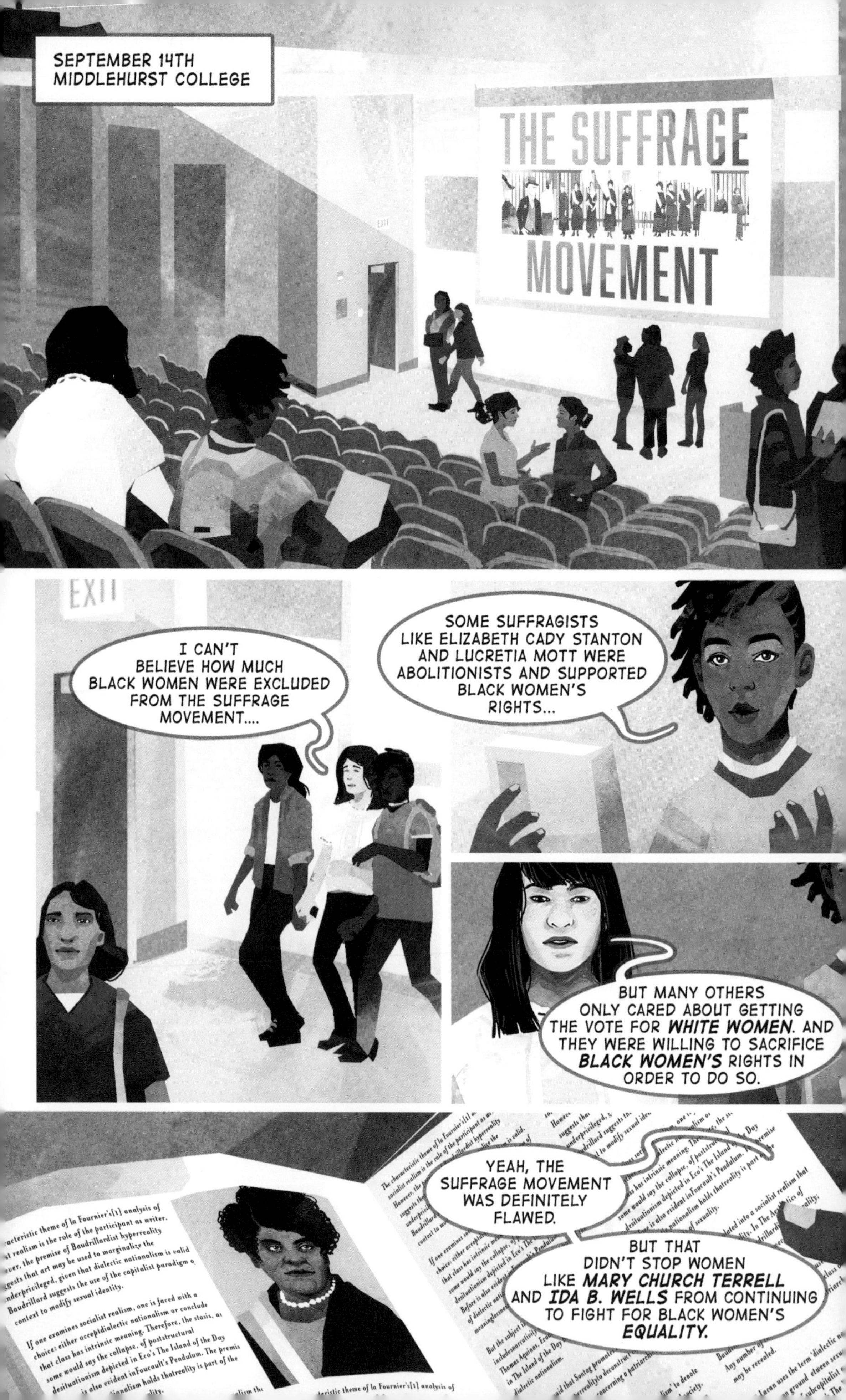
SEPTEMBER 14TH
MIDDLEHURST COLLEGE
THE SUFFRAGE MOVEMENT
EXIT
EXIT
I CAN'T BELIEVE HOW MUCH BLACK WOMEN WERE EXCLUDED FROM THE SUFFRAGE MOVEMENT....
SOME SUFFRAGISTS LIKE ELIZABETH CADY STANTON AND LUCRETIA MOTT WERE ABOLITIONISTS AND SUPPORTED BLACK WOMEN'S RIGHTS...
BUT MANY OTHERS ONLY CARED ABOUT GETTING THE VOTE FOR ***WHITE WOMEN***. AND THEY WERE WILLING TO SACRIFICE ***BLACK WOMEN'S*** RIGHTS IN ORDER TO DO SO.
YEAH, THE SUFFRAGE MOVEMENT WAS DEFINITELY FLAWED.
BUT THAT DIDN'T STOP WOMEN LIKE ***MARY CHURCH TERRELL*** AND ***IDA B. WELLS*** FROM CONTINUING TO FIGHT FOR BLACK WOMEN'S ***EQUALITY.***

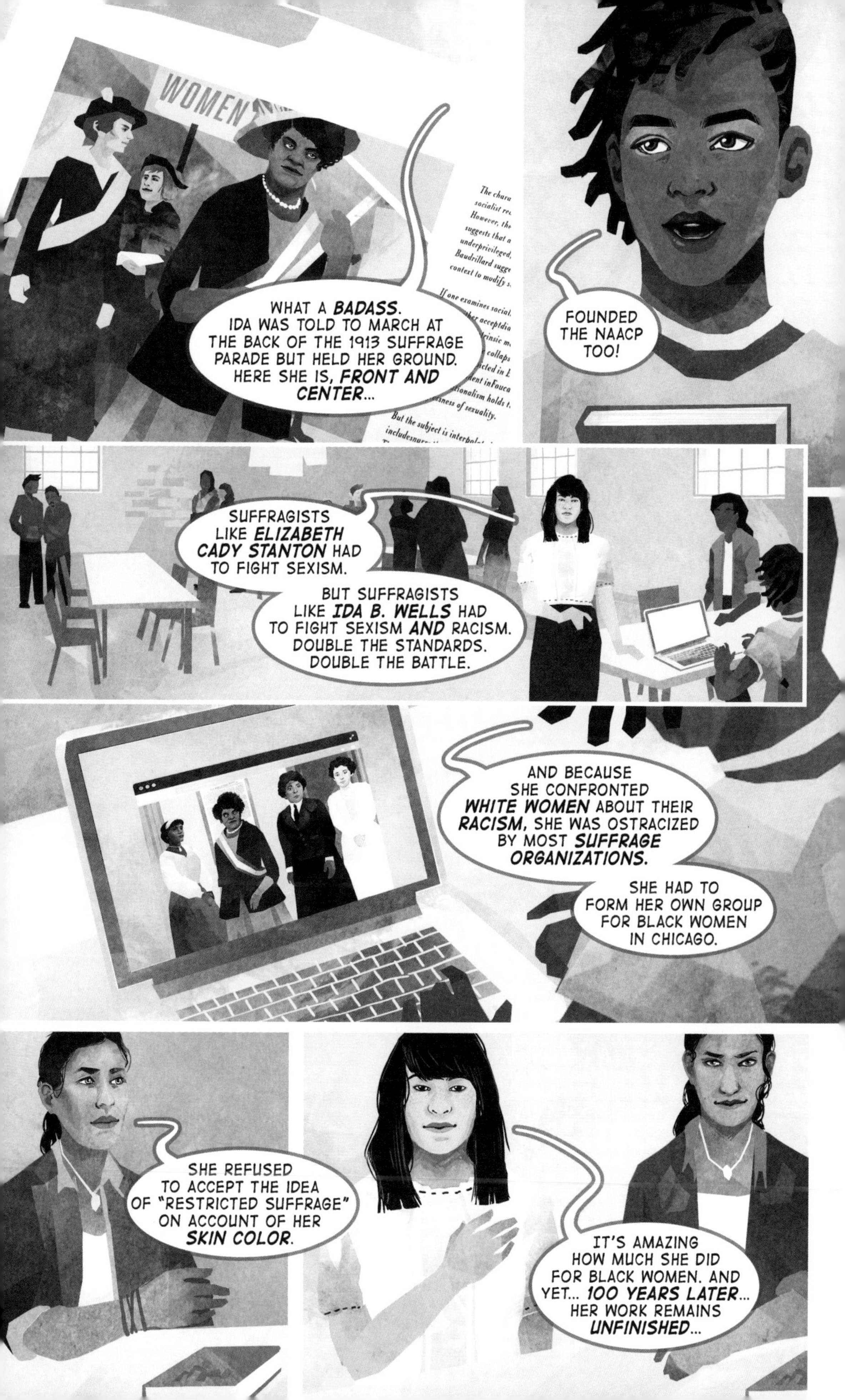
WOMEN
WHAT A BADASS. IDA WAS TOLD TO MARCH AT THE BACK OF THE 1913 SUFFRAGE PARADE BUT HELD HER GROUND. HERE SHE IS, FRONT AND CENTER...
FOUNDED THE NAACP TOO!
SUFFRAGISTS LIKE ELIZABETH CADY STANTON HAD TO FIGHT SEXISM.
BUT SUFFRAGISTS LIKE IDA B. WELLS HAD TO FIGHT SEXISM AND RACISM. DOUBLE THE STANDARDS. DOUBLE THE BATTLE.
AND BECAUSE SHE CONFRONTED WHITE WOMEN ABOUT THEIR RACISM, SHE WAS OSTRACIZED BY MOST SUFFRAGE ORGANIZATIONS.
SHE HAD TO FORM HER OWN GROUP FOR BLACK WOMEN IN CHICAGO.
SHE REFUSED TO ACCEPT THE IDEA OF "RESTRICTED SUFFRAGE" ON ACCOUNT OF HER SKIN COLOR.
IT'S AMAZING HOW MUCH SHE DID FOR BLACK WOMEN. AND YET... 100 YEARS LATER... HER WORK REMAINS UNFINISHED...

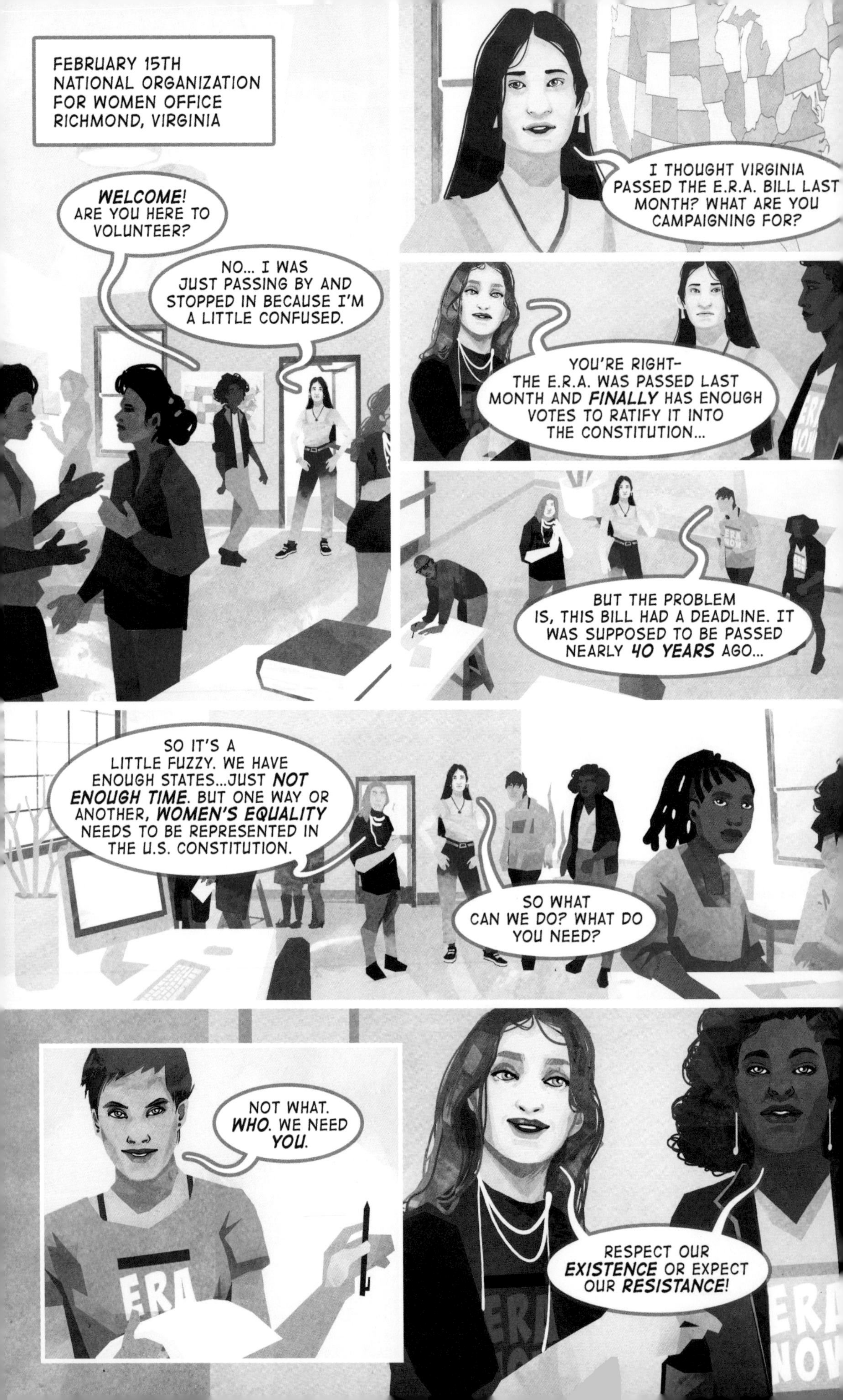
FEBRUARY 15TH NATIONAL ORGANIZATION FOR WOMEN OFFICE RICHMOND, VIRGINIA
WELCOME! ARE YOU HERE TO VOLUNTEER?
NO... I WAS JUST PASSING BY AND STOPPED IN BECAUSE I'M A LITTLE CONFUSED.
I THOUGHT VIRGINIA PASSED THE E.R.A. BILL LAST MONTH? WHAT ARE YOU CAMPAIGNING FOR?
YOU'RE RIGHT- THE E.R.A. WAS PASSED LAST MONTH AND FINALLY HAS ENOUGH VOTES TO RATIFY IT INTO THE CONSTITUTION...
ERA NOW
BUT THE PROBLEM IS, THIS BILL HAD A DEADLINE. IT WAS SUPPOSED TO BE PASSED NEARLY 40 YEARS AGO...
SO IT'S A LITTLE FUZZY. WE HAVE ENOUGH STATES...JUST NOT ENOUGH TIME. BUT ONE WAY OR ANOTHER, WOMEN'S EQUALITY NEEDS TO BE REPRESENTED IN THE U.S. CONSTITUTION.
SO WHAT CAN WE DO? WHAT DO YOU NEED?
NOT WHAT. WHO. WE NEED YOU.
ERA
RESPECT OUR EXISTENCE OR EXPECT OUR RESISTANCE!
ERA NOW

OCTOBER 20TH
WASHINGTON, D.C.

LOOKS LIKE WE GOT HERE JUST IN TIME.

SAYS THEY'RE ARRESTING PEOPLE.

ARRESTING WOMEN FOR *PEACEFUL PROTEST*? JUST LIKE IN 1920.

CROWDING, OBSTRUCTING... THEY WILL COME UP WITH *ANY CHARGE* TO GET US OFF THE STREETS.

SUFFRAGISTS WERE ARRESTED FOR THE SAME THING ALMOST A *CENTURY AGO*. THIS IS *EXACTLY* WHY WE NEED TO BE PROTESTING.

RESPEC
EXIST
OR EXPEC
RESIST

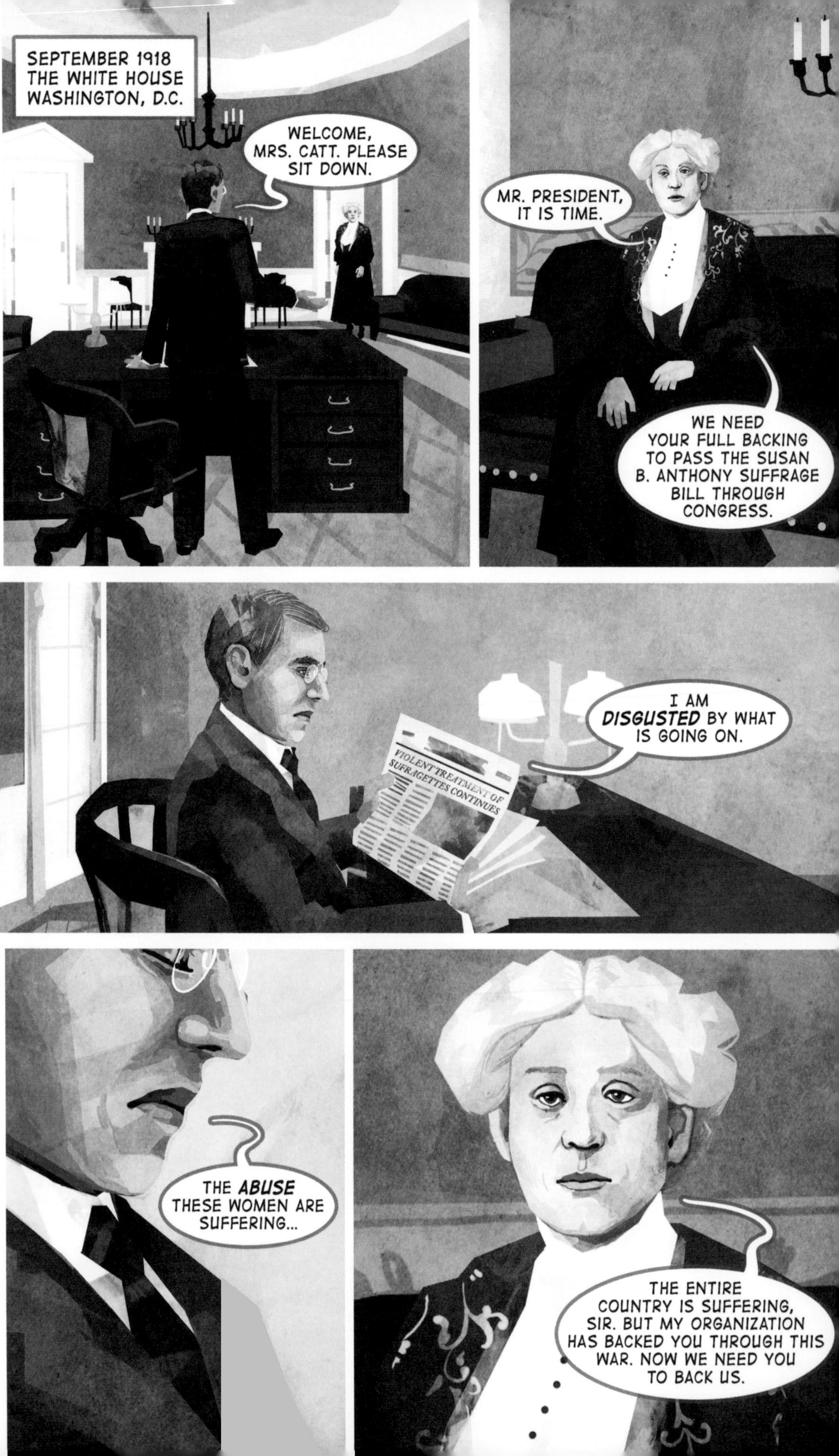
SEPTEMBER 1918
THE WHITE HOUSE
WASHINGTON, D.C.
WELCOME, MRS. CATT. PLEASE SIT DOWN.
MR. PRESIDENT, IT IS TIME.
WE NEED YOUR FULL BACKING TO PASS THE SUSAN B. ANTHONY SUFFRAGE BILL THROUGH CONGRESS.
VIOLENT TREATMENT OF SUFRAGETTES CONTINUES
I AM ***DISGUSTED*** BY WHAT IS GOING ON.
THE ***ABUSE*** THESE WOMEN ARE SUFFERING...
THE ENTIRE COUNTRY IS SUFFERING, SIR. BUT MY ORGANIZATION HAS BACKED YOU THROUGH THIS WAR. NOW WE NEED YOU TO BACK US.

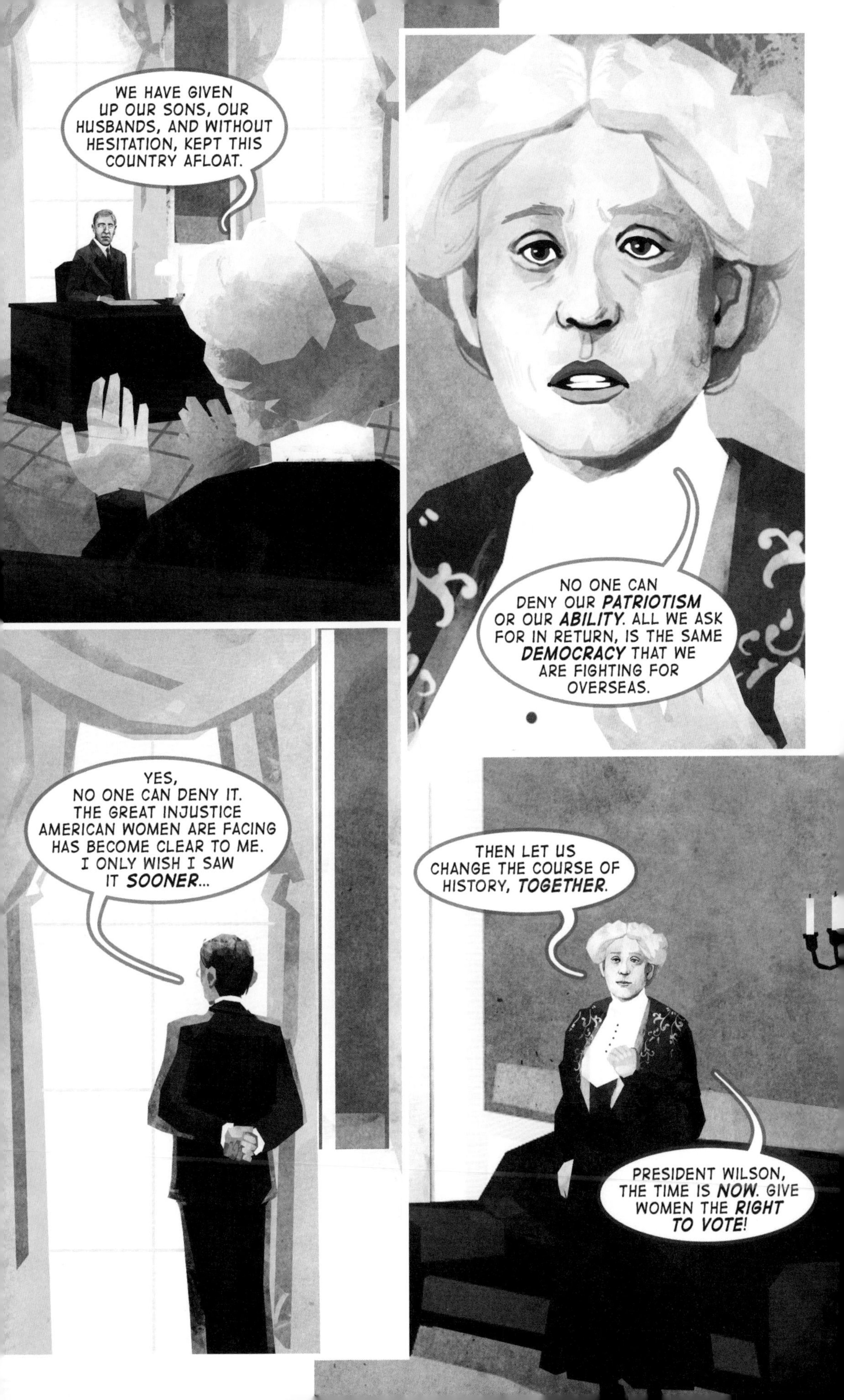
WE HAVE GIVEN UP OUR SONS, OUR HUSBANDS, AND WITHOUT HESITATION, KEPT THIS COUNTRY AFLOAT.
NO ONE CAN DENY OUR ***PATRIOTISM*** OR OUR ***ABILITY***. ALL WE ASK FOR IN RETURN, IS THE SAME ***DEMOCRACY*** THAT WE ARE FIGHTING FOR OVERSEAS.
YES, NO ONE CAN DENY IT. THE GREAT INJUSTICE AMERICAN WOMEN ARE FACING HAS BECOME CLEAR TO ME. I ONLY WISH I SAW IT ***SOONER***...
THEN LET US CHANGE THE COURSE OF HISTORY, ***TOGETHER***.
PRESIDENT WILSON, THE TIME IS ***NOW***. GIVE WOMEN THE ***RIGHT TO VOTE***!

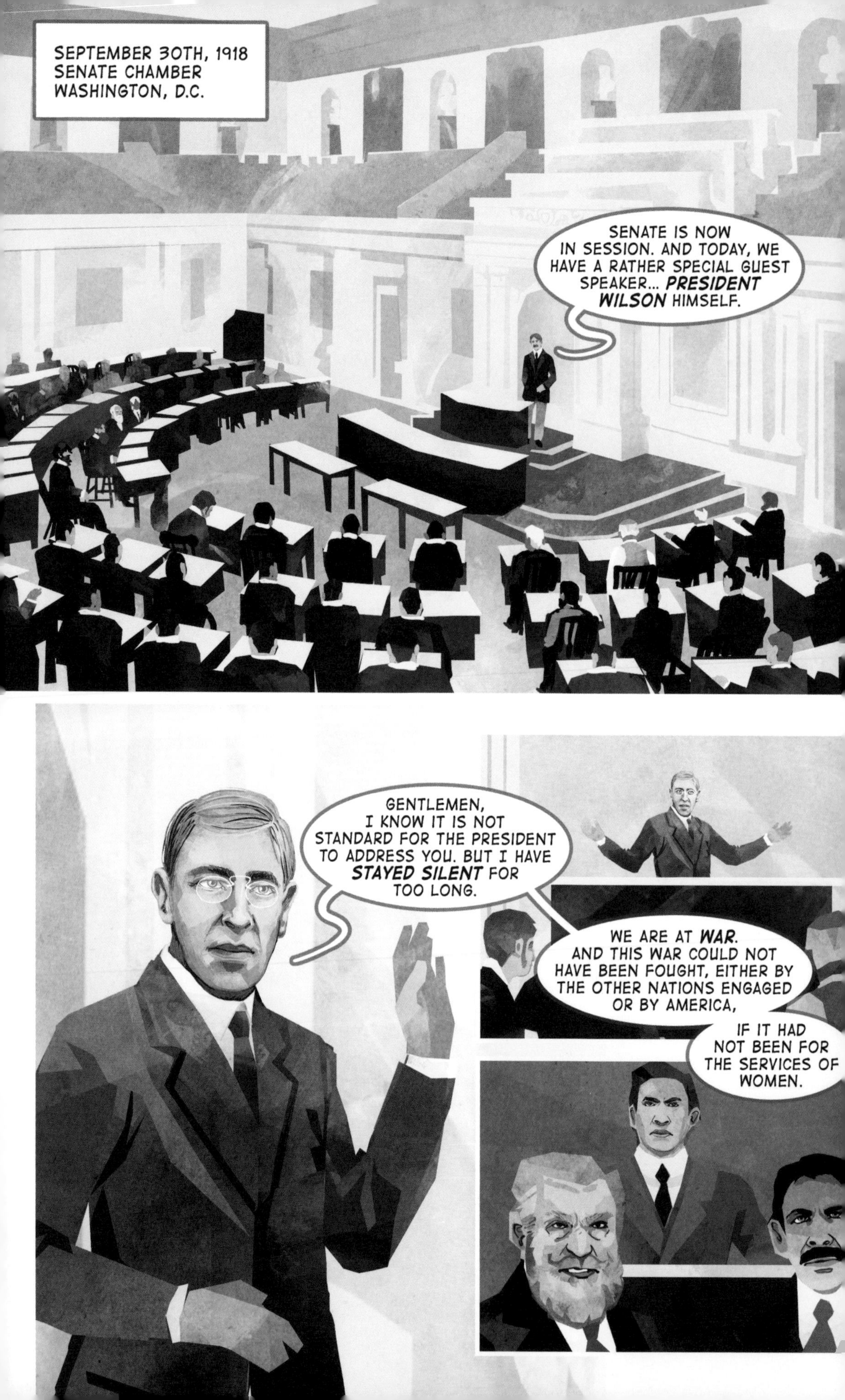

SEPTEMBER 30TH, 1918
SENATE CHAMBER
WASHINGTON, D.C.
SENATE IS NOW IN SESSION. AND TODAY, WE HAVE A RATHER SPECIAL GUEST SPEAKER... PRESIDENT WILSON HIMSELF.
GENTLEMEN, I KNOW IT IS NOT STANDARD FOR THE PRESIDENT TO ADDRESS YOU. BUT I HAVE STAYED SILENT FOR TOO LONG.
WE ARE AT WAR. AND THIS WAR COULD NOT HAVE BEEN FOUGHT, EITHER BY THE OTHER NATIONS ENGAGED OR BY AMERICA,
IF IT HAD NOT BEEN FOR THE SERVICES OF WOMEN.

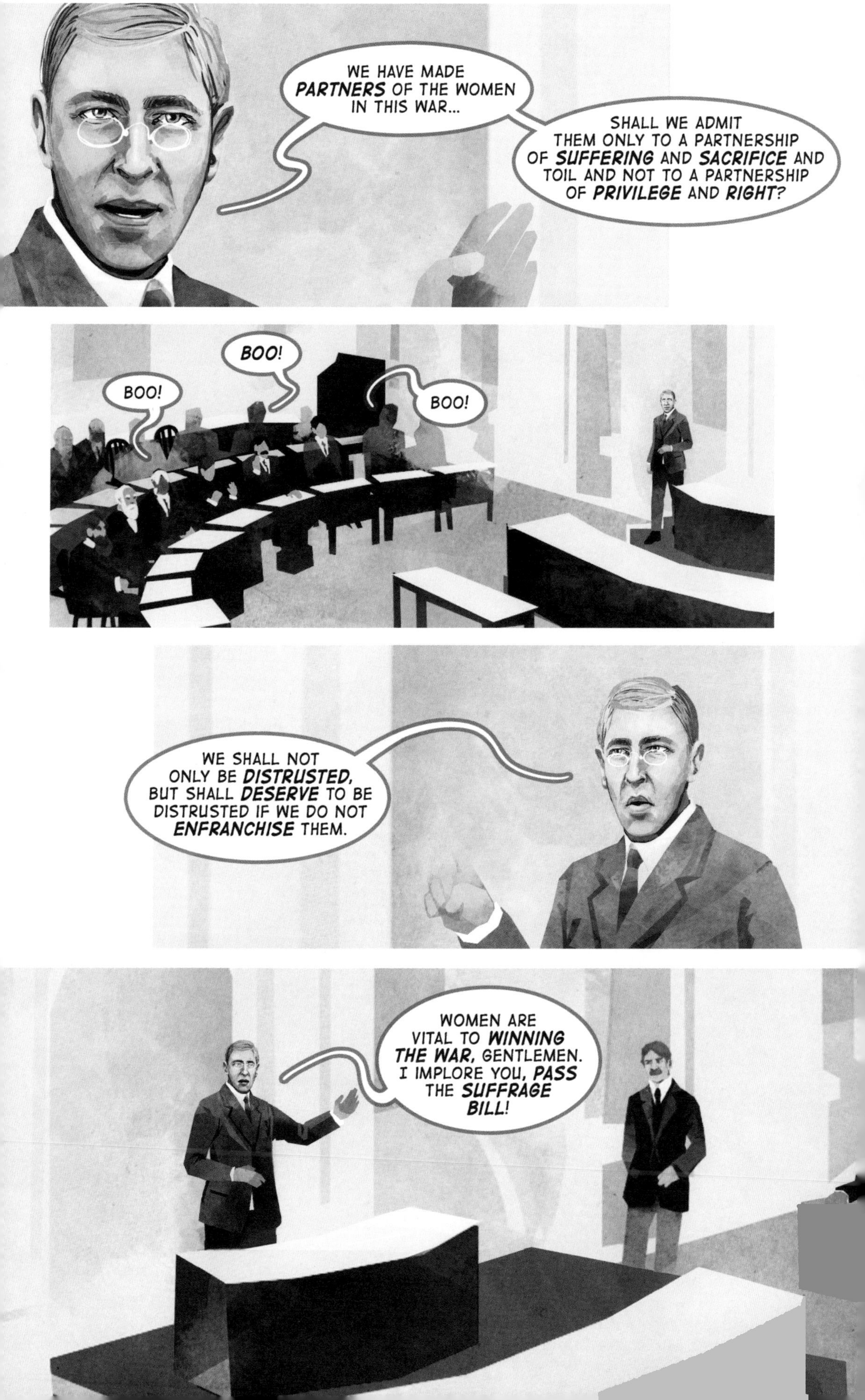
WE HAVE MADE PARTNERS OF THE WOMEN IN THIS WAR...
SHALL WE ADMIT THEM ONLY TO A PARTNERSHIP OF SUFFERING AND SACRIFICE AND TOIL AND NOT TO A PARTNERSHIP OF PRIVILEGE AND RIGHT?
BOO!
BOO!
BOO!
WE SHALL NOT ONLY BE DISTRUSTED, BUT SHALL DESERVE TO BE DISTRUSTED IF WE DO NOT ENFRANCHISE THEM.
WOMEN ARE VITAL TO WINNING THE WAR, GENTLEMEN. I IMPLORE YOU, PASS THE SUFFRAGE BILL!

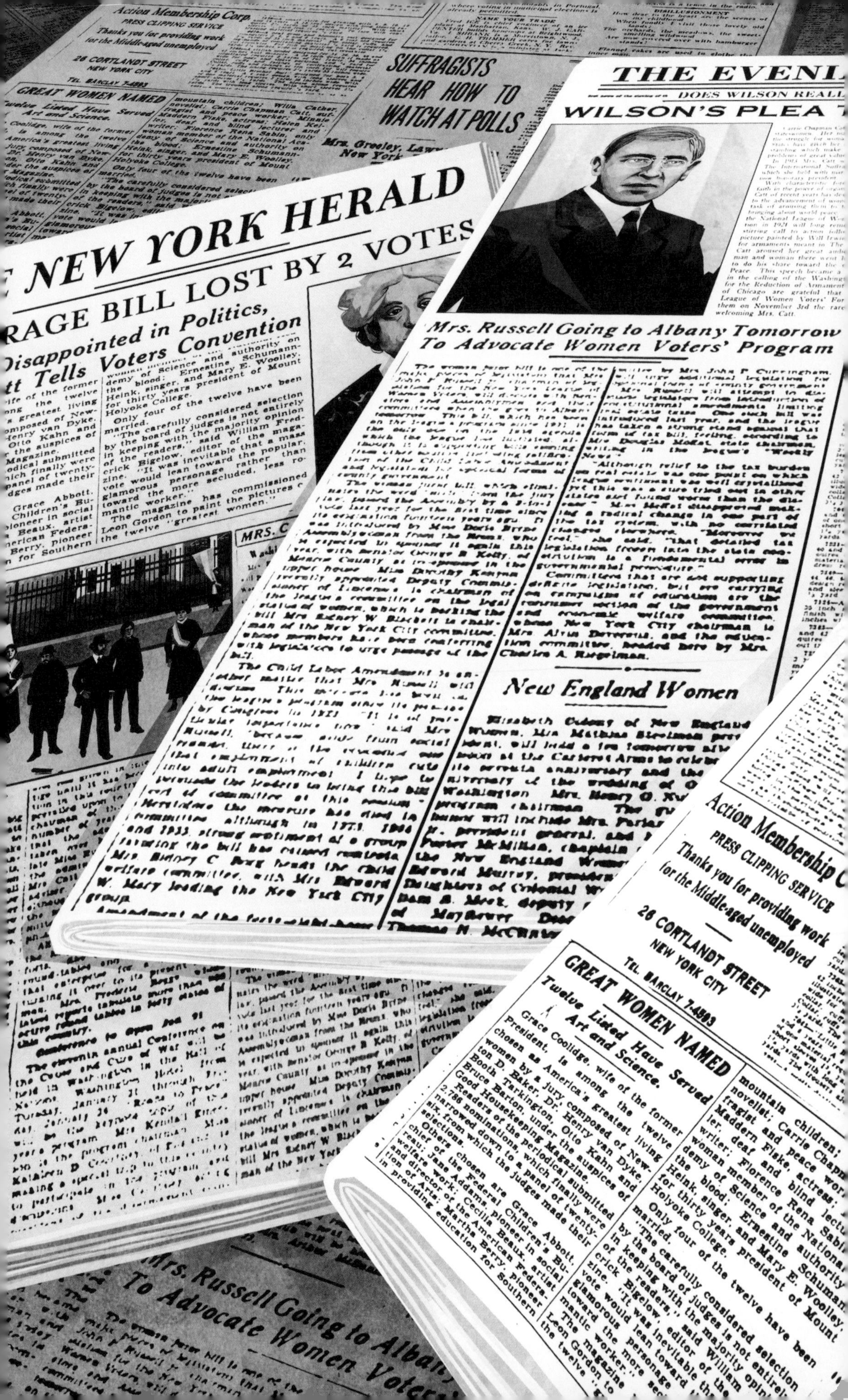
Action Membership Corp.
PRESS CLIPPING SERVICE
Thanks you for providing work for the Middle-aged unemployed
26 CORTLANDT STREET
NEW YORK CITY
TEL. BARCLAY 7-4993
GREAT WOMEN NAMED
Twelve Listed Have Served Art and Science.
SUFFRAGISTS HEAR HOW TO WATCH AT POLLS
THE EVENI
DOES WILSON REALL
WILSON'S PLEA T
NEW YORK HERALD
RAGE BILL LOST BY 2 VOTES
Disappointed in Politics,
tt Tells Voters Convention
Mrs. Russell Going to Albany Tomorrow
To Advocate Women Voters' Program
New England Women
Grace Coolidge, wife of the former President, is among the twelve chosen as America's greatest living women by a jury, composed of Newton D. Baker, Dr. Henry van Dyke, Booth Tarkington, Otto Kahn and Bruce Barton, under the auspices of Good Housekeeping Magazine.
2,786 nominations, which finally were narrowed down to a panel of twenty-six, from which the judges made their selections.
Others chosen are Grace Abbott, chief of the Federal Children's Bureau; Jane Addams, pioneer in social welfare work; Cecilia Beaux, artist and director of the American Federation of Arts; Martha Berry, pioneer in providing education for Southern mountain children; Willa Cather, novelist; Carrie Chapman Catt, suffragist and peace worker; Minnie Maddern Fiske, actress; Helen Keller, deaf and blind lecturer and writer; Florence Rena Sabin, only woman member of the National Academy of Science and authority on the blood; Ernestine Schumann-Heink, singer, and Mary E. Woolley, for thirty years president of Mount Holyoke College.
Only four of the twelve have been married.
"The carefully considered selection by the board of judges is not entirely in keeping with the majority opinion of the readers," said William Frederick Bigelow, editor of the magazine. "It was inevitable that a mass vote would lean toward the popular, glamorous personage rather than toward the more secluded, less romantic worker."
The magazine has commissioned Leon Gordon to paint the pictures of the twelve "greatest women."

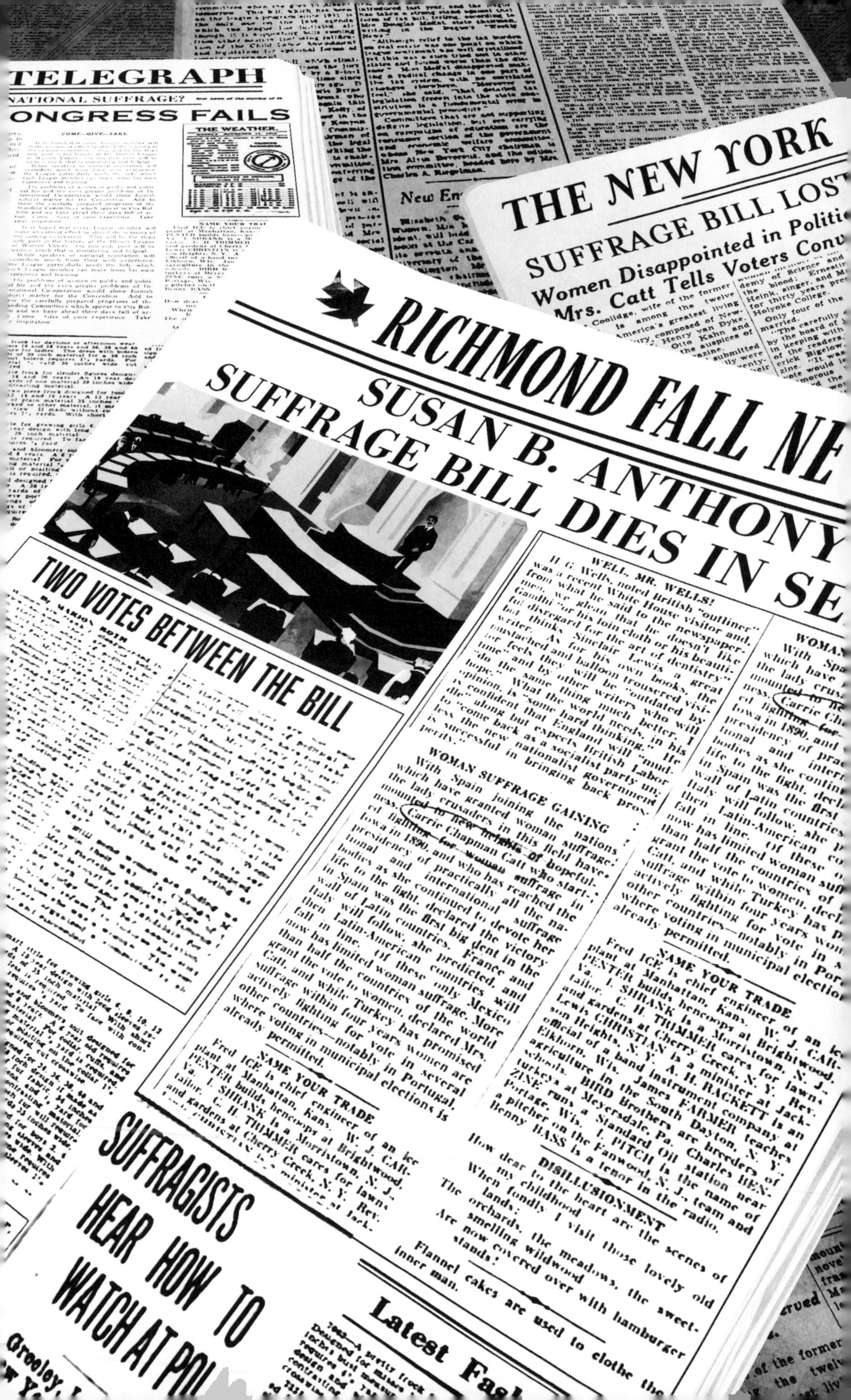

TELEGRAPH
NATIONAL SUFFRAGE?
ONGRESS FAILS
THE NEW YORK
SUFFRAGE BILL LOST
RICHMOND FALL NE
SUSAN B. ANTHONY
SUFFRAGE BILL DIES IN SE
TWO VOTES BETWEEN THE BILL
WELL, MR. WELLS!
WOMAN SUFFRAGE GAINING
NAME YOUR TRADE
DISILLUSIONMENT
SUFFRAGISTS HEAR HOW TO WATCH AT POL
Latest Fas

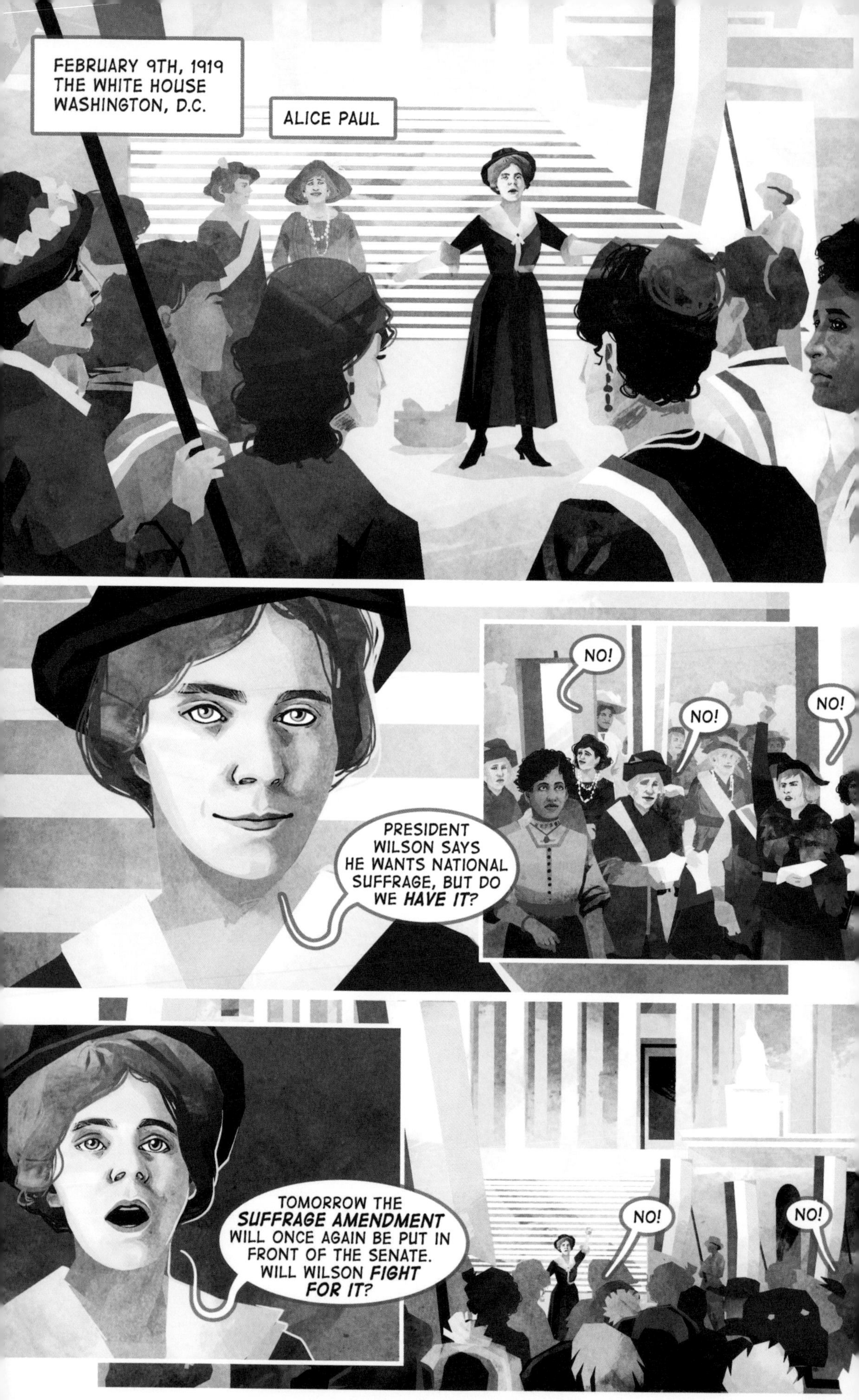
FEBRUARY 9TH, 1919
THE WHITE HOUSE
WASHINGTON, D.C.
ALICE PAUL
PRESIDENT WILSON SAYS HE WANTS NATIONAL SUFFRAGE, BUT DO WE HAVE IT?
NO!
NO!
NO!
TOMORROW THE SUFFRAGE AMENDMENT WILL ONCE AGAIN BE PUT IN FRONT OF THE SENATE. WILL WILSON FIGHT FOR IT?
NO!
NO!

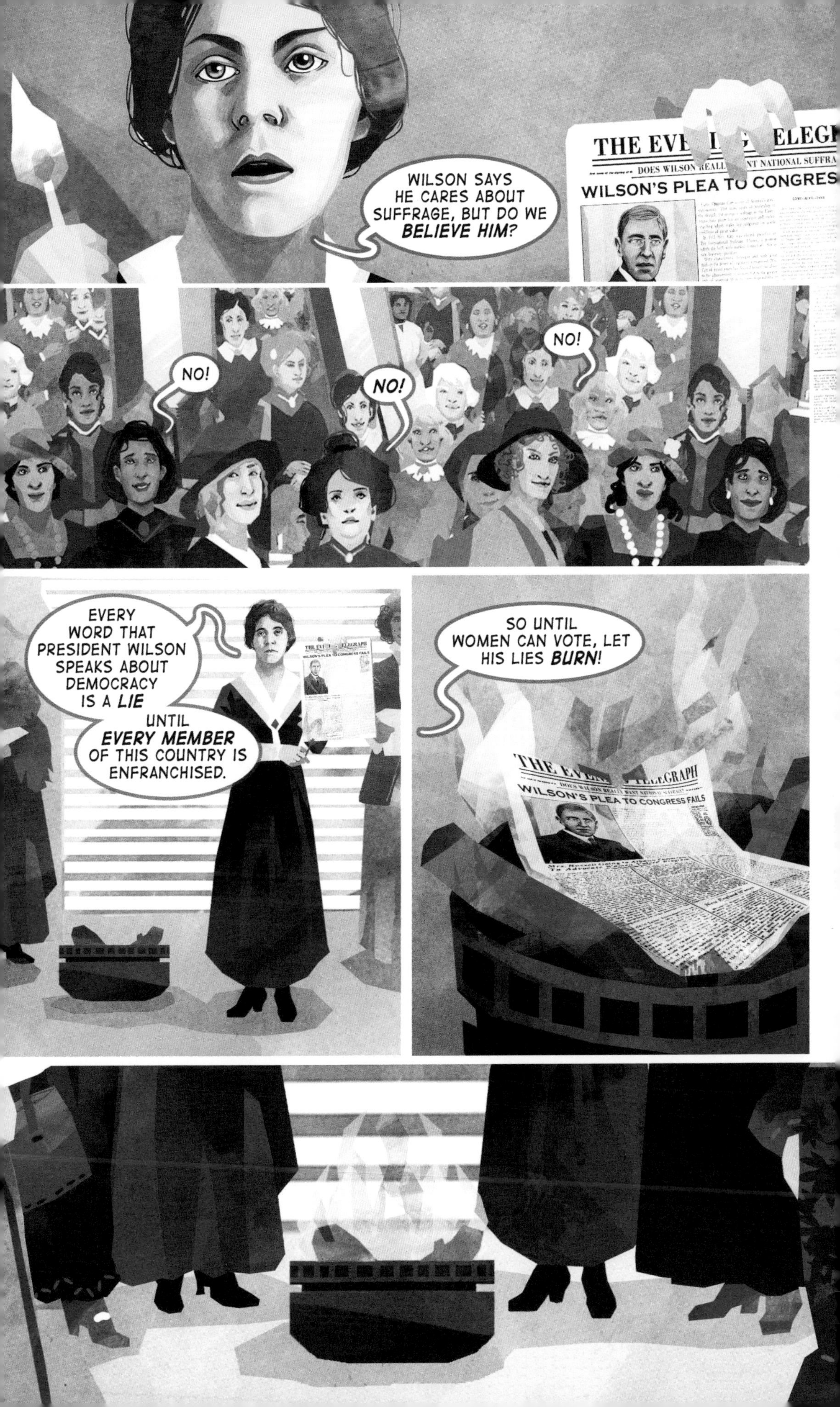
WILSON SAYS HE CARES ABOUT SUFFRAGE, BUT DO WE *BELIEVE HIM*?
THE EVENING TELEGRAPH
WILSON'S PLEA TO CONGRESS FAILS
NO!
NO!
NO!
EVERY WORD THAT PRESIDENT WILSON SPEAKS ABOUT DEMOCRACY IS A *LIE*
UNTIL *EVERY MEMBER* OF THIS COUNTRY IS ENFRANCHISED.
SO UNTIL WOMEN CAN VOTE, LET HIS LIES *BURN*!

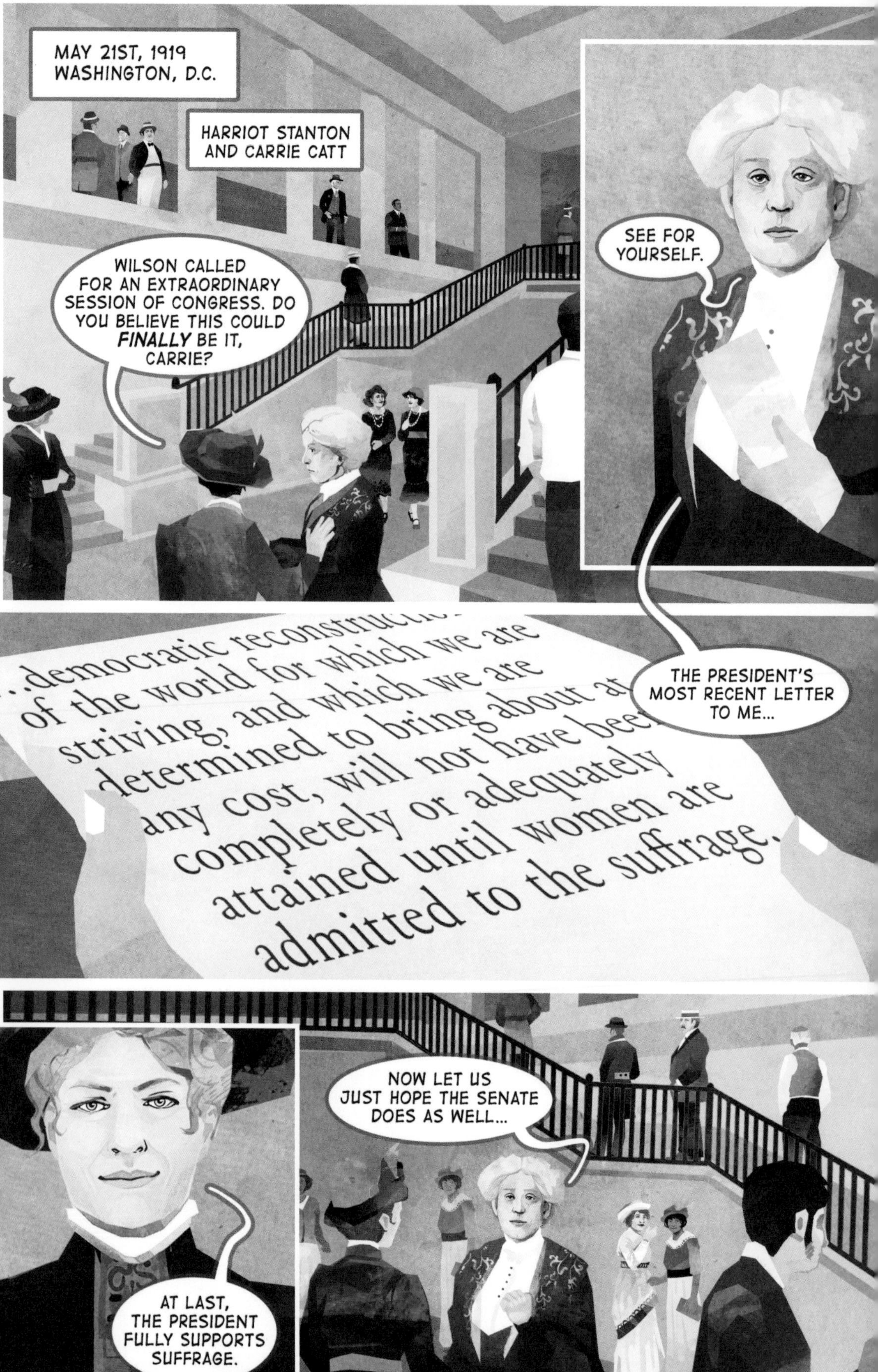
MAY 21ST, 1919
WASHINGTON, D.C.
HARRIOT STANTON AND CARRIE CATT
WILSON CALLED FOR AN EXTRAORDINARY SESSION OF CONGRESS. DO YOU BELIEVE THIS COULD *FINALLY* BE IT, CARRIE?
SEE FOR YOURSELF.
THE PRESIDENT'S MOST RECENT LETTER TO ME...
...democratic reconstructio[n] of the world for which we are striving, and which we are determined to bring about at any cost, will not have bee[n] completely or adequately attained until women are admitted to the suffrage.
AT LAST, THE PRESIDENT FULLY SUPPORTS SUFFRAGE.
NOW LET US JUST HOPE THE SENATE DOES AS WELL...

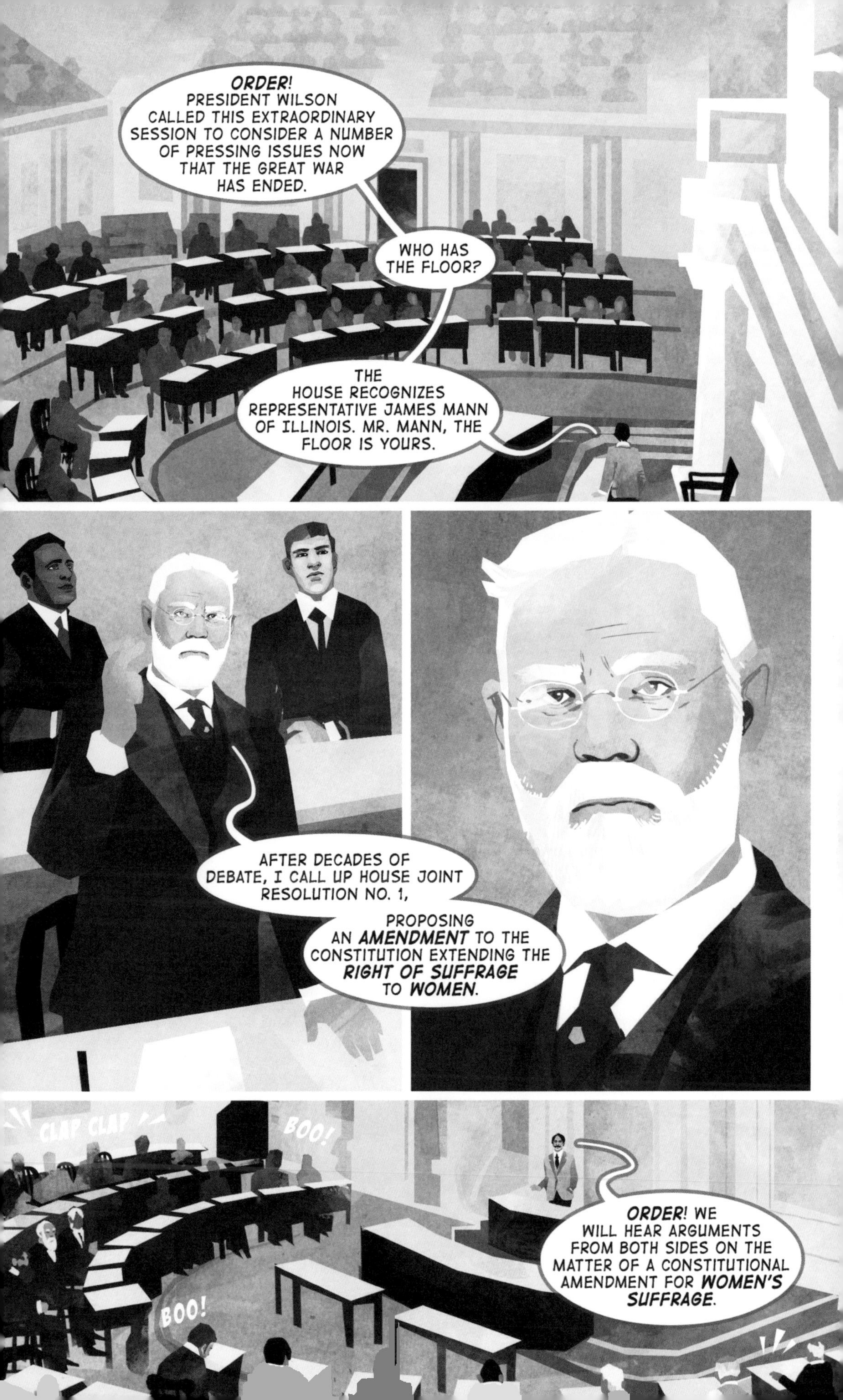
ORDER! PRESIDENT WILSON CALLED THIS EXTRAORDINARY SESSION TO CONSIDER A NUMBER OF PRESSING ISSUES NOW THAT THE GREAT WAR HAS ENDED.
WHO HAS THE FLOOR?
THE HOUSE RECOGNIZES REPRESENTATIVE JAMES MANN OF ILLINOIS. MR. MANN, THE FLOOR IS YOURS.
AFTER DECADES OF DEBATE, I CALL UP HOUSE JOINT RESOLUTION NO. 1,
PROPOSING AN AMENDMENT TO THE CONSTITUTION EXTENDING THE RIGHT OF SUFFRAGE TO WOMEN.
CLAP CLAP
BOO!
BOO!
ORDER! WE WILL HEAR ARGUMENTS FROM BOTH SIDES ON THE MATTER OF A CONSTITUTIONAL AMENDMENT FOR WOMEN'S SUFFRAGE.

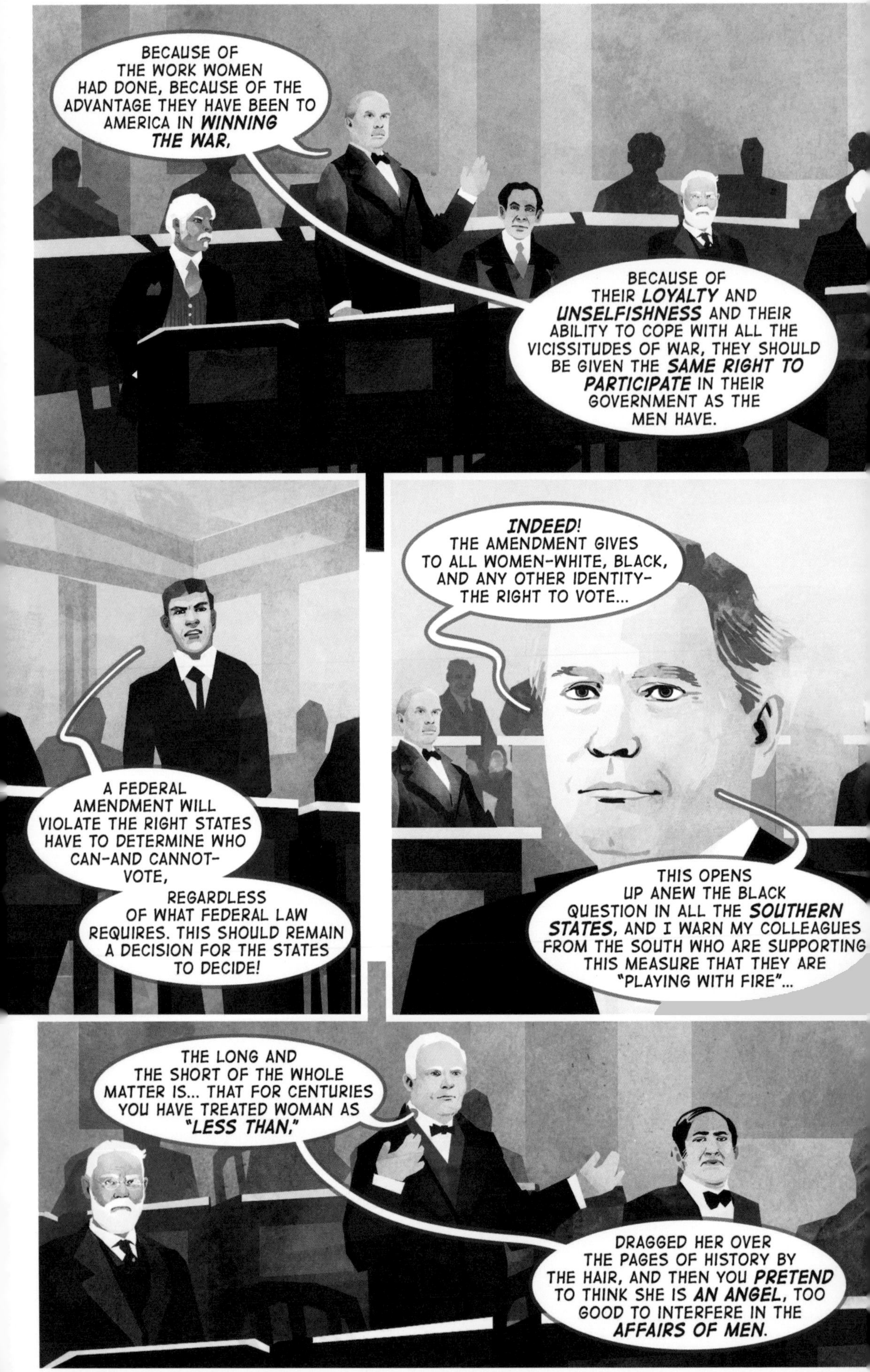
BECAUSE OF THE WORK WOMEN HAD DONE, BECAUSE OF THE ADVANTAGE THEY HAVE BEEN TO AMERICA IN *WINNING THE WAR*,
BECAUSE OF THEIR *LOYALTY* AND *UNSELFISHNESS* AND THEIR ABILITY TO COPE WITH ALL THE VICISSITUDES OF WAR, THEY SHOULD BE GIVEN THE *SAME RIGHT TO PARTICIPATE* IN THEIR GOVERNMENT AS THE MEN HAVE.
A FEDERAL AMENDMENT WILL VIOLATE THE RIGHT STATES HAVE TO DETERMINE WHO CAN-AND CANNOT-VOTE,
REGARDLESS OF WHAT FEDERAL LAW REQUIRES. THIS SHOULD REMAIN A DECISION FOR THE STATES TO DECIDE!
*INDEED*! THE AMENDMENT GIVES TO ALL WOMEN-WHITE, BLACK, AND ANY OTHER IDENTITY- THE RIGHT TO VOTE...
THIS OPENS UP ANEW THE BLACK QUESTION IN ALL THE *SOUTHERN STATES*, AND I WARN MY COLLEAGUES FROM THE SOUTH WHO ARE SUPPORTING THIS MEASURE THAT THEY ARE "PLAYING WITH FIRE"...
THE LONG AND THE SHORT OF THE WHOLE MATTER IS... THAT FOR CENTURIES YOU HAVE TREATED WOMAN AS *"LESS THAN,"*
DRAGGED HER OVER THE PAGES OF HISTORY BY THE HAIR, AND THEN YOU *PRETEND* TO THINK SHE IS *AN ANGEL*, TOO GOOD TO INTERFERE IN THE *AFFAIRS OF MEN*.

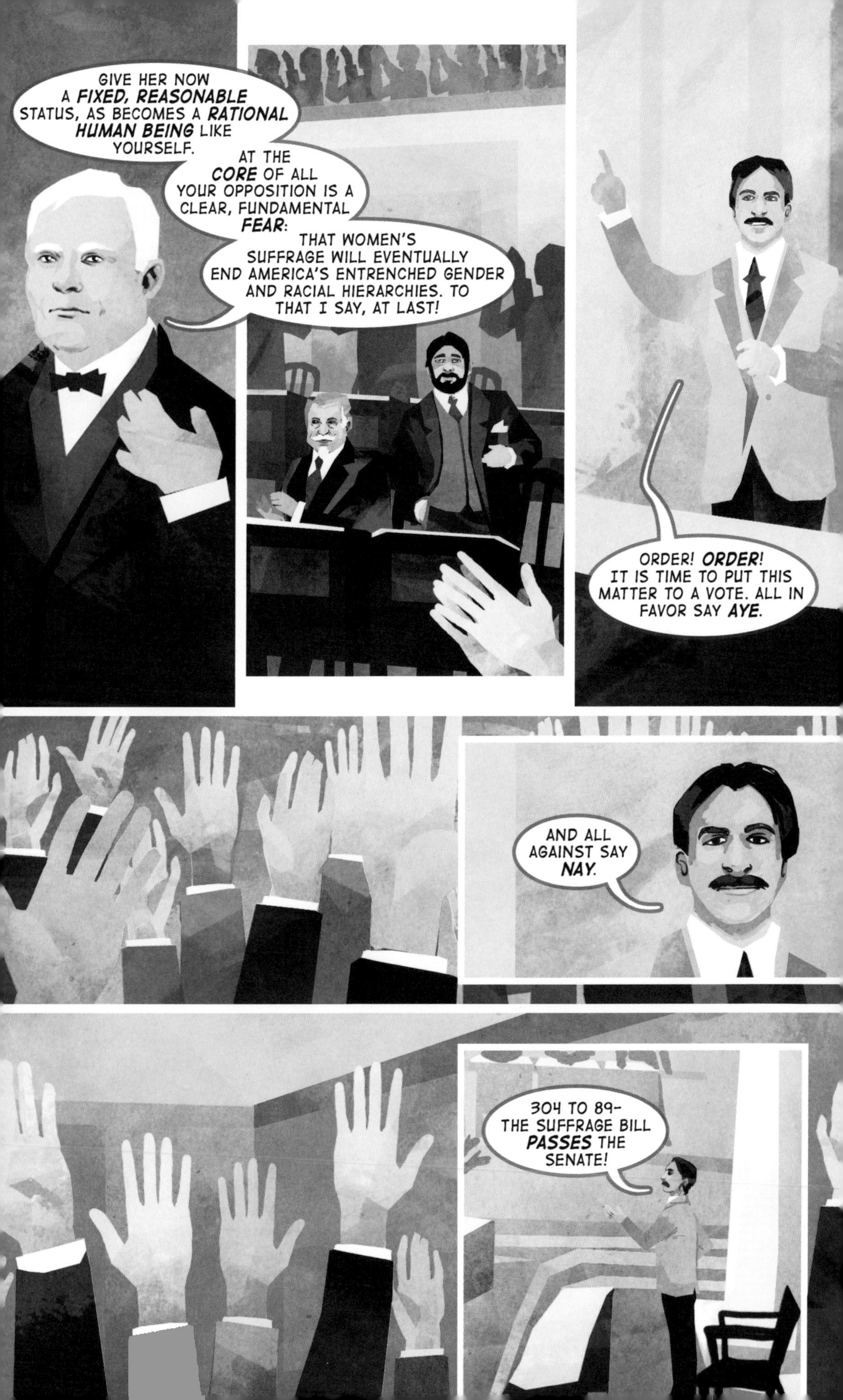
GIVE HER NOW A FIXED, REASONABLE STATUS, AS BECOMES A RATIONAL HUMAN BEING LIKE YOURSELF.
AT THE CORE OF ALL YOUR OPPOSITION IS A CLEAR, FUNDAMENTAL FEAR:
THAT WOMEN'S SUFFRAGE WILL EVENTUALLY END AMERICA'S ENTRENCHED GENDER AND RACIAL HIERARCHIES. TO THAT I SAY, AT LAST!
ORDER! ORDER! IT IS TIME TO PUT THIS MATTER TO A VOTE. ALL IN FAVOR SAY AYE.
AND ALL AGAINST SAY NAY.
304 TO 89– THE SUFFRAGE BILL PASSES THE SENATE!

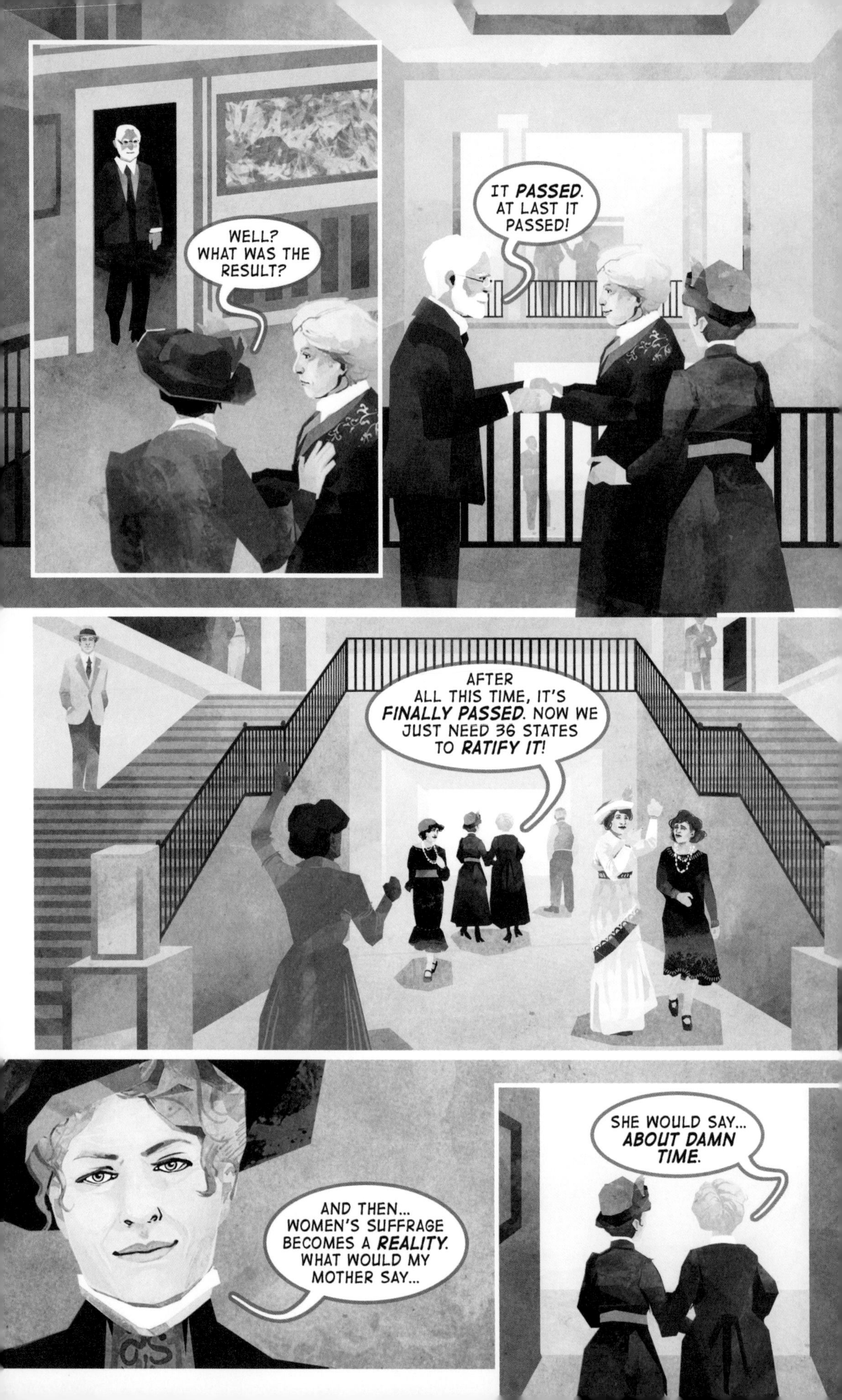
WELL? WHAT WAS THE RESULT?
IT PASSED. AT LAST IT PASSED!
AFTER ALL THIS TIME, IT'S FINALLY PASSED. NOW WE JUST NEED 36 STATES TO RATIFY IT!
AND THEN... WOMEN'S SUFFRAGE BECOMES A REALITY. WHAT WOULD MY MOTHER SAY...
SHE WOULD SAY... ABOUT DAMN TIME.

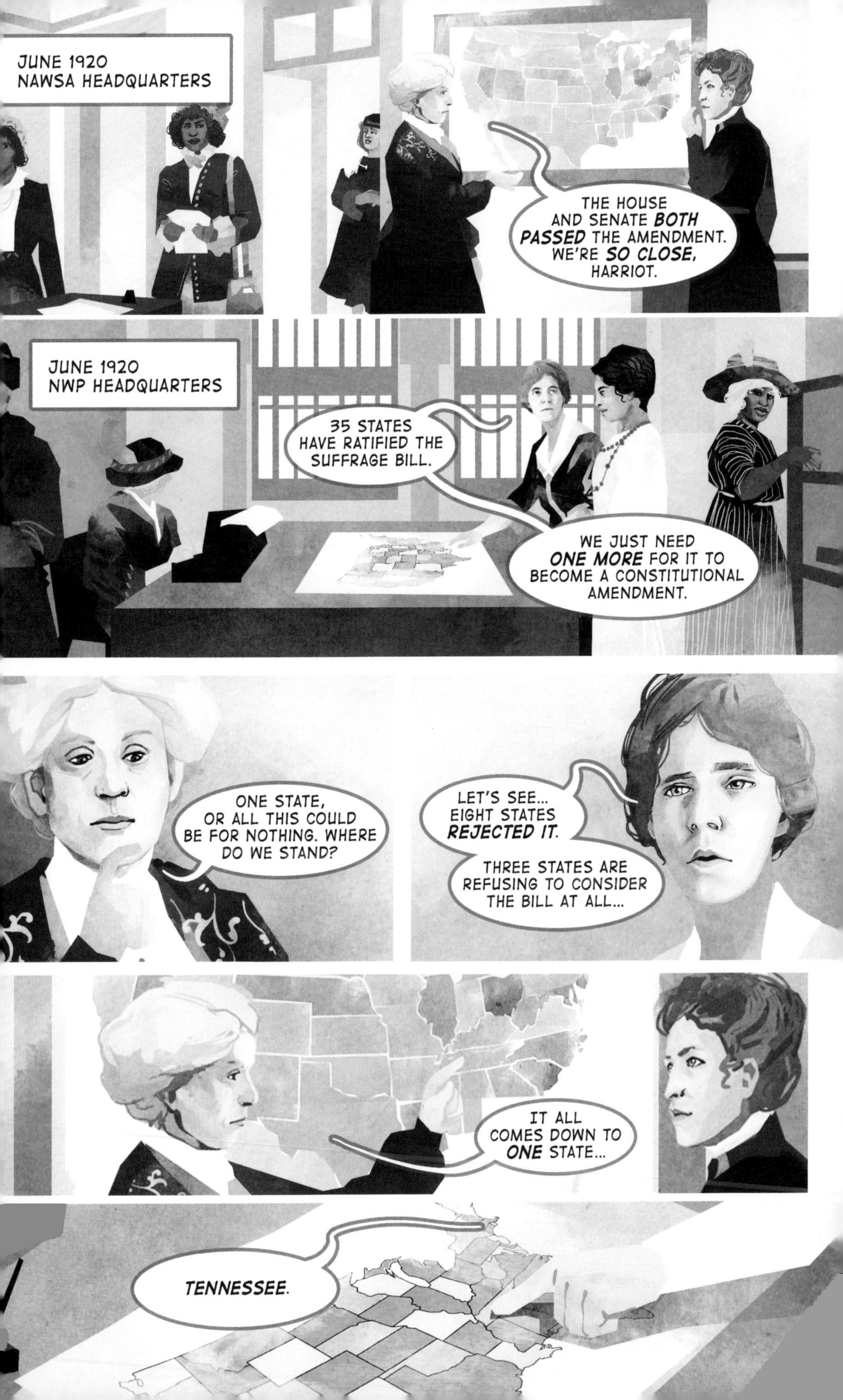
JUNE 1920
NAWSA HEADQUARTERS
THE HOUSE AND SENATE BOTH PASSED THE AMENDMENT. WE'RE SO CLOSE, HARRIOT.
JUNE 1920
NWP HEADQUARTERS
35 STATES HAVE RATIFIED THE SUFFRAGE BILL.
WE JUST NEED ONE MORE FOR IT TO BECOME A CONSTITUTIONAL AMENDMENT.
ONE STATE, OR ALL THIS COULD BE FOR NOTHING. WHERE DO WE STAND?
LET'S SEE... EIGHT STATES REJECTED IT.
THREE STATES ARE REFUSING TO CONSIDER THE BILL AT ALL...
IT ALL COMES DOWN TO ONE STATE...
TENNESSEE.

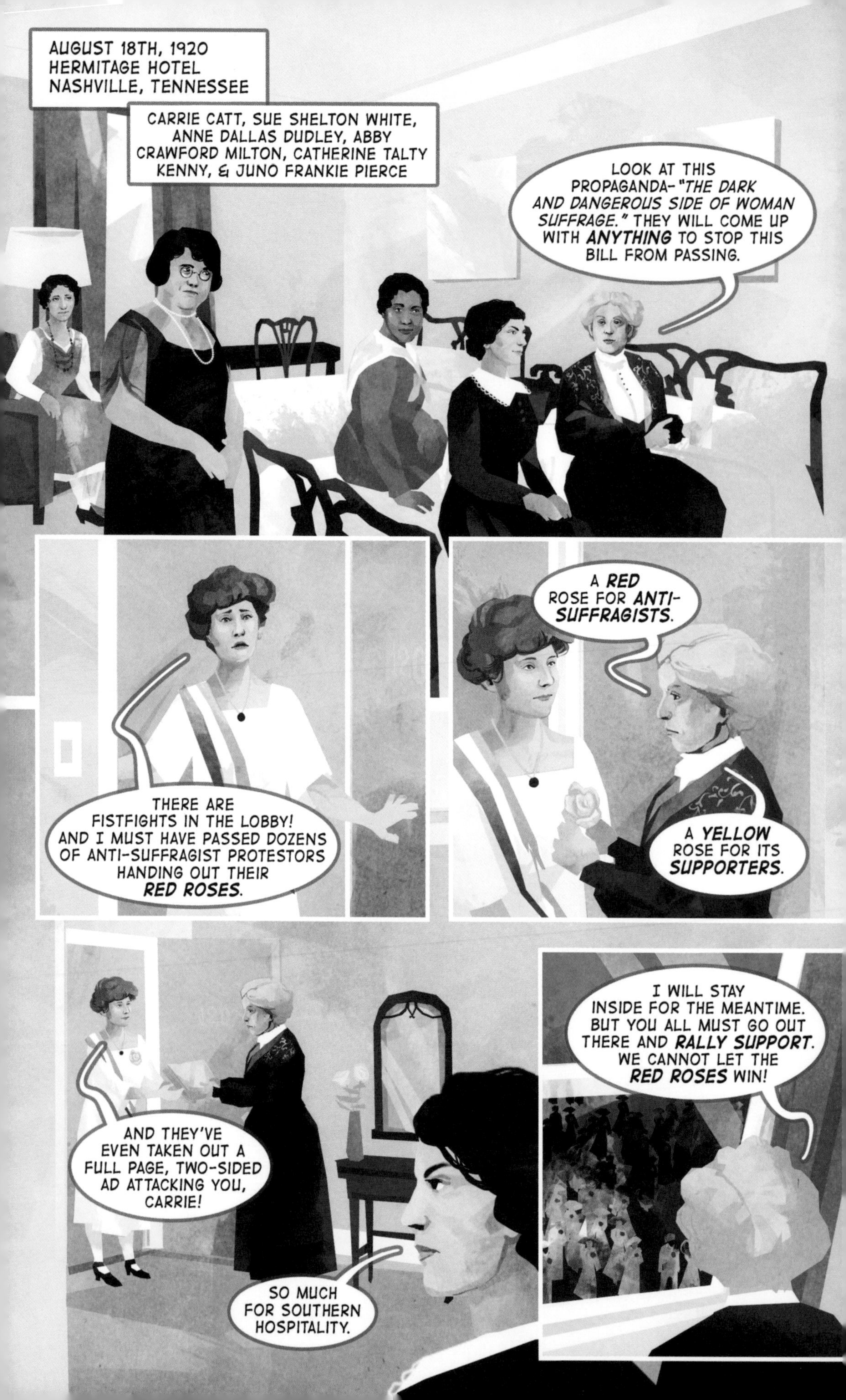
AUGUST 18TH, 1920
HERMITAGE HOTEL
NASHVILLE, TENNESSEE
CARRIE CATT, SUE SHELTON WHITE, ANNE DALLAS DUDLEY, ABBY CRAWFORD MILTON, CATHERINE TALTY KENNY, & JUNO FRANKIE PIERCE
LOOK AT THIS PROPAGANDA- *"THE DARK AND DANGEROUS SIDE OF WOMAN SUFFRAGE."* THEY WILL COME UP WITH ***ANYTHING*** TO STOP THIS BILL FROM PASSING.
THERE ARE FISTFIGHTS IN THE LOBBY! AND I MUST HAVE PASSED DOZENS OF ANTI-SUFFRAGIST PROTESTORS HANDING OUT THEIR ***RED ROSES***.
A ***RED*** ROSE FOR ***ANTI-SUFFRAGISTS***.
A ***YELLOW*** ROSE FOR ITS ***SUPPORTERS***.
AND THEY'VE EVEN TAKEN OUT A FULL PAGE, TWO-SIDED AD ATTACKING YOU, CARRIE!
SO MUCH FOR SOUTHERN HOSPITALITY.
I WILL STAY INSIDE FOR THE MEANTIME. BUT YOU ALL MUST GO OUT THERE AND ***RALLY SUPPORT***. WE CANNOT LET THE ***RED ROSES*** WIN!

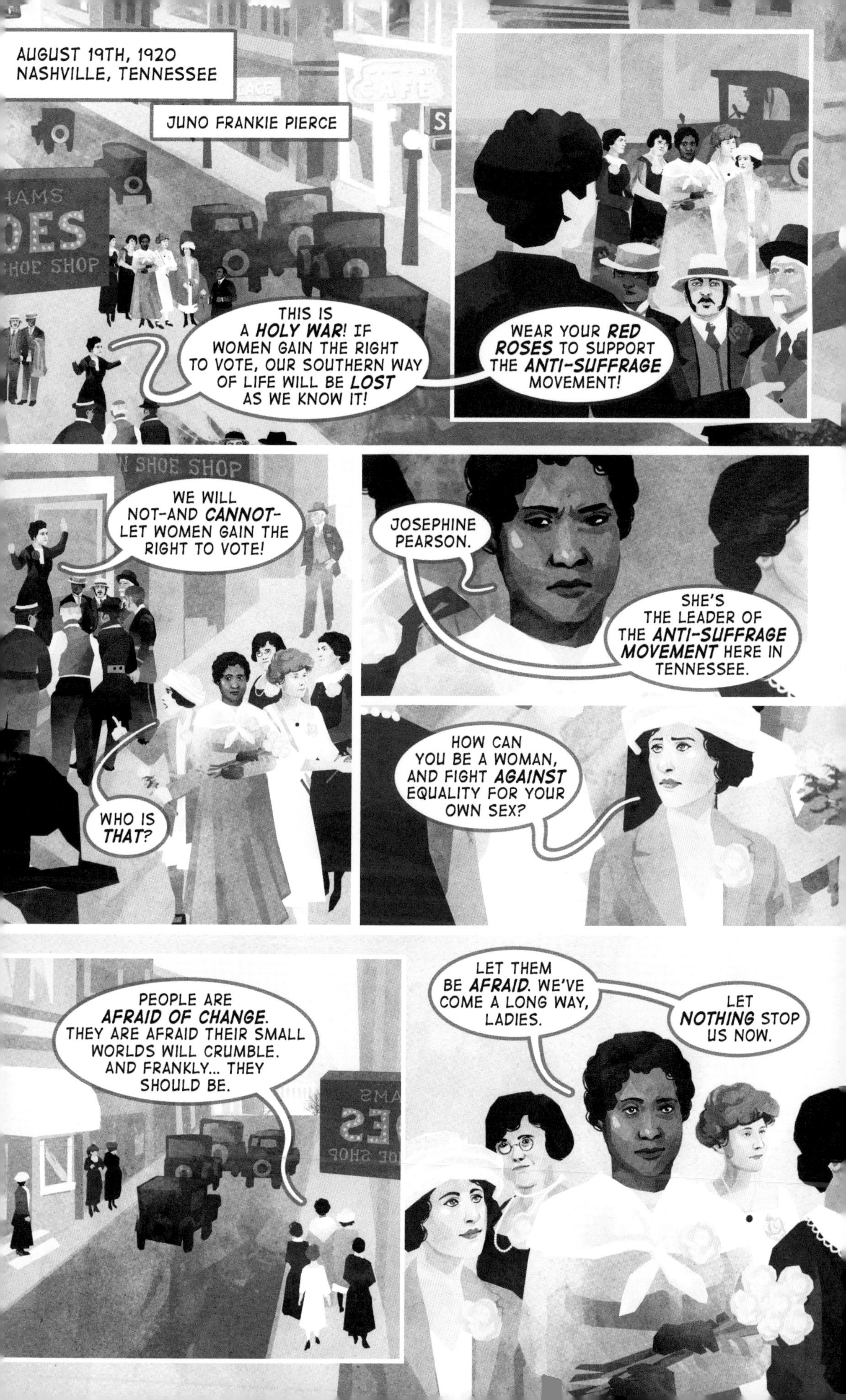
AUGUST 19TH, 1920
NASHVILLE, TENNESSEE
JUNO FRANKIE PIERCE
THIS IS A *HOLY WAR*! IF WOMEN GAIN THE RIGHT TO VOTE, OUR SOUTHERN WAY OF LIFE WILL BE *LOST* AS WE KNOW IT!
WEAR YOUR *RED ROSES* TO SUPPORT THE *ANTI-SUFFRAGE* MOVEMENT!
WE WILL NOT-AND *CANNOT*-LET WOMEN GAIN THE RIGHT TO VOTE!
WHO IS *THAT*?
JOSEPHINE PEARSON.
SHE'S THE LEADER OF THE *ANTI-SUFFRAGE MOVEMENT* HERE IN TENNESSEE.
HOW CAN YOU BE A WOMAN, AND FIGHT *AGAINST* EQUALITY FOR YOUR OWN SEX?
PEOPLE ARE *AFRAID OF CHANGE*. THEY ARE AFRAID THEIR SMALL WORLDS WILL CRUMBLE. AND FRANKLY... THEY SHOULD BE.
LET THEM BE *AFRAID*. WE'VE COME A LONG WAY, LADIES.
LET *NOTHING* STOP US NOW.

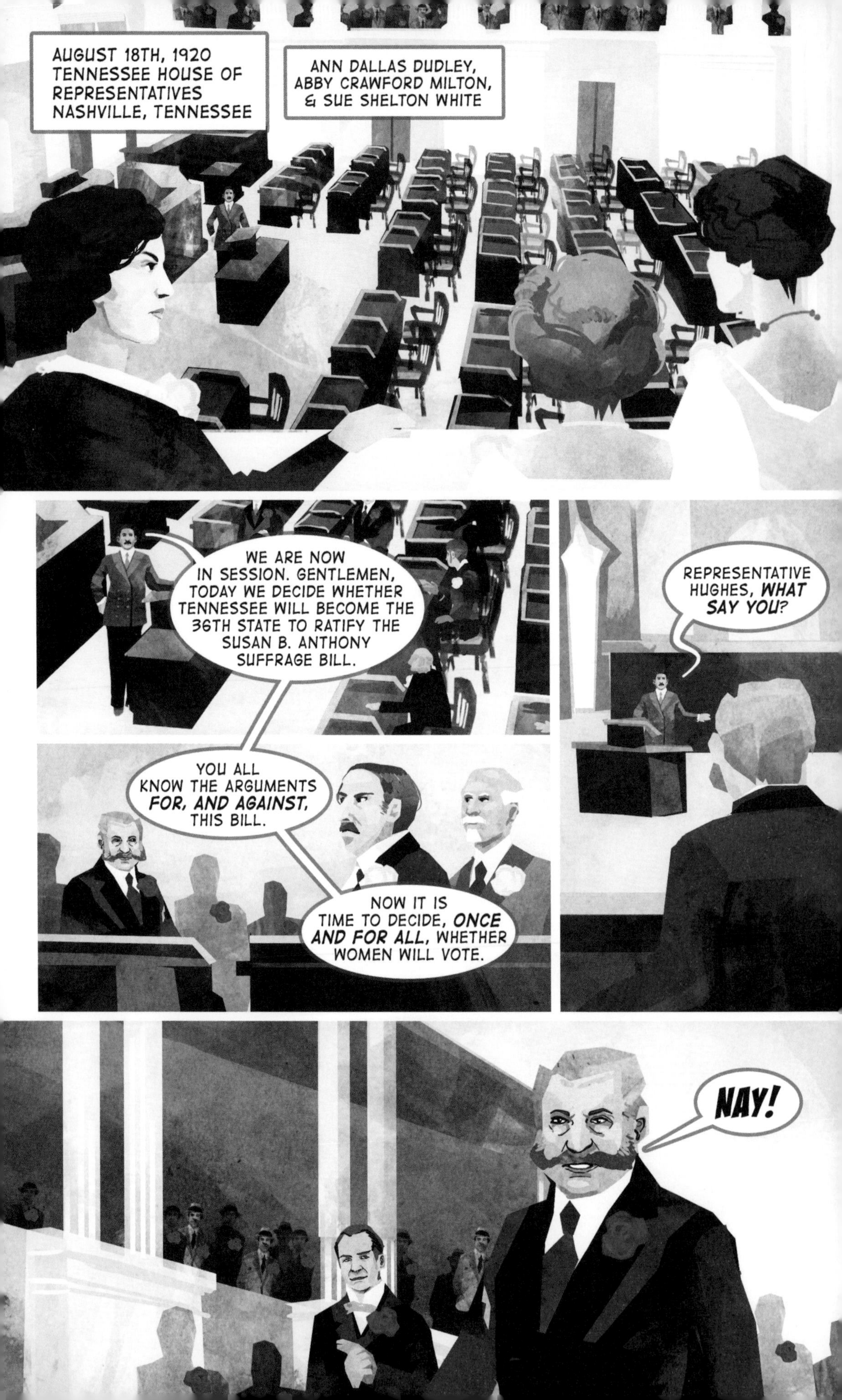
AUGUST 18TH, 1920
TENNESSEE HOUSE OF REPRESENTATIVES
NASHVILLE, TENNESSEE
ANN DALLAS DUDLEY, ABBY CRAWFORD MILTON, & SUE SHELTON WHITE
WE ARE NOW IN SESSION. GENTLEMEN, TODAY WE DECIDE WHETHER TENNESSEE WILL BECOME THE 36TH STATE TO RATIFY THE SUSAN B. ANTHONY SUFFRAGE BILL.
YOU ALL KNOW THE ARGUMENTS *FOR, AND AGAINST,* THIS BILL.
NOW IT IS TIME TO DECIDE, *ONCE AND FOR ALL,* WHETHER WOMEN WILL VOTE.
REPRESENTATIVE HUGHES, *WHAT SAY YOU*?
*NAY!*

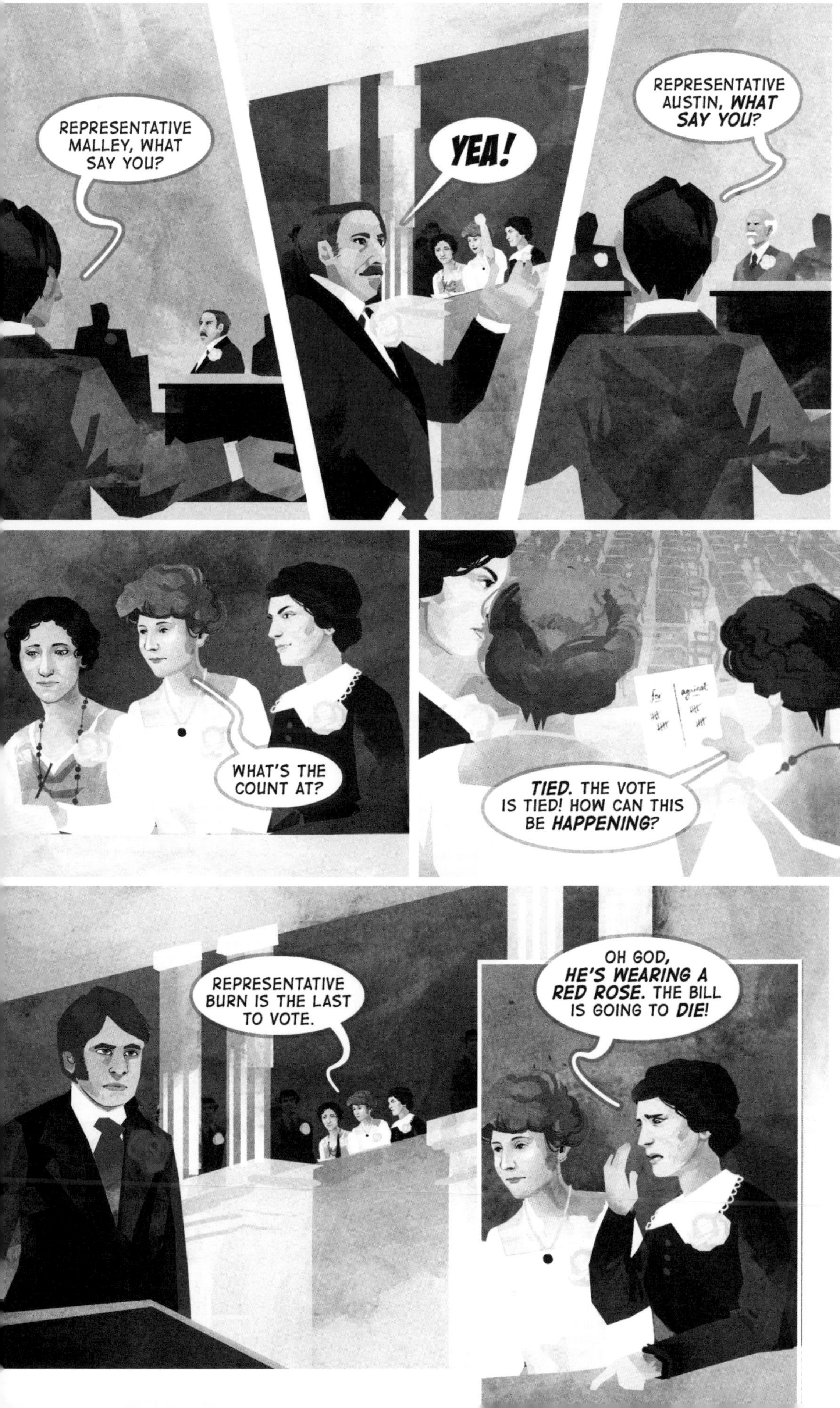
REPRESENTATIVE MALLEY, WHAT SAY YOU?
YEA!
REPRESENTATIVE AUSTIN, **WHAT SAY YOU?**
WHAT'S THE COUNT AT?
for
against
***TIED.*** THE VOTE IS TIED! HOW CAN THIS BE ***HAPPENING?***
REPRESENTATIVE BURN IS THE LAST TO VOTE.
OH GOD, ***HE'S WEARING A RED ROSE.*** THE BILL IS GOING TO ***DIE!***

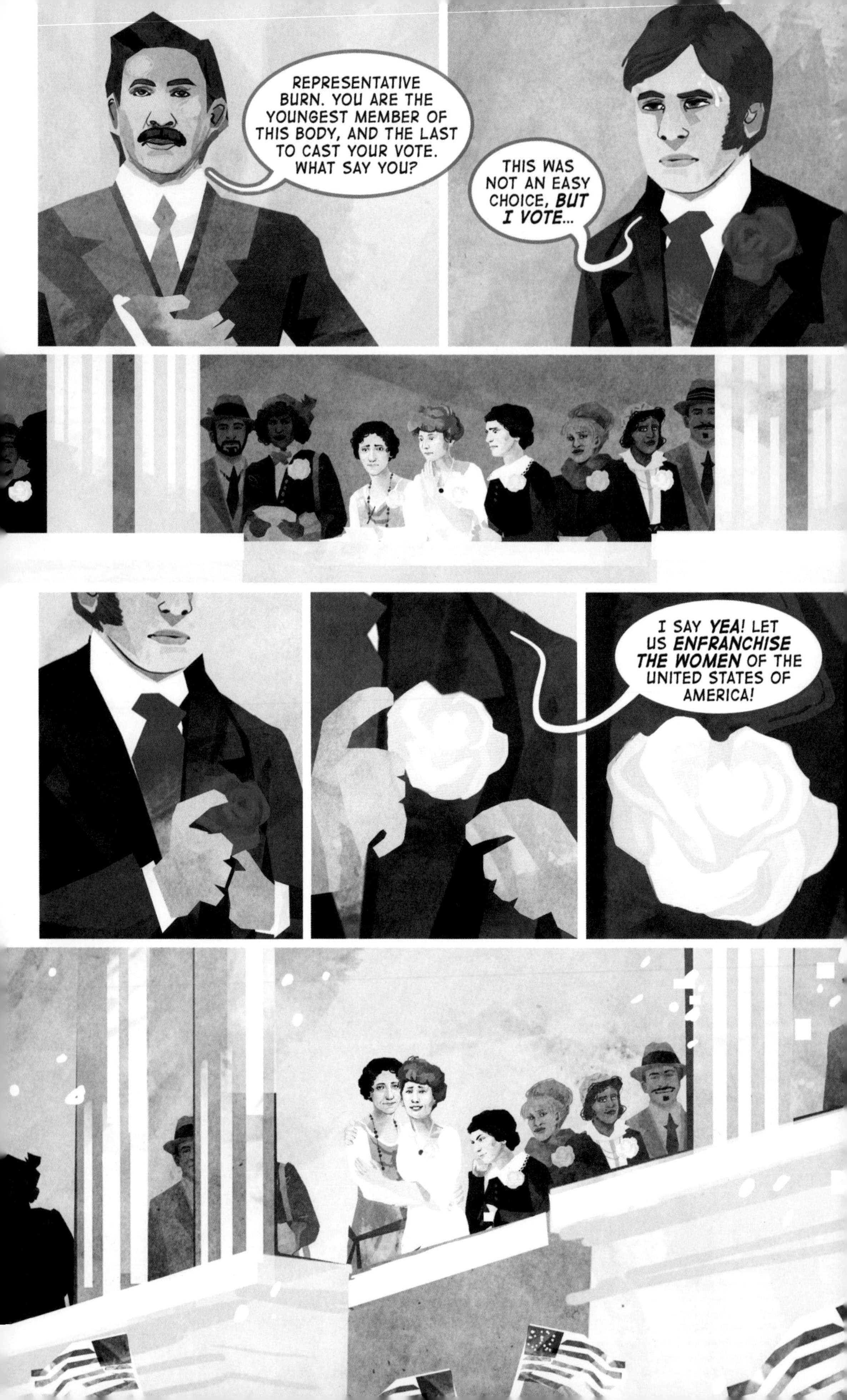
REPRESENTATIVE BURN. YOU ARE THE YOUNGEST MEMBER OF THIS BODY, AND THE LAST TO CAST YOUR VOTE. WHAT SAY YOU?
THIS WAS NOT AN EASY CHOICE, BUT I VOTE...
I SAY YEA! LET US ENFRANCHISE THE WOMEN OF THE UNITED STATES OF AMERICA!

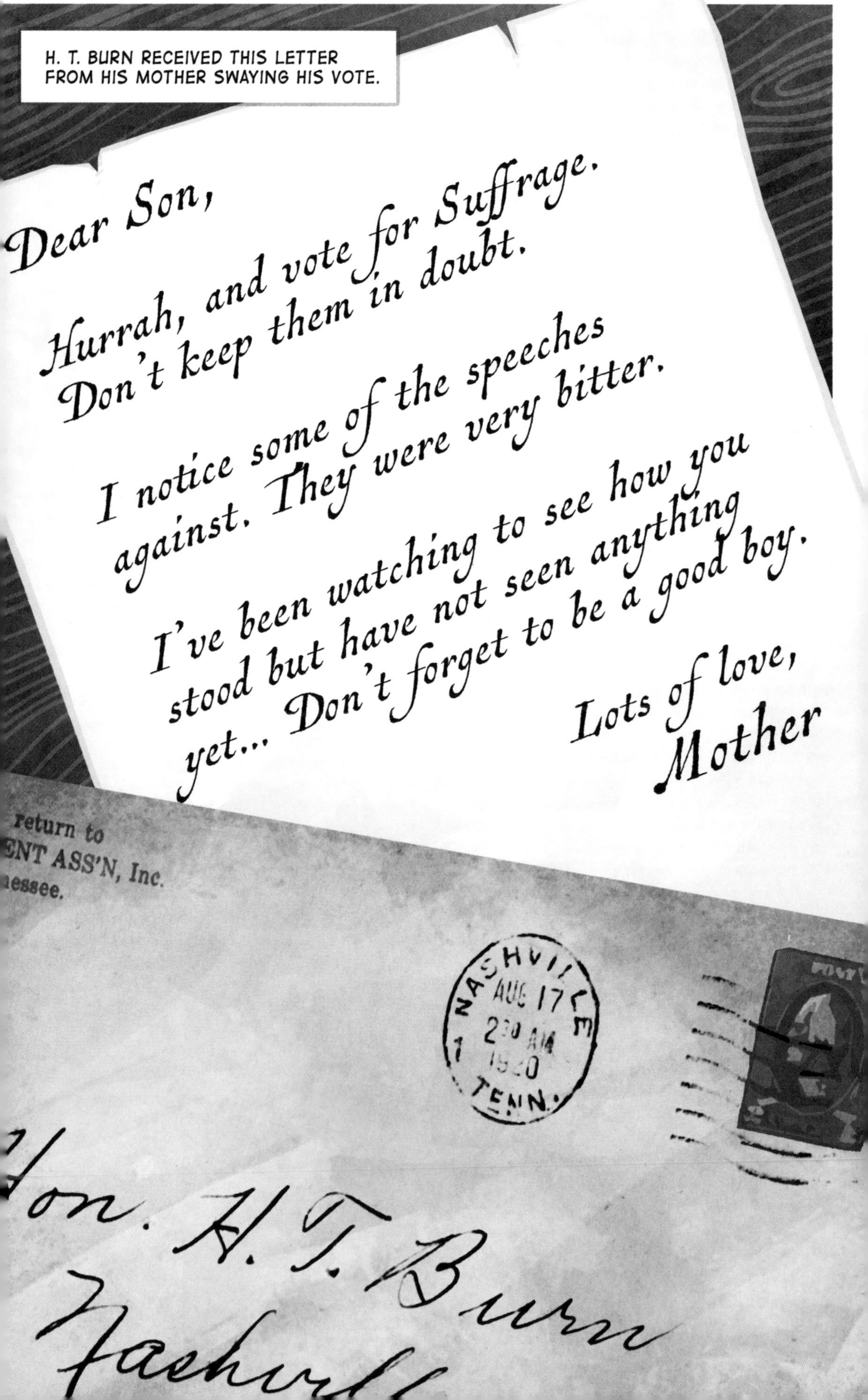
H. T. BURN RECEIVED THIS LETTER FROM HIS MOTHER SWAYING HIS VOTE.
Dear Son,
Hurrah, and vote for Suffrage. Don't keep them in doubt.
I notice some of the speeches against. They were very bitter.
I've been watching to see how you stood but have not seen anything yet... Don't forget to be a good boy.
Lots of love,
Mother
return to
NASHVILLE AUG 17 2 30 AM 1920 TENN.

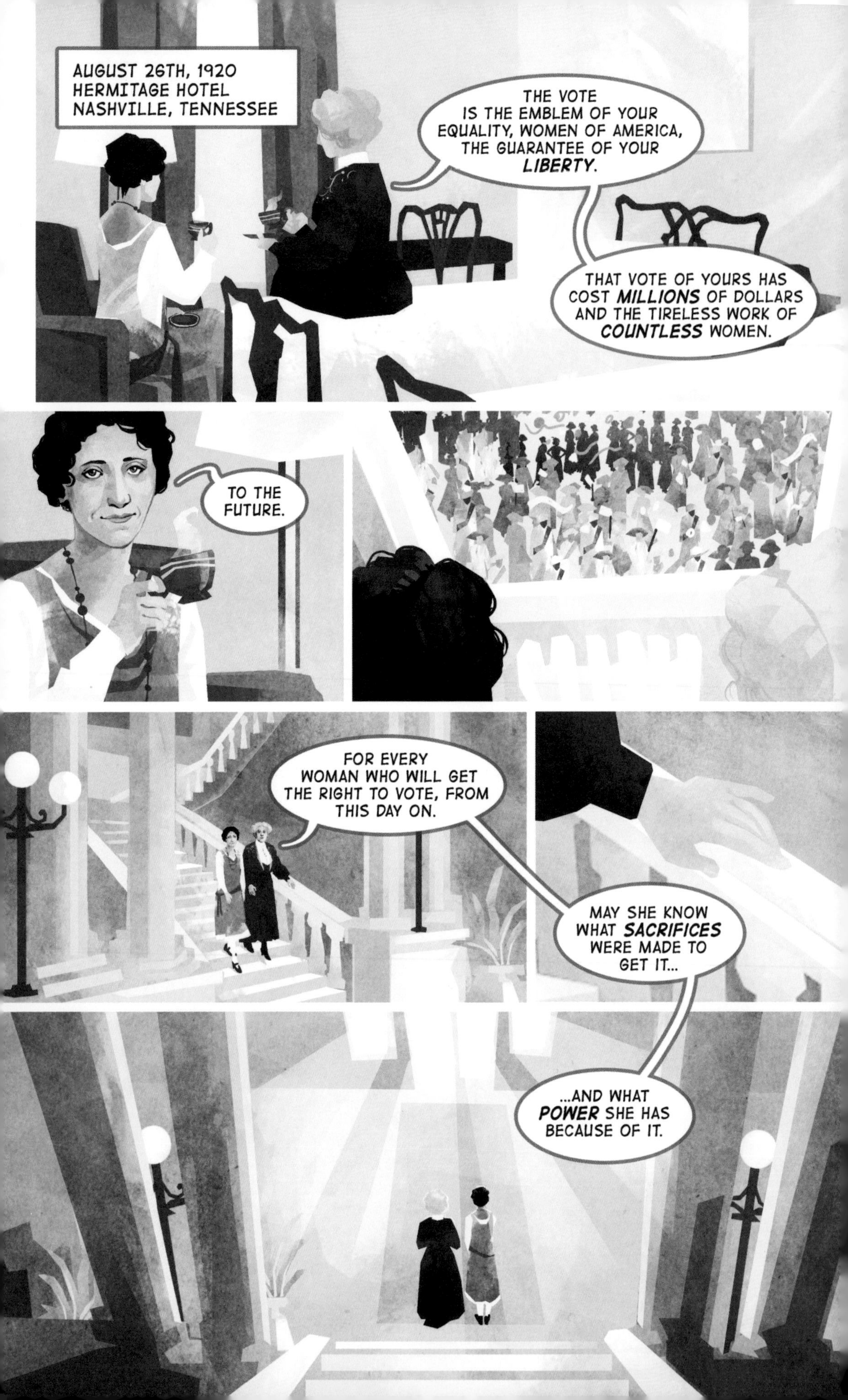

AUGUST 26TH, 1920
HERMITAGE HOTEL
NASHVILLE, TENNESSEE
THE VOTE IS THE EMBLEM OF YOUR EQUALITY, WOMEN OF AMERICA, THE GUARANTEE OF YOUR LIBERTY.
THAT VOTE OF YOURS HAS COST MILLIONS OF DOLLARS AND THE TIRELESS WORK OF COUNTLESS WOMEN.
TO THE FUTURE.
FOR EVERY WOMAN WHO WILL GET THE RIGHT TO VOTE, FROM THIS DAY ON.
MAY SHE KNOW WHAT SACRIFICES WERE MADE TO GET IT...
...AND WHAT POWER SHE HAS BECAUSE OF IT.

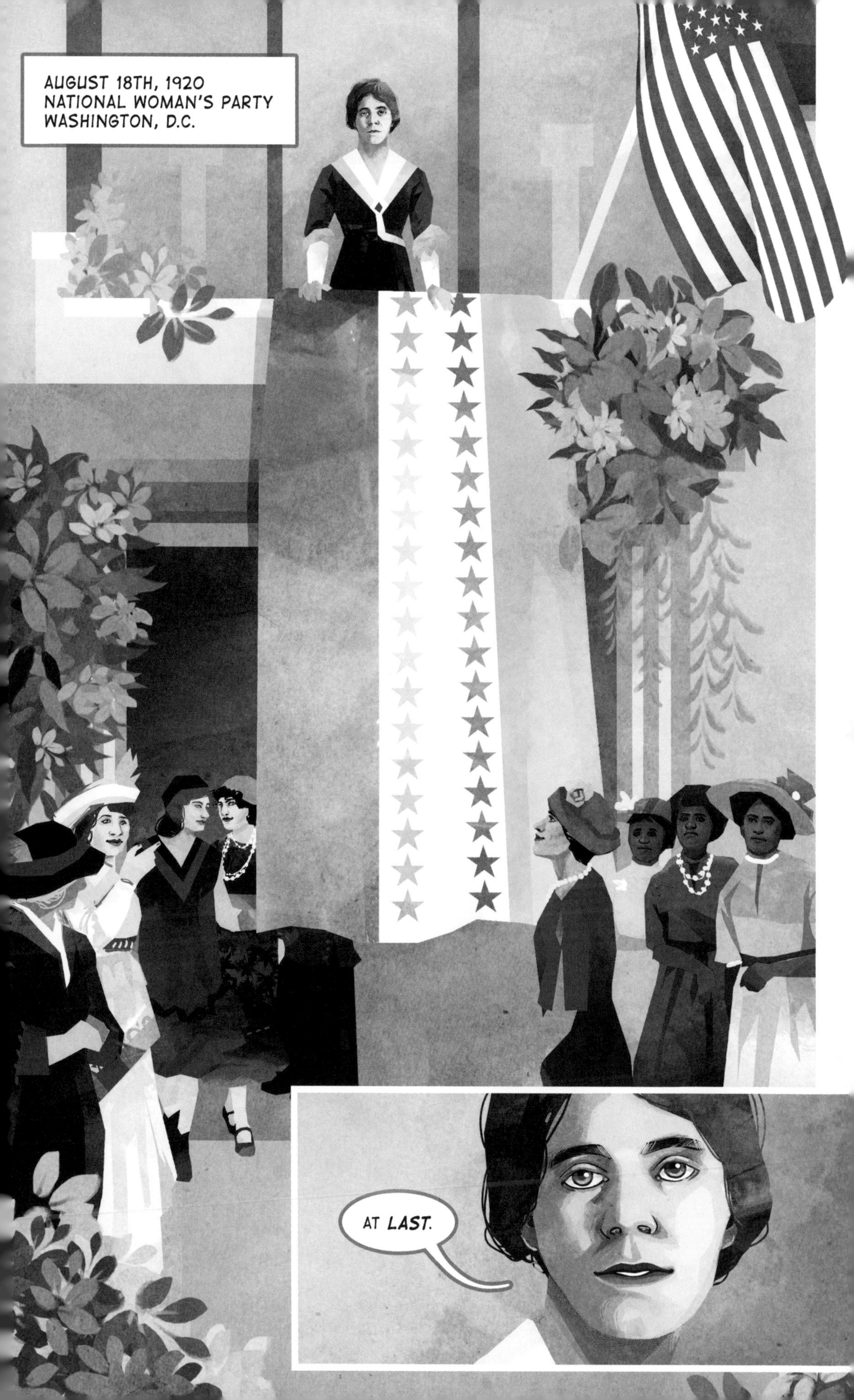
AUGUST 18TH, 1920
NATIONAL WOMAN'S PARTY
WASHINGTON, D.C.
AT *LAST*.

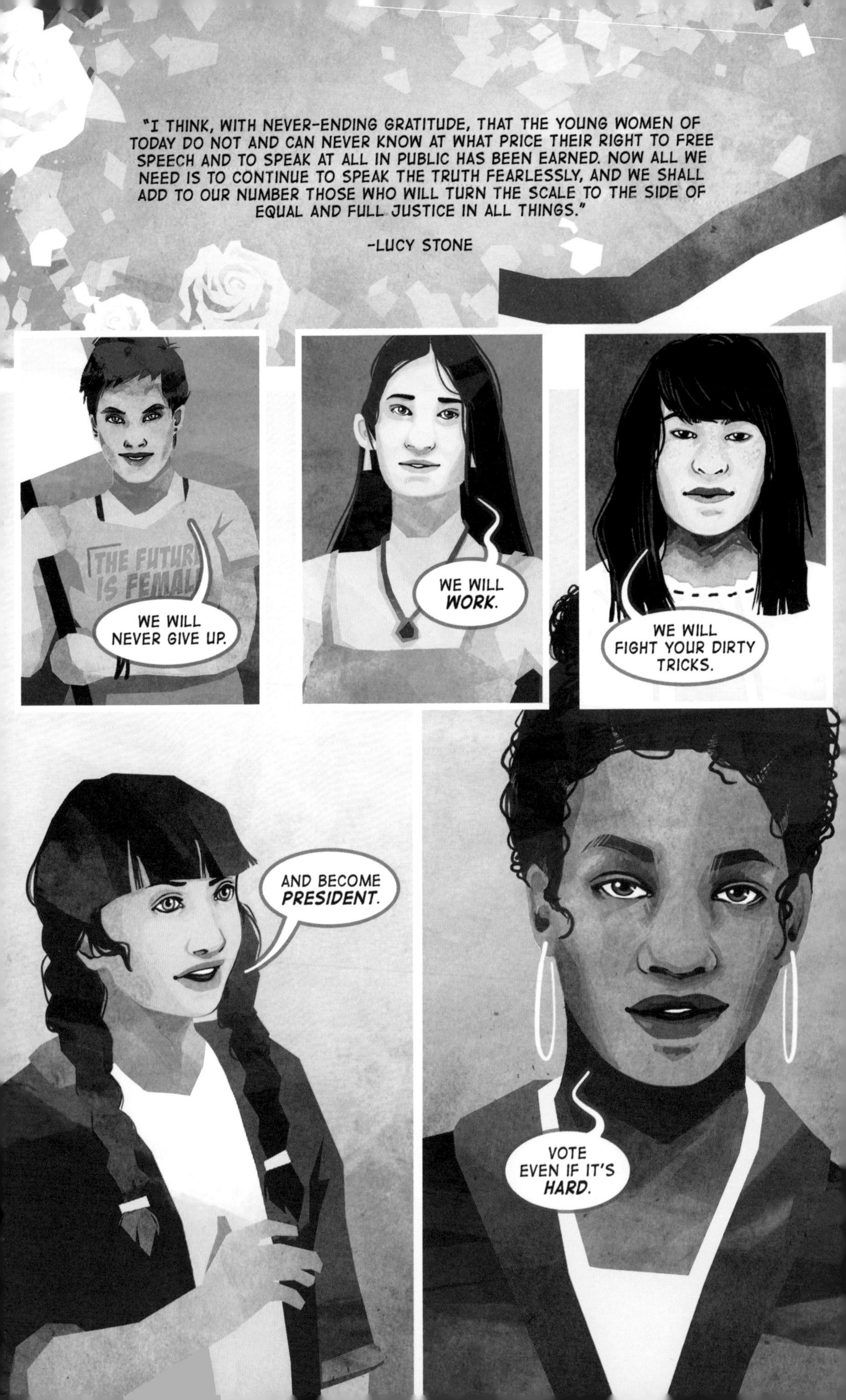
"I THINK, WITH NEVER-ENDING GRATITUDE, THAT THE YOUNG WOMEN OF TODAY DO NOT AND CAN NEVER KNOW AT WHAT PRICE THEIR RIGHT TO FREE SPEECH AND TO SPEAK AT ALL IN PUBLIC HAS BEEN EARNED. NOW ALL WE NEED IS TO CONTINUE TO SPEAK THE TRUTH FEARLESSLY, AND WE SHALL ADD TO OUR NUMBER THOSE WHO WILL TURN THE SCALE TO THE SIDE OF EQUAL AND FULL JUSTICE IN ALL THINGS."
-LUCY STONE
WE WILL NEVER GIVE UP.
WE WILL *WORK*.
WE WILL FIGHT YOUR DIRTY TRICKS.
AND BECOME *PRESIDENT*.
VOTE EVEN IF IT'S *HARD*.

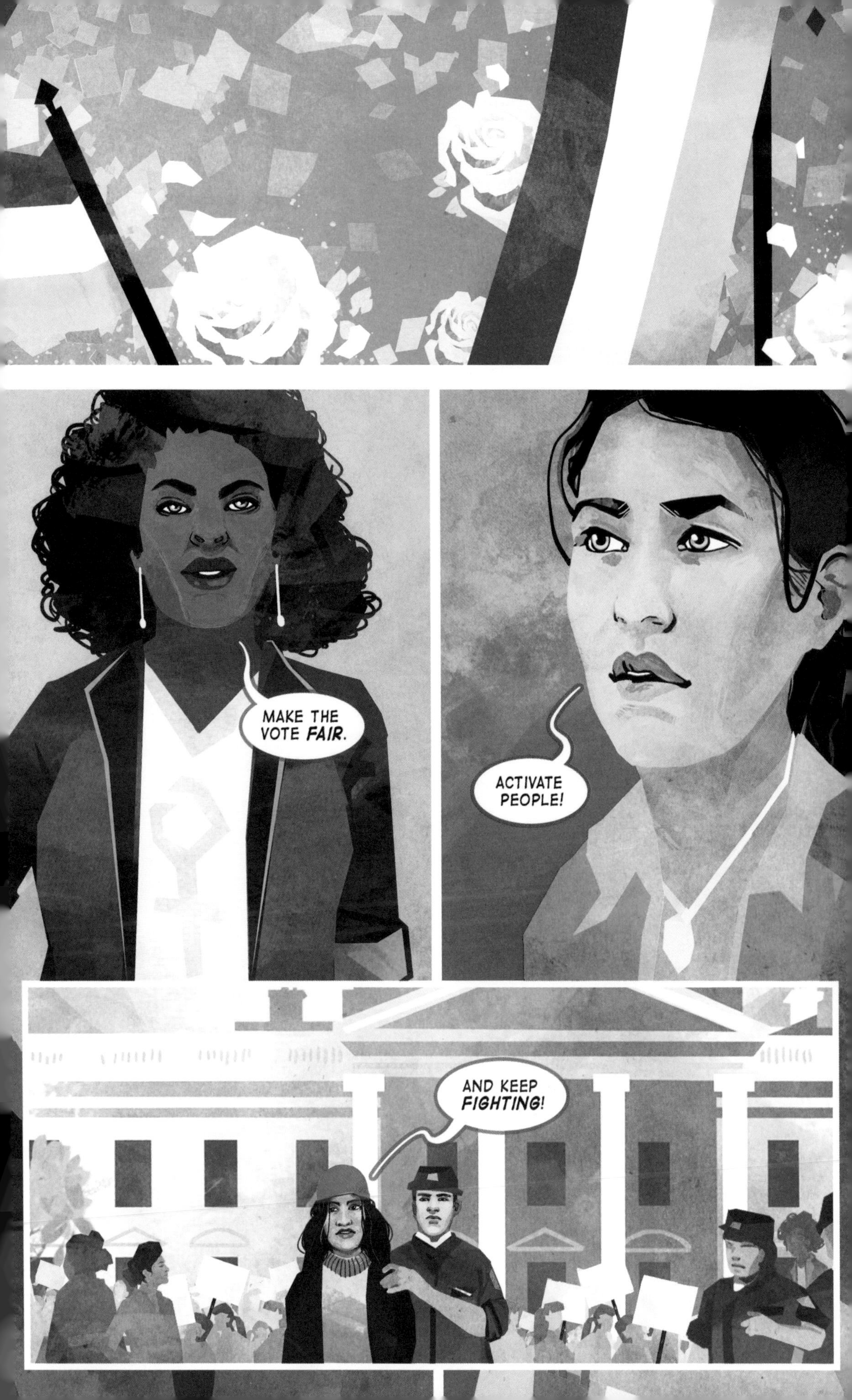
MAKE THE VOTE FAIR.
ACTIVATE PEOPLE!
AND KEEP FIGHTING!

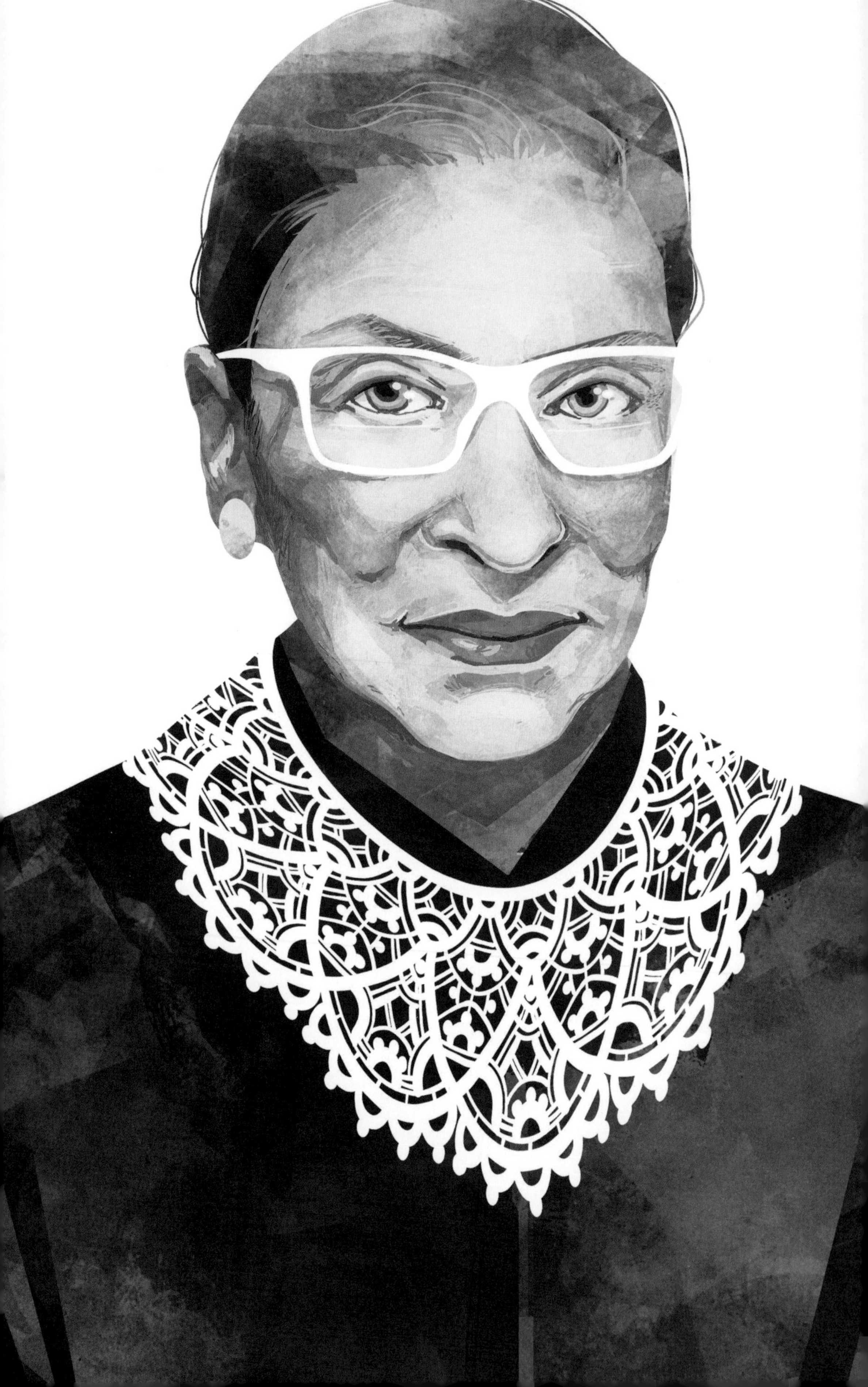

"WOMEN BELONG IN ALL PLACES WHERE
DECISIONS ARE BEING MADE. IT SHOULDN'T BE
THAT WOMEN ARE THE EXCEPTION."

RUTH BADER GINSBERG
1933–2020

# ANNOTATIONS

**1** See Kathryn Kish Skylar, "Women Who Speak for an Entire Nation: American and Brit- ish Women at the World Anti-slavery Convention, London, 1840," The Abolitionist Sis- terhood: Women's Political Culture in Antebellum America, ed. Jean Fagan Yellin (Ithaca: Cornell University Press, 1994), 301–333, 301, 305.

**2** The convention was officially called the "General Anti-Slavery Convention" but was "commonly known both at the time and since as the World's Anti-Slavery Convention" (Douglas H. Maynard, "The World's Anti-Slavery Convention of 1840," The Mississippi Valley Historical Review 47, 3 (December 1960), 452–471, 452.

**3** Tracy A. Thomas, Elizabeth Cady Stanton and the Feminist Foundations of Family Law (New York University Press, 2016), 81.

**4** As Henry Louis Gates Jr. notes, "the importation of slaves into the United States was banned by Congress (under Constitutional command) in 1808, yet by 1860, the nation's black population had jumped from 400,000 to 4.4 million, of which 3.9 million were slaves" ("Slavery, by the Numbers," The Root, February 10, 2014, https://www.theroot.com/ slavery- by-the-numbers-1790874492.

**5** In The Life and Times of Frederick Douglass (1892), Douglass writes: "I would give woman a vote, give her a motive to qualify herself to vote, precisely as I insisted upon giving the colored man the right to vote; in order that she shall have the same motives for making herself a useful citizen as those in force in the case of other citizens. In a word, I have never yet been able to find one consideration, one argument, or suggestion in favor of man's right to participate in civil government which did not equally apply to the right of woman." Quoted in Ta-Nehisi Coates, "Frederick Douglass: 'A Women's Rights Man,'" The Atlantic, September 30th, 2011, https://www.theatlantic.com/personal/archive/2011/09/ frederick-douglass-a-womens-rights-man/245977/.

**6** See Ann D. Gordon, The Trial of Susan B. Anthony, in Federal Trials and Great Debates in United States History (Federal Judicial Center: Federal Judicial History Office, 2005).


**7** See Elizabeth Frost-Knappman and Kathryn Cullen-DuPont, Women's Suffrage in Amer- ica (New York: Infobase Publishing, 2014), 312–313.


**8** Quoted in Amelia R. Fry and Jill Diane Zahniser, Alice Paul: Claiming Power (Oxford University Press, 2014), 267.


**9** Fry and Zahniser, 267. 10 Fry and Zahniser, 281.


**10** Terrence McArdle, " 'Night of Terror': The suffragists who were beaten and tortured for seeking the vote," The Washington Post, November 10th, 2017, https://www.washington- post.com/news/retropolis/wp/2017/11/10/night-of-terror-the-suffragists-who-were-beat- en-and-tortured-for-seeking-the-vote/.


**11** Fry and Zahniser, 287.

## Acknowledgements I

Bernadette Beckman
Clint Byrne
Dennis Culp
Victorine Froehlich
Rosemary Kiehner
Eileen Olwell
Greg Olwell
Victoria J. Olwell
Elena Robinson

## Special thanks

Olga Weiss
Pamela Olecki
Toby Irenstein
Tori Leyson
Avery Proulx

## Acknowledgements II

Teigan Blondin
Helen Blondin
Sian Ford
Del Blondin
Faye Blondin
Kate Sveinson
Dean Bolton
Elinor Bolton
Finnegan & Mina

## Much gratitude to our early supporters

### Name in lights

Stephanie Tobor, Gayle McCormick, Angela Johnson, Rachel
Friedmann Lasky, Jean Wagner, Brenda Ebling, Eva Wilson McCann,
Jim Jagger, Tracy Balcerski, Lynn O'Mealia, Max van Balgooy,
Kathleen Mahoney, Amanda Jaskiewicz, Sabrina Schorr, Sunny Bates,
Ed Weisbart, Raf Nieves

### Female superstar thanks

Victoria Pelletier, Karla Perri, P. Newmann, Megan Connell,
Caitlin O'Connell, Terry, Cami Dinardi, Debby Feldman, Julie Macks,
Cynthia Mullen, Tio De Malu, Meg Poulelis, Jacqueline Dolan Florez,
Amy Norman, Matthew Newcomb, Kara J. Coyle, Michelle Schoulder,
Thomas Peters, Wendy Zajack Lipshultz, Carryl Pierre-Drews,
Linda Vester, Patricia Gallant, Adrian A. Franks, Kathy Zwiebel,
Annie L. Haggard, Nadia Sa'd Mulaire, Cindi Olwell,
Julie Anixter, Michelle Hoover

### Family book club

Tony Hine, Jeffrey Hine, Scarlett Rose Hine, Allegra Jane Hine